Driven

Crazy

**A Female Trucker Dishes on
Fun,
Danger,
and Quirkiness in a Semi**

by Karen Greenhill

Visit: drivencrazybook.com
Like: facebook.com/drivencrazybook
Follow: twitter.com/DrivenCrazyBook
Review online at Amazon.com or Goodreads.com

Driven Crazy:
A Female Trucker Dishes on Fun, Danger, and Quirkiness in a Semi
Copyright © 2015 Karen Greenhill

ISBN: 9780985071509

~ This book is dedicated to courteous and safety-minded truck drivers everywhere who make the convenience and comfort of modern life possible for all of us.

Foreword

This book is a memoir of the author's experience while driving tractor-trailer trucks over a large part of the United States for a period of years and contains her perceptions and opinions stemming from those experiences. All of the occurrences reported in this book actually happened. All names and some identifying details of individuals have been changed. Conversations have been reproduced faithfully as possible, but with accommodations for pseudonyms. The destinations of some trips have been changed or omitted, for instance when a co-driver turned a big rig around in the front yard of a farmhouse. Not every trip taken or co-driver encountered is mentioned in this book, nor are trips necessarily presented in the order they occurred. For narrative reasons, truck stops have been given fictitious names that lend them character so they might stick in readers' minds.

Driven Crazy is also a story of journey, not just in the sense of travel, but in the sense of growing as a person who just happens to be a woman working in trucking. From a nervous rookie to a seasoned driver, this is the story of how a person mastered some of the biggest trucks on the road while learning about life.

Because so few books have covered trucking, *Driven Crazy* may help fill a bit of a gap in cultural knowledge and provide the public with at least partial information about life in the trucking world. After all, the world of trucking affects all of us daily by providing needed services while sharing our roadways and sometimes risking our lives. Ultimately, the author and publisher hope the reader will find the telling of these true accounts to be agreeably entertaining and illuminating at the same time.

Acknowledgments

My thanks to the following for their help and moral support:

To my co-drivers:

To the men and women I drove with, genuine heartfelt thanks to each of you who do your jobs with the dedication that kept me safe while I drove with you and keeps millions of motorists safe year after year. Thank you for all the kindness, patience, and camaraderie you shared.

To my proofreaders:

Prof. Candace Justice, at the University of Memphis: Thank you for reviewing early chapters, offering encouragement, and taking me seriously as a writer.

Marcia: Thank you for your honest, no-nonsense approach to reviewing and for suggesting I picture the text like a film. I hope the results don't give readers "narrative whiplash." If they do, I am solely responsible.

Thanks to my brothers, Jeff and Greg, for reviewing technical information and providing feedback. Their insights were incorporated within the text.

Last but not least, thanks to Susan, one of the world's best co-drivers, for reviewing early efforts and keeping me in check on how another driver views trucking in general and our jobs in particular.

Table of Contents

Chapter 1: "Don't let the back trailer wag the truck."

Heading into a west Texas sunset I steered a Kenworth semi-truck pulling two trailers from Fort Worth, Texas to Phoenix on my first ever professional driving gig. At the same time driving a truck as a rookie was fun, it also felt scary. This truck was, bar none, the biggest vehicle I'd ever driven, the heaviest and longest. Most semis pull one long trailer, but a set of doubles reaches farther. At my level of experience just keeping an entire doubles rig on the pavement and heading in the right direction took my full concentration. The motorists, those driving four wheeled vehicles, darted swiftly around the big truck, while I did my best simply to maintain the speed limit. Seated high above cars and pickup trucks felt like guiding a horse along a path shared with kittens who have no clue what dangers lurk around them. One touch of the truck on the bumper or fender of a four wheeler and that might be all she wrote for the motorists, according to one instructor at the truck driving school I'd attended.

The view through the windshield showed grasslands giving way to more and more sparse plant life. Ahead of us the sky gradually turned from blue to golden then to scarlet. In time the stars and moon took over for the night. For the first couple of hours my co-driver, a friendly guy called Dutch, sat next to me, giving instructions and advice. I'd already graduated from training, but still had a lot to learn from my first co-driver. I had just met Dutch, but he would become one in a long line of co-drivers who would teach me a truism or two about trucking: little bits of advice or observations that stuck with me long after climbing from the cab of a truck.

Right then just getting used to sitting in the pilot seat of one of the largest vehicles on the road took some doing. From here my point of view began at about eight feet above the ground outside. To my right between the driver and passenger seats the gear shifter rose from the floor a good two feet and had a grip the size of an orange to hold onto while changing gears. Over the side windows and windshield, storage cubbyholes or bins wrapped around from the immediate left, across the front of the truck and all the way over to the right of the passenger seat. Nylon mesh nets covered the openings of the cubbyholes to prevent stored items from bopping the driver or anyone else on the head while the truck jostled down the road. Between the seats and behind us in the sleeper compartment, room enough to stand made the inside of the cab feel less claustrophobic. In front of me the steering wheel lie horizontally, as large as a Thanksgiving Day platter. The extravagant looking dashboard, filled with banks of gauges, wrapped around the driver seat in a semicircle like an airplane's cockpit controls, enhancing the sense that a truck driver *is* a pilot.

I could hardly believe that after a few weeks of training I had become that pilot. Every new driver has a case of rookie nerves, and I felt no differently. Yet, caution has advantages when a driver is still learning how to maneuver up to 80,000 pounds of metal, glass, rubber, and freight at up to 80 miles per hour. Many people get a case of nerves just learning to drive a car. Driving a truck certainly isn't like driving the family sedan.

Many new things about driving a big truck were unexpected. The sensitivity of the steering wheel still surprised me while I sat next to Dutch. Something about big trucks had made me think the controls would respond slowly and deliberately like an awkward dinosaur. But on the contrary, whatever you ask of these machines they respond, and quickly. Even the ragamuffin training trucks I had learned in had driven like finely tuned equipment.

Like most new drivers I went down the highway steering slightly side to side to maintain control even when all went smoothly.

But then every once in a while the truck would come across a subtle change in the road surface. Responding instinctively, I would steer in one direction in order to correct the truck's bearing and find myself overcompensating, steering too far. Then to make up for that overcompensation, I steered too far in the opposite direction, almost like a kid at an amusement park swishing back and forth on a bumper car's steering wheel. I couldn't think of a worse catastrophe then bumping a real car. So at this early stage, I felt real alarm each time this happened. Then I turned the steering wheel back and forth, until equilibrium returned, and the truck simply headed down the road again. The sensation felt disconcerting to say the least.

Such things reminded me that years ago I had read the books by James Herriot describing his work as a veterinarian. He'd explained that his profession often resulted in feeling foolish or looking that way to others. So with apologies to that author I must say that trucking also provides nearly endless opportunities to look and feel foolish. I would rediscover this phenomenon on many occasions.

"What do you do when that happens?" I asked Dutch, feeling embarrassed that he had seen my most recent display of overcorrection.

"Just keep on top of it," Dutch advised calmly like a father teaching a kid how to ride a bicycle. His relaxed attitude would be reflected in other drivers I drove with starting out. Any driver puts his life in the hands of whomever takes over the wheel, experienced or not. We all had to trust in fate and our co-drivers to get us to our next destination in one piece.

Earlier in life I wouldn't have dreamed I would really and truly drive a semi anywhere. Bookish and bashful, I'd graduated from college with a major in English, but with the economy not producing many desk jobs I then sought a job in the real world. Trucking is definitely real, though naturally not quite like I'd imagined. For as long as I could remember I had looked in wonder at the big trucks going up and down the highways. I can see myself in our old blue Chevy peering out the window at behemoth trucks pulling long silver vans or flat bed trucks that carried giant, yellow, earth moving equipment, and I felt the earth, well, move. Sort of. I lost myself in the adventure of dreaming what piloting a powerful truck might feel like. I imagined a sense of drama when I eased a big truck around tight turns, taking heroic pains not to obliterate all the tiny cars. The drivers and passengers of those cars would look on in awe, resisting the urge to break out in applause. That's what I had pictured at any rate when I was a kid simply intrigued by the big trucks. Musing about driving had been one thing, but did I really have the skills to drive? Everyone *thinks* they drive well.

As a grownup, I also knew that truck driving involved long hours, dangerous conditions and sometimes traffic collisions that took lives. Colliding with a car full of people would be a nightmare for everyone. Though truck drivers are many times less likely to be killed in a collision with a car or pickup than the motorists, I wondered how many motorists really appreciated that fact. Anyway, most truck drivers are men. If I just happened to be a girl, should that stop me from pursuing such a career? I had never been particularly frilly. Not that I have anything against frilliness or lack thereof. We are all the same under our skin, though I may have pictured a woman who drove a truck looking like a tattooed, tough gal. I could envision her slouching, a cigarette dangling from her lower lip, her face in a permanent grimace, just this side of female. If that was the case, then the men must be even tougher. They must make that tough gal look like Cinderella. Could I even stand to be within a quarter-mile of the testosterone emitted by a burly dude in a tattered jacket and thick-soled boots who had more hair on his back than a malamute? In other words did I have the backbone to drive a truck?

As a bashful bookworm, I wondered if truckers could accept a female from a quiet suburban life as one of their own. Yet despite these misgivings I also found myself driven to have that intriguing job, to be paid to travel, to steer the biggest vehicles on the road, and to conquer my fears. Driven to find out who I would share the cab of a semi-truck with, man or woman.

Don't wag the truck

In time I would drive with Hilda, a co-driver who often drove while distracted, for instance texting at the wheel and weaving in the lane as she went. And with Romeo, a would be ladies' man, who ultimately tried to bully me into driving our truck with a brake repair a mechanic said would certainly fail. Later on there was Nick, a seemingly mild mannered guy who confessed that he had stolen anything he could get his hands on in his previous jobs. Then he began to muse aloud about what he might take from the sorting centers of the carrier we both drove for. Our carrier often left dock doors to their facilities open at all hours with unattended packages sitting on conveyer belts, whether workers were present or not. The only guards on duty worked in a small building beside the gate and never patrolled the dozens of acres of ground at each facility. Only a chain link fence with some barbed wire strands on top kept anyone out.

Or consider another random trio of rodeo clowns. For instance, Ernesto, a young guy with a wispy moustache, decorated the bunk in the sleeper compartment with half a dozen small pillows of polyester leopard prints and a spritz of cologne. When my ten hour shift ended I turned the wheel over to him. After all of three hours driving, he pulled over onto a shoulder marked off by painted stripes between rushing highway traffic on the left and a busy exit ramp to the right. There he announced he felt too sleepy to go any farther. Or Simon, a seemingly cheerful guy if you met him out on the terminal yard. But driving with Simon left more than one co-driver feeling truly "restless," as I later learned.

But most memorable of all had to have been Dopey, a Dr. Jekyll and Mr. Hyde type. On our first week driving together Dopey had acted remarkably cheerful and full of fun. Then one day on the company lot, he forgot to set the truck's parking brakes, thus letting tens of thousands of pounds roll across the pavement near people and equipment with no one at the wheel. Later, he said he couldn't read our trailer numbers, and he acted lost driving around places we had driven just days earlier. I can still picture his bleary eyes searching my face to see if I could tell something was amiss with his behavior. The longer he and I drove together the more his personality took on an edge of meanness.

These drivers and others joined me in steering not 18 wheelers, but 22 wheelers, hauling two trailers at a time all over this country's highways.

First, I attended a week of classroom instruction at a truck driving school run by a community college. We watched videos and read from a booklet to pass a couple of written tests. Then two other students and I worked for three weeks with a driving instructor. Looking out the windshield of a truck those first weeks felt like being stuck in a real life video game. I learned the control station, seeing the super-realistic graphics whiz by. The game had an edge of fun, but if I wiped out the stakes had become much higher than losing a couple of quarters in an arcade game or losing face in front of friends.

The second day of class we went to a medical office for a DOT physical. Every CDL holder has to pass a physical exam under Department of Transportation standards. I would later learn that even diabetics, whose condition can cause a driver to black out, are allowed to drive big trucks if they pass the physical. Eventually, I would see and hear of more than one diabetic driver whose health caused sores to cover their bodies and wondered how fit they really were. In addition, if drivers were being treated for depression or other psychological problems, if a doctor certified their condition as under control and would agree they posed no danger then they, too, could be qualified to drive. In short, if a physician declares anyone fit enough, he or she can get the required medical certificate to drive a truck.

Each training day we walked out to the parking lot to the school's truck and made a cursory show of inspecting the vehicle by checking the oil and coolant levels. We never really checked anything else except the brake lights and turn signals. My questions in later training days about a more thorough inspection or about what precisely I should be looking at when discussing different parts of the engine or suspension were brushed aside with comments that my employer, whoever that might be some day, would show me what I needed to know once I drove professionally. Or so I was told.

Don't wag the truck

My classmates and I gradually built up just enough driving skills to pass the licensing test. Then we each had a commercial driver license, which is a sort of hunting permit for a trucking job. Being a newly minted Class A CDL driver, I imagined all trucking jobs to be so-called over-the-road trucking where drivers take an eighteen wheeler out for two or three weeks at a time. During that time a trucking company dispatches a solo driver or a team from one random location to another. A team might start out in Dallas and be dispatched to, say, San Diego then to Milwaukee on to Boston and next to Atlanta and so on before driving toward home. At the end of the 14 or 21 day work period, drivers usually get all of one or two days off before hitting the road again. Jobs with local delivery companies usually require experience, which I clearly didn't have. Other more strenuous jobs included hauling sand or water to remote locations for oil drilling companies. All of these jobs required long hours. All trucking jobs do.

Luckily, the head of the truck driving school, Mr. Spears, had a suggestion I wouldn't have dreamt of. He knew of a company that utilized rookie drivers. Unlike over-the-road driving, this carrier was one of many that employed drivers hauling trailers along designated lines from hub to hub on a regular schedule. That meant I would get to know the roads I frequently drove on. Mr. Spears gave me the names and phone numbers of three or four men who hired drivers. I knew of no such women, though I would later hear of one in California and another in Tennessee.

I phoned a driver-manager named Sam who invited me to come to his office to fill out an application. A driver-manager is the go-to guy for any issues drivers have from hiring to firing and everything in between. One morning at his office in Fort Worth I met Sam, a handsome, forty-something guy with wavy brown hair and a friendly, almost gentle way of talking. I sat in a plastic chair in the waiting room between a potted plant and a gumball machine and balanced a clipboard on my lap, a pen in one hand and a fan of pages in the other. With the application turned in, questions milled around in my mind. Was being female still considered a disadvantage or had our society outgrown those old notions? Was being a rookie a deal breaker after all? I would have

7

to wait to find out. First they had to review and verify my job history and check my background.

After some weeks, the carrier decided that I was neither a crook nor a villain, and I got a call from Sam. If I passed a drug test, they would hire me. More or less. Drivers may start as part-time or substitute drivers so that when another driver falls ill or gets called to jury duty or so on, someone is available to step in. Then when a full-time driver retires, changes jobs, or wins the lottery, the manager has someone ready to fill in permanently. Being a relief driver also gave a rookie a chance to prove himself and, hopefully, the opportunity to find a compatible co-driver. Because I would learn co-drivers can cause mixed emotions, from comedy to drama. They could make you feel safe while you hunkered down in the sleeper bunk to catch some zees while they drove down the highway. Or they could make you lie awake staring into the darkness hoping to God and the universe that all went well before the trip ended.

Once I had passed the drug test, Sam called again and arranged for us to meet at the trucking company's facility called a terminal or a yard. Before he could entrust me with one of the trucks, Sam needed to see me drive. I didn't know it yet, but if I drove well enough, he would show me how to set up a pair of double trailers, instead of a regular 53 foot trailer. With rare exception this carrier pulled double trailers or, more simply, we just called them doubles.

On the appointed day I got in the driver seat, started up the engine, and drove the truck around the building. Like a typical driver I set off in second gear. Only with a particularly heavy load or starting from a standstill on a steep grade might a driver start in the granny gear, as first gear is known.

"I hope I'm not too rusty," I told Sam. "It's been months since I've driven a training truck."

"You're doing pretty good for someone who hasn't driven in a while," Sam answered, while I shifted gears smoothly.

"I don't know how to float the gears, yet," I admitted, referring to the way drivers shift from gear to gear without the clutch while the truck is moving.

"You'll have to learn floating soon, but it's easier than using the clutch."

I hoped so. In truck driving school we were required to double-clutch. That is to bring the clutch up and back down again twice before engaging the gear that supplied the engine's power to the wheels.

"See that trailer right there?" Sam asked, pointing at the one whose number matched our dispatch slip. "We're going to back the dolly up to it. That's the back trailer for this set."

The dolly is essentially another set of wheels with a hitch called a fifth wheel on top. Just like the fifth wheel immediately behind the truck's cab the dolly has an identical heavy duty fastener that connects to a trailer via a thick metal pin that sticks out underneath the leading edge of the trailer. On a set of doubles the dolly's fifth wheel latches on to the back trailer. That fifth wheel latch on top of its wheeled axle has a frame in front that comes to a point. The point attaches the back trailer to the front trailer via a different type of hitch on the rear of the front trailer. Simple as pie, right?

Truckers call the back trailer on a set of doubles the wiggle wagon because that trailer drifts or wiggles from side to side while the rig moves down the road. Naturally, the cab heads in the direction that the driver steers, and the front trailer immediately follows. But the back trailer, with its dolly attachment and no steering component, wiggles along behind.

Sam had a couple of points of advice. "When you get out on the road and you're checking back in the mirrors, you'll see that back trailer drift from side to side. Be sure to keep steering by what you see in front of the truck. Don't steer to try to correct the drift. You've heard, 'Don't let the tail wag the dog.' Well, don't let the back trailer wag the truck."

"Another thing," Sam continued. "I don't know if they told you this at driving school, but you can't swerve for animals in these things."

They had. I remembered Larry, our instructor, telling our class when we practiced shifting gears along the highway service roads west of Fort Worth where our vehicle had rolled past fields of grazing cattle. Barbed wire stretched from wooden fencepost to wooden fencepost. On a typical day a large red-tailed hawk had perched on the topmost wire. When I slowed down to practice downshifting, I caught a glimpse of the hawk. The bird may have spotted a field mouse because he used his muscular legs to cata-pult upward and soar into the sky leaving the wire bouncing up and down in his wake.

"No matter what," Larry had instructed, "You do all you can to stop in time, but swerving a big truck is only going to make things worse. If you have to, it's better to run over an animal than to collide with a car."

Other drivers I worked with early on likewise mentioned this necessity. With those reminders out of the way, Sam showed me how to connect the lifelines. That is, all the brake lines and power cords that connect the cab to the first trailer and go between the front and back trailers. A thick electrical power cord called the "pig tail" because of its spiral shape had to be attached between the two trailers so that the back trailer would have signal and brake lights. Very important. The brake lines must be connected to truck and trailers by a sort of clasp called a glad-hand. Brake lines on the dolly had to be attached to just the right locations on each trailer so the rig could stop. Even more important.

If that wasn't enough, bulky metal hooks, each of which could fill a dinner plate, attached by chains to the dolly and clipped on a u-shaped bar under the hitch at the rear of the front trailer in case the hitch failed. The chain hooks are a precaution to prevent the back trailer from rolling away completely detached. Sam showed me how to cross the chains so that the tip or point of the dolly might be cradled by them, if they had to serve their purpose.

The entire rig included a cab with a sleeper compartment – often simply called a sleeper. The sleeper cab alone weighs about 16,000 pounds. A dolly and two trailers weigh thousands of pounds empty. Add to that several thousand pounds of freight. Normally a tractor-trailer can have a total weight of 80,000. The heaviest rigs I ever drove, including freight, weighed between 60,000 and 65,000 pounds.

With all the attachments linking the rig together, what even-tually became easy as child's play, looked like spaghetti junction the first time Sam demonstrated. Much of the procedure of that first set up had flown right over my head, and I said so.

"I know," Sam acknowledged. "The first few times you drive your co-driver will already have the set built. After a few runs, whoever you drive with will build the set with you."

"You mean I might remember everything *and* do it in the right order."

"You'll learn. It just takes some time," Sam smiled.

I looked back at the length of the rig. Just driving one 53 foot trailer had felt challenging enough in training school. All together a set of doubles extends five feet longer than a standard semi rig. Each doubles trailer reaches 28 feet in length and the gap between the two trailers makes about another 2 feet for a total of 58 feet. The full size sleeper cabs we drove added another 15 feet. That made the whole rig 73 feet long.

"How can I turn corners with that much truck behind me?"

"It's actually a bit easier in doubles," Sam said. "You see, between the first and second trailer you have another articulation or bending point. The trailers you'll be pulling may make the whole rig a few feet longer, but it has some give in the middle."

Sam continued. "If you come to the yard at 2 o'clock Thursday afternoon I have a guy named Dutch who drives to Phoenix. His co-driver is taking a couple of days off, and Dutch would be a real good guy for you to drive with the first time. He'll meet you outside the front gates."

Sam advised me to bring along a sleeping bag for the bunk and one or two items to make life on the road a bit more comfortable. During training school I had already pulled out an old bookbag from my earliest college days to serve like a sort of rugged purse. While our driving practice had progressed I found the green bookbag with brown trim handy for carrying along bottles of water, food, and clean toilet paper that a truck stop or tiny hole-in-the-wall gas station might not have available when we had stopped for a break. From Wordsworth to water. From Faulkner to food. From T.S. Eliot to TP, like me, my little green bookbag's life had taken a new turn.

11

Chapter 2: "Take up all the real estate God gave you."

A few days later I walked up to a Kenworth parked outside the gate of the Fort Worth terminal with its blinkers flashing. The number on the side of the truck matched the number Sam had given me earlier. The contents of the little green bookbag were supplemented by a travel carrier with things like a change of clothes, ear plugs, and a toothbrush. I also carried a sleeping bag, a light jacket and a pillow in a blue plastic recycling bag. I had bought a gray, hard plastic clipboard with a storage compartment for my logbook. At least so far it wasn't a lie-book, as drivers often call them.

Dutch opened the passenger side door, and I felt the cool air conditioning waft out into the warm, late May afternoon.

"Are you Karen?" asked a cheerful-looking 40-something guy with dark brown hair, a baseball cap and glasses. I nodded my yes. "I'm Dutch," he said. "Let me help you load your gear."

Then he stepped into the sleeper compartment and opened the side door hatch at the foot of the bunk. Standing outside on the grass I handed my bags to Dutch through the hatch opening. Then while Dutch closed the hatch I went back to the passenger door, climbed in and took a seat.

Once I sat down Dutch wanted to know what Sam had told me about him. Most drivers don't get much feedback from managers unless they do something wrong. I told him truthfully that Sam had said he was a good driver who would be patient with a new driver. Naturally, I hoped relaying this information to Dutch would encourage patience, too, though I trusted Sam's judgment.

"You'll be driving out," Dutch informed me, meaning I would drive the first ten hours from Fort Worth to a small town east of El Paso. I had no idea at the time, but brand new drivers often drive out first so that the experienced driver can see if he or she wants to work with them.

Much later a different driver told me that he had a rookie go around the block once before he instructed him to return to the terminal. Once there he called his manager on his cellphone and told him the rookie couldn't drive. With no one to replace the rookie the run had to be cancelled, costing the money that would have been earned by those drivers. Because good drivers were in high demand, the experienced driver said he could do that.

Safety, I would find, is a major concern of drivers more so than anyone else. Drivers put their lives on the line every working day. A driver had the right to say whether he or she would run with another driver based on how safely they thought another driver performed, in addition to compatibility issues like whether another driver smoked or not. In that case the manager may have known the rookie was no good, but he just wanted the truck to roll. I didn't realize it then, but I too would see the desire to roll despite risks play out for various reasons.

Dutch and I switched seats. I sat on the driver side getting re-acquainted with the surroundings of a big truck. In addition to the large mirrors on each side of the cab I noticed a small one just above the passenger window that pointed almost directly downward. Our training truck in driving school had the same type of mirror. It looked like an odd place for another mirror, and I'd never known its intended function.

"Dutch, what's that mirror for?" I said, pointing outside at the reflective oval.

"That's a lane checker," Dutch answered with some authority. "If you look into it, you can see how close or far you are to the paint stripe."

At this stage I felt lucky to be able to look in just the side mirrors while I struggled with the sensory overload of driving a truck with little practice. But Dutch's answer didn't quite fit in my mind. I would ask other truckers the same question over the next several months. Some said that small mirror helped reveal whether a car drove in a blind spot right next to the cab before a trucker changed lanes. Many passenger side doors have a small window at the bottom and toward the front, supposedly for the same reason. Others thought the mirror showed a driver who stood next to the door before he unlocked it from the driver seat. Some confessed they didn't know its purpose. Perhaps all the suggestions combined to explain the use of that odd little side mirror, but not many drivers knew for sure.

I steered the truck away from the gate and down the street toward the highway. Once again I found myself a bit surprised that I sat behind the wheel of a big rig and this time in a truck emblazoned in large letters with the company logo. My employers had given me the responsibility of driving down busy highways and streets next to vehicles of all descriptions in all sorts of weather at any time of the day or night. We didn't circle back after the first block. I must have been doing something right.

I entered the highway, double-clutching as I had been taught. Dutch helped guide me through the choice of exits and ramps until we left the city and headed west on I-20. Then he sat up with me for a couple of hours, though he must have been tired after the first two day run of the week that he and his co-driver had just completed. Drivers awaiting their shift frequently retire to the bunk to sleep or at least to rest, regardless of the time of day. But a driver might also sit up and talk for a while with his co-driver. Or he might eat a snack, smoke a cigarette or call his wife or girlfriend or both – at different times obviously.

This being my first run, Dutch wanted to make sure I drove well enough for him to sleep behind me, the trucker's way of saying he can trust your driving. Clearly, he had a vested interest in making sure I could point the truck down the road with a reasonable degree of safety.

As the truck headed down the highway, I recognized the bittersweet limbo of the fun of driving and the stress of handling this big vehicle at a fast speed. This particular truck could only go 70 miles per hour because of a mechanism on the engine called a governor. In fact, all but one truck in my experience had a maximum speed of between 68 and 72 mph. Starting out I still didn't feel comfortable getting up to a mere 65 mph. So when the truck approached each curve I slowed down to a speed I felt safe driving at, even if that meant only going 60 or even 55.

West of Fort Worth scrubby rangeland goes on for miles with a mix of trees and grasses hearty enough to thrive in the semi-arid climate. Most landowners use such acreage for grazing cattle or, if they're fortunate, harvesting oil and gas from beneath. Out in the distance oil wells that looked like bareboned hobbyhorses pumped up the dark fluid that made diesel and gasoline possible. Gradually, the land became more and more arid closer to El Paso. Then the desert of the American southwest extended pretty much all the way to the Pacific Ocean, though our run reached only to Phoenix.

For now, I just had to get through the allegedly flat, smooth surfaces of west Texas to our switch out point, the place where Dutch would take the wheel while I took a turn resting in the sleeper compartment. Engineers design Interstate Highways with an eye toward minimizing curves or hills. Though west Texas is certainly not famous for topographical extremes, the highway in that region does have some inclines and curves. Each one felt like a challenge on my first full day of driving. Each time the truck approached a curve, I slowed to a speed that made me feel in full control.

"Drive as fast as you feel you can safely go," Dutch said encouragingly.

While the sun set and darkness descended over the landscape, Dutch wrote down a list of exit numbers and town names so that I would know where I could stop for a break.

"Here's the list," Dutch said, leaning up to the dashboard and attaching the paper to the gray clipboard that carried my logbook. "These exits have truck stops that are easy to get in and out of with doubles."

"Okay," I agreed. "The last thing I want to do is get the truck stuck."

Sam had told me that double trailer rigs can't back up much.

"You do know to park in the fuel lanes, right?" Dutch asked, referring to the diesel pumps that trucks pull up to. Unlike the gasoline pumps where motorists pulls up to the pump in whatever direction they find momentarily convenient, truck fuel lanes all have only one direction to enter and exit.

"Won't the station mind if I park there and don't get fuel?" I asked.

"The truck stops know we can't back these things," Dutch asserted.

Many of the parking spaces at a truck stop require backing a semi rig at some point, whether upon arrival or when leaving. While a standard trailer can, at least theoretically, be backed up all day long, a set of doubles can only back up a few feet at a time and then with limited flexibility. Simply put, the back trailer of a set of doubles cannot be steered in reverse. In a short distance the back trailer takes on a mind of its own and veers to one side or the other. If a driver keeps backing under these circumstances, the trailers will jackknife against each other, possibly causing damage to the brake lines and other components between the front and back trailers. Or if a doubles rig was parked nose-in at a parking spot against a curb, backing to get in or out of the spot could cause the back trailer to strike the trucks parked on either side.

Though other drivers might bristle at the suggestion when they walk in from more distant parking accommodations, driving double trailers frequently necessitates parking in one of the fuel lanes for breaks. Spaces reserved for doubles are rare and are usually occupied by standard rigs. Naturally, doubles drivers never park in a fuel lane overnight. The truck stops would have something to say about that! When stopping overnight a doubles driver either found one of those rare pull-through spots or pulled nose first into a parking space in the middle of the lot, far from curbs. Being a longer rig, the back trailer takes up part of the space behind, essentially taking two spaces.

Later, I would learn to judge for myself when to find a pull-through space where a doubles driver could roll forward both arriving and leaving a spot that didn't block a fuel lane. But starting out, I'd follow Dutch's advice lest I put us in a jam. If I drove into a spot where the truck couldn't pull forward or back up, we would have to break down and rebuild the whole set. That wasn't my idea of fun and games when the set might be blocking the way of an angry truck driver or two or three. Of course, some drivers would get great entertainment value out of such a scenario. But I didn't want to be a diversion for some bored and lonely truckers with nothing better to do than to peer out of their cabs at the rookie doubles driver that drove nose-in to a back up spot.

"Do you have a spare key?" I asked. "So I can lock the door while you're in here sleeping?"

"We all pretty much trust each other out here," Dutch said with a nonchalance that some drivers exhibit on the road. Personally, I didn't want to be left in an unlocked truck at night in a station and would later learn that leaving the doors unlocked was against company policy. After all, truck stops are famous for being hotspots for theft and mayhem. However, this being my first run I felt I had little say in the matter. Or I just didn't have enough backbone right then to say differently.

Like many new drivers my hands moved the steering wheel slightly back and forth more than needed while simply heading down the road. Keeping in mind Sam's admonition about the tail wagging the dog, I still had to get used to the sensitivity of the steering wheel. Looking back along the length of the rig in the side mirrors, perhaps, I let the dog get wagged a bit on the first trip or two. Yet, it stood to reason that the back trailer could wiggle all it wanted, but the laws of physics would ultimately bring that back trailer wherever the front trailer pulled it, every time. Incontrovertibly.

"There are armrests on the seat," Dutch said and pulled them down on the passenger seat to show me. He demonstrated how they clicked in position. "Sound the horn if you need me, and use your armrests," he said, eyeing my novice steering technique.

Dutch retired to the sleeper and zipped up the heavy vinyl fabric that hung like a curtain, separating the driver compartment from the sleeper compartment. Left alone in the gloom of the sunset to continue my westward journey, the headlights picked up the reflective paint and markers on each side of the lane, forming a welcome visual aide. More than ever before, my eyes hungrily sought out any highway signs. White or red or yellow, if a sign stood, I wanted to know what it had to say, what warning or instructions it could impart so that I might be prepared for what lie ahead. I never saw a road sign that didn't give good advice.

As I piloted the truck through the growing darkness, I gradually became more and more distracted by a light to my left, just outside the driver window. I couldn't figure it out. Cars and other trucks came up beside me and passed, but the lights kept a steady pace right next to me. I remained stuck in the hyper-attentive mode of driving this behemoth during the *nighttime* for the *first* time. I could barely peel my eyes from the view in front of me to see what odd light hovered next to the window. Finally, when the moment felt right, with no traffic nearby, no impending curve ahead, I glanced over to my left in the driver side window and saw it: the reflection of the dashboard lights in full glow. I heaved a sigh of relief. Glancing over again I saw the green digits on the driver side mirror reflecting the numbers 76°, the evening's temperature.

A few hours later, I stopped for a break at one of the truck stops on Dutch's list. When I got out of the truck, a man in a pickup did a double-take, looking twice at me. Yes, a woman had driven this semi with a sleeper and double trailers into this station, I smiled to myself. When I returned to the truck I drove back onto the highway. The video game display in front of my windshield looked all too real again. I sat, looking out and steering along the curves of the highway for hours and hours. I didn't have time to get bored. The experience felt too new, the responsibility too awesome.

After a few more hours, I noticed another light. This time a warning light in a squiggled shape appeared in red on the dashboard. I couldn't tell what it meant. Was the engine about to fail? Tell me it doesn't have anything to do with the brakes, I thought.

"Dutch!" I called. No answer. I waited a few minutes. The warning light persisted. "Dutch, sorry to bother you," I called louder once more, my voice still trailing off amid the road noise. Again no response. I didn't know what to do. Maybe I should pull over, I thought. Well, he had told me to honk the horn so I pressed the center of the steering wheel and the horn honked. Still nothing and still the light glowed red. The road noise in a semi drowns out a lot of sound. Yet I found myself surprised that Dutch couldn't hear the horn.

Oh, my God, I thought. He didn't get out of the truck when I stopped for a break did he?

The curtain had remained zipped up and Dutch had told me he'd leave his logbook on the driver seat, if he got out. His logbook hadn't been there when I had returned. What if he'd forgotten to set it there? I called his name again, not quite sure what to do next. But finally, Dutch poked his head out from between the curtains.

"What's up?"

I explained the light that had come on.

"Oh, don't worry about that. Sam knows about it. The transmission runs warm. It's nothing."

"I thought I'd left you back there when you didn't answer to the horn honking."

"Next time use the air horn," Dutch said, pointing to the metal wire loop that hung down near the top left edge of the windshield next to the side window. "The city horn is like a gnat biting a rhino," Dutch said casually, referring to the quieter horn that a driver sounds by pressing the center of the steering wheel. Then he zipped back up the curtain while I continued onward, ignoring the dashboard light.

I never did relax enough to use the armrests that first drive.

We eventually came to a tiny town near El Paso where we would switch out driving. Dutch would drive us the rest of the way into the Phoenix hub while I lie down in the bunk. I pulled off at the highway exit looking for the tiny gas station that Dutch had described. I halted at a stop sign, but couldn't see any station. In every direction the streets disappeared in the gray and black of nighttime gloom. I felt wary of driving farther into the small town streets where I might wind up lost or stuck. I heard Dutch stirring in the bunk. Like many drivers Dutch slept with his clothes on so he quickly exited the sleeper. He greeted me cheerfully and plunked down into the upholstery of the passenger seat.

"I should have given you directions to the station," he said.

19

I didn't say anything, but I preferred having him seated next to me while I navigated the narrow, dark streets to the small fuel station that Dutch and his regular co-driver stopped at every night and day, going and returning along the line they drove. While I steered the truck, I looked in the side mirrors watching the back tires. Combined with the length of the trailers and sleeper cab, the back tires reached more than 60 feet away from me as they edged around every turn on the way to the station.

Then Dutch gave me a bit of driving advice that stood me in good stead for many tens of thousands of miles to come: "When you make these turns or drive around stations or truck stops, take up all the real estate God gave you," he said. "That's what an old guy told me when I started so I'll pass it on to you. It doesn't cost you anything to make big turns and it can save getting into a bad situation so take up all the real estate God gave you."

I drove the truck to a fuel lane at the station, stopping by a diesel pump and climbed out. I had driven ten hours, all the way from Fort Worth to far west Texas all by myself. I could hardly believe it.

In a few minutes I would unroll my sleeping bag in the bunk and try to get some rest. But first we went into the station to take a break. Half an hour later I sat down on a bench for a moment while Dutch chatted to the station clerk and noticed something I'd never felt before. While sitting I involuntarily leaned forward. I realized I had been pushing against the force of being pressed back into the seat of a moving vehicle at highway speeds all those hours. I'd never driven that far, for that long, and certainly never with such pent up tension. I would feel this phenomenon for the first and last time that night. I had become a trucker. I would get used to driving.

Chapter 3: "The driver is the captain of the ship."

Dutch sat down in the driver seat to start the next leg of our trip over the Texas border to New Mexico and then on to Arizona. The clock read past midnight. I negotiated my way around the giant gear shifter that stood between the seats, opened the curtain, and stepped into the sleeper compartment. The next thing I knew I became airborne. My gut suddenly filled with the deep anxiety that grips a rollercoaster rider during a downward plunge. I quickly bounced into the bunk, landing hard on the sheets of the mattress and producing a vocalization along the lines of, "Unhf!"

"Are you okay?" Dutch asked, calling over his shoulder.

Lifting myself, face first off of the bunk, I sat on its edge. "What the hell happened?" I asked, rubbing my right arm where it had whacked against the desk when I fell. I had been lucky not to hit my head on the edge of the top bunk.

"Maybe I should have mentioned, there's a step down from here to the sleeper."

I pulled back the curtains to look at the culprit. On the black rubber matted floor a metal step did indeed rise up from the sleeper into the driver compartment.

"Are you sure you're okay?" Dutch asked kindly, though I noticed his shoulders shrugged rhythmically in a dance of politely silent laughter.

"Yeah, I'm okay."

"I should have told you."

"Well, now I'll never forget."

21

I zipped up the curtain soon after I entered the compartment. Though Dutch seemed like a nice guy, something weighed on my mind. I had never been this far from civilization and alone in a vehicle with a man I'd just met. Supposedly, the carrier checked out every applicant and approved no drivers who had even a minor criminal history. What went through my mind, however, were the stories I'd heard from other women who recommended female drivers climb into the sleeping bag with the zipper on the underside between herself and the bed. These women explained, if a male co-driver turned out to be a would-be lothario, a woman would have time to awaken and resist before the male could reach her nether regions. Some of these cautions came from male drivers, too. No one ever said they knew of an actual assault. Nonetheless, the risk of finding myself in such a circumstance was just one of the reasons I found the prospect of driving a truck worrisome.

What I really should have been most concerned with, however, was my next night's sleep. Because for the first time I faced one of the major difficulties of team driving: getting adequate sleep in a truck while it moves down the road with the co-driver at the wheel. Disruptions and noise can awaken anyone whether they like it or not, and being in a truck with sounds and movements one can't control pose a significant and ongoing challenge.

Dutch drove back to the highway before I learned the importance of having your bunk ready before your co-driver takes off. No one but husband and wife teams share the same bedding. Most drivers sleep on or in a sleeping bag. While the truck made its turns through the streets of the town on its way back to the Interstate, my feet and legs worked hard to balance on the floor while uncurling and flattening my sleeping bag on the bunk and digging my pillow out of the blue plastic bag.

The sleeper had two bunks, top and bottom. The bottom bunk is always the one used when a co-driver remains at the steering wheel, heading down the road. The top bunk may be snapped into place against the back wall. Most often drivers keep the top bunk folded down and use the surface for storage. When drivers switch out they stow their own sleeping bag and pillows on the unused top bunk while their co-driver sleeps. The degree of complication of a driver's bedding supplies corresponds to how long they have driven in that truck. For a driver on his regular route the truck became a home away from home. One driver I later worked with had a body pillow his spouse had given him that he called his "work wife." Nuf sed. I made sure he set that one on the top bunk before I rolled out my sleeping bag.

In trucks with a so-called condo cab a driver could stand up to full height inside. I stand just a couple of inches short of six feet tall, and I could raise a hand over my head and still have plenty of space between my fingers and the ceiling of the sleeper. I felt glad to be in this type of truck because the older conventional cabs required a driver to crouch when he or she moved from the front seats to the bunk. Once in the sleeper compartment, old-timers told me, the drivers of yore had to lie down on the bunk to change their clothes or attempt to do so while standing almost bent over at the waist.

The small floor space between the edge of the bunk and the seats was about the size of a large bath mat. To stay balanced while putting down bedding, dressing or undressing when the truck moved down the road required contortions like an amateur circus performer, tipping this way and that. Occasionally, I grabbed hold of the hand grip on the edge of the upper bunk while struggling in the dimly lit interior. If anyone could have seen this dance, they might have thought they were witnessing an advanced case of ants in the pants.

Finally, with all the sleeping gear in place I sat on the edge of the bunk itself, facing toward the curtain to take off my shoes and looked around. A writing surface with two cup holding indentations on top and a drawer underneath stood just behind the driver seat and to my left. Below the drawer a storage compartment awaited supplies or equipment. About a foot above the desk a shelf with more storage reached all the way to the top of the truck's ceiling.

On the floor to my right short plastic walls sectioned off a squared area likewise covered with a flat plastic surface. In the resulting boxed area a small refrigerator hummed. Some driver-managers supplied drivers with refrigerators and some didn't. If not, drivers could buy a refrigerator at their own expense. Above the refrigerator even more storage cubbyholes held food, clothes, logbooks, and so on in every available nook and cranny. Wherever an item could be stored, protective nylon mesh held the supplies securely, preventing objects from falling on passengers or on the floor.

Drivers customarily keep the head of the bed behind the driver seat. Thus, every time someone lies in the bunk, they rest their head on the same end, not where someone has rested their feet. I laid back on the bunk with the side of the desk to my left and the back wall of the cab to my right and looked up at the bottom of the bunk above. To my right and above my head a panel gently glowed with a digital clock and buttons to operate the compartment lights, temperature control and volume for overhead radio speakers in the sleeper.

Unbeknownst to me while I lay on my rolled out sleeping bag and tried to drift off into dreamland, a three segment storage area for tools, tire chains, bottles of windshield wiper spray and so on lie underneath the bunk. One segment is under the head of the bunk with a hatch on the outside behind the driver door. Another segment is under the feet of the bunk on the passenger side with another hatch door on that side. In between a third segment can only be reached from inside the sleeper where drivers release a latch and lift the bunk to reveal the entire storage area. To get into storage from outside a driver releases one of two latches behind either seat, opening a small handle-less door on the outside of the truck for the storage bin on the corresponding side. So if a trucker releases the latch behind the driver seat, only the storage segment on the driver side opens.

In the trucks Sam's drivers used, window hatches looked out from both the head and foot of the bunk. They had no curtains, but were heavily tinted so passersby could not see in. The hatches could double as emergency doors. In the event of a crash, if the driver in the bunk can't get to the front of the cab these hatches can be removed. If the front of the cab is crushed or on fire, they may provide the only escape. Hence, this truck came better equipped than most that only have small vents on the sides of the sleeper.

24

While I lay there with closed eyes and tried to surrender to sleep, I couldn't help but notice how the truck shifted and lifted, bounced and jounced my hapless body while the wheels rolled over every texture of the pavement beneath us. All the noise and vibrations couldn't be felt to the same degree while sitting in the front seats. Both seats floated on a pneumatic cushion of air that absorbed the shock of each bump. Not so the bunk.

Someone once said, if you can't sleep, rest, and that often leads to sleep. Usually. Though I felt tired, I had also been filled with adrenalin from several hours of driving for hundreds of miles at night for the first time. I nestled into the sleeping bag, adjusted the air conditioning and closed my eyes again in the mostly darkened sleeper. In the great American desert few street lights pervade the dark of night. But some narrow gaps in the curtain let in headlights from passing vehicles. Yet, somewhere along the next several hundred miles sheer exhaustion finally overtook me. I slept lightly then woke again while the truck bumped along. Then I would doze off for a while more, perhaps for a few minutes or for an hour.

After several hours of catnaps, alternated by long moments of staring into the dark of the moving sleeper, I woke to the feel of the truck slowing and exiting the Interstate. I lay blinking into the darkness while the truck continued on and on. I could hear the faint sound of Dutch talking on his cellphone. I unzipped the curtain and blinked back the bright desert sun. "Good morning," Dutch said, folding his phone and setting it in one of the cupholders on the dashboard. "Let me get this stuff out of your way."

Strewn across the dashboard and passenger seat multiple CDs reflected their silver rainbows of digitalized music out of the truck cab and, one could imagine, into the stratosphere. Without missing a beat Dutch gathered up his belongings with his right hand while steering with his left. By contrast I couldn't stand to take my eyes off the road in front of me for more than a second while driving. In the meantime Dutch could set out CDs in an array as far as his arm could reach.

Once Dutch had scooped his CDs into a large carrier case I sat down in the passenger seat and put on my shoes. I glanced around. We rolled through a flat valley. While looking at maps of different states over the years I'd noticed if the roads looked straight and the rivers crooked, the land usually lie flat. If the roads looked crooked and the rivers ran straight, the land often contained mountains. But no rivers flowed nearby. Arid, reddish mountains, unlike any I had ever seen, rose on either side of the roadway. The truck could have been on the surface of Mars except for the clumps of bushes and the ribbon of asphalt that led off into the distance. Several miles ahead a group of buildings soon formed a smudge on the horizon.

"This is the reservation," Dutch explained. I looked around at small whirlwinds of sand that danced across the ground between the road and the mountains.

"What are those?" I asked

"Dust devils," Dutch said and explained that hot air rising caught some of the sands in an upward vortex, like tiny, harmless tornados. He continued. "They're not the only devils out here, though."

"What do you mean?"

Dutch pointed to a fracture in the windshield of the truck that glinted brighter in the sunlight. A series of rings expanded from the central point of a small hole in the glass caused by a bullet.

"Last month while my co-driver, Miguel, drove to the hub we took a pot shot."

I looked at the plains of red sands punctuated with dark green shrubs and cacti. I looked into the remote edges of the mountain-sides and wondered if someone stood out there with a gun aimed at the truck right then.

"What did they do that for?" I asked.

"For the hell of it."

We arrived at our terminal hub in Phoenix at about ten in the morning and went about the business of making a turnaround. We dropped the trailers, meaning we drove them to spaces in the drop lot and disconnected the lifelines, leaving them for a termi-nal employee to pick up with a so-called yard dog, a piece of equipment that moves the trailers up to each dock door. The yard dogs were tiny cabs designed for one worker to hook up a single trailer at a time and ferry it within the grounds of the terminal.

Next, Dutch and I took each trailer's paperwork to the dispatch office and received the papers for our set of returning trailers. Before building a new set of trailers, we drove over to the terminal's fuel pumps. Fueling at the terminals could be quicker and easier than fueling at a truck stop, but not every terminal pump could be found in good repair. Drivers often had to fuel elsewhere when pumps were closed or their run took them too far afield to use a company facility.

We both climbed down the metal steps of the truck to set the pump handles into the tanks on each side. Climb being the operative word. The truck's steps descend so steeply a driver faces the truck when getting in or out of the cab, as if on a ladder. Some drivers insist on learning the hard way. If a driver descends the steps while facing away from the truck, as if walking down a set of stairs, just a slip of one heel on a step and he introduces himself to the ground pretty abruptly.

To get into the truck a driver has to step straight up onto a long silver running board with a textured metal surface meant to grab the soles of the shoes. That silver grid-like surface goes around the back of the cab to a catwalk. The catwalk is a work platform where a driver can climb up to attach or detach stubborn electrical cords or brake lines whose glad-hands don't want to slide together easily. Usually, the lifelines can be attached while standing on the pavement next to the truck.

With the driver door open a trucker puts his right foot on the lowest step, reaches up and takes hold of a vertical grab bar on the side of the truck just behind the door, and hoists himself up. Usually with his left hand on the door, he then places his left foot on the higher step and hoists again. Then he swings his right foot onto the truck cab floor between the seat and pedals and, turning to face the windshield, sits down on the driver seat.

On terra firma Dutch showed me how he set each fuel pump handle under a rubber cargo strap to hold it in place while fuel surged into the side tanks. While we waited for the tanks to fill Dutch asked me what I began to call "the question," a question

27

that almost every male co-driver would ask me for the next few years. "So what made you decide to drive a truck?"

Many co-drivers asked this nearly universal question simply in a friendly attempt to make conversation with the "girl" co-driver. So, while the reason appeared obvious to me, I explained my desire for a good job. Yet, I couldn't help but wonder if any guys ever heard this question themselves. So I started my own little tradition: I asked Dutch why he drove.

Of course, he had the same general reason. He also explained that like many drivers he had first sought a trucking job where he could come home from work at the end of every day. A home-daily job is a privilege that most people take for granted, but it is a coveted gig in trucking. At first, Dutch drove for a rock hauler, a company that supplies gravel for construction sites where workers pour concrete. Like many drivers involved in that type of work Dutch earned pay, not by the hour, but by the load.

"I'm lucky," he said. "My wife has a job. But even so, and though I didn't own the truck, didn't have to maintain or fuel it, we couldn't make it."

"What do you mean?"

"After about six months, I looked at our books and realized we would have to go bankrupt in another six months if I kept hauling rocks." Instead, Dutch had gladly accepted this job, where he spent every weekend at home and made good money for a working man or woman.

Fueling completed, we drove onto the yard to build our new set of trailers. I looked at the temperature reading on the driver side mirror. The numbers glowed 108°. Once our set was built, I had to drive first, since I had driven first the day before. Again Dutch gave me a list of exit numbers with suitable truck stops, this time from Phoenix to El Paso. Following regulations, Dutch had to log himself into the sleeper in his logbook.

"I'll stay up until I guide you back to the Interstate," Dutch said. "Later today you'll see some canyons with rocks bigger than this truck. Some places look like giants just walked away after playing a game of marbles. You'll love the scenery."

I liked Dutch's optimism, but I couldn't imagine being able to enjoy the scenery just yet and told him so. I still found it a challenge simply to open a water bottle and take a sip while driving. While we rolled along, Dutch taught me the first truism of truck driving: "The driver is the captain of the ship." Therefore, I had a right and privilege to drive at the speed I felt most comfortable with.

I got the truck onto the Interstate and up to speed. Then Dutch went back to the sleeper and once again my nerve-wracking video game began. Even with more practice, each moment felt like an adventure. Each curve held a challenge, but I managed to make it down the road.

Dutch had been in the sleeper bunk for a couple of hours by the time I drove through the canyons he had mentioned. Steep hills and curves lie ahead. I could only glimpse the surroundings every now and then while cautiously keeping control of the truck. What astonished me more than boulders and mountains, however, were the other truck drivers. I doddered along doing the best I could in the slow lane while other truck drivers swept by, taking curves at high speeds, plummeting down the mountainous roads in the hammer lane, as the fast lane is called. Cautious of distractions, I kept the CB radio off, but in retrospect wouldn't have been surprised to hear a good-natured ribbing from another driver.

"Hey, ___" the voice of a trucker might say, calling other drivers by company name, the way they do. Then with a note of friendly challenge and humor the voice might ask, "You out for a Sunday drive?"

Several hours later our rig had crossed the state of New Mexico and approached a point along the west Texas Interstate that dipped very near our border with the country of Mexico. Along the highway a US border patrol station checked all traffic that drove through. On the approach to the facility, bright yellow lights flashed alternately next to large traffic signs that warned: Be Prepared to Stop. Traffic slowed nearly to a stop, yet agents simply waved most vehicles through. Cars and trucks of all sizes snaked through a tall yellow metal building shaped like a giant letter U turned upside down onto the highway.

Wearing a light smile on his face an agent waved through the semi immediately in front of us, just like he had the cars before.

29

When I rolled up, I hadn't come to a complete stop and so needed to downshift into a lower gear. In my inexperience, I hesitated. I stepped on the brake in order to start out from the lowest gear. The agent's smile quickly faded from his face, and he put his hand up, indicating he wanted me to stop. Perhaps, he had seen my lack of smooth moves as some sort of reluctance. I stopped the rig and lowered the window.

His brown slacks and short sleeved shirt were topped off by a broad-brimmed hat like Smokey the Bear. Smokey walked up to the window with thumbs tucked into a black leather belt decorated by a pistol, ammo clips, and a can of pepper spray. Without further ado, he spoke.

"Are you a United States citizen?" Smokey asked, his eyes hidden behind reflective sunglasses.

"Yes," I answered.

"Where were you born?"

"Dallas."

"Where are you driving to?"

"Fort Worth."

"Do you have a co-driver?"

"Yes."

"Where was he born?"

I paused a second. "I don't know him well enough to know where he was born," I answered, then added. "I'm subbing for his regular co-driver."

Smokey looked at me thoughtfully for a split second then continued.

"What are you carrying?" Smokey asked.

"Um," I hesitated. We didn't carry a single commodity. I couldn't truthfully say, 'Why yes, officer, we have a load of toilet paper.' Or photocopiers or cantaloupes or any other tangible object on earth that can fit in a truck trailer. We carried whatever people shipped in their packages. That's it! "Packages," I replied at last.

Without articulating anything, Smokey seemed to say, "Humph!"

"How long you been driving?" asked Smokey, a frown creasing his face. He glanced down at his shoes, balanced on his left foot and polished the top of his right shoe on the back of his pant leg.

"This is my first run."

Smokey set his right foot back down and looked up quickly, a surprised expression on his face. He laughed a gravelly, deep-voiced laugh. "How long then?" he persisted.

I thought another second. "Less than twenty hours."

"You're not doing too bad then." Smokey pointed down the road. "You can go on." I set the truck in gear and drove out from under the roof of the U-shaped building with Smokey's blessing.

As we pulled away from the border patrol station, traffic that had been slowed by the station gradually uncoiled and sped up then came to a near stop over and over again. Each time the cars ahead performed a stop and start, I guided the great truck to a halt and then geared back up once we moved again. Dutch stepped out of the sleeper and sat in the passenger seat.

"Did you hear all that?" I asked, nodding my head back toward the border station.

"He give you a hard time?"

"I thought he was gonna have me pull the rig over for a search until I thought to tell him that we're carrying packages."

Dutch laughed. "That's what Miguel told them when they questioned him before. They know we haven't got anything exciting. He was just playing the big man." Then Dutch asked, "Have you ever floated gears before?"

"I don't know how."

"When you hear the engine rev up to the point you would normally clutch, just pull the shifter out of gear and slide it into the next gear."

"Sounds too easy."

"Try it."

Driving across the flat, straight desert highway the engine roar increased. Instead of pushing in the clutch pedal to pull the shifter from one gear to the next, I simply pulled the shifter out of gear and quickly pushed it into the next highest gear. I did that again and again, into the next gear each time. I found floating gears to be about as easy as it sounded. Also, it saved my left foot and leg the stress of pushing in the clutch each time, except for when I had to stop and restart from a standstill.

Traffic slowed to a stop again. Then the cars and trucks began to move down the highway once more. I floated the gears back up yet again, instead of using the clutch pedal. Dutch called Sam on his cellphone and reported the news.

"Hey, Sam! This girl you got here's floating gears." Sam must have asked how I did. "Like a duck to water." I heard Dutch say into the phone.

Hmm, I thought. I did that well? Better than expected, anyway? I'd gotten almost no rest during our trip. We hadn't stopped to shower or to eat a real meal. And driving a truck the first few times took real courage. Though I was still green as a leprechaun on St. Patrick's Day, my back quietly and gradually began to form a new trucker's backbone. Maybe I *can* do this job for the long haul, I thought. But my next co-driver seemed to think otherwise or maybe he wanted *me* to think so.

Chapter 4: "The captain doesn't sink the ship!"

Truckers earn every penny they're paid working long hours in a dangerous job, and my next co-driver seemed bent on reminding me of those dangers. One co-driver would later tell me that a highway patrolman had said he wouldn't drive a truck because he thought the job too dangerous. On top of that the difficulty of sleeping on a moving truck can be one of the worst problems, especially starting out. I had been lucky to get any rest at all on the first trip. Plus, drivers on the move have little chance to shower or even brush their teeth. If I wanted those civilizing influences, I'd have to carve out the time with my co-driver. But would my next co-driver cooperate?

A week later Sam called me again. "I got another run for you."

"Where to?" I asked.

"This time you'll be going to sunny Orlando," Sam chimed, making it sound almost like I'd won a vacation on a game show. Hotel not included.

"How long does that take?" I answered, not really wanting to go through the uncertainty and exhaustion of another run, but feeling I ought to make some use of my new CDL.

"One run is out a day and back a day."

"Okay, sure," I answered with feigned enthusiasm, more to encourage myself to go than for any other reason.

"You'll meet Buster at the Dallas terminal at noon on Tuesday. He'll have the trailers ready to go. All you have to do is show up."

"Not Fort Worth?"

"No. There's a terminal in Dallas, too."

Sam gave directions to the Dallas facility and our call ended with me silently wondering why the first few co-drivers had the rig built already. I theorized that Sam let a brand new driver get used to driving before anything else. Maybe he experienced a higher retention rate that way. Perhaps, Sam also waited to see whether a new driver meant to stick around. Maybe, driver-managers, who are often drivers themselves, remember how overwhelming learning to drive can be and try to ease new drivers in. Or, at least, Sam did.

At the appointed hour I met Buster, an older man with a bushy moustache and shaggy hair gone gray. He wore a plain navy blue tee-shirt, instead of the uniform shirt we drivers were supposed to wear. He greeted me with a country-fried voice made rough by decades of chain smoking, a voice that he shouted in as much or more than he spoke. Not, it appeared, because he felt angry. But from speaking over the roar of road noise year after year, and perhaps, from going a bit deaf. The result: Buster often sounded unduly excited, whether he was or not.

We met and I loaded my things into the truck. Then I drove out of the Dallas terminal. Seated in the passenger seat smoking a ciggy, Buster showed me the path to the Interstate from the front gate. Once on the highway I asked Buster if he and his regular co-driver, Buddy, ever took a shower break at a truck stop. By then I had heard truck stops had showers that really amounted to private bathrooms. I didn't yet know that each company terminal also had showers, until Buster mentioned it.

"One thing's for sure," Buster said. "You'll get a chance for a break on this run. Me and Buddy always stop and get cleaned up at least once a week. But we use the terminal showers, either here or in Orlando. They want eight to ten bucks at most truck stops." Buster said, leaving out the tidbit that truck stops don't charge truckers to shower when they purchase fuel, usually amounting to hundreds of dollars.

After a beat or two, Buster spoke again. "You know what they say about the driver being the captain?" Buster asked, flicking the ash of his cigarette into an empty cup.

Don't sink the ship!

"Yeah, the driver is the captain of the ship," I answered.
"You know the second part?"
"Don't swerve for animals?"
"Close. It's related."
"What's that?"
"Don't sink the fucking ship!"
Hence, Buster unceremoniously introduced a truism of trucking, though we'll neaten it to: The captain doesn't sink the ship!

I had driven about three hours when a heavy rainstorm struck near the Texas-Louisiana border. I turned on the wipers, and in true ironic form, the wiper over the passenger side swept the windshield wonderfully clear. The windshield wiper on the driver side chose that moment to go on its own vacation. Not only did it not clean the window worth a damn, but after a few strokes the rubber wiper blade totally spazzed out and bent against the window at a bizarre angle. Then the metal wiper arm scratched the glass like fingernails on a chalkboard. I turned the wiper off to limit the damage it might do to the glass, besides the wiper could no longer clear the view. Then heavy raindrops splattered blindingly against the windshield. Luckily, an exit with a truck stop drew near just then. I pulled in and stopped in a fuel lane, and Buster reattached the wiper blade. With the crisis averted I went inside to get a soda.
When I returned a few minutes later the rain had stopped and Buster sat in the driver seat. This became the first run, but certainly not the last one, where I would meet a driver who wanted to do what truckers commonly call "driving off the book." In this case I thought Buster wanted to drive, for one thing, because he could go faster. He had been steering trucks since my childhood, and naturally, driving had become second nature to him by this point. While I still learned the ropes Dutch had told me to take my time. Buster had a different notion.
"What are you doing?" I asked, looking up at Buster through the open driver window.
"I'm gettin' ready to roll," Buster answered in his loud, twangy voice.
"I haven't driven ten hours yet," I pointed out naively.

35

"Aren't you tired?"

"Not yet. It's still the middle of the afternoon," said I, the up-start, persnickety female.

"You don't wanna drive a whole ten hours," Buster declared. "Buddy and I always switch out after a few hours," Buster added, describing his routine with his regular co-driver. At the time I didn't know, but would later find out that he and Buddy did indeed drive that way. But right then I persisted.

"I know I'm supposed to drive more than three hours," I answered, standing my ground.

Buster relented. He stood up, stepped back and sat on the edge of the sleeper bunk. "If you get tired, just holler," he said, pulling the curtain closed.

I drove I-20 across northern Louisiana for a couple more hours. While heading down the road something on the dashboard emitted a slow beeping noise. Remembering the light that had come on during my first trip, my eyes searched the dashboard in vain for a warning light or any indication of what the beep meant. "Buster?" I called over my shoulder. "Do you hear that?"

As if he were already awake, Buster came out of the sleeper like a boxer out of the corner of the ring. He sat down heavily in the passenger seat, lighting another cigarette. "That's the scale house pass," Buster explained, referring to an electronic device that beeps a code telling a driver either to pass or to pull in for a vehicle weight check.

More commonly called weigh stations, scale houses are located every so often on all major highways. They measure the weight of trucks to make sure they are under the legal 80,000 pound limit. However, trucks that illegally haul more weight can simply exit before they get to a station and take local roads around. Often this isn't necessary, since many weigh stations remain unmanned most, if not all, of the time.

Like many trucks ours came equipped with a PrePass device. The device is a transponder in the form of a square, light brown, plastic box about the size of a cigarette pack that adheres to the top of the windshield. The system uses the same type of technology that automatic toll road readers do. In this case, about a mile or so before a weigh station the transponder sends a signal to scales buried in the highway that tell a computer how much the truck weighs.

When we drove by a weigh station the box emitted a slow beep and flashed a tiny green light, if we were permitted to pass. If we were required to drive onto the scales, it emitted a rapid beep and flashed a tiny red light. If for any reason the device didn't work, we also had to stop and drive into the station for a weight check.

Not that anyone had told me any such details yet.

Buster continued. "You're lucky it beeped you through."

"Why am I lucky?" I asked.

"If you pass a scale house, they fine you $2000," Buster practically shouted.

Though unaware of PrePass, I knew we had to stop at scales or risk getting ticketed, but I had never heard of such a high dollar amount attached to any driving offense. Later, I would drive with someone who said he had been fined $500 for passing a scale. That amount could certainly take the wind out of any driver's sails, but Buster quoted a figure four times higher.

Buster continued. "They don't even have to stop you with the police car."

"What do you mean?"

"They usually have a flight man come after you."

"A flight man?" I asked.

"Uh-hunh, he ought to come after you and ticket you for passing that scale back there."

"Um, I was beeped through with a green light."

"One day you'll just get it in the mail, a big old fine for running a scale," Buster continued unabated. "You'd better hope it doesn't get lost in the mail, too. 'Cause they'll issue a warrant for your arrest." Buster looked out his side window and shook his head. "Yep, I tell you. This is a miserable job."

I didn't point out to Buster that if they didn't pull the truck over, they wouldn't know who to ticket! But also I noticed that these dire warnings came on the heels of my refusal to let Buster drive on my book.

"If the cops don't get you, other drivers will," Buster went on.

I pointed out the obvious. "Other drivers can't give tickets."

"No, but they get up to all kinds of things at truck stops. Robbery. Murder. *Rape.*" Buster said, adding an extra flourish to that last word, as a scarcely veiled intimidation tactic.

"Gosh, you'd think there's no drivers just trying to earn an honest living," I answered with a tinge of irony that escaped Buster.

"There are!" Buster shouted.

"Well then, I'll just have to drive with those guys."

"Doesn't matter if they're with us or not," Buster answered, just in case I might think drivers from our company would be safe to work with.

"Everyone has to pass a strict background check and drug test," I replied.

"That don't mean nothing!" Buster countered. "I drove on this very truck three months ago when the cops busted a guy right in front of my eyes for carrying drugs," Buster shouted, dramatically pointing his right index finger down at the floor of the truck. "Not only that," he continued. "There's a driver who works out of the Dallas hub who killed a man." He gave me a name. "If you ever see him coming, drive the other way."

Then Buster asked "the question."

"Why do you want to drive, anyhow?" he asked.

"You mean why does a *woman* want to drive?" I asked with a laugh.

"Nah, nah," Buster tried to backpedal, but I was just having fun with him. I didn't really mind the question. I just thought it kind of obvious why anyone drove a truck.

"Truck driving is not a hobby," I explained. "It's a good job." Then for the second time I returned the favor. "Why do you drive?" I asked.

"Because I *love* it," Buster answered.

I couldn't help but laugh again. Apparently, Buster didn't detect the contradiction of admitting he loved a job he had just so eagerly described as a dismal and dangerous existence.

Buster nodded towards an upcoming exit sign. "Go ahead and stop up here at the café. That's where we eat," Buster exclaimed.

I parked the truck in a rare pull-through spot at a gas station that had been converted into a burger joint. I tugged my little green bookbag onto my shoulders. Then we went in and each ate a lackluster meal of a burger and fries. I made a pit stop in the ladies' room before returning to the warm sun of the parking lot.

Back at the truck Buster sat in the driver seat once again. I stood outside the truck with my thumbs tucked around the shoulder straps of my bookbag and looked up at Buster. His tanned arm leaned on the window ledge of the door while the shit-eating grin on his face shone through the constant haze of tobacco smoke.

"Go ahead and take a break," Buster said, pointing his thumb toward the sleeper compartment. A little column of ashes detached itself from his cigarette and fell silently onto the silver running board outside the driver door. True, I felt a bit fatigued from the stress of starting my second run with another unknown guy to another unfamiliar place, but in the early evening hours I still felt wide awake.

"I'm not that tired yet," I protested.

"You're tired enough you don't wanna drive for another five hours," Buster said. He turned off the parking brakes and set the shifter into gear, making the truck roll forward slightly. "Besides, up here we get off the Interstate and take local highways. You don't know the way."

There we were parked at a small store in a small town somewhere in northern Louisiana, and a man thirty years older than me insisted that he drive. I wondered what I could do. I could refuse again, like I had done earlier. If the thought had occurred to me, I could have insisted he tell me which highways to take and written their numbers down. But Buster's ruse worked. Right or wrong, this time I relented.

I climbed aboard and entered the sleeper compartment. Later I covered this run with Buddy and learned that he and Buster usually took an all-Interstate route. But technically, their instructions were to take the route Buster and I drove the first time. Not doing so could get us in trouble for not following the suggested route. Maybe Buster thought I'd tattle on him otherwise, but then again he had no compunction about switching out driving. So maybe, I reasoned, he thought he would show the new girl driver a more challenging path.

Once unpacked, I lie down on the bunk on my sleeping bag and tried to rest. The early hour and the lingering energy of paying full attention to driving left me feeling wound up. In time Buster drove off the Interstate onto a Mississippi state highway. The constancy of motion on the Interstate evaporated. Dotted with traffic lights the local roadway guaranteed a stop and start rhythm to our once steady progress. Each time we came to a light or a stop sign I felt the truck slow and jostle with the gears changing. If I dozed in the darkened interior of the truck cab for those hours, I don't remember it. Finally, we pulled over at a small truck stop along the state highway where night had fallen.

I went inside and bought a drink and some chips. Back out at the truck Buster sat in the driver seat watching a police car with flashing lights atop its roof that had pulled in to the parking lot. Upon my return Buster went into the truck stop while I sat in the cab. He returned carrying a bag with chips, cookies, candy, and sodas that he arranged in the cubbyholes above his head. While he drove if Buster didn't puff on a cigarette, he snacked on cakes, cookies or crackers. Like a lot of drivers Buster indulged in snacking more for stimulation than nourishment, not that much nourishment resided in most snacks. The only meals we ate on this run came from the café that had seen better days. I plead guilty to this type of dietary foolishness, too. I didn't possess Buster's repertoire of calorie enhancers, but I sometimes bought bags of chips or packets of orange crackers with peanut butter filling to eat during the long journey.

"They caught a drug dealer," Buster said, jerking his head toward the police car.

"How do you know?"

"That gal in there told me," Buster said, referring to one of the truck stop clerks. Knowing how gossip works more on imagination than fact, I doubted the reliability of his source, but said nothing.

Buster continued. "Last month they arrested a truck driver in this very spot," he said, pointing directly at the truck cab floor again.

"Oh? Did he buy drugs?"

"No, he run somebody off the road back there," Buster paused. "He didn't even know it."

"How could he not know it?" I asked.

"He didn't see them on these dark little roads." Buster stood up. "You want to drive for a while?" he asked.

Again I doubted Buster, but kept my thoughts to myself. Even I already knew that, if paying attention, a driver couldn't unknowingly drive a car off the road. Plus, his immediate offer to let me back into the driver seat added an interesting garnish to his comments. Buster directed me to keep heading down the two-lane state highway until we hit the Interstate. Then he went back to the sleeper bunk.

For what felt like several hours I drove along a narrow highway trying to see as far in front of the truck as possible. I squinted at what lay ahead in the inky blackness. In this different and less illustrious brand of truck from the one Dutch and I had driven, the headlights of Buster's truck shone weakly into the night. Yet, the lights of other vehicles looked more like glare than illumination. And while the stop and start of traffic lights offered good practice, I still felt relief when the truck could go through a green light so I didn't have to shift gears up or down.

At one point when driving along, struggling to see, the windshield and side windows fogged up in an instant. Suddenly, I found myself steering a big rig with two trailers down a highway at night with cars driving all around us, and I couldn't see! Then I had no choice but to take my eyes from the road while fumbling with the window defroster. In a few seconds the glass cleared again. Naturally, the cleared windows were a vast improvement over the near sightlessness of a few seconds prior, but darkness still seemed to close in on the path in front of us.

More time passed, and the adrenalin rush caused by the unexpected fogging of the windows wore off. The end of a long day approached. At about the time Buster should have taken his first shift and I should have headed to the sleeper, I began to feel drowsy. I struggled, not only to see, but to stay awake. I moved my eyes from side to side the way my driving instructor had suggested during training. I checked the mirrors and looked at the dials on the dashboard. But my eyelids felt heavier every time I blinked. Though driving certainly felt stimulating, I started to relax *too* much.

"Buster!" I called in the direction of the sleeper.

"Yeah?"

"Do you wanna drive?" I asked.

The curtain to the sleeper compartment opened. "Pull over at the next stop."

The next morning Buster drove the rig through what looked like a maze of toll roads to me until we reached the Orlando terminal where we dropped our trailers and picked up two new ones. I stepped out of the truck cab to see again what Sam had shown me and how Buster did the work of the yardman: unhooking and re-hooking the brake lines at the back of the cab and between the trailers and the dolly, retrieving the pig tail power cord to put between the new set of trailers, connecting the chain hooks from the dolly to the front trailer's hitch, and lowering and raising the landing gear on either trailer. Drivers turn a crank handle to lower the sturdy metal legs of the landing gear on either side of a trailer. If a driver doesn't lower the gear before driving away from a trailer, the trailer will fall hard, first onto the back of the truck then, ultimately, onto the pavement. Neither of which is good for either the truck or the trailer.

Once the landing gear has been lowered the fifth wheel pin that attaches the trailer to the dolly or to the back of the truck cab must be pulled open. Starting out, I worried that releasing the fifth wheel would be too difficult. I wondered to what physical excesses I may have to go to get the release pin to cooperate. For that matter, what if I had a flat tire or a mechanical breakdown? I couldn't fix a truck with no mechanical training.

Weeks after Buster and I had parted ways, a different co-driver said he had trouble with the fifth wheel release. "Can't get this damn thing loose," he had called out. "You grab hold of it, too, and let's see if we can loosen the mother."

I did as directed, leaning over with that co-driver, and with a gloved hand, grabbing the fifth wheel's release pin under the trailer. I braced my feet against the ground and tugged with all my might, like my co-driver that day. We huffed and we puffed and finally got the pin out.

"You know, that didn't want to come out," he had chuckled.

Don't sink the ship!

I innocently agreed, thinking in wonderment how I might ever
do a solo run, if even a guy couldn't release the pin easily. But the
days of such challenges remained ahead of me.

Buster and I eventually had our set built and drove to the
terminal offices where I wanted to shower before our drive back
over the next 24 hours. Buster insisted we didn't have time, and
once again I just didn't have enough backbone to argue. In my
naiveté and weakness I got back on the truck after merely changing clothes and headed back out.

When Buster and I started the return journey, how, I asked,
should I fill out my log for the previous day. I needed to know,
considering the haphazard way we had switched out driving. Like
anyone on a regular route, Buster and his co-driver had worked
out where the halfway point on the route is. Buster told me what
time to show our switch out and gave me the name of the town to
write on the log. I penned both in my logbook before we hit the
road again.

On my first trip I had driven what I logged and logged what
I'd driven. No deception there. Regulations allowed us to drive up
to eleven hours a day. We could do other work like setting up the
trailers or fueling for up to three additional hours a day. The legal
limit for the full work day remained at fourteen hours. Not every
day required that many hours, but in trucking along designated
routes a typical day's drive lasted about ten hours for each driver,
if they didn't drive on each other's shift. But almost half of my co-
drivers and I did. In that case, we couldn't be truthful on our "lie-
books" without repercussions. If we accurately represented who
had driven at different times during our trip, we would be fined,
fired or both.

Though I had felt doubtful about Buster's eagerness to trade
out driving, I would learn that the main reason drivers defy
logbook laws is for safer driving. Only drivers can decide for
themselves if they feel too tired to drive or not. Guidelines are
needed, and drivers do need protection from some unscrupulous
employers who would have them drive themselves, and motorists,
off the road. Yet, where the rubber meets the road, genuinely in

this case, no one can legislate from a distant time and place what a driver's level of readiness truly is.

On paper a driver may be ready to go, having taken a ten hour break. The reality is that team drivers, particularly, often awaken throughout their rest period due to bumpy roads, a random horn honking, a siren going by, a co-driver who makes frequent stops or who plays the radio or CB too loud, or any number of unpredictable distractions and noises. Nor can all the noises be managed by using ear plugs. It's just tough for most people to get good rest in a moving truck, especially when still a rookie.

Most new drivers don't even make it one year on the road. Having already found the first two days on the road with Dutch surprisingly tiring and stressful, I could see why. Part of the reason, I mused, must be that many team drivers never adapt to the difficulty of sleeping in a moving truck. I didn't want to become one of the statistics. I wanted to last a respectable amount of time in this extraordinary job.

Thus, it helped a great deal that when I first started driving professionally experienced colleagues often expected to drive part of my shift. They did this as a matter of course and without my asking. Older drivers acted as if they understood that a new driver felt nervous and tired out more quickly. They wanted the truck to keep going down the road at a fairly quick pace. The sooner the week's work ended, the sooner they could get home. On those first few runs, because I could drive until physically or mentally exhausted and then my co-driver willingly took over, that helped me get gradually acclimated to commercial driving.

Anyway, the consensus among drivers I worked with was that the logbook rules had been decided by bureaucrats who had never stepped into a truck in their lives. Sitting behind a desk in Washington, the pencil pushers couldn't judge when someone needed rest or how long someone could safely drive. The bureaucrats who wrote the regulations may have pictured a truck driver all cozy in his sleeper bunk, a smile on his face, his blankie pulled up around his neck, snoozing peacefully for a solid eight hours within the allotted ten hour break while his co-driver works. That, of course, is far from the reality.

Don't sink the ship!

Gradually, I heard from other truckers, that they had once been permitted to switch out drivers every five hours. The schedule of the so-called five and five worked best for the short, intermittent sleep a driver could get on the road, followed by a rested period of driving. But somewhere along the way the government had made the five and five illegal. Many drivers found it the safest way to drive, however, and kept it up anyway.

By and large, the drivers are correct. No one can predict, never mind regulate how a person feels, whether he's been sick or didn't sleep well. Switching out drivers when needed is a part of the nature of the beast when it comes to trucking. Truckers must decide what's safe, whether their actions match regulations or not. The alternative, having an exhausted colleague struggle to stay awake at the wheel while their rested co-driver impatiently waits out the end of a ten hour shift in the bunk, could lead to a crash. Due to their practical nature, most truckers wouldn't let that happen.

Buster drove us back from Orlando to the Florida panhandle where we switched out again. I took the wheel while our rig headed toward Pensacola Bay. Buster sat in the passenger seat again and proceeded once more to fill my ears with tales of woe on the highways and byways of our great land. The bridges over the bay fast approached, and one had been badly damaged years before. A large section of the bridge had fallen into the water after being buffeted by debris during a hurricane. Temporary repairs had allowed the old bridge to be reopened while workers constructed a new bridge several yards to the north of the original structure.

"You know, a truck driver discovered the bridge had washed out," Buster volunteered. He spoke about this driver like he had been an acquaintance. "Yep," Buster continued, "He had breakfast at a truck stop just the other side of the bay when the hurricane came in. They had the roads closed, but he went anyway."

The reports of the unfortunate driver's death had been in the national news. I didn't ask Buster how he might know any details. Probably part gossip, part jumping to conclusions, though I doubted if any difference exists between the two.

"He barreled through there going about 75 mph," Buster continued. "He couldn't see the road in front of him. Then his truck went off the end of that bridge and sunk like a rock."

"Or like a semi," I quipped.

"He never had a chance," Buster ignored me, enjoying the sound of his own loud, scratchy voice. "Even if he coulda got out of that truck, he couldn't have got to shore in that storm."

Inwardly, I shuddered at the thought of being trapped in a truck when it plummeted to depths that must guarantee any driver or co-driver a one-way ticket to oblivion in fair weather, never mind during a hurricane. Drowning to death trapped in a vehicle must be a particular horror. The weight of a rig must send it so deeply into the water so quickly that even the driver at the steering wheel might not make it out in time. Even if he did get out of the cab and attempt to swim upward, falling trailers could easily thwart his escape.

The thought of being the co-driver in the sleeper bunk who has no warning of the plunge into darkened depths didn't bear thinking about. Just when he or she might awaken and realize what had happened, going from even a catnap to being ready to flee sounded unlikely at best. Not all trucks have the escape hatch doors in the sleeper compartment that Dutch's truck had. Buster's truck, like most, had small openings about the size of an envelope that didn't even open all the way. They just provided an air vent, if opened while going down the road.

I didn't want to give Buster the satisfaction of reacting to his words. I simply kept my eyes on the road ahead.

"You know, there are hundreds of old bridges all over this country," Buster stated, as if implying they all waited tremulously to plunge unsuspecting drivers to an early and watery grave.

"Not many of them get struck by loosened oil well rigs," I countered, mentioning the particular reason the old bridge had given way.

"They're still out there!" Buster commanded in his twangy shout.

I slowed down to cross the bay at the posted speed limit. With Buster's doom-laden message still hanging in the air I saw all that remained of the old bridge was a metal framework set on top of concrete posts sunk into the ground far beneath the water's surface. While I realized the bridge would have been closed if the crossing had been dangerous, the structure looked fragile. I could see the wavelets under the grid of the damaged bridge. They proceeded in their unending march to the shoreline underneath both bridges and our truck. A driver couldn't help but think about the dangers of steering tens of thousands of pounds over a wide stretch of seawater, even over a bridge of solid concrete. If a bridge gave way, it *would* be a catastrophe. Yet, what could any of us do? The old expression of "Keep on trucking," took on a bright, fresh meaning!

A while later our rig rolled into Alabama and this time *under* a bay. Thankfully, not due to any failed bridge. Rather, a tunnel directs the Interstate traffic beneath Mobile Bay. I had slowed for both the bridge and the tunnel. With my lack of experience I drove much more slowly than Buster would have in either Pensacola or Mobile. Back out on the open road of southern Alabama headed toward the Mississippi state line Buster decided to show me a thing or two.

"Let's see," Buster said. "The governor on this truck only goes to 68, but with the cruise control you can trick it a bit and get up to 71."

"I'm not using the cruise."

"Why not?"

"I'm just getting used to driving," I explained.

At this stage the minute I got the cruise control set, I'd be 'breaking' it almost immediately to slow for a curve, a safely distant motorist or some other reason that wouldn't make a seasoned driver hesitate. But then Buster reached over to the dashboard in front of me. Touching the controls when you're not in the driver seat is a major breach of trucking etiquette, regardless of whose name is on the logbook at the moment. Buster knew this, of course, but he turned on the cruise control anyway. Then he pressed the lever upward to make the truck go beyond 68. I tapped the brake, canceling the cruise. Buster turned on the cruise again, revving the engine back up. I tapped the brake again.

"What'd you do that for?" Buster asked, in his characteristic shout.

"I'm just getting used to driving," I repeated. "You want to know what else they say about the driver being the captain?" I asked, discovering another trucking truism.

"What?" Buster rose to the bait.

"Only the captain operates the fucking controls."

"Humph," Buster responded, slumping back into his seat.

Just then a new vertebra in my rookie trucker's backbone popped into place.

Eventually, I exited the Interstate in Mississippi and headed back up the state highway. Then I pulled into the same small truck stop we had visited on our way down. In the early summer weather our windshield had collected a variety of bugs. The sun had set and visibility became decreased further by the fine coating of what remained on the glass from colliding with many an unfortunate specimen. At truck stops the squeegee window cleaners have a long broom handle so drivers can clean the truck windows that stand high off the ground. I steered the truck into one of about half a dozen fuel lanes, got out and took one of the squeegees from the bucket of soapy water where it rested in front of a diesel pump.

While I cleaned the windows I became aware that a man stood nearby in an empty fuel lane. He hadn't driven up in a truck. In fact, no truck stood parked nearby. The man merely loitered while he spoke to drivers that walked by him on their way into the building from the parking lot. He stood too far away for me to hear what he said to other drivers. After a glance, I never looked at the man again. While I washed the truck's windows, however, I could see Buster sitting in the truck looking intently at him. With the windows cleaned I went into the truck stop.

When I came back out I saw that Buster had waited in the truck for my return. Possibly, Buster and Buddy took turns going inside in lieu of locking the truck's doors. Buster never did leave the truck unattended. While on the surface that makes some sense, it makes even more sense to lock the truck and carry a key. We were not obligated to have someone with the truck.

Don't sink the ship!

When Buster climbed back into the truck he reported that the man by the pumps had stared at me the entire time I had cleaned the windows. I couldn't really do anything with that information. "So, what?" I answered.

"There was something really strange about it," Buster said.

I shook my head. Buster must be trying to creep me out, I figured. "He's probably selling drugs," I suggested.

"He probably is!" Buster shouted.

I don't use drugs so I don't buy them. Therefore, the man's activities had nothing to do with me. The truck stop staff, working on the other side of a large glass window that overlooked the fuel lanes, must have been aware of the man's presence. If they felt the situation warranted it, they could do something about it.

Buster drove out and I returned to the bunk to try to get some sleep. "Try" being the key word. The state highway's bumps and stop lights interrupted our progress for hours. Eventually, we returned to the Interstate where the continuous ribbon of pavement made the going smoother. Then later in Louisiana we stopped at the same café and had another uninspiring meal.

In due course we made our way back to our home terminal where Buster let me off at the parking lot. I set my coiled sleeping bag and plastic logbook holder on the passenger seat where I could grab them easily when exiting the truck. Then I edged around the shifter and the passenger seat until I stood on the first step outside the passenger side door facing into the cab.

As I began to climb out of the cab, I caught sight of a couple of leftover packets of orange crackers that I had bought at one of the truck stops. They rested in their open box on the dash to my right. After days with little decent food I just wanted to go home, shower, rest, and eat a real meal. Right then, even if I'd been starving, I would have rather thrown those crackers into Pensacola Bay than eat any of them.

"Do you want these crackers?" I asked Buster.

"Sure," he answered. Then with an exaggerated emphasis on the first and last words, he cheerfully yelled over the rumble of the engine. "Fooood is fooood!"

I left the crackers with Buster and climbed down the truck with my gear. While I walked to my car and drove home I thought about my most recent adventure. Though Buster's words may have been meant to discourage me with his food for thought, I decided I wouldn't give anyone the satisfaction of making me run away by the telling of horror stories, whether fact or fiction. I had earned my CDL so I would drive a truck come hell or high water.

Sometimes a job is a job! Or is it?

Chapter 5: "No one can get used to it for you."

A couple of weeks passed before Sam had another run I could or would take. I hadn't told Sam anything about Buster's discouraging words. Maybe Sam just tried to ease me in since I was a new driver or maybe he heard the reluctance in my voice when he did call. Besides Sam only managed a few trucks. When a run became available and I'd already committed to an office temp job elsewhere, I'd turn down the run to honor the prior commitment. Now and then I drove that summer again to both Phoenix and Orlando, and also up to Virginia, each time with different co-drivers. Driving a couple of times a month I wasn't setting any records on adding mileage to my logbook. Then one day with summer drawing to a close Sam called with another run.

"Hey, Karen," Sam's voice came over my cellphone. "I got a run with a guy I think you'll really enjoy driving with. He's making a run to the truck stop in Virginia you went to before."

I remembered the first trip to that state when Sam had said he had a run that didn't go to a company hub. "Where? To a truck stop?" I had asked, not knowing then of the common practice of drivers from different hubs meeting and exchanging trailers at such places.

"To a truck stop along Interstate 81," Sam had explained. "You meet a team from another terminal hub. They bring trailers from their terminal and you trade trailers. It's called a butthead."

"A what?" I had laughed. "Do they call it that because drivers are buttheads?"

"It just means one team butts heads with another," Sam had laughed agreeably. "One more thing you'll like about this run: it only takes about forty hours. Then there's a gap of about eight hours before heading back out for a second run."

That had sounded good on the first run and still did. Part of me wanted to stay home with the comforts and conveniences we all normally take for granted. Yet, a break in the work week like that meant a few hours respite to shower in my own home and get some brief, but solid sleep before returning for another couple of days of punishment. Because that's what driving a big truck still felt like. Trucking didn't seem all bad. Just moving down the road and going through the truck's gears successfully did have a satisfying sense of accomplishment. Still, while driving, I felt a bittersweet combination of fun and fear. Driving was fun, but undeniably dangerous. Scary, but adventurous. A more determined part of me didn't want to give in to fear. I decided privately that nothing would succeed at making me fail.

"Okay, I'll do it," I said.

"Good deal. Meet Coach outside the gate at Dallas at six in the morning."

"I'll be there," I replied.

I met Coach at the Dallas terminal as planned where he had the trailers ready and the truck parked just outside the gate. I loaded my sleeping gear, little green bookbag and logbook and greeted my co-driver. Coach had a bald pate with a gray rim of hair around his head, revealing the maturity of his years. I could tell he stood shorter than me when he walked by on the way to his own car. Oddly enough, most male truck drivers I met were shorter. At 5'10" in sneakers I stand at about the average height of an American man. So about half the guys I meet are shorter anyway. But about three out of four guy truckers stood 5'9" or less. I mused about Napoleon complexes and the size of semis, while setting my things in the top bunk. I drove out and Coach sat up with me to see how his rookie co-driver handled the truck. While we talked I soon discovered that Coach approached life from a completely different perspective than Buster. Clearly an intelligent man with a quick wit, I found Coach to be a well-adjusted dude – no complexes.

We headed eastward along I-30 on the never ending strip of concrete. Fewer vehicles shared the road while the sun rose. My hands still moved the steering wheel more than a seasoned driver would. I wondered if Coach noticed. So far I only had a few thousand miles of commercial driving experience. Each trip had contained innumerable lessons of how to drive and what the job really involved, Buster's tall tales notwithstanding.

Yet each time so much as a single moment at the wheel arrived when I felt more relaxed, something would happen to gain my full attention again. Another trucking truism begged to be acknowledged: Expect the unexpected!

Driving along, the road might start to head down a slight decline with the momentum of thousands of pounds going at 65 mph only to have a four wheeler with a boat trailer pull onto the entrance ramp in front of us at 45 mph. Though I had right of way, I would change lanes as soon as possible rather than risk colliding with an inattentive motorist. Or a road gator, the remains of a ruptured tire, would appear on the pavement around the next curve. I would change lanes quickly, once the coast was clear. No sooner had I thought about road gators than we came upon one. I looked in the mirrors and signaled a lane change.

"I see you know to steer around the gators," Coach said. "You know why, don't you?"

"Other drivers avoid them. It just seems like a good idea to go around them."

"There's more to it than that. I once drove to Denver with this one girl," Coach said, referring to a female co-driver. "She ran over a big, old strip of rubber in the mountains of Colorado and took out the brakes to the back trailer."

The heavy, metal-reinforced rubber of the tire had flown up in the rapid air current created by the truck's motion and torn the dolly's brake lines. Because of this the emergency brakes engaged, bringing the entire rig to a halt.

"We waited beside the road for eight hours until a repair truck got there to fix the brakes," Coach explained.

Without even mentioning logbooks Coach and I simply started alternating driving every few hours. I drove until we reached the

Covered Wagon, a small truck stop just west of Texarkana, the city joining Texas and Arkansas. Here we switched out driving.

The Covered Wagon had barely enough room for our rig to maneuver through the parking lot, up to the fuel pumps, then back out again onto the tiny, two lane country road that intersected the highway. Double trailers must be headed straight into the fuel lanes, in order to drive through a lane without scraping the sides of the trailers on the fuel pumps or the bollards. Even gas stations often have bollards, or protective posts meant to prevent autos from striking the fuel pumps. At a truck stop these short posts are meant to prevent a semi or trailers from running into the pumps, so they are much heavier and taller.

If the trailers were driven into the fuel lane crooked, the driver would have to back up what few feet a doubles rig could go to attempt to straighten them. If that didn't work, the set might have to be rebuilt right there in the tight parking lot with an accompanying blockage of fuel lanes for both amused and angered fellow drivers. Otherwise, the trailers would scrape along the bollards that stood about four feet tall and three feet in diameter at this truck stop. These posts, marked with the scratches and scrapes left by wayward trucks, were visual reminders for us drivers, in addition to preventing the fuel pumps from being scraped off the ground like crumbs off a table. I imagined diesel spraying into the air along with the odor and fire hazard that accompanied such a mess. That's to say nothing of the cost to the driver's employer or an insurer, and to the driver himself or herself upon reaching the status of unemployed. Happily, Coach sat next to me and gave me instructions while I made a wide sweeping turn to pull into the narrow fuel lanes with both of our trailers in a reasonably straight line behind us.

Having gone inside to buy a mini-pizza, I sat up in the passenger seat to eat. Coach sat at the steering wheel and drove out from the fuel lane. He looked ahead to where the narrow driveway curved. He would have to negotiate the exit to the truck stop parking lot. Other trucks had lined up in the few parking spaces and still others parked in the driveway itself. Coach thought the way ahead looked blocked. He didn't want to find out the hard way and wind up where he could neither turn around nor exit. We couldn't return the way we had come either, but we still needed to get out.

"This will piss 'em off, but it beats getting stuck," Coach said. Then he steered the truck in a broad arcing turn toward the truck scale. Lots of truck stops have heavy duty scales so drivers can weigh their rig to make sure it's within the legal limit of 80,000 pounds. The long, broad scale sat without a truck on it, the perfect out for our predicament. The truck stop staff wouldn't like a driver using the scale as an exit, but slowly and carefully Coach drove over the huge instrument then back onto the small country lane.

While Coach steered us back onto the Interstate ramp, he got a call on his cell. Before he answered, he made an unorthodox request. "It's my wife. I never tell her when I'm driving with a female. She's real jealous," Coach explained. "So if you don't mind not talking when she's on the phone, I'd appreciate it." I nodded my agreement, since I intended to eat anyway. I simply didn't talk while Coach chatted with his missus. Coach would be the only driver ever to make this request.

In a few minutes Coach ended his call. Then he asked me "the question." "Why did you decide to drive a truck?"

I explained that I wanted a good job, especially one with companies that were hiring. Then I asked Coach why he drove.

"It gets me out of the house," he answered. Coach had a retirement income, but he liked the extra money. Like me he drove part-time to cover for other drivers and stayed home when he felt like it. Unlike me, he didn't hope for a permanent route.

Our truck crossed the border at Texarkana into Arkansas on the way to Little Rock. Park-like stretches of piney forests lined the Interstate like a boulevard. In places the land rippled with hills and valleys, looking like a forested picnic blanket had been spread out by a giant. Our truck tugged uphill then soared downhill at 75 mph. "That's about as fast as you want to take doubles," Coach said, referring to our trailers.

While he drove, I marveled at the beauty I couldn't always appreciate while driving. Going along the highways I had often caught glimpses of towns, restaurants, and billboard signs advertising touristy places. I wanted to eat at the diners, browse the souvenir shops, and see the sights. I often wanted to stop at all the beautiful natural places, too. I dreamt of tall forests that hid sunlit glens untouched by human footprints for decades, or maybe forever. But I had to go to an intended destination in a certain amount of time in a vehicle that had a decidedly limited capacity for touring.

"It's nice to take a look around while someone else is driving," I commented. "All these places make me want to stop. I sometimes feel like a prisoner in a wheeled box."

"I felt that way, too, starting out. I've gone back and seen some of these places on vacation."

"You mean, though you're a driver, you drive on vacation?"

"Sure. Lots of drivers do. And while we work we get to see more than the inside of a cubicle or a factory wall," Coach said. "We get to work in the great outdoors without a supervisor breathing down our necks."

We crossed a wide river with a long shallow shore. Water-loving trees grew along the edges of the banks. "Did you see that leprechaun sitting on a cypress knee?" Coach asked, pointing outside at the passing foliage.

Without missing a beat, I answered, "Yep, and he's shooting the finger at us."

Coach laughed, as we discovered a common affinity for creativity that wove through some of our conversations.

We switched out driving again somewhat east of Little Rock. I drove across the rice flats of eastern Arkansas. Small airplanes crop dusted grassy fields that reached to the horizons. After a couple of hours we crossed the M bridge on Interstate 40 over the Mississippi River into Memphis. Technically, it is called the de Soto Bridge for the 16th century Spanish explorer christened Hernando. But the superstructure of the bridge, where it edges up to the Tennessee shore, is shaped like a giant, rounded letter M, which may as well stand for Memphis.

Immediately after we crossed the river, traffic slowed due to construction. Over the next few years on frequent trips to and from the city, I drove along the curves of I-40 in the city called the Home of the Blues, the Birthplace of Rock and Roll. The highway loop curves around the northern edge of the city to rejoin the straight east-to-west direction of I-40 on the other side of town. At first, I disliked these curves because of the attention and care it took to swoop around them at highway speeds in a truck. But then I learned that in the 1970s Memphis citizens had caused federal highway officials to design the curves around the city rather than plow the path of the Interstate through acres of centuries old trees and well-maintained historic homes. It is a happy fact that so far we still live in a country where ordinary citizens can sometimes make the most powerful government in the world do the right thing.

Right then the interchange underwent massive improvements where I-40 began its turn joining the I-240 loop. Traffic detoured onto narrow, temporary lanes that curved sharply while I guided a rig not less than 73 feet in length around what looked like impossible angles. Signs directed trucks to remain in the right lane. It soon became clear why. While we bumped along on these winding, temporary lanes, the trailers behind the truck's cab flexed from side to side. Then another truck came along going our way in the left lane, the one for cars only. The other truck's one long trailer moved side to side, just like our doubles did. The two rigs could easily bump each other or scrape one another down the sides along this detour that felt like a rollercoaster.

"Uh, oh," Coach said. "Let's hope we don't swap some paint."

"What?" I said, more as a declaration than a question. I might be about to have an "incident" involving another vehicle. I did the only thing I could, I kept steering in my lane and hoped for the best. A few tense seconds later the other truck passed by uneventfully, though our trailers had come too close for comfort.

"That guy thinks it's funny," Coach observed.

"What guy?" I asked.

"The other driver. He was looking over here and grinning."

I'd been too busy concentrating on maintaining our lane to spare a glance. Unfortunately, some truck drivers act as if they are unaware or unconcerned about suggestions made by any highway signs. I would come to learn that while some drivers have a slapdash attitude about anything others mask fear or aggression by joking around. Such is life.

In time we left the loop and headed towards Nashville.

While I drove further into Tennessee I hoped to learn what Coach thought about truck driving. Many would-be drivers found the realities of truck driving more demanding than they had expected. Truckers often have to cope with little sleep, poor food, driving in all kinds of weather and occasionally with a co-driver who just might drive them up the wall, if not off the road. Also, the job took a driver away from home and family for long stretches of time. To top it all off, no driver ever knew for certain whether he or she would return home in one piece or at all.

First, I asked Coach for his honest opinion of my driving. I knew I moved the steering wheel back and forth too much, one of the marks of a new driver.

"You'll get over that," Coach advised.

"I hope so. It's just hard to get used to driving."

"Why do you think so?"

"For one thing there are days or sometimes even weeks between the trips I take," I answered.

Here we were already in late summer, heading into autumn. I had worked a clerical temp job for several weeks in June and July, partly because Sam didn't have very many trucks. Consequently, he didn't need a substitute driver very much of the time. Partly due to my own reluctance.

"I don't blame Sam," I added. "Driving scares me."

"Tell me what it is about driving that scares you." While he spoke, I drove slowly around a curve, as I had on other early runs. Too slowly. "See now," Coach said. "You don't have to slow down that much to get around these bends."

"You're right, but that's as fast as I felt safe going. It's even worse when the curve goes downhill," I said.

A lot of the routes we drove had only a few curves or hills. But occasionally we had to drive in mountainous areas. Later this run went through the mountains of eastern Tennessee and Virginia.

"You haven't had a lot of practice and you don't like curves, what else?" Coach asked.

"After that has to be driving at night," I answered.

Nighttime made it tougher to see everything and lent an aura of heightened danger to unpredictable roads with even more unpredictable auto drivers.

"What else?"

"Next has to be rain. It's hard enough to drive in clear, sunny weather," I explained. "Rain is even worse. The pavement's slick. I already think of this truck as being hard to stop, but when it rains you can tell it takes farther to slow down or stop."

"There's less traction between the tire and the road," Coach said.

"The worst would be all three: mountains, at night, in the rain," I said. "Driving a truck just feels so precarious."

"That's a good five dollar word, but what do you mean?"

"It feels so unstable," I searched for a way to describe what I meant and remembered how I'd described it to another co-driver. "It feels like I'm driving a bowling ball balanced on a pair of pool cues over a pane of wet glass!"

Coach laughed good naturedly.

"It feels like this whole rig might tumble onto the shoulder, into a ditch, or into another vehicle with little warning and not much resistance. The way the truck moves side to side, the way the tiniest adjustment of the steering makes the truck go so fast in any direction," I continued, remembering with irony how I'd thought the truck's controls would feel slow and deliberate.

"You want it to respond to you quickly. That's a good thing," Coach said.

"It feels like it could turn over easily and like I'm not in complete control."

"A truck this size takes a helluva lot of momentum to turn over. A driver would have to be asleep or on something or just going too damn fast. You're in no danger there," Coach laughed again.

I nodded, knowing Coach knew what he spoke about.

He continued, "Now, you will feel a little bit of sway to the truck while it goes along. That's the springs giving the truck a better ride. You have everything you need to be in total control at your fingertips."

Coach decided to take a nap in the bunk. Alone again at the controls I steered along for an hour or so more until a bottleneck came into view in traffic up ahead. Two trucks each hauled a half of a manufactured house. Rolling down the highway the structures looked like someone's abode had decided to go for a drive. All traffic gradually made its way around the heavily laden trucks, while they eased along in the slow lane.

Though the drivers carrying the house kept part of their load over the painted shoulder stripe on the right side of their trucks, still a portion of the house also jutted over the center stripe between the two eastbound lanes. Thus, while cars, vans, and pickups slipped by like leaves darting down a narrowed stream, the big trucks passing the house had to drive partially on the shoulder to get past both halves of the wide load. That was the only way. A trucker could either pass on the shoulder or stay behind the slow moving trucks.

I certainly wasn't going to remain behind them going only 45 mph. Though I still didn't like passing any vehicles, by then I had developed just enough backbone to take on the rumble strip, that grooved line dug into the sides of the highway shoulder. Running tires over the strip makes a loud noise designed to awaken tired drivers or get a distracted driver to stop messing with the radio or cellphone and look ahead when they are in danger of going off the road. Perhaps why they also may casually be referred to as the idiot strip.

When my turn in traffic came, I checked the side mirrors and moved into the passing lane when it finally cleared. My front bumper approached the house movers' outsized cargo. I moved over as other trucks had done until my left tires were on the rumble strip of the passing lane. BRRRAP! Coach popped his head out of the sleeper."What's the matter?" he called out drowsily.

"Just passing a wide load," I answered.

"Okay," he said and opened the curtain.

Sitting behind me on the edge of the bunk Coach watched the proceedings. BRRRAP! The tires continued calling out their constant alert, like they would to an unaware driver, but I felt very aware. Aware that I had to drive over the edge of the left lane. Aware that my trailers could scrape along the side of the manufactured house and cause a wreck, if I lost control. Aware that I had to attune every fiber of my body to passing the house on wheels. My eyes wanted to rivet to the lane in front of me and shut out all the danger. But I forced myself to glance in the mirrors, too, and make sure my truck moved where it should to pass the house movers' cargo.

The long highway lay in front of us. The rumble strip roaring beneath eleven of our truck's twenty two wheels made quite a din. To add to the sensory overload, through the heavy plastic cover over the house's middle, surreal glimpses of a bedroom door, a kitchen counter, a fireplace mantle came into view. Finally, the house on wheels lay well enough behind us. I steered off of the rumble strip and back into the driving lane.

"If you want to switch out again, there's a pickle park about ten miles further," Coach said.

"A what?"

Coached laughed. "A rest area. Or there's a truck stop about another thirty miles beyond. It's your choice."

"You know where all the truck stops are?"

"Oh, yeah," Coach answered.

Remarkably, truck drivers get to know the Interstate System to an extreme level of familiarity. Just like a cab driver gets to know every block and street of a city, many truck drivers know every curve and bump of the nation's highways. Not only did drivers learn what stops lie ahead, many could open the curtain after spending hours in the bunk and immediately know precisely where they were down to the nearest town or exit or even the mile marker. Unlike city cab drivers, truckers' territory of intricate knowledge just happens to span a geographic area comprising a rather large chunk of a rather large continent.

We approached the rest area and I pulled in and parked. Coach called the rest area a pickle park for reasons that sounded obvious, so I didn't ask for further explanation. Rest stops are, of course, a place where a man can drain his pickle. They are also places where some men try to pick up other men. "Pickle park" must win in the name game because it is alliterative. Dick park or cock park wouldn't have the same ring to them. Dick drain or cock curb, possibly.

Rest areas and their goings-on edge along the seedy side of trucking life. But many well-meaning people frequent these places, too. Many years ago, Coach explained, he had been on a long, solo run and stopped at a rest area to use the restroom. A desperate-looking young woman had approached him pleading for help. She had been stuck at the rest area for a couple of days, begging change from the few people who would speak to her so she could get food from a vending machine. She had found herself largely disregarded by most passersby who mistook her for a substance abuser or a prostitute.

Coach had let her tell her story. She had eloped with a man who had pledged his love for her. But once the man had gotten her away from her family, he had raped her and abandoned her at the rest area. At a time when cellphones were not yet common, she had used what little change she could get for food. Filled with shame and fear, she had not contacted her family from the one pay phone at the rest area. Even when cellphones were still unusual, many truckers already had them. Coach called her family on his cellphone with the number she gave him and ex- plained he was a trucker who had found their daughter at a rest area. Did they want to talk to her?

"Yes!" they had answered.

He reassured her and handed her the phone. Following a tear- ful conversation between the young woman and her family, Coach talked to the woman's father. Coach would let her ride along in the sleeper while he would park and nap in the driver seat when tired. Following her father's instructions, she agreed not to exit the truck except for restroom breaks. In a couple of days, before Coach took the trailer to the truck yard of the company he worked for at the time, he would stop at a shopping center just off the Interstate and reunite his passenger with her family. That he did.

"When I got there her father offered me a $100 dollar bill as a thank you," Coach explained. "But I didn't take it."

That's the sort of kindness the good people who drive trucks carry out from time to time. Not for money or recognition. But just because, it's the right thing to do.

After our pit stop, Coach drove us back onto the road. I sat in the passenger seat and told Coach some of the things Buster had told me. Coach chuckled. He, too, seemed to take Buster's warn- ings and whinings as an attempt to scare off the "girl driver."

Then I told Coach about the difficulty a different co-driver and I had experienced releasing the fifth wheel pin. Coach gave me a sort of sideways grin. Then he explained that the driver should have backed up with the trailer brakes on to put a modicum of slack in the connection. Then the pin would generally release without any trouble.

"Oh," I said, shaking my head because then I realized. Perhaps, that other driver had enjoyed being alongside a female while she, um, exerted herself. Perhaps, he didn't get enough huffing and puffing at home.

Next, I explained my worry about what to do if the truck broke down. "I have no mechanical training," I said.

"Almost none of these drivers do," Coach answered. "If you need anything, you call your manager. Then he calls fleet service or has you call them. A mechanic comes out to do the work."

"Of course," I said, seeing how obvious that was. We were drivers, not mechanics.

"Not only that," Coach said. "You couldn't carry all the tools needed to work on a truck with you. And if it can't be fixed roadside, they tow it in."

I had seen the biggest tow trucks on the road occasionally. With cabs the size of a semi, they could tow an entire loaded rig.

I continued sharing my concerns with Coach. Like any driver, being in the sleeper when a wreck occurred had become one of my worst fears.

"At least up front we have seat belts," I mentioned. "I can't even imagine what might happen to the driver who's in the sleeper during a wreck."

"I hope you never find out," Coach replied.

On a drive years ago Coach had been in the sleeper compartment when his co-driver had gone off the highway. The force of the accident had lifted Coach several feet into the air, all the way to the ceiling of the cab. Then he plunged downward with such force that his left foot tore the door from the truck's refrigerator off its hinges. In addition to his wounded foot, he had several broken ribs, a burst spleen and numerous cuts and bruises. He felt lucky to be alive. The doctors had kept Coach in the hospital for two solid months.

If there had been safety belts or a safety net on the bunk of the sleeper, Coach might have still had some injuries, but they wouldn't have been so severe. Sleeper belts are long enough to cross the bed with someone in it and snap into place like a seat belt. Bunks with this equipment have three belts. Drivers find them more restricting than the safety nets that are designed to keep someone from being tossed around, but don't hold them directly down on the bed.

Such safety equipment is required on bunks, but many didn't have any. Drivers often disabled or removed the belts or netting. Possibly, some drivers want to be seen as tough by other drivers and, evidently, being belted in during sleep doesn't display a badass attitude in their opinion. Others ignorantly fear a sleeper belt in the same way some fear a seat belt. They want to be "thrown clear" in an accident, even if that means kissing the pavement or the windshield at 70 mph.

Yet, more drivers and passengers survive while wearing belts. If the truck starts to go out of control a seat belt can keep a driver in his seat and, therefore, in control. No one can reach the steering wheel after being thrown against the passenger window or the ceiling or onto the floor.

In my experience driver-managers never checked to see if the sleeper belts or nets existed or if they functioned. No one ever told me to use the sleeper belts or nets. Prior to Coach explaining his accident, I hadn't even known these safety features existed.

"Always click yourself in when you're in the sleeper, even if it's a pain in the ass," Coach said.

Almost all trucks we drove had netting rather than belts. Later some of my co-drivers took offense when they saw that the sleeper netting had been unfurled and used while they drove. Perhaps, I'd had to untangle the netting from the back wall. Using the sleeper's safety equipment didn't constitute a comment on another driver's skills, though some took it that way. I simply didn't want to wake up being thrown around inside the sleeper compartment, if they had a front tire blow out or were struck by another vehicle. Or if they experienced any of the countless possible situations that might cause the vehicle to move abruptly or even to go off the road.

Fortunately, another nascent vertebra formed in my new trucker's backbone with the strength of Coach's advice. I didn't ever want to suffer what he went through during that accident. Using the safety equipment simply signified an acknowledgement of the laws of physics. I would use the safety equipment in every truck that had it from then on.

"And be ready to take pictures," Coach advised.

"What? Why?"

"If you're ever in an accident, a picture can be worth a thousand words."

Listening to him, I felt struck by how none of Coach's comments were designed to strike fear in my heart. They always included reasons why things happened and solutions to problems. After driving with him a few times, I came to see Coach as one of the smartest people I had ever met. He just happened to be driving a truck. Again and again I would find living proof that you never really know who's behind the wheel of a big rig.

Then Coach told me about a rookie driver he had run with who drove out for a couple of hours and pulled over. The rookie said he felt tired and got in the sleeper. Coach took over the driving for him, the way he would have for any co-driver, but this run turned out differently.

"I drove all the way to the other terminal," Coach said. "I dropped the trailers and built the new set. I stopped for fuel and to eat. I pulled over at a pickle park to sleep sitting in the driver seat. That guy never did show his face again until we pulled back into the home terminal a couple of days later."

Well, I thought, at least I hadn't turned out that bad. Maybe I had more courage than I realized. Courage is not a lack of fear, after all. Courage is enduring in the face of fear. A trucking truism, if ever there was one.

I tried to get some sleep in the bunk while Coach took us the rest of the way to our destination. Close to midnight we arrived at the truck stop in the Virginia mountains. Coach phoned in to the company's computerized system to get the trailer numbers we were assigned to return with. Frequently, when we pulled into a large truck stop we saw some of our company colleagues, even more so where drivers frequently exchanged trailers.

Any driver should find out for sure which set of trailers he or she needed to take back. If a team took a set of trailers destined for, say, Chicago to Fort Worth by mistake the company probably wouldn't pay for that run and the tenure of the drivers might be up for some serious reconsideration. Since neither Coach nor I were regulars on this run, we wouldn't recognize the drivers we were meeting, nor they us. Anyway late at night most drivers already at the truck stop were tucked in their bunks, not looking for newly arriving drivers to trade trailers with. The computer system gave Coach the trailer numbers we needed, and we coasted along until we located the rig that had those trailers.

However, the driver we were meant to trade trailers with had a problem. Arriving early, he had decided to take a nap. Since the temperature felt fine up here in the mountains and he needed neither heat nor air conditioning, he had turned off the engine to his truck. That had caused the truck's refrigerator to drain the batteries. He already had a buddy helping him out when our rig pulled up. We dropped our trailers and waited while he and his buddy gave his engine a jumpstart from another truck. Eventually, they got the truck started and the driver drove out from in front of the trailers he had brought from New Jersey. Then Coach backed up to hitch our cab to those trailers so we could pull them all the way to Texas.

The trailers stood in a long line of trucks whose drivers had parked for the night. Some of the engines rumbled to keep the drivers cool or warm. Others lay silent. Late at night most drivers had closed the curtains to their sleeper compartments. The curtains close with a zipper or by pressing together strips of Velcro or by connecting long, thin magnetic strips, which are the best. Magnetic strips let in the least light or prying eyes, and they are the easiest and least noisy to seal and unseal. Some trucks have curtains that can cover the windshield and side windows, too. This way a driver could use the driving area like a private living room, albeit a very small one.

Coach backed up until we heard the click of the fifth wheel pin. I got out of the cab, put on my gloves and wound up the landing gear while Coach attached the brake lines and power cord. When I stood between the trailers of our truck and the one parked beside us, I looked up into the dark sky between them. The lights from the truck stop parking lot provided a glow overhead that illuminated a fine mist falling down. If I hadn't been preparing to drive in the mountains at night in the rain, the sight might have inspired poetic thoughts.

With the common courtesy of a driver who already knows a run, Coach sat up just long enough to guide me back onto the highway from the truck stop. Almost in a daze, I drove the big rig back onto the highway service road heading south and steered the truck onto the entrance ramp.

We had been on the road almost twenty four hours. Coach had to get some rest in order to drive again later. He got up from the passenger seat to go into the sleeper. Then Coach gave me some final advice: "Go only as fast as you feel you safely can, and let me know if you get too sleepy to drive." Then he uttered words I realized must be another trucking truism for all the challenges facing every rookie driver. "Just remember, no one can get used to it for you."

Thus, I sat once again guiding a truck along the highway at night, this time along the hills and curves of the Appalachian Mountains. Once the truck reached highway speed, the mist that had fallen gently back at the truck stop pelted the glass. In front of my eyes the windshield wipers kept up a steady beat. High though we were in the mountain atmosphere with nightfall and rain, the air had cooled and become saturated with moisture. Fog stretched up into the nooks and crannies of the mountains and occasionally spilled onto the roadway. From time to time I found myself immersed in ground level clouds. I slowed down so that if someone or something appeared in front of the truck there would be time to stop.

Driving toward the Tennessee border, a light flashed up ahead. For a few moments it looked like an emergency vehicle parked next to the road. But this light didn't shine red and blue and didn't flash quickly like police and ambulance lights. Instead, a bluish-white beam of light periodically burst forth with brightness. Then the light spun around and flashed the same illumination in other directions. A couple of seconds later, here it came again. Flash! Spin. Flash! Spin. Over and over again. Driving closer, I could see that the light wasn't alongside the road, but on a hillside above the highway. I wondered what the light meant. I would later learn it signaled the presence of an airfield. Right then it simply added to my sensory overload.

The truck chugged up hills and seemed to plummet down them. I pressed the brakes when it felt necessary. Coach had reminded me what they had told us in truck driving school: a driver can wear out the brakes with overuse. They call that fanning the brakes. If the brakes get too hot, they stop working! I hadn't yet mastered the use of the engine brake along with gear selection and pedal braking to slow the rig. Often called Jake brakes after a brand name, engine brakes reduce the affect of two or four cylinders, limiting the power of the engine and slowing the vehicle without having to use the pedal brakes. Anyone near roads that big rigs frequent has likely heard the loud, steady rhythm of engine brakes in use. Some roadways have signs forbidding their use, but engine brakes can come in awfully handy in slowing a rig.

Cars zipped casually by on terrain easily mastered in such small vehicles. Once again, I envied the comparable ease of steering a sedan or a pickup at any time or in any weather rather than guiding this colossal rig. That night I watched the auto drivers exit the highway and pull their vehicles into restaurant and hotel parking lots. I looked with longing at the illuminated signs that advertised food and places to rest. Right then I didn't want to be in a metal box high over the road struggling to control a big rig, driving unrelentingly to complete the run. I didn't want to struggle for snatches and grabs of sleep on a bouncing, noisy bunk while someone else sat at the wheel. I wanted so much to stop at one of those restaurants, eat a delicious meal, and climb into a warm and cozy bed for the night. I wanted to feel safe and rested.

In time, I steered the truck into Tennessee. The mountains gradually receded, and the rig headed toward Nashville. Every so often the road would straighten out for a while. Along such stretches I didn't have to exercise the pointed concentration of driving on uneven terrain. That's when I started to experience an optical illusion. Something about being on the highway at night made it appear as if the portion of sky visible below the top of the windshield formed an arch. At first, I thought I saw a bridge ahead, but the image always stayed the same distance away. The truck never got closer to the phantom bridge. I lowered my head to glance up at the sky. Stars and moonlight peeked through the rain clouds. No bridge awaited. Like a lot of things in trucking, appearances can be deceiving.

Eventually, the rain abated, and I turned off the windshield wipers. Guiding the truck along the road became relatively peaceful while the night wore on and traffic diminished. My eyes scanned the road in front. Reflective paint and plastic markers outlined the path in front of the truck, and I could make out the shapes of trees alongside the road against the nighttime sky. A firefly hit the windshield and disintegrated. My eyes flicked over to the spot of its demise. The once internal cocktail of juices lit up in a little mass of phosphorescence on the outside glass. I drove along in the dark while the remains of the firefly glowed for a long time.

Chapter 6: "She might not want to drive with *me.*"

A couple of weeks after my last drive with Coach had ended, I sat in my car at a drive-in enjoying a burger and Coke when my cellphone rang. Sam's name came up on the phone's little screen. I had made progress getting comfortable behind the wheel on the last few runs. On my last run with Coach I'd taken the wrong ramp at Nashville and had to rouse him from the sleeper to guide me back to our intended path.

"I recognize these streets," Coach had said. "You're not the first driver to do this."

While that had made me feel a bit better, nothing helped later on yet another run with Coach. Struggling to change gears going up a hill on a Tennessee Interstate, the truck had crapped out on me. Or rather I'd crapped out trying to switch gears while rolling up the incline. I missed the intended gear then couldn't engage any gear at all. Coasting, I'd set the hazard lights flashing to alert motorists approaching from behind while the truck came to a stop on the highway. Then I had to start out from a low gear. That hadn't happened since driving school. Later Coach made an oblique remark about how weak the engine of our rig was.

"I wouldn't be surprised if this truck came to a standstill going uphill with either one of us driving." I could have confessed. But I knew and Coach knew that he had been awake. He just lent some perspective out of the kind camaraderie many drivers show each other. Now, sitting at the drive-in I contemplated pressing the ignore button on the phone. But I wanted to maintain an association with Sam. I answered his call.

"Hi, Sam. You've got a run you need filled?"

"Not me, but I know someone who does. He's got a lady driver who goes to Ohio. It's a good run with a lot of miles." I had to agree when I heard the numbers, over 1000 miles one way. "They just lost the co-driver on this run," Sam explained further. "He had his license revoked so they need someone permanent ASAP."

Sam still didn't need a full-time driver and had no way of knowing when one of his regular drivers would leave the job. Autumn had arrived, and I had accumulated a lot less driving time than would have been completed with a regular run. Doubtless I would have gotten more comfortable more quickly with a twice weekly run, week after week. For a week or two with Sam's blessing I could work with a driver I'll call Hilda. If everything worked out, I might work the run permanently.

Hilda worked with Wayne, a goofily jocular, wheeler-dealer sort of guy, who oversaw several trucks with a guy named Wil. Wayne, who had been a driver himself, acted as Wil's right hand man. Sam had arranged for me to meet Wayne on Monday morning at the dispatch office. On the appointed day I entered through the gray metal doors and asked one of the dispatchers, Carol, where I could find Wayne.

"You just passed him," Carol answered. "He's the guy outside who looks like he's talking to himself."

When I stepped back outside I found Wayne, a skinny, mustachioed guy in blue jeans and a shiny, black nylon jacket. He stood under a small gray awning with a cigarette in one hand, a stream of smoke rising heavenward. Wayne talked seemingly into thin air. Just the blue tooth of his cellphone peeking out from one ear signaled that he conducted business and didn't belong in a straightjacket. Wayne could strike a passerby as the kind of guy who liked to spend his free evenings boot scooting with petite blondes who wore bright red lipstick.

Wayne kept up a friendly bravado while he talked on the phone that chilly early autumn morning. I waited for a break in the sometimes relentless series of calls that rang into his earpiece. He had to be available twenty four hours a day to many drivers

71

for whatever issues might arise on the road: mechanical break-downs, collisions, questions about a dispatch, complaints about co-drivers, reminders from drivers who needed time off to visit the doctor or attend a funeral or any of the myriad of issues that could occur. I almost never spoke to Wayne either on the phone or in person when he didn't try to sound like my best friend. If I said anything just intended to be mildly humorous, he laughed out loud. If a problem arose, he could be both sympathetic and syco-phantic.

During a gap in his phone calls, Wayne said hello. "Are you the driver Sam sent?"

I nodded.

"I guess he told you about the run."

"Yeah," I acknowledged.

"It's a pretty good run. Pays well. You'll be driving with Hilda. Meet her here tomorrow at noon," Wayne instructed.

I would meet Wil weeks later, a blondish, shortish, bespecta-cled 40-something who appeared a bit bashful perhaps or maybe just inscrutable.

The next day, Tuesday, I showed up at the dispatch office and climbed into the passenger seat of a truck driven by Hilda. While she steered the vehicle around the yard, Hilda soon told me that her previous co-driver had just been let go because his license had been revoked for not making timely child support payments. A truck driver by trade, the one tool he needed most to make those payments had been taken from him. If the state revoked a driver's license for any reason, the company would not take that driver back for at least a year.

Shortly before we headed to the terminal yard's fuel pump, Wayne telephoned Hilda, possibly to make sure the unknown rookie had shown up for the run. From the driver seat Hilda spoke to Wayne on her cellphone, while I sat in the passenger seat and the machine pumped up to a hundred and fifty gallons of diesel into each of the truck's two side tanks.

"Maybe he'll commit suicide," Hilda chuckled into Wayne's ear from her phone. In fact, Hilda sounded especially pleased that it had been her who had let Wayne know about her co-driver's license revocation, a bit of information she had gleaned from him during the prior week. Right then I only heard her side of the phone conversation. Yet, from the way she spoke with Wayne, I got the feeling the two were in cahoots: she the informer, he the enforcer.

"You're right. She might not want to drive with *me*," Hilda laughed softly into her phone. She darted one eye over to me where I still sat, work gloves in hand, ready to turn off the fuel pump on my side of the truck when it clicked full.

While we built our set of trailers I saw that Hilda stood about 6' tall with large, bulky shoulders. She had slightly wavy hair and piercing eyes that looked as if she was trying to figure me out. Suddenly, I felt a surge of longing for a happy-go-lucky guy for a co-driver. Growing up with four brothers and no sisters, I felt comfortable with most guys. Whether I enjoyed a specific guy's company or not, I almost always understood where he was coming from. I couldn't figure out Hilda.

Possessing the strength of a man, Hilda clearly didn't need my power to assist her in pulling the dolly into position or in placing it onto the hitch on the rear of the front trailer. She backed up our trailers and the dolly with the practiced hand of someone who had been driving for years while I gamely did my best to help build our set. I whirled the handle to the landing gear or plugged in the electric cord, slipped the brake lines into their glad-hands or clicked the chain hooks onto the hitch.

When we were done Hilda drove out of the terminal, and I prepared the sleeper bunk by setting out my pillow and bedding. Hilda kept the top bunk filled with her sleeping bag, numerous pillows and blankets. I noticed that the storage cubby behind the passenger seat, big enough for a mini-refrigerator, remained empty. I decided to store my sleeping gear in the unused space when needed, instead of up above. Also, on Coach's suggestion, I could take a picture. If we had an accident, I could take pictures of a dented fender or anything else that needed recording.

After prepping the bunk, I took a seat up front again, waiting for our arrival at an eatery of some sort. Unlike many drivers who will buy a quick sandwich at a truck stop, often eating while they drive, Hilda said she normally stopped to eat. We had met on the yard at noon in order to head out the gate before two. However, driving around the terminal, fueling, setting up trailers, loading the truck with sleeping supplies, and preparing the first day's logbook page chewed up a couple of hours before we knew it. Thus, we left at half past two and drove about an hour to get out of Fort Worth and across Dallas. Another half hour later we came to a tiny truck stop diner that called itself a pancake house. The clock would be bumping up to evening by the time we finished eating.

At about four in the afternoon Hilda pulled into the back lot of the small truck stop that looked more like a glorified gas station. Hilda parked the truck in an unobstructed spot where she need only pull straight ahead to leave. Then she locked the doors of the truck and handed me a spare key. Refreshingly, Hilda was pragmatic about locking doors. I preferred knowing that no one could explore what goodies they might steal from the truck while we were eating. Also, if I fell asleep when she stopped somewhere along the way, I wouldn't wake up with a stranger in the cab about to explore my goodies.

We walked into a diner that looked like it had been decorated during the Eisenhower administration and sat across from each other in a booth. A waitress walked over, and we each placed an order. I requested breakfast for lunch or maybe breakfast for dinner. Sometimes a driver even eats breakfast at breakfast time. Hilda ordered a burger and fries.

While we waited for our food I couldn't help but study Hilda. Beneath her brow she possessed stern looking eyes with tanned wrinkles around the edges. Her mouth contained silver caps along with regular teeth. The hands she held her drink with had heavy palms and thick fingers with blunt fingertips. By contrast, at my height and build I have never been accused of being petite, but sitting across from Hilda with my comparatively light features and small hands, I felt downright dainty.

Hilda spoke in a husky, rural accent. She could definitely be described as "country," not that being from a rural or country background is a negative thing. Any self-respecting linguist, especially the cunning ones, will tell you that different speech patterns do not denote higher or lower qualities; they merely reflect the shared history of different groups of speakers. Anyway,

I mention Hilda's manner of speech because whenever I think of our time as co-drivers I always recall especially the way she spoke. Her voice often had an urgency or an almost plaintive quality to it, which is ironic because otherwise Hilda didn't appear in the least bit vulnerable. She appeared to know exactly who she was and made no apologies. Yet, often, her ordinary comments or questions sounded like a distressed entreaty.

For the moment I merely sized Hilda up since we might be sharing a truck for a while. I try to give each new person I meet a fair shake and believe in letting people be who they are. If someone didn't suit me, behaved rudely or drove badly in my opinion, after finishing the run I had agreed to, I could simply be too busy when Wayne called the next time he needed a co-driver to work with that person. Once or twice I had offered to drive with someone else so Wayne had arranged that instead.

Hilda, the senior driver on the run, also had the option to approve or disapprove of driving with me. It's human nature to think of oneself as a good companion. Upon occasion I've had that belief confirmed by others. But, if for any reason something about me irritated Hilda, she could call Wayne and tell him she needed a different co-driver. Yet, I really hoped for a steady run. Doing the math, I figured the drivers on this run each earned an excellent wage for a working person.

Eventually our repast ended, and we climbed back in the truck, she to the steering wheel and I to the bunk. I stretched out on the sleeping bag and closed my eyes. I drifted a bit then dozed. I might have fallen into deeper sleep, but couldn't rest long. The first day out most drivers are wide awake, full of rest from the weekend. Though it is difficult to get *solid* sleep on a truck, I found myself surprised at how often I might be able to doze even in the middle of the day if my co-driver drove steadily while I curled up in a cool, dark sleeper and closed my eyes.

When working with a co-driver it is generally easiest to sleep when the truck is moving. Of course, some drivers could sleep standing up. Chalk it up to youthful vigor or what have you, but I usually had too much energy to fall asleep at a moment's notice. At the start of the week especially I needed the truck to either head down the road continuously or stand still in order to doze off.

Stopping and starting almost always woke me. If I was lucky enough to be sleeping deeply and my co-driver pulled over at a truck stop for a break, I often felt disappointed by an enforced wakefulness when my brain noted the slowing of our truck, and the uneven sounds of the gears downshifting replaced the constancy of road noise.

About thirty minutes after we had left the diner I felt the unmistakable slowing of the truck followed by jostling from side to side while we made our way down an exit ramp and across an intersection. Of course, lying in the bunk, I could see none of this, but clearly we were off the highway. Finally, the truck stopped. I poked my head out from between the sleeper curtains like a prairie dog surveying its terrain. We were in the parking lot of a Wal-Mart.

"What's up?" I asked.

"I need to get some things," Hilda answered in her breathy, almost apologetic-sounding voice. Hilda explained that her wife didn't always run errands to supply Hilda with what she needed for the upcoming week. "If I don't have the things I need, I'm hell to live with," Hilda confessed.

Great, I thought silently.

Through the grapevine I'd learned Hilda had a rep that she "Can't get out of Texas." Now I knew precisely what was meant by that. If we had headed straight through, buying sandwiches for a quick lunch and only stopping for restroom breaks, we would have been in Arkansas by the time we stopped to shop. Usually, drivers start the week with whatever they need. Shopping during the work week for what could be acquired on the weekend was unusual in line-haul driving when everyone has the weekend off. The clock read after five in the evening and Texarkana lie another ninety minutes away. That city, that straddles the Texas-Arkansas state line, marked "Getting out of Texas."

I looked out the windows. In this parking lot in a small town the big rig looked strangely incongruous sitting slashed across a score of parking spaces striped off for passenger vehicles. Even if I could have fallen asleep while Hilda shopped, the knowledge that in some undetermined, but brief amount of time, I would be awakened when she got back in the truck and lumbered onto the highway kept me from resting. So I, too, climbed out of the cab and entered the store. I bought a few things and returned to the truck. The intrepid Hilda remained nowhere to be seen.

I sat down in the passenger seat and looked around for something to occupy my time. Our trucks had a satellite radio, something I'd never used before. I tuned the set and scanned channels just to hear the programs offered while watching people come and go in the parking lot. Most of them ignored the big truck parked in their midst. A few glanced my way while they parked or loaded goods into their cars.

After a while I checked my watch. Thirty minutes had passed since we'd stopped. I surfed more stations and checked again. Forty five minutes. Looking around the inside of the cab I found a disconcerting lack of reading material, but flipped through a couple of truck stop magazines, mostly filled with ads for driving jobs. I glanced at my watch. In total an hour had passed. Finally, as amber beams from the setting sun slanted across the asphalt, the driver door opened and Hilda climbed into the seat.

Hilda steered the rig onto the highway while I returned to the sleeper and earnestly tried to get some rest. I put in ear plugs and curled up with my sleeping bag to get comfortable. I dozed a couple of times until I fell into a deeper sleep. Then BRRRAP! A harsh sound arose from the tires below the sleeper. Sounding like a monster fart, all eleven right tires of our twenty two wheel, double trailer rig scraped the rumble strip. The same sound had stirred Coach from the bunk weeks earlier when I drove partway on the shoulder to pass a house being transported on flatbed trailers. Just like in a car, the noise echoed through the truck's entire cab.

The truck swerved gently to the left and the sound went away. In the sleeper compartment I couldn't see what had happened, but supposed in a moment's inattention Hilda had driven onto the rumble strip and then back off again. Oh well, she had corrected it. Even good drivers occasionally veer onto the strip. Providing they didn't make a habit of it, it didn't much matter. I glanced at the glowing numbers on my watch. I closed my eyes and dozed off again. BRRRAP! The noise of the rumble strip echoed through the cab. I looked at my watch. About twenty minutes had passed.

Shit! I thought. Pay attention. I'm trying to get some sleep in here.

I tried to relax my mind. I tugged on my bedding, readjusted my ear plugs and closed my eyes, hoping to get at least a solid nap before we reached the point between Memphis and Nashville where Hilda would bunk down in the sleeper while I took over the driving. I would have to drive overnight on my own, the longest single drive I'd undertaken since running with Dutch.

One good thing, Hilda never wanted to drive on each other's logbook. She required a solid break for rest, which is every driver's privilege, if they can doze off anyway. She would drive her shift, and I would drive mine. That seemed like a good idea. I could trust myself to protect my own reputation and felt better about not depending on someone else to drive any part of my shift. True, I still found driving a challenge, especially in bad weather or at night. And while some of the curves and hills still gave me the chills, I improved with each run. So far I had grown gradually more confident without becoming careless. Most new drivers who are going to mess up have an incident about a year into their work, when they become less vigilant about driving.

I wouldn't knowingly do anything to mar my record. Some drivers might blast through a construction zone with a 50 mph speed limit at 70 mph. Or they could change lanes without looking, thus raising the righteous indignation of an auto driver who might be forced onto the highway's shoulder. Further, not only could a driver be pulled over for a ticket, but our company employed what we called "spy vans" that sometimes monitored our speed and driving in urban areas. I don't know if a van ever measured my driving, but drivers who received a negative report always heard the results. If a driver accrued enough bad reports, we were told he or she could be let go.

Right then, lying in the bunk trying to sleep, at length my mind drifted off. BRRRAP! Yet again Hilda had swerved onto the rumble strip. I checked the time. Another fifteen minutes had passed. Falling asleep was hard enough with all the random noise we were subject to, but the thought that Hilda might be so distracted she could drive us off the road occurred to me. I looked up at the bunk above, at the shelves and the ceiling several feet

78

overhead and wondered what it would be like to be in the sleeper compartment if Hilda had a wreck. With Coach's warnings in mind I reached up and pulled down the unused safety netting that had been crammed between the top bunk and the back wall and clicked it into place just in case. Then I turned over facing the back wall of the cab and tried to settle down enough to doze off once more.

But then, yes, again: BRRRAP! This time curiosity got the better of me. I got out of the bunk and stood next to the Velcro closure on the heavy vinyl curtains that blocked light from the sleeping compartment. The Velcro didn't quite seal near the top. Feeling like a bit of a sneak, I peeked into the driver compartment. The sun had set. In addition to the glow of the instruments on the dashboard, I could see the glow of Hilda's cellphone. Hilda's thumb flitted over the alphanumeric pad while she texted someone on her phone.

Fucking great! I thought, shooting the breeze with someone when she should be driving the damn truck.

The fledgling vertebrae I'd grown on my trips with Buster and Coach weren't strong enough to open that curtain and ask Hilda to hang up and drive. Though, who's to say she would have? Eventually, Hilda gave up her correspondence, and I settled back down as best I could.

Hours later, we arrived at a truck stop in Tennessee partway between Memphis and Nashville where we switched out driving. The dashboard clock showed past 1:00 a.m. Hilda had taken thirteen hours for what should have been at most a ten hour drive.

We each took a break. I walked to a nearby gas station that still made fresh sandwiches even at this late hour. I had gotten a bit of fitful sleep, not much. But my turn to drive had come. Ready or not. So for the first of many times in my career I walked up to the driver door of a 73 foot long, 22 wheeled set of double trailers and sleeper cab that weighed in at over 60,000 pounds while *shaking* with exhaustion. Then I sat behind the wheel and drove for ten hours straight.

For staying awake, a caffeinated drink gave a short burst of energy, but that quickly dissipated. Besides, soda and coffee just increases the number of times a driver has to pull over into a truck stop. The so-called natural energy boosters for sale by the truck stop registers had no affect on me. I wasn't about to start popping any other sort of pill. That just seemed like a bad idea. The pure adrenalin of driving this big machine would have to keep me awake overnight and into morning.

With Hilda in the bunk I settled into the driver seat, entered the highway and headed into the blackness of the night. A few minutes later the driver of a white van pulled in front of the truck a bit abruptly and stepped heavily on his brakes. I had to work hard not to rear end him. Naturally, I wondered what went through the van driver's mind. Did he have an engine problem? With no exit nearby, did he need to pull over onto the shoulder? Had something in his van distracted him? Maybe he'd just spilled some hot coffee on his lap. That might make a motorist slow or brake hard unexpectedly.

Once it was safely possible, I passed him and continued driving. The weather remained clear and the highway contained only a few cars and other trucks. The night looked good for driving. Then about a half an hour later it happened again. The same white van pulled up fast along the left side of the rig. Before he swerved into the right lane I picked my foot up off the accelerator, slowing the truck's progress. Once more the van pulled in front of the truck and leaned heavily on his brakes. This time, since I'd already let up on the fuel, I didn't have to brake as hard to avoid a collision.

Clearly, this was no coincidence.

My mind tried to come up with more explanations. Had Hilda encountered him already and somehow pissed him off? Maybe her swerving had nearly caused a collision that Hilda was oblivious to. Without realizing a different driver sat at the wheel, the van driver might be trying to exact some form of revenge for being cut off or forced onto the shoulder earlier in the night. Of course, he might have confused our truck for another one from our company or even for a different company altogether. I could only speculate.

But nearly causing a wreck? Did he have some sort of vague suicidal wish? Was he trying to create the basis for a lawsuit? Or maybe he was just some random jerk who liked to play cat and mouse games with big trucks. People like that are out there. I would never know his story unless we collided, and I wasn't going to let him mess up my record. I drove onward after passing him, fast as the truck's limited speed allowed. Our truck topped out at 71 mph. I tried to put some distance between our vehicles.

Well, the third time's the charm, they say.

Another thirty minutes and along came the same white van. He pulled the same stunt. I readied myself for him, but this time an exit with a truck stop came into view. Instead of braking then speeding past him, I pulled off into the exit ramp. If he wouldn't let me pass him and stay ahead, perhaps he'd feel he had won his game if he got ahead. Let him. I just wanted a safe trip.

The most foolhardy thing about that van driver or any other motorists doing this type of thing rests in the fact that just one brush of the truck's bumper against his van, and he could have been killed. Most people have a limited understanding of just how much momentum a big rig truly has. While a truck is far less heavy than a train, the old PSAs about railroad crossings that say, "if it's a tie you lose," pretty much describe many a motorist who tangled with a semi, too.

But to this day I remain in awe of the number of motorists who don't appear to understand that if our vehicles did collide, the motorist in a passenger vehicle of any size has much less chance of survival than the truck driver. I thought of it like this: Which is stronger, a 15 lb. infant or a 250 lb. man? If the two fought, who would win? The answer is so obvious it makes the question ridiculous. If a 5,000 lb. automobile and an 80,000 lb. tractor-trailer collide, the same principles apply. Yet, many motorists drive around trucks as if they believe they are equal in weight and momentum.

Perhaps, something had angered the van driver. As a truck driver, I never once did anything to deliberately anger a motorist and never knew of any other driver who knowingly did so. Not that that kind of thing can't happen, but it's very much the exception rather than the norm. Often motorists don't know what trucks need to do on the road or why. One of the strongest and most often expressed sentiments among truck drivers is that the public doesn't know how to drive. Often that sentiment is expressed almost angrily itself. Yet the loved ones of truckers, their spouses, kids, parents and so on, usually drive four-wheelers. So it would benefit us all to realize most motorists are *never taught how* to drive near trucks.

Some motorists might not believe it, but a lot of truck drivers' time is preoccupied with keeping auto drivers safe. Often I heard truck drivers strategizing with each other on the CB about lane changes, since one of the most frequent challenges with motorists occurs when these necessary maneuvers take place. Unfortunately, some motorists look upon trucks changing lanes as a game of one-upmanship.

Lane changes in a truck always had a valid reason – most often for safety. A stalled car may block the lane ahead or a police cruiser might stand parked on the side of the road with emergency lights flashing. Or maybe the lane ahead tapered off or closed due to road construction. Many other things could be blocking the lane ahead: an animal crossing or the remains of one that failed to cross, or a chunk of tire rubber or other debris might lie before us. I once had to change lanes to avoid a car bumper lying horizontally across I-40 in Memphis in the middle of the night. I then phoned the police with the lane direction and mile marker to let them know about it.

The list can go on and on.

I never once in many thousands of miles of driving changed lanes or signaled to change lanes just for the hell of it. Frequently, I wished motorists didn't see a lane change signal like it's a chance to prove they missed their career as an Indy driver. I wanted to say to them, 'Please don't race around the truck or drive alongside, making my choices either to hold my lane when it's no longer safe or to crash into you.' Of course, most motorists who drive near trucks with a lot of bravado suddenly become great pragmatists when they realize they really are between a rock and a hard place, or a concrete barrier and the side of a fast moving trailer. Some motorists then must re-discover the presence and function of their brake pedal and develop the humbleness to use it.

When I drove my own car after becoming a trucker I could see when and how to cooperate with big rig drivers. I cringed when recalling my own clumsy driving next to trucks on the highway, even on my way to truck driving school. I became conscious of avoiding blocking their way or sometimes even helped them move over, if I could do so without endangering myself. Truckers and sometimes even motorists use headlights to signal a lane change can be made safely. When that's the case the vehicle behind flashes their headlights. When a trucker moves over in front of the signaling vehicle he shows his thanks by flashing his brake lights two or three times.

I also learned that one of the best things to do is simply to stay far away from trucks when possible. A future co-driver later described the advice he had given his own mother thusly: "If you can help it, don't drive too close in front of a truck or too close behind one. If you have to drive beside one, make that time as brief as possible." After becoming a truck driver, if I could safely do so in my own car, I slowed down or sped up or changed lanes to avoid being alongside a rig any longer than necessary.

Even if the truck driver is attentive and skilled, things can go wrong. For instance, a truck tire can shred and peel off large pieces of rubber so close to a car the motorist loses control if struck by them through an open window or driving over them. Or if a front tire on the rig blows out, the truck could swerve suddenly into another lane. Even a strong blast of wind can move a truck into adjacent lanes before the trucker can react.

Becoming a driver made news stories about crashes with trucks really stick in my mind. I'd heard a report of a car with four passengers whose driver had pulled out in front of an oncoming truck rather than wait for the semi to pass. The truck driver did all he could, but the rig couldn't slow or stop in time and ran over the car killing everyone in it. Or there was a bus full of students that had a fiery crash with a big rig that killed several passengers. Another semi crossed the median and killed the passengers of a van and the trucker. And on and on. I'd heard that some motorists believe trucks have a sort of super braking system that helps trucks stop more quickly with all that weight. But, no, the laws of physics apply. More time and distance are needed to bring a semi-truck to a stop than a passenger vehicle.

The opposite also applies. Since a semi-truck weighs much more, acceleration is slower. Most truckers are aware of how frustrated motorists can feel behind a slowly advancing semi, and many avoid pulling out closely in front of motorists for that reason. True, sometimes a motorist gets stuck behind a slow moving truck anyway. The trucker wants to go faster, too. But getting a heavier vehicle up to speed simply takes time. In the meantime, a motorist who whips around a truck without looking can put himself and any passengers in danger of colliding with another vehicle when a little patience could have saved the day and maybe even the motorist.

Both truckers and motorists could avoid more collisions if they remembered three simple ideas. First, slow down! Plan ahead so you don't have to rush and be humble enough to slow down when it will help in traffic instead of only speeding up. Next, look up ahead on the roadway so you can be ready for stopped traffic or whatever else fate has in store. If you cultivate this practice, you will notice you are ready for what lies ahead while other motorists charge forward obliviously. And last, but not least: Don't drive for your ego! Next to controlling speed this would probably make the biggest difference in reduced collisions. The point of driving is not to put your car in front of everyone else's. Just drive to get to your destination and enhance your sense of self-worth in a safer venue, like a racquetball court, not a roadway. One thing is for sure. Trucking made me a more mellow driver. I began to drive cool, so to speak. Not like a hothead. As a result, ordinary driving or commuting became much less stressful, even enjoyable.

Chapter 7: "I could call Wayne."

Back on the road the driver of the white van was nowhere to be seen. I drove for over an hour to Nashville then northward to Kentucky. A few hours later I hooked a right at Louisville and headed east on I-71 toward Cincinnati. There I found the type of road I dreaded. Hills and curves. At night. At least it wasn't raining. The stretch from Louisville to Cincinnati had fewer towns. Mile after mile of roadway pierced into an impenetrable inky darkness. The road surface and the tall trees that ran alongside were just about all I could see. Parts of the highway carved through the sides of mountains where jagged, rocky walls fell under the beams of the headlights. Other trucks hammered past me while I drove this new stretch of road for the first time. With just a few thousand miles under my belt, I found the terrain the most dramatic I had come across up to that point. I struggled to help the truck climb the hills and to control the "fall" downhill. Uphill curves weren't so bad because climbing a steep roadway, I felt more in control of the rig. Flat land curves were bad enough, but I especially hated curves that were on a descent. At those times the rig felt like a rollercoaster that might go off the rails, if I failed to combine speed and steering just so.

Trees along the highway had started to lose their autumn leaves and a wind kicked up. The brown, yellow and red leaves whirled across the highway like evil little pixies dancing tauntingly across the headlight beams. Each time another truck passed by a curtain of leaves rose and blew across the windshield like a school of fish swimming in the same direction for a second or two before dispersing into chaos until the next truck drove by. The wind pulled on the trailers, too, like sails catching the breeze.

A truck may be powerful and have a lot of momentum, but nothing man-made is ever a match for the strength of nature. Gusts of wind could make the trailers, the back one especially, inch over with each blast. I worked to hold the trailers steady in their lane, edging close to the paint stripe next to the shoulder. If the wind pushed the rig hard enough, I wanted it to be onto that shoulder and not into the other lane where cars passed by.

The whole scene reminded me of the Wizard of Oz. The winds, like the tornado that picked up Dorothy's house and tossed it around like a toy, could do the same to any rig. Plus, I imagined the dark and deserted-looking trees along the edge of the highway belonged to the forest where Dorothy and her companions wanted to pick apples. Instead, the trees themselves had scolded them. The trees here, too, must wear scowls and have sharp limbs for hands. While the trees scowled, surely the rock walls laughed cruelly. Next to those rock walls yellow triangular signs read: Fallen Rock. Not Falling Rocks or Watch for Rocks, but rather laughably, rocks disgraced from the presence of Eden. What poem might Milton have written for them?

After almost an hour more of what felt like a scary carnival ride that wouldn't end, I drove around a sharp curve and spied a large green sign with white lettering. The words commemorated the tragic Carrollton, Kentucky bus accident that had taken more than two dozen lives along this path many years before. More than ever, I just wanted this road to end.

Finally, about ninety minutes after driving past Louisville our highway merged with I-75. A short while later I negotiated a steep descent toward the Ohio River with Cincinnati's earliest commuters. The predawn sky gave off a golden and purple blush that projected light onto the land while cars jostled for position, approaching the bridge that crossed the river. Nervously, I made my way along the different lanes, making sure not to get side-tracked into one of the lanes that exited onto local streets where I could get trapped with the cumbersome rig. Nor did I want a lane that might whisk us away in the wrong direction, toward some unintended destination. Occasionally, a school bus with a bright flashing light atop the roof sidled along. Filled with more vulnerable passengers than most vehicles, I couldn't get away from a school bus too soon.

Leaving the city, the highway continued across farmlands while the sun rose. Green fields lined a highway with a speed limit of only 55 mph for trucks. Plodding along the flat plains, just the novelty of driving somewhere the first time made the trip of many hours feel short.

Eventually, we neared the company facility and Hilda sat up in the passenger seat to show me the way to the terminal. On my first order of business at Cleveland I stopped by the restroom to attend to one of life's little necessities. Hilda only had to make sure she had stored her overnight pee bag where it wouldn't leak until she could ditch it at a truck stop trash can. Yes, I may as well tell you the whole ugly truth about driving and peeing. Not, hopefully, at the same time, though that happens with male drivers, believe it or not. Anyway, this subject brings on a host of issues that we'll call, "Fun with Urine."

As all drivers discover, one of the most inconvenient things about trucking is the nearly ever present reminder that one has a body. Outside of a truck we usually take for granted being able to sleep when we're tired, drink when we're thirsty, eat when we're hungry, and use the restroom when needed. Once truckers are driving down the highway, however, they find themselves chained to the limitations of normal bodily care in a moving vehicle with a limited number and type of stopping places available and strongly budgeted time. A few, rare sleeper compartments include an RV style toilet. The vast majority of big trucks contain no such luxury. So many truckers use alternative methods.

Once eliminated, liquids can be stored temporarily in a truck in suitable containers. Anything else really calls for a restroom break where genuine porcelain is involved. Truckers consider it bad form to crap in a truck. Now you know. If you think it's bad form for Hilda to toss her "pee bomb" in a trash can, consider that one of the guys I drove with to Los Angeles in later days threw a large plastic trash bag out the passenger window every day somewhere in Arizona or New Mexico. I'm not sure why he didn't just have a pee bottle like most guys. Maybe I don't want to know.

Though it might sound ridiculous, male drivers have an option that can sound almost like a luxury to female drivers, that of whizzing in a bottle. This is a comparatively simple matter for your average dude, and a host of plastic bottles with secure caps exist. A male driver can whip it out and pee in a soda bottle with a screw-on lid so the liquid "cargo" can't spill out. One team of drivers used empty laundry detergent bottles. Each had his own color coded receptacle in order to avoid whizzing in his co-driver's bottle by mistake. Unfortunately, they disposed of their pee bombs by upending the partially filled bottles onto the pavement at our company's facilities when they dropped or picked up trailers.

Indeed, our manly colleagues may chose from a plethora of options, including the unexpected. Every driver has heard of rowdy truckers who claim to drive sixteen hours or more each day without stopping. Legend has it such drivers punch a hole in the rubber boot where the stick shift meets the floor, insert tubing that leads to the outside, and attach a funnel to the top of the tube. That way they can pee and drive at the same time without bothering with later liquid disposal.

Another legend holds that for the management of solid waste some drivers drill a hole in the bunk floor that's not big enough to step through and is kept covered by a mat when not in use. Some drivers claimed to know this because they had heard of mechanics who refused or resisted working on the undercarriage of rigs outfitted in this way due to the resulting problems of residue. Like many legends this one may not be so.

When it comes to liquid management, clearly us females are not streamlined like the males. As usual, we're more complicated. What to do, then? Without impeding the truck's progress, how might one deal with the inevitable results of drinking water, soda or tea, and of just having a pulse? Until driving with other females I had always asked any male co-driver to stop if I needed to use the restroom while he drove. Then Hilda explained that some females use gallon size plastic bags with a seal at the top, the type used in millions of homes to store food or other items. Name brands, she advised, store brands were not to be trusted. Like any, this method has its flaws. I would find this out later to my deep chagrin.

On my own I worked out that while standing and leaning a leg against the bunk to steady myself, the bag could be opened in an elliptical shape. After doing what has to be done, the clear plastic bag is then sealed and placed in a plastic shopping bag with a knot tied in the top for an extra layer of leakage protection. The shopping bag, one of many accumulated from truck stop purchases, usually came in a solid color. Thus, the white or tan bags helped disguise the contents of the clear sealed bag, if it had to be walked across a truck stop parking lot to reach a trash container.

Later another lady trucker would advise of a more secure method involving a small plastic funnel and a bottle of isopropyl alcohol. Put the funnel into the neck of any suitable plastic bottle and whiz away secure in the knowledge that you can easily twist that cap closed over the contents in the same way male drivers do. Dispose of at will. The alcohol cleans the funnel both before and after use, thus helping avoid bladder infections, a not infrequent female concern.

Much later I would figure out a supplementary method that worked well for a quick solution on solo runs. Before arriving at work, I bought the biggest Styrofoam cup some fast food joints provide, one that I couldn't possibly pee enough to overflow. Unlike paper cups, foam doesn't break down so easily. The cup could be securely placed with its cover on in one of the deep cup holders on the sleeper compartment desk until disposal. Some women use a large plastic or metal travel mug with a screw-on lid in the same way.

This brings us to: once you've done your dirty, what next?

Instead of throwing a bottle or cup away, both men and women at times dump the contents of a pee receptacle on the ground somewhere along the back of their truck once they've parked where they can "check the tires." Many times I detected the smell of urine when walking to or from my parked truck at a truck stop. Some drivers toss pee bottles alongside the road, but the people who mow the shoulder grass can tell you they don't want a shower in anyone's pee when the blades of the mower slice through a thin plastic bottle that has been roasting in the sun for no one knows how long. Thus, the lesser evil is to throw pee bottles away in trash cans at truck stops or rest areas.

To wit, some drivers specifically choose plastic drink bottles composed of a solid color. If one has a clear bottle with a yellow fluid in it, the contents can be obvious. But if the plastic is tinted, a driver could simply appear to be disposing of some unwanted soda. Many use bottles from soda brands that look a bit like pee anyway. The soda, that is.

Some drivers were quite blatant in disposing of their pee bottles, sometimes even discarding them at our company's terminals next to overfilled waste baskets where security cameras were supposedly trained on their every move. This didn't seem like the wisest move considering the phrase, "Don't shit where you eat." Maybe one shouldn't pee there either.

Other drivers were more cautious, since, though it is seldom enforced, all the methods of disposal just mentioned are illegal. Anyone could be fined beaucoup bucks, in fact, for using any of these methods. I heard the sum of $1000 mentioned, a lot of dough to the working man or woman. But I never encountered anyone who had received any fine for personal waste disposal.

If you find this whole phenomenon disturbing, you are not alone. Yet, it is one of the many hard facts of life about trucking. Perhaps, if truck stops or rest areas had containers specifically designed to receive human waste in whatever ad hoc packaging it arrived in, that would be more hygienic and better for the environment. Don't blame or punish drivers for an unavoidable bodily function, just provide a better solution.

We dropped our trailers and built a new set bound for Fort Worth. Then I waited to see if Hilda could get out of Ohio.

"We always fuel at a truck stop on the way back," Hilda explained, taking the wheel while I sat next to her in the passenger seat and updated my logbook. I logged myself in to the sleeper bunk.

"If you stop, I'd like to take the time to shower."

"My co-driver and I always shower and eat," Hilda said.

I felt glad to hear it. We would fill the truck's fuel tanks and our bellies. Each of us also could use one of the truck stop's many showers for free due to our fuel purchase of several hundred dollars. If I had a co-driver who made it a part of the regular routine to stop for at least one decent meal and a shower, perhaps this run could work out for both of us. I didn't feel quite myself unless I could shower and put on a clean set of clothes at least every other day. Another plus: Hilda didn't text anyone that morning. Perhaps, I thought, the day before had been a onetime thing. Since edging onto the rumble strip pretty much ruined a co-driver's opportunity to sleep, I certainly hoped so.

Somewhat over an hour later we pulled off amid grassy fields, crossed the highway via an overpass and pulled into a fuel lane at a large truck stop. We filled up once a day, since like most big rigs our vehicle only got about six miles a gallon. Our truck took on over $500 of diesel each time. Most truck stop chains have a driver incentive program of a point per each gallon purchased. Eventually, the points add up to a cash rebate. Hilda swiped her driver loyalty card through the reader to cop the points.

While Hilda parked the freshly fueled truck I went inside to the counter, signed for our purchase and got a key to one of the shower rooms from an attendant. Ideally, truck stops have multiple showers available at any time. During busy times drivers may have to wait, but large truck stops like this one had a dozen or more showers. Our team typically arrived at a slow time, in the early afternoon on a weekday, so showers were always available.

A modern truck stop's shower can be a clean and spacious place to relax in private and wash off the road grime and sweat of a couple of day's work, changing out of clothes that have often become greasy while building sets of trailers. Each shower is really a single bathroom with a toilet and sink in addition to the shower itself. The good ones always include a bench with enough room both to sit and to place your luggage at the same time. The smart managers also provide a couple of sturdy hooks on a wall or the back of the door so drivers can hang up a coat and shirt or trousers. The truck stops provide towels and soap, but I preferred to bring my own. I also packed toiletries like a toothbrush and toothpaste, deodorant, and enough clothes for the trip or the week.

Just like using the restroom when you want, I had taken brushing my teeth and having a daily shower for granted before driving a truck. I could almost understand why many drivers had bad teeth or had given up and gotten caps or dentures. Simply keeping one's teeth clean can get lost in the grind of drive and rest, drive and rest, day in and day out with little respite. Between shower times I used an empty plastic bottle to spit toothpaste and water into. Then tossed it at the next stop.

After my shower I walked across the gaudy red carpet of the truck stop's restaurant to see if the buffet foods looked merely dull or actually alarming. Past a smattering of men here and there I walked back, having decided to order instead. It is customary for team drivers to sit together when they eat. Hilda sat, her wet head hovering over a plate of steak in a nearby booth. Lowering myself into the seat opposite Hilda, I took a menu from the waitress who hurried away to refill coffee cups.

"Do you want to borrow my hair dryer?" I asked Hilda when she glanced up at me.

"Why?" Hilda said, looking up fully and directly with a strong gaze into my eyes, such that I wondered if she took the offer as a slight.

"It's just that your hair is wet, and it's cold out," I explained.

"Doesn't bother me," Hilda shrugged.

Handing the menu back to the waitress, I placed an order.

"So what made you want to drive a truck?" Hilda huskily asked "the question." So even a woman wants to know why I'm driving a truck, I thought.

"I wanted a good job," I explained. "When I graduated from college almost no one was hiring, but I wanted to do something real world so here I am." Then I asked Hilda why she drove.

Hilda had much the same answer, but with a twist. She had, she said, once lived on easy street, paying cash for any car she wanted. Then her fortunes took a turn for the worst. Now she drove because the job pays well.

While we continued to chat Hilda gave me what she thought were a couple of pointers. "You don't want to piss off the girls,"

Hilda intoned in her hushed, whispery way, referring to Wil's office staff. "They control your paycheck."

I hadn't developed the habit of pissing people off deliberately, but I decided to keep that little nugget of insight to myself. We finished our return journey then drove out and back again on another run to end the week together. Hilda ran the solo butthead run for her route alone that weekend while I went home.

Many team routes went out and back in two days two times per week. Then on a third trip one driver went on a solo butthead, exchanging trailers with a driver from the location they usually drove to. So that a driver that went to Cleveland, for instance, changed trailers with another driver based in Cleveland on the third trip of the week. On the third trip each driver met partway, spent the night in his own truck, then drove back the next day. This way every other week a driver drove six days, and on alternating weeks he or she drove four days. Thus, everyone had a long weekend every two weeks, but a longer work week just as frequently.

The next week Hilda's truck went out every day, but without me in it. I substituted on another route while, I speculated, Hilda drove with at least one other candidate for her run. In the end Hilda may have decided that I was the least troublesome co-driver. Or perhaps I had unintentionally given the impression that if pushed, I wouldn't push back. Whatever the case, Wayne called me on Monday and told me to meet Hilda at the Fort Worth terminal on Tuesday afternoon. I would be running with her until further notice. Wayne became the guy to call if a problem occurred or a question arose.

Every week most team drivers trade who drives out first. Thus, the one who leaves the home terminal behind the steering wheel is in the sleeper bunk starting out the next week. Typically for most runs, on any given week Hilda drove out from Fort Worth, going until her legal limit of hours had been reached at a usual place where a driver trades out the bunk for the steering wheel or vice versa. Then her co-driver drove the rest of the way to the destination terminal. Afterwards Hilda drove out from Cleveland, returning partway to the same trade out location. Then her co-driver brought the truck back home. The next week the co-driver started the run. That week I drove out from Fort Worth. Let's see, I thought, if *I* can get us out of Texas.

Hilda and I had agreed to meet earlier so we could leave the yard at noon. If we reached the switch out in Tennessee at about 10 or 11 p.m. instead of midnight or later, we would be making some headway. Yet, Robbie Burns might have written the truism, "The best laid plans of mice and men often go awry" for trucking. If that's the case, we just might say, "The best laid plans of trucks and drivers often go awry."

I drove out of Fort Worth and across Dallas. We had cleared the suburban clutter until our truck passed through countryside between small towns. The truck rolled speedily eastward on I-30 when the engine, that typically chugged along for days at a time, suddenly died. The temperature needle pointed into the red zone, thus the engine had overheated and shut itself down.

I had just enough driving practice not to panic. Nonetheless, a sense of alarm rose up in my chest and through my arms while I struggled with weakened steering power. Thankfully, the truck had been in the slow lane. With the hazard lights blinking, the momentum of tens of thousands of pounds still moved forward. I coasted the truck gingerly onto the shoulder. I tugged on the wheel to pull over out of traffic without putting any tires on the grass next to the highway. Visions of getting stuck in mud and requiring a wrecker to pull the rig out danced in my head. We hadn't stopped for lunch yet so Hilda still sat beside me rather than bunking down.

"I guess you checked the radiator fluid level before we left the yard," Hilda said in what I took for a mocking tone, hinting that I hadn't inspected the truck. In a way, Hilda was right, like her and every other driver I'd built a set with, I never did a true pre-trip inspection. For one thing I didn't know how. Some drivers I'd worked with had already built the set and, presumably, had inspected the equipment. Coach had showed me how to make sure the brake system worked correctly. Another driver had told me that the trucks are maintained well enough that inspections weren't necessary. Yet, inspections were still required by law. We had been on the yard almost two hours before leaving the terminal and neither of us had done more than check that the lights worked. I had driven out, so technically, inspecting the truck had been my responsibility. I had let it slip. No excuse.

We got out of the truck and opened the hood only to find the coolant at the normal level. Something else had gone awry.

"See? I told you the radiator was filled," I grinned.

Still no excuse.

Not only did I still not know how to inspect a truck, we drivers never had any sort of face-to-face safety instruction or meetings in the years I drove. Instead of safety meetings, every so often dispatch clerks handed each driver a collection of stapled pages and had us sign a list acknowledging receipt. Drivers were supposed to read the pages on their own time. Mostly the pages had simple reminders like: slow down in the rain. But on at least one occasion several pages contained nothing more than gobbledygook spewed from a computer file gone wrong.

Right then Hilda and I found ourselves miles from a truck stop, fuel station or store of any kind. I picked up my phone out of a drink holder on the dash. I would call Wayne so he could send assistance to the hinterlands when Hilda took action.

"I'm not waiting out here for a tow truck," Hilda said, standing up.

We traded seats. After the engine cooled a bit, Hilda turned the key. The engine started. She eased back into traffic then took the first exit and continued along the service road. The needle soon hit the red zone again. The engine died. We'd rolled just minutes and a few hundred yards further.

Hilda steered the truck close to the edge of the service road and turned on the hazard lights again. A few cars made up the sparse traffic that drove around our disabled rig. About fifteen minutes later Hilda started the truck again. She drove down the service road to a traffic signal where we lost precious seconds waiting for a green light to appear while the engine grew hotter and hotter. The light changed and we headed down the road again. The needle neared the red zone. Just when the engine gave up for the third time Hilda pulled off into the empty parking lot of a new building that still had the construction company's signs out front.

Stop and start. Stop and start. Over an hour passed before we reached a small truck stop with a barbecue restaurant next door. In a normal truck the drive would have taken minutes. If it had been my truck engine, I would not have liked the treatment this one had received. But personally, I felt glad to be in a place with food, beverages, and toilets. Hilda had impressed me with her skill and determination. She had made it to a haven of comfort. I would have waited on the side of the road.

Parking the truck, Hilda called Wayne on her cell, and he decided to bring another truck to hitch up to our trailers. In the meantime we went inside the restaurant. By the time we had finished dining Wayne pulled up in another truck. Hilda and I each moved our sleep gear, logbooks and whatever else we didn't think we could live without for the next couple of days into the other cab. Then our usual ride got towed to a mechanic's shop for what turned out to be a thermostat replacement, something that couldn't be caught during an inspection, as it happens.

All told our little interlude with the overheating truck had cost us a few hours. It looked like I couldn't get out of Texas any faster than Hilda, at least not in the truck she usually drove. We got to the switch out site at the truck stop in Tennessee at about 2 a.m. I felt so beat I even slept uninterrupted for a few hours while Hilda drove. In our type of trucking, driving a regular route over and over, a setback in time tends to last the whole week because most runs have little or no down time to catch up. My experiment with speedier driving would have to wait until another week.

We made our run up to Cleveland and returned to Fort Worth again. Twenty four hours after our turnaround in Ohio we readied ourselves to head back out on our last run of the week. But payday had arrived. Though Hilda had been making good money for years in this job, she always said she ran low on cash. Following her routine, she hightailed her pickup truck out of the parking lot to cash her check and stop at a fast food joint. I could sit in the truck and listen to my hair grow or retreat to the shower at the terminal.

Starting out I hadn't been aware the terminals *had* showers, but each includes both men's and women's showers. The quality and even the cleanliness appeared to have a lot to do with the age of the facility. The Fort Worth terminal's tiny shower was in a private bathroom that appeared to be several years old. The door stood just off the sorting area for packages. The room's toilet paper dispenser dispensed paper when it felt like it. The room felt cold in the winter and steamy in the summer. Puke colored, yellow tile covered the whole grimy looking place, but a driver could shower there.

I carried my shower bag, really a full-sized piece of soft-sided luggage with a week's clothes and grooming supplies, to the women's private bathroom and locked the door. I didn't want to be caught with my pants down. I felt glad, too, that Hilda and I did our turnaround in broad daylight. At times, I would have to use a terminal shower at night, and it always felt a bit creepy without many people around the dispatch office or the yard. Not every shower has a solid floor-to-lintel door with its own lock, which they should all have. Some terminals have a shower within a multiple person restroom with a door like any other stall with open space above and below the door. I always felt concerned about vulnerability in places like that. Fortunately, I didn't experience any problems, but never felt entirely secure in such showers.

I set my bag down on a bench seat, took off my clothes, and put on a set of flip flops to prevent catching athlete's foot off of the sticky floor. Then I took a little bar of soap and a bottle of shampoo out of my bag and placed them on a wire frame caddy just inside the shower stall. I stepped over a tile ridge that helped the shower's water to go down a drain in the middle and pulled the shower curtain across a gap between the walls.

Humming a tune I wet my sweaty hair and worked the shampoo into a lather when my eyes froze on an unexpected sight. I was not alone. Only the instinct not to scare him prevented me from screaming and running right back out of the shower again. Less than a foot away he moved, looking at me. Was he a man or a mouse? No. He was Super Roach! From the surface of the shower wall a giant, squash-resistant cockroach wiggled his antenna at me. Then he reared his ugly head from the surface of the yellow tile.

But then instinct failed me: I screamed. Responding to the sound he ran onto the shower curtain that I then so desperately wanted to open so I could run past my unexpected companion lest his six creepy little legs landed on the soft skin of my naked body. I screamed again. That only made things worse because then Super Roach ran around in circles on the curtain. Shampoo seeped into my eyes as I struggled to pull off a flip flop, while trying valiantly to refrain from falling ass first onto the wet, dirty floor.

Whoosh! I swiped the dripping wet shoe against the soft material of the curtain hoping to catch the creature that dared so rudely to intrude upon my efforts at personal hygiene. Mr. Roach – it must be a guy, after all it hid out in the ladies' shower – simply ran deeper into the folds of the curtain. Still balancing on my one shod foot, I hadn't even thought to put both feet on terra firma. I pulled on the curtain, straightening the folds and saw him again.

Whoosh! The little sucker ran again, this time onto the tile. I had a clear shot at him. Whack! Splat! Take that you little bastard! I opened the curtain and let Mr. Roach's remains fall from the bottom of the flip flop into the trash can nearby. All wildlife issues resolved, I continued my shower.

A couple of hours later Hilda returned from her errands. Preparing to leave, we sat in the truck and updated our logs with the numbers on the trailers and noted the numbers on the anti-theft seals that closed the trailer doors. Even when driving legally truckers often take a moment to make sure their logs match. If a team is pulled over by police and the times and places on their logs differ, explanations would be due. Cleveland was the first regular run I'd been on, and filling out logs can be a bit of a puzzle, especially for a novice. So I asked Hilda a question to make sure we had recorded our switch out at the same time.

"We got to Sugar Tree at two," Hilda answered.

"Sugar Tree?" I said in surprise because a truck stop at the exit where we switched out had a large sign over their door that read, 'Welcome to Holladay, Tennessee!'

"You don't call it Holladay?" I asked.

"I've been running this route for five years and never had a log come back for the town name," Hilda answered. Hilda's delivery did sound a bit temperamental, but still looking at my logbook I persisted with another comment, not yet realizing I might be poking a hornets' nest with a stick.

"I put today's PTI at noon," I said, referring to the abbreviation for the usual imaginary pre-trip inspection.

"I don't need to know that."

"Oh. I wrote down a PTI on my log when you drove out," I said. "I guess I didn't need to do that."

"Why would you? You're in the sleeper," Hilda answered.

Though truthfully I had helped build our set and fuel and whatever else needed doing. Then I had sat up until we got to wherever Hilda wanted to eat.

"Okay, I won't do that anymore," I said.

"You need to show your PTI."

"For today, yeah. I won't show it when you're driving out."

"You just said you did."

"I mean from now on," I explained.

Out of sync with our conversation Hilda responded haughtily. "I guess I just don't have your education," she said, commenting on the bit of background information that I had shared with her. "But I have been filling out logbooks for a long time."

I looked up. "No offense intended," I said sincerely.

"Maybe I should get a co-driver who doesn't question me," Hilda continued in her non sequitur. "I could call Wayne. That's all it would take!" she commanded, pitching her logbook on the dashboard and retreating hastily into the sleeper.

I didn't reply, for one thing the issue clearly wasn't me or the logs. For another, I didn't think anything I could say would be helpful. But the fact that a simple conversation could awaken such temper threw me for a loop right then. Would another innocent comment or question bring on a similar response?

But one of Hilda's remarks had brought up an interesting point. If any driver went over the hours of service on the day's log, one of Wil's staff returned a "corrected" log to him or her. The returned log instructed the driver how to change the original page in the logbook from what had been driven to what wouldn't get the driver in trouble from dispatch management or if pulled over by a police officer who inspected the logbook. If a driver had mistakenly driven too many hours, however, no one ever spoke about it.

We started our trip. I drove out and stopped per her request at Hilda's favorite store where she bought supplies again. With Hilda's errands done, we stopped at a pizza buffet. Then over several hours I drove the rest of the way to the switch out. Midnight drew near when I pulled into the darkened truck stop at Holladay.

I parked the truck in an empty fuel lane and picked up my little green bookbag. Climbing down from the truck, I pulled the bookbag over my shoulders and looked at the truck next to ours. Unfortunately, the only clear lane had been next to a truck hauling a trailer full of cattle. Livestock trailers are made of metal slats open to the outside so that the transported animals can breathe. A consequence thereof is that everyone in the vicinity also breathes in the perfume of their manure. As a result, truck drivers and motorists can often tell when a cattle truck is ahead on the highway before the vehicle even comes into sight. When it does one often can see the cowbell still dangling from the back bumper. Used to call cattle to feeding, loaders strike the bell to encourage the animals to walk up a ramp and go inside. The bell that had signaled food and comfort to the cattle continues to dangle and sound its peal, swinging back and forth with the sway of the truck's movement.

After a break in the truck stop I returned and walked briefly around the rig glancing at all the lights to see they were on. I didn't do much of a PTI at the terminal, mainly because I didn't know what to check beyond the lights and making sure the gauges on the dash were within range. No needles pointed to red and no dashboard lights were on. However, I had picked up a bit of intelligence from other drivers. Turns out it's a good idea to check both the fifth wheel pin behind the cab and the one for the dolly that attaches the back trailer to make sure they're still in place before leaving a truck stop or pickle park. On more than one occasion a trucker has pulled away from a parked location to find that an unknown colleague or passerby has pulled the release pin, thus loosening the connection. Without that vital attachment the trailers will fall off of the truck. Sometimes that doesn't happen until after entering the highway, and the aftermath may involve multiple vehicles. A loosened trailer has been known to run into other vehicles, at times with deadly consequences. God only knows why anyone would do such a malicious thing, but that's the world we live in.

Finding everything secure, I turned around and walked back between our rig and the cattle truck. October had given way to November. In the autumn nighttime coolness my breath turned to mist that floated in the air. Just a few feet away that mist joined the breath of dozens of cattle, jam-packed against the slatted walls of the trailer next to us. Some such truckloads headed for the slaughterhouse or feeding lot. Even if merely being transported from one farm or ranch to another, ultimately most cattle share one fate.

Some cattle, especially in western states, have been reared in the open range with little or no contact with humans. I could only imagine their terror and discomfort when they are loaded aboard a filthy vessel by strange creatures and pushed in until no more room is left for another hoof to stand. Drivers told stories about animals trodden to death by others if they fell to the floor in these trailers. In the crush, the standing animals can't make room for the fallen animal to rise. Or if a wooden floorboard breaks and a cow's leg falls through, one driver explained that the limb can be dragged and reduced to a stump while the creature calls out in agony unheard above the rush of road noise.

In addition, cattle are transported without water or feed in all kinds of weather: hot or cold; rain, snow or shine. One of my driving instructors had told our class about a cattle hauler who had reached his legal driving limit for the day thirty minutes away from a destination on a hot summer day. According to regulations, he should have stopped for a ten hour break, leaving the cattle hungry and thirsty in the trailer that entire time. Some of those cattle would have perished from neglect due to heat and dehydration. The driver didn't think that the right thing to do so, well able to make the delivery, he brought the cattle in and got fired for his efforts. In his case, no mercy, he had deliberately gone over his hours. Maybe such things should be judged on a case-by-case basis where the humane treatment of animals is concerned.

In the dimmed atmosphere of the truck stop's lights I could see the cattle trying to push away from the side of the truck where I walked next to them. Perhaps these were free range cattle, tantamount to wild animals. I paused and turned to look at them. The one nearest me peeled its eyes back into its head and called out in fright. The creature's beautiful light brown hide stirred less than an arm's length away behind the slats in the trailer's side while the cow shifted weight and moved restlessly. Its fellow occupants shuffled a few inches closer to the center of the trailer. I turned again and, finishing my walk, climbed back into the cab of our truck.

Chapter 8: "Let's go find Wayne."

Once Hilda steered the rig back onto the highway I had no idea of the covert operation I would undertake on the tail end of this run. While Hilda prepared to drive through the rest of Tennessee and across Kentucky then into Ohio I laid out my things on the bunk and retired to sleep. I dozed off for a bit then woke again before dozing some more. After a couple of hours I awoke with the familiar discomfort of needing to pee, made worse by the constant bouncing of the truck on the road.

To see where we were I opened the tiny vent that made a sort of window in the side of the truck's sleeper compartment and looked outside. Once opened, the small vent hatch's metal grid blocked debris from coming in the truck, but allowed air to enter swiftly with the speed of highway travel. The truck rolled along the Kentucky highway in what I called the scary forest, the stretch of road that had reminded me of Oz. We had already passed the few truck stops near Louisville and were at least an hour away from any others near Cincinnati.

If I wanted to relieve my bladder of its burden, I would have to resort to the plastic bag method. This wasn't the first time I had performed this venial sin, but it always made me a bit nervous. Since road noise levels make it impossible to hear a container being filled, what if my co-driver, oblivious to my actions, hit a large bump or made a sharp lane change and I fell over, open pee bag and all onto the floor or into the bunk? What if I fell, trousers at the ankles, through the curtains and between the seats in the driver compartment? What if I struck the gear shifter, knocking the truck out of gear and with pants at the ankles, caused a catastrophe? That would be some way to go!

Hoping for the best, I turned on a dim light then dug through my things to pull out the plastic bags I had brought for just such an occasion. While I performed the balancing act of standing in a moving truck, I carefully filled a bag. Then, as I'd done before, I cautiously sealed the warm, bulging plastic bag and set it down on my sleeping bag so I could pull up my trousers. Next, for safer storage, I dug out a plastic grocery store bag to place the pee bag inside. Then I picked up the pee bag that I'd just sealed and set down a moment ago. I raised the bag to eye level, and my expression morphed from confusion to increasing concern to hopeless astonishment. The once bulging bag contained only a couple of ounces of yellow fluid.

"What the hell!" I hissed to myself. "Where's it all gone?" I wondered with deepening panic. Oh my, God! I thought: my pee has soaked into the bunk mattress. What the hell am I going to say to Hilda? I wondered. I wouldn't have blamed her one iota for calling Wayne. She might not believe the moisture came from a plastic bag that leaked, after I took a leak *in it*. I sure wouldn't want to drive with someone who I thought wet the damn bunk!

My hands skated around on the top of the sleeping bag. The nylon surface felt surprisingly dry, but little lakes of yellow fluid stood between the folds of blue fabric. I rolled up the sleeping bag and stuffed it into the blue plastic bag I normally kept it in. I cleaned and dried my hands then felt around on the sheet over the cheap, thin mattress of the bunk. The sheet felt dry! Was I witnessing a miracle? No, but luckily for me, the sleeping bag had absorbed the whole embarrassing mess.

I tied closed the blue bag that stored the sleeping bag and shoved it into the empty cubby behind the passenger seat where it normally waited for use. Then I lay back down on the dry sheets and, after all these shenanigans, tried to get some rest. For a couple of reasons, I determined to deal with the results of the leaked pee bag without telling Hilda what had transpired. Partly, I thought it sensible not to draw her disgust and unpredictable reaction. But another reason formed in my head: I simply wanted to see if I could get away with it.

Somehow I got a little more sleep before Hilda arrived at the Ohio terminal where we switched out trailers. Once again in the driver seat, I headed for our regular truck stop for fuel and food, hoping that my sleeping bag didn't lend any atmosphere to the sleeper compartment that Hilda now occupied.

After filling up the truck's tanks with diesel, I pulled our long rig past the head-in parking spaces toward our usual space beside a stretch of curb next to a tall sign that announced the truck stop's name to highway travelers. The parking space sat out of the way of other trucks, yet not far from the building. I steered up to the space, keeping an eye out for a place to deposit the ultimate pee bomb when I spotted a previously overlooked dumpster. Funny how things can become obvious when we seek them. The green metal receptacle stood near a delivery entry to the building and out of sight of any windows that customers might look out of.

I put the truck in neutral and applied the parking brakes then lollygagged in the driver seat, fiddling with my logbook until Hilda vacated the truck to go take a shower. I watched the passenger side mirror until her sizeable figure disappeared into the truck stop door several yards behind our rig. Then I waited fifteen minutes. Give her time to get situated, I thought, to make sure she hasn't forgotten anything. Luckily, Hilda usually took her time doing any task set before her.

Finally, I stepped through the open curtain to the sleeper compartment, ostensibly to get my shower bag. But first, my giant pee bag fetched my attention. I pulled the plastic covered sleeping bag out of the truck and, along with my shower bag, carried the heavy burden toward the truck stop. When I arrived at the dumpster I slung the blue bag with all its contents into the dumpster. Then I proceeded into the building to get my own shower and meal before starting the long drive back home again.

I didn't yet know, though, if Operation Pee Bag had been a success or not. I couldn't detect any scent in the sleeper compartment, but maybe Hilda would. When Hilda returned to the truck she got back into the sleeper without saying a word. If she had detected my secret, I'm positive she would have been more than happy to speak up. Yet, evidently she never detected the presence of the leaked pee bag and its superabsorbent companion. And why had it leaked? On the side of the bag, the folded crease contained an imperfection, a small opening. Name brand and all.

Following a couple of days off we started another week of driving. We drove up to the Cleveland terminal and back again. Then we set out on the exact same run. That's the way in line-haul driving, out and back, out and back until you've finished the week. This Tuesday we left the terminal at about two in the afternoon, and Hilda drove out at her usual pace. Plus, construction delays in Texas were followed by a couple of auto drivers in western Arkansas who decided to swap a little paint, rather than yield. The post-collision traffic jam set us further behind. The clock already neared midnight when we approached Little Rock. Hilda pulled off into a truck stop I'd never seen before.

"I don't think I can go any further just now," Hilda lamented, sounding like she thought I might disagree.

I felt more than rested and glad to drive. Anyway, regardless of where we were on the map, the time for a switch out had come. We wouldn't reach Holladay until about three in the morning, placing Hilda over her legal driving hours for the shift.

Before assuming the wheel I went inside the truck stop for a break. Hilda did, too. Like any other team we split up and each took care of our business separately. I selected a bottle of soda and a candy bar then stood at the check out to pay for it. When I stepped up to the counter the cashier brushed back a string of hair from her forehead. With tired eyes she set a small plastic bag containing a snack and another bottle of soda in front of me.

"You came in with that other driver, didn't you?" The cashier asked, not unkindly, tilting her head toward our truck parked just outside the window, the company's logo matching the one on our uniform shirts. She had seen that both Hilda and I drove for the same company. I nodded. "Your girlfriend forgot the other stuff she bought," the clerk said, gently pushing the items toward me.

Girlfriend? I wondered if my face betrayed any surprise. It would have felt childish to correct her. And, no, she didn't mean it like previous generations meant, friends who are girls. I just thanked her and moved on. But I had figured some people would mistake Hilda and me for an item. I had seen it from the start, though many people either didn't seem to make the assumption or didn't indicate that they had. Others simply clocked the pair of us, as if taking in some matter-of-fact information, then carried on with their business. That's the way it should be – without judgmentalism, even if they were mistaken about our status.

What I found odd is that in the 21st century one can be presumed to be gay because of one's occupation. Like many people I hold a 'Live and let live,' philosophy towards gays. After all, more and more evidence suggests that being gay is simply a trait some people happen to have, like eye color. Anyway there's something wrong with the need to label people. Often those who label women obsess over our sexuality. Such labels seldom match reality. Of the female drivers I met, Hilda was the only one who identified as homosexual. Most others were married and drove with their husbands. Some single women had a boyfriend whom they drove with. Other women, like me, drove with platonic co-drivers of either gender just like most guys who drive a truck. Of course, the real problem with labels is the people who use them as a springboard to mistreat others.

More than once I found these types of experiences to be deeply evocative of the Bob Seger song, "Turn the Page," where the lyrics describe onlookers questioning the gender of someone they don't know and don't understand. While most people treated me fairly, I got a distinctly negative attitude from some of the truck stop clerks, other drivers, or random members of the public. For instance, one day I had waited my turn in line in a restroom of a fast food burger place in Arkansas. I stood there in my trucking uniform with my sturdy work shoes on when a woman jerked her thumb in my direction and volunteered loudly to anyone listening, "This is the women's room. I don't know what *that* is."

Some of the other women had merely looked embarrassed for me. Others smirked. Had I been in any of their sandals or slingbacks, it was just the type of situation that normally would have elicited a remark right back to her from me. After all, truck driver or not, when a woman wears comfortable shoes what it *really* means is she has comfortable *feet*. But no one came to my defense. Nor did I. Sometimes it's easier to smart off on another's behalf than for one's own sake.

The clothes we wore no doubt encouraged some attitudes. Naturally, I had expected some built in strictures of how being a driver would affect my appearance, regardless of who I drove with. That didn't bother me too much. After all, having grown up with four brothers and no sisters, feeling comfortable with boyishness was inevitable. However, the clothes we drivers wore were clearly for work. Understandably, some of the things we wore had to fit the needs of our job functions. For example, we had to wear rugged shoes for gripping the pavement when adjusting the dolly and simple black trousers to hide the oil that got on our clothes when we built a set of trailers. I learned that the hard way one day when I only had a pair of light brown trousers available.

The only thing I liked about our company shirts was that the insignia made it obvious why I, a woman, visited a truck stop. That didn't stop some male drivers from offering money for sex anyway, when I walked to the building from the truck or shopped or ordered food at a truck stop restaurant. But most had the sense to see a driver working her job, too, not someone looking to give them a job. I wondered how much more frequent those offers might have been if I had had no uniform with insignia to wear.

The manner some people treated me because of my appearance while performing a traditionally male occupation was so outdated, or at least, it certainly should be. When I had first walked into truck stops, stores or restaurants wearing a man's uniform shirt after climbing out of one of the largest vehicles on the road, initially, I marveled at the straightforward and unprejudiced way most people treated me. You may think it odd to anticipate anything different, but if we're honest many of us know that people treat and mistreat others based on appearance all the time. Women especially know that. Some average-looking guys who wear presentable clothes, frankly, may not. Us girls know if we look less than well-groomed or nicely dressed we often get bad service, bad attitudes directed toward us and, sometimes, really shitty wisecracks intended to hurt.

In a different incident I remembered the manager, no less, of a fast food establishment at a Dallas truck stop who provided shoddy service and openly derided me to her staff. She pointed at me angrily and said, "She hasn't had her sex change operation yet." Just because I was a woman working as a trucker. Due to her senseless hatred, I never stopped at that truck stop again and never spent hundreds of dollars for fuel there after that.

On one especially memorable occasion, a comment made my blood run cold, leaving me genuinely concerned for my life. At an Arkansas truck stop I, clad in my uniform with my little green bookbag over one shoulder, exited my truck and walked alone toward the building across the fuel lanes, the way drivers typically do. A random truck began to pull forward from a fuel pump just when I started to step across its path. I paused and quickly looked up at the driver to see whether he noticed me. He did.

"I'll stop this time," he said out the open window. Looking right at me, he continued, "But I should run you down."

Mystified, I looked up at him. An evil expression glinted from his eyes and laced the grin on his face. Abruptly and wordlessly, I made a sharp right turn to walk alongside the fuel pumps, placing the pumps between me and his truck. I planned to walk around and behind his rig, instead of in front. Technically, he could have tried to back over me, but he might have risked hitting the truck behind him. Anyway, I didn't think he'd make the attempt. He proved me right. Instead, he stepped hard on the accelerator, going forward much faster than is customary in a fuel lane. His final remark whirled through the air above the roar of his engine. "Fucking cunt!"

He didn't know me or anything about me other than what he could see, a woman trucker. I didn't know him either. Neither of us had ever seen the other before, nor would we encounter each other again. The only reason for his behavior? He hated seeing a woman in trucking and quite possibly he assumed a woman driver must be gay. At such times I felt like I had become one of millions of innocent people caught in the so-called "culture wars" created by those who worry about who is gay or straight, who is masculine or feminine enough to match the stereotypes of their gender.

Rampant suspicion over sexuality and gender is not healthy for a society. A person is a person. That's enough. No one has to justify their masculinity or femininity, their height, build, looks, grooming, clothes or who they find attractive. Nor should they have to explain their interests, hobbies or choice of occupation. Expecting people to apologize for or to ask permission to be who they are shows disrespect for the freedom we, as a nation, love to claim we fight for. But lately in our country there is an arrogance among some who rush through life being rude and obnoxious to others based on assumptions over categories that people may or may not even belong to. Such rudeness should be regarded with the same disdain as any other ill-mannered behavior.

If wearing the clothes of my job meant I looked more masculine than the driver who threatened me liked, it appeared that in his mind that gave him God's permission to do whatever he wanted to me. As is often the case with people who think like him, they mistake *their own egos* for God. People like that can fall into a life of casual evil, recklessly harming and disrupting the life journey of others due to their twisted thinking. The fact that I refused to make myself vulnerable to him infuriated him. There I was a woman driving a truck, and there's nothing he could rightfully or legally do about it. Such experiences brought me to the conclusion that we must work to keep our civilization civil and not let bitter and potentially violent individuals feel they are permitted to harm, mistreat or even to threaten others.

On the less disturbing day that a clerk mistook us for a couple, I returned to the truck and handed Hilda the shopping bag the clerk had given me. "I wondered where that went," Hilda said, grabbing the items before she entered the sleeper compartment.

Since we were running late, I took the wheel many miles before our usual switch out and headed across eastern Arkansas toward the city of Memphis. A couple of hours later, at about two in the morning, I drove across the Mississippi River on I-40's M bridge and halfway around that city's loop when an orange Schneider truck pulled up beside me, the driver honking his horn and pointing back over his shoulder. I looked over at him while he wildly gesticulated. What now? I wondered.

Occasionally, truckers gesture at each other. Not the middle finger salute, but truckers often wave hello to each other. Going up and down the highways and byways truckers frequently give a brief three finger wave of thumb, index and middle finger. I called it the trucker's wave, T-Rex style. In addition, sometimes drivers signal each other when a tire is flat or something else is wrong.

"Hilda?" I called out, over the road noise. "I'm sorry to bother you. Are you awake?"

The other truck's horn had woken her.

"What should I do?" I asked in my still naïve rookie way.

"Pull over and look at the truck," Hilda suggested patiently.

Something must be wrong with the rig, but I couldn't tell what. I looked back in the mirrors at the sides of the truck and couldn't see anything exceptional. Fortunately, we were coming up on the point where the loop met I-40 on its way to Nashville. The left shoulder is particularly wide and lengthy there. Not only did the shoulder have room to stop, but even some distance to accelerate before reentering the highway.

I slowed down and turned on the hazard lights. They flashed rhythmically in my face while I steered the 73 foot truck onto the shoulder. Cars and trucks whipped by quickly in the lanes next to us. I climbed down from the cab and walked along the side of the truck farthest away from the traffic, looking for a problem. Nearing the end of the rig, the problem became obvious. The back trailer had no lights.

The front trailer, hooked directly up to the cab, displayed its full array of illumination. The power cord that led from the front trailer to the back trailer, however, had either jostled loose with road vibrations or had never been plugged in correctly to begin with. I pushed the plug in all the way. The back trailer lights blinked on like a Christmas tree. Without lights on the back trailer, we were lucky no one had rear ended us in the dark.

Now to get us back on the highway. I walked back up to the driver seat and put the truck in gear. Three factors came to mind. One, getting tens of thousands of pounds moving from zero to 55 mph takes time and space. I stepped on the accelerator, and the truck slowly gathered momentum. Two, a concrete retaining wall stood a few dozen yards ahead. I had to accelerate while driving straight toward it. Three, traffic on the highway drove at, well, highway speeds. And everyone who wanted to take I-40 eastward had to get in the lane I needed.

The hazard lights still flashed in my face while I geared up the engine. I had to merge into traffic or hit the wall. Obviously, the wall was not an option. Or I supposed it could be, if the alternative meant striking a car. After several yards of gradual acceleration, the giant truck reached 45 mph, the minimum highway speed. I turned off the hazard lights in order to signal entry back onto the highway. A break in traffic presented itself, and I pulled back into the driving lane. Then along with the motorists and other trucks I took the curving ramp eastward and onward.

I drove my ten hour shift overnight through Nashville and into Kentucky before pulling in at a truck stop about an hour south of Louisville. I felt exhausted and ready to bunk down for a few hours though the sun shone on a bright autumn morning.

Hilda put her sleeping gear away and wandered into the truck stop for a break. Though tired, I knew enough to put something in my stomach or risk waking from precious sleep in an hour or two with hunger gnawing at my insides. I went inside and bought a breakfast sandwich to eat then sat in the passenger seat with it while Hilda prepared to drive. In between bites I answered Hilda's questions about my stop along the shoulder in Memphis the previous night, not realizing what would come next.

"It's your fault," Hilda said, her eyes narrowing, deepening the lines on the sides of her face.

"What?" I asked in perplexed surprise. I wondered if she intended to joke, but looking into those eyes, I could see she meant business. It seemed like an attempt to place blame for an event that required no blame that I could see.

"You didn't inspect the truck," Hilda said. By this time I had grown weary of Hilda's attitudes.

"That's rich considering you have years of experience, and I've never seen you do a single inspection," I countered.

"Oh, I inspected it," Hilda insisted.

The fact is Hilda and I always built the set and left the terminal soon thereafter. I'd never even noticed Hilda checking the lights. I'd also never seen her check the fifth wheel pins when leaving a truck stop or rest area. Further, neither of us had noticed anything wrong with the truck in Little Rock. Nor had she when she drove out from Fort Worth the previous afternoon. Officially, the first driver of the run, the one who drove from the terminal, marked the required 24 hour inspection on her log. Legally, that driver should perform that inspection, also. Of course, ironically, if it hadn't been for our delay, Hilda might have been driving when another trucker sounded his horn in warning.

"You may not see it," Hilda persisted. "But every time I get in or out of this truck I double or triple check everything."

I couldn't help but laugh."I don't see it because it doesn't happen," I managed to assert.

"You were driving last night," Hilda continued stubbornly, a hard tone straining her husky voice. "If I called Wayne and told him you drove last night without brake lights on the back trailer, do you have any idea how fast he'd take you off this truck?"

My trucker's backbone still had too many weaknesses. Besides my mind felt too addled by Hilda constantly and needlessly vying for the upper hand, instead of enjoying an even partnership of co-drivers. While Hilda steered back onto the highway I rose from the passenger seat and entered the sleeper compartment without answering. Conversation over.

Then I looked at the sleeper bunk. Dammit! I hadn't laid out my things. I did my circus balancing act while setting out sleeping bag and pillow. After laying down and snapping the safety netting closed, I tried to rest. Though I still felt exhausted, being blindsided by these little snares of Hilda's took their toll. I had gone from feeling cheerfully sleepy when I pulled into the truck stop at the end of my shift, to feeling angry, frustrated and fully awake.

Unfortunately, Hilda and I were not the only drivers who didn't really perform inspections. While I still wasn't sure what an inspection should entail, my lack of training wasn't Hilda's responsibility. I supposed the carrier and its managers bore the responsibility of making sure we drivers knew how to conduct inspections and verifying periodically that we did so. Nevertheless, we all signed the bottom of each day's log stating that we had inspected our vehicles. Though of the dozens of drivers I would work with, most didn't do much more than check that the lights worked. Clearly, that included checking to make sure the brake lights worked before we left the terminal. Day or night. If it rained, having the lights on proved especially helpful. Taking a cue from other drivers, I kept all lights on anyway for that little extra edge of visibility to other drivers, rain or shine.

As for the errant power cord that night, inspections or no inspections, such things sometimes happened. A cord could become loose when the truck simply moved along. Once again it became clear that it's just good practice to look up and down the rig carefully each time the truck stops and, when possible, even in the mirrors while driving.

Lying in the sleeper bunk after our latest conversation and several weeks of similar dramas, I wished I'd never agreed to take on the run permanently. I began to think about leaving. Then, unexpectedly, the next week Hilda let me in on a little secret. Perhaps figuring she wouldn't be with the company for long anyway, she explained she had applied for a local job delivering fuel to gas stations. With her years of driving experience she stood a real chance. The job would pay less, but would be adequate for her needs. She only had to go in to see them one more time on Monday, she said.

"Great!" I said to Hilda. "I hope you get the job."

"Oh, I will. I've already talked to them," Hilda insisted.

I really did hope Hilda would get the job she wanted. This opportunity could prove to be the turn for the better we both needed. If another company hired Hilda, I might stay on this run. Perhaps, I could work with a more compatible co-driver. Perhaps. I worked that week with a renewed sense of hope.

The following Tuesday I showed up at the dispatch office ready to rotate. This might be the day Hilda handed in her notice. Maybe she already had. Maybe Wayne would call later to say that Hilda would only work the next week or two at the most. I waited my turn in line then walked up to the window. Jane, one of the clerks, looked through her thick glasses at the computer screen. Jane's appearance would strike anyone as odd on her best day. I liked Jane, and she acted friendly enough. But frequently, she looked like her hair might harbor a rat's nest. I gave Jane our truck number and asked for the dispatch slip.

"Hilda's got your slip. She's already out on the yard."

"Okay, thanks." I exited the office and walked through the break room. Hilda and the truck were somewhere out on the yard, likely on the far side of the building where our trailers usually stood parked or awaited loading. In retrospect, I probably should have just waited for Hilda to finish the job and return to the office. But naturally, hindsight is 20/20. Like an eagerly helpful dummy I walked around the huge building and spotted our truck where Hilda backed up the front trailer to the dolly that stood in front of the back trailer.

Reaching the rig I tried to wave Hilda in and gave her the hand signal to stop before the trailer struck the dolly. The trailers looked aligned to me, but Hilda had other ideas. She pulled forward to realign her approach to the back trailer again. If Hilda didn't want my direction, I would happily ride in the cab while she worked. I decided to walk around some other trailers well clear of where she repositioned the rig and walk up to the passenger side door. A couple of minutes later I made my way around to the other side of the cab. The passenger door stopped right in front of me, as Hilda rolled the rig back to a halt. Due to the height of the cab, I couldn't see Hilda ten feet up and five feet over in the driver seat. She must have seen me in the small side mirror over the passenger window, I reasoned. I climbed into the cab and sat in the passenger seat. Inexplicably, Hilda exploded.

"Don't you ever get in a moving truck while I'm driving!" Hilda shouted, slamming the gear shifter into drive and lurching the truck forward again.

"What?" I asked my usual brilliant question when she directed her aim toward me. Hilda went on making exclamations about my irresponsibility and general worthlessness with fire in her voice. If she had hit me with the truck, she said, leaving the sentence hanging.

If I had stepped onto truck while it rolled, Hilda would have had a valid point. But no one could mistake me for Speedy Gonzales *or* the Road Runner. I couldn't have jumped onto a moving truck, if I had wanted to. Hilda had backed up in order to pull forward again. Any driver knows you can't switch from forward to reverse on the fly. All those gears in the transmission have to come to a stop before they can start moving in the opposite direction. She had stopped to switch gears while I thought she had stopped to let me in the cab.

"One minute you were back there waving me in. The next minute you're up here," Hilda exclaimed.

Once again I sensed that Hilda's outburst had nothing to do with anything I had done. Quickly I asked, "You didn't get the job with the fuel company, did you?"

"No, I didn't," Hilda paused, then added. "That's got nothing to do with it."

Sure, I thought. Nothing at all. At the same time I felt amazement at the typical frank artlessness of Hilda's responses.

"I could call Wayne on you, and he'd take you off this truck right now," Hilda continued, raising her voice again.

Finally, I'd had enough of being Hilda's verbal punching bag. "Is he here now?" I asked, calling her bluff. "Let's go find Wayne. We can tell him you're looking for another job while we're at it."

That suggestion suddenly took the wind out of Hilda's sails. She slumped in her seat. With those words not just one, but two or three vertebrae materialized in my trucker's backbone to make up for the weeks I'd given Hilda too much latitude in the way she talked to me.

We completed the set up and drove out to start our week's run. I'd won a small victory by standing up to Hilda. Yet, I still found it hard to cope with working alongside a deeply incompatible co-driver. The experience illustrates how important respect is for the safety and well-being of team drivers. That respect cannot be one-sided though. To be effective and to build a team, respect must be mutual. Another trucking truism. In our case, enough was enough. After some reflection, I determined to call Wayne during the weekend and tell him I didn't want to run with Hilda anymore. Drivers were in demand. It would be better to work as a relief driver again than to remain miserable.

Chapter 9: "I'm a cocky bastard!"

The next Monday while running errands and preparing to drive out for the week I thought about how to approach Wayne. I decided to tell Wayne that I'd work the run until he could find a replacement for my spot. Before I got a chance to phone him, however, Wayne called me. Hilda had personal business to attend to and would be gone for at least a week, Wayne reported. My co-driver in the interim would be a chap I'll call Romeo for reasons that will soon present themselves.

That Tuesday I met Romeo at the dispatch office at mid-afternoon. A blond-haired, short, heavy guy leaned against the counter. When I entered the office, he looked up at me and lifted his glasses further up on his nose.

"You must be Karen."

"Guilty. How did you know?"

"You're the only chick to walk in here for the last half hour," Romeo answered, adding an odd laugh that sounded just this side of a heckle.

Romeo immediately referred to me as "Beautiful." Fleetingly, I wondered if he might genuinely consider me beautiful or, perhaps, he had been struck in the head with a heavy object. Then I noticed that he called Jane, our cosmetically challenged office clerk, "Beautiful," too. Bless her heart, as we say in the south, and not always with irony, as has often been reported.

Jane handed a sheet of paper through the window, and Romeo swaggered outside with our paperwork. Romeo manfully built our set of trailers. I rode along in the cab, but I simply stayed out of his way. Romeo knew he could build our set faster than I could, so he simply got on with the task. I knew I needed to be able to build a set on my own eventually. Just then I'd take a break from the process to speed our departure.

With trailers in tow we left the dispatch office and stopped outside the employee parking lot. I stood in the sleeper compartment and made room for Romeo's things next to Hilda's sleeping bag, blankets and pillows in the top bunk while he retrieved his things from his car. Then I sat in the driver seat while he sat in the passenger seat, and we each updated our logs. I noticed Romeo kept glancing at me out of the corner of one eye. He wanted to talk. Naturally, "the question" arose.

"What's a pretty lady like you doing driving a truck?" Romeo finally asked in what sounded like the truck driving version of "What's a girl like you doing in a place like this?"

Once again I explained my wish for a job. Then I returned the question, and Romeo explained that he did the job mostly for fun. He didn't need the money, he said. For heaven's sake, I thought, laughing to myself, another would-be millionaire?

I drove out the gates and headed into east Texas on our way up to Ohio. Many co-drivers rest in the sleeper, unless perhaps, they want to stay up on the way to a meal stop or to smoke a cigarette. Romeo wanted to stay up and talk. To make conversation I asked him what he thought about drivers breaking up their schedule to suit themselves, not following the regulations for logbooks.

"Only if I knew the other driver really well would I even consider that," Romeo said.

I didn't like the idea that another driver could do something illegal or simply inconsiderate while our log entries showed I drove. If someone complained about a driver and the logs we had turned in made it look like I was at the wheel, whatever the issue, I could get the blame. The reverse held true if I did something foolish while my co-driver was the official driver of record. Drivers could only really trust themselves to protect their own reputations. However, as a time and rest management method, the five and five worked well for an awful lot of drivers, if the widespread and regular use of the practice is any indication. Drivers could often control fatigue better dividing their work this way. One wonders if the bureaucrats who decided to make the five and five illegal asked many drivers their opinions.

I drove along I-30 for about an hour out of the DFW area, as Dallas-Fort Worth is often called, stopping at a truck stop where we could each get something to eat. Though I always felt uneasy about blocking the fuel lanes with our long, un-backable rig, we were in and out of truck stops fast as possible. I'd chosen this stop because they had room to park without blocking a fuel lane. Not every truck stop happened to have such a place. Having a parking spot where our rig could rest out of the way of fueling or other truck traffic felt like a luxury. Knowing we didn't block lanes, I could relax and not rush to get back out and move on.

I parked alongside another truck. Romeo and I walked across the fuel lanes toward the truck stop building. Once inside I bought a chicken sandwich from the fast food place at this stop and returned to the truck. Sitting in the driver seat I saw Romeo inhale a burger while he walked back out to the truck. He opened the passenger door and put a large soda in a cupholder. Then he climbed into the passenger seat and polished off another burger and an extra big portion of French fries.

"I'm gonna look under the hood," Romeo announced and started to re-open the door.

"Gonna do an inspection out here?" I asked.

"I'll just check the oil and top off the windshield wiper fluid."

With that Romeo climbed down and undid the latches on each side of the truck's hood in an unnecessarily grand manner. Then he stood in front and tugged on the handhold at the top of the hood pulling down the shell of metal and the chrome grill that covered the engine, peeling the hood forward, not backwards like on most cars. While he checked the oil, I stepped down to throw away my sandwich wrapper.

"That was a little tougher to open than I expected," Romeo said, pointing his thumb at the truck's hood.

Semi-truck hoods have both a handhold at the top and a foot-hold on the bumper for a reason. Drivers work to open them on occasion, but I played along. "What do you mean?" I asked.

"I forget I don't have as much weight to throw around any-more," Romeo said.

"You've lost weight?"

"About fifty pounds."

"Wow! Congrats."

"Yep. I only weigh 230 now."

We climbed back on board the truck and prepared to leave. I began to roll forward, pulling past the truck parked to our right before turning toward the driveway of the truck stop. In order to make sure the back trailer didn't hit the other truck, I kept an eye on the right side mirror. Oddly enough, some drivers will put their head in front of the side mirror while they're sitting in the pas-senger seat. Two things don't occur to the lump of gray matter inside. First, the driver steering the truck cannot see through another driver's cranium. Second, the point of view in the mirror's reflection is altered by sitting in a different location in the truck cab. Thus, what looks clear from the passenger seat might not look that way from behind the steering wheel. Just that little nudge over in visual geometry can make a difference in judging distance.

"You're clear," Romeo proclaimed, leaning back in his seat.

From my point of view it didn't look like that was the case. Re-lying on the newest vertebrae recently added to my growing trucker's backbone, I continued to pull forward. I turned when it looked clear to me. If I struck the other truck, Romeo wouldn't be at fault. As a motorcycle cop once reminded me during a friendly conversation, "Don't drive where you can't see." Good advice.

I steered the truck back on the road toward Arkansas while Romeo remained in the passenger seat again and made a point of telling me why he thought he hadn't remarried since his divorce. Naturally, I hadn't known he'd been married and couldn't imagine wanting to straddle a guy who looked like he could deliver quad-ruplets at any moment. But there's someone for everyone they say, at least until the divorce.

"I suffer from Nice-Guy-Syndrome," Romeo proclaimed.

"Oh," I said with polite disinterest. Really I wished Romeo would bunk down so I could enjoy glimpses of the late November autumn scenery that still decorated the landscape. While gaining experience I had gradually become able to look around a bit while driving instead of riveting my eyes solely to the road ahead or on other traffic. Plus, without Hilda, we were making pretty good time. No sit-down meals or stopping to get supplies.

But while we traveled along, Romeo explained he couldn't get a girl to go out with him beyond a date or two because he just wasn't a mean, tough sonuvabitch. Finally, the necessity of getting some rest before driving overnight occurred to Romeo. He retired to the sleeper compartment, parting with a trite trucking expression that I'd never heard before. In fact, I didn't understand the first half dozen times he employed the phrase: "Keep the shiny side up!" Or in other words, don't crash the truck. If the grubby side of the truck faced skyward, we would both be in big trouble. No doubt, Romeo thought himself witty.

That left just me, the road and the radio turned down quietly. A couple of hours later we crossed into Arkansas, rolling past the forested edge of the highway. The foliage looked lovely in the lingering sunset. The light began to wane and take on that glowing quality of early twilight. I kept an eye on traffic while stealing looks along the edge of the forest. Here and there deer already edged out from the trees to graze on the wide grassy swathes that sweep up and down the Interstate between the pavement and the trees. Then I saw them. Several yards off of the highway in a flat, shallow creek bed next to the stream of water stood a proud buck with his rack of horns pointing majestically upward. Several does stood with him, their heads bent down to the grass. The buck surveyed his kingdom with complete confidence. Being a child of one of the media generations I couldn't help but think the scene looked like something out of a Disney flick. Idyllic.

Tidbits of beauty and wildlife regularly presented themselves along the roadways. One day while rounding a curve on the highway east of Little Rock the view through the windshield suddenly consisted of flocks of geese and ducks in a roadside field. Many of the birds grazed. Some fluttered upward. New arrivals, too, found a spot to land on grass or water, resting or feeding before continuing their migrations.

We eventually reached our switch out in Tennessee. While filling out our logs I explained to Romeo that Hilda logged this town by the name Sugar Tree.

"Why?" Romeo asked. "It says Holladay right over the door."

After giving Romeo directions to the Cleveland hub, I retired to the sleeper. I got some solid sleep and awoke when our truck neared the terminal. We switched out trailers at the yard. Then I drove to the truck stop where we routinely fueled while Romeo prepared the sleeper for his rest period.

Driving between the northern and southern parts of the country the difference in temperatures becomes more obvious once the seasons change. When we left Texas and drove to northern Ohio we covered a span of over a thousand miles. Some of those miles reached eastward, but quite a few went in a northerly direction, too. Thus, in late autumn I stepped out of the warm truck into the bracing chill of the Ohio wind to pump fuel into the truck for the return journey. Wearing a heavy coat and gloves I started the fuel pump then climbed back aboard and sat down in the driver seat.

"I've got this covered out here. You can go on inside, if you want," I said to Romeo who had exited the sleeper and flopped down in the passenger seat. I pointed out to him the location where we normally parked so he could find the truck, if he went inside.

"I'll stay here and wait," he said. "Unless you want to join me in the bunk."

"What?" I asked.

Romeo repeated his offer.

"No, I don't think so." I stood up to get my shower bag out of the sleeper. Stepping around the gear shifter, I stumbled. "Oops, I nearly fell over," I exclaimed needlessly, one of those meaningless, throw away remarks everyone makes.

"I wish you'd fallen on me," Romeo said dreamily.

Oh, brother, I thought. Then I said, "If you don't mind, I'll go ahead inside and start my shower, if you want to wait here."

"We could take a shower together."

I'm a cocky bastard!

"Nope, we couldn't," I answered. "When the fuel tanks are full, if you'd pull the rig up next to the truck stop's sign near the highway." I pointed to our regular parking space again. "It's close to the building and has room for doubles without blocking anyone else."

"Are you sure you don't want to shower together?" Romeo persisted. "It saves water."

"See you in a while," I replied and carried my heavy bag inside to warmth and cleanliness, sans Romeo.

After showering I went to the truck stop's restaurant for a bite to eat. In a few minutes Romeo sat down across from me in the booth.

"Did you enjoy your shower?" Romeo asked with a silly grin.

"Sure."

"Did you get all your *parts* clean?" Romeo asked with an even wider grin. I decided to ignore where he might be steering the conversation.

"Did you have a shower?" I asked.

"I almost never take a shower on the road."

"You don't?"

"Nah. I figure anything that challenges my immune system is good."

I'd just spotted at least one more reason Romeo might have trouble getting a girl.

As we dined, Romeo appeared bent on impressing me with what a nonchalant and jolly fellow he was. He whipped off his glasses, thinking perhaps that made his countenance more pleasing. Then he looked at me to gauge my reaction.

When our meal ended Romeo decided to make one last trip to the men's room. Thus, I started back out to the truck alone. Turning the corner to where we usually parked, I saw nothing. The truck wasn't there. I pivoted around and looked out at the vast expanse of the parking lot. Our rig could have been anywhere. Then I spotted it, about a football field away pulled between two of the many trucks that had begun to crowd the lot for the night.

I lugged my shower bag out to the spot Romeo had chosen. Due to the length of our truck, the rig took up two parking spaces, one in front and one behind. What's more Romeo had parked so close to the truck on one side that the gap between looked almost razor thin. On the other side of our rig sat an empty cattle truck. However, the aroma left by the truck's most recent occupants filled the air.

I walked up the length of our truck to the driver door and got my key ready. An instinct told me not to bother. I had given Romeo a spare key and asked him to lock up whenever he stopped or left the truck. I tried the handle. The door was unlocked. Hopefully, nothing had been stolen and no stranger waited inside. I climbed aboard and waited for Romeo to return.

I sat down in the driver seat that I would occupy for the next several hours and updated my logbook. In a few minutes I heard someone trying to open the passenger side door. I looked in the mirror over the passenger window and saw Romeo. I pressed a button on the driver side door to unlock the passenger door.

While I steered the rig back onto the road Romeo insisted on staying up and sharing some of the CDs he had brought along. He liked the soundtracks to musicals, perhaps an unusual interest for a guy so obviously gagging for female attention. I listened politely, but Romeo must have sensed his selections didn't exactly set me on fire. He resorted to CDs by country music artists.

"Oh, no," I exclaimed. "You're not going to play country music are you?"

"What? You don't like country?" Romeo asked with a shrug of disappointment.

"You might not know it to look at me, but I'm more likely to listen to classic rock."

"But country's good music."

"Some of it's good. A lot of it's great," I answered, thinking of the country CDs that nestled in my little green book bag next to rock CDs. "But some of it bores me to tears, or it's too twangy."

"Twangy?"

"You know the kind of thing. When a guy sings about how his dog left him and his wife stayed?"

"I've never heard that one," Romeo replied humorlessly.

Nonetheless, he continued to sit up front and talk while playing deejay with his CDs. This was okay up to a point, but only up to a point. When you are driving you can't exactly decide whether your co-driver stays up front or goes into the sleeper. If he wants to sit up and talk, you are a captive audience. After all, when it's your turn to drive the truck where else can you be, but at the steering wheel?

Finally, about an hour later Romeo returned to the sleeper while I drove on across the fields of Ohio at what had begun to feel like the super low truck speed limit of 55 mph. A speed that, even with only a few months driving experience, I found so slow that my mind wandered with boredom. Ironically, I would have been able to focus on the road better going 65 mph.

To keep my mind active I turned on the CB and listened to chatter. The truckers heading our way warned that a policeman, also called a bear, waited ahead. Then seemingly unnecessarily one trucker on the CB said, "He was white." Then paused. "That means he was a *polar* bear," the trucker added with a sparkle of humor to his voice.

Since we were completing this run much more quickly than usual, I felt pleasantly surprised to reach Cincinnati in the afternoon and set across the Ohio River on the way to Louisville with a couple hours of daylight left. I would be driving along the highway of the scary forest. At night the path stretched for over an hour through darkness with what looked like heavy tree coverage on both sides of the highway and little else visible other than the headlights of cars and trucks.

I steered westward and drove along, but not past grimacing trees and scowling rock faces. Instead, a mix of fields bordered by woods and dotted with farmhouses comprised what I had thought of as the scary forest. Clearly, people out here lived ordinary lives. Not one single, mean-faced tree came into sight. In fact, halfway along on the north side of the Interstate someone had fastened a giant yellow smiley face to a fence post. The "Have a nice day" style of smiley face grinned across the highway. That face had been smiling happily out into the darkness each time I'd driven warily past.

Hours later I pulled into the switch out in Tennessee. Next, Romeo would drive homeward while I bunked down. Every so often Romeo stopped, like all drivers do. Romeo pulled into a truck stop in the wee hours of the morning, and I awoke wondering if I lie alone and vulnerable in an unlocked truck. I rose and parted the curtain of the sleeper. Sure enough Romeo hadn't locked the door again. So I decided to try an experiment. I reached over and locked the door. Then I lay back down and tried to relax for a few minutes. In a while I heard a knock on the driver door. It was Romeo. After opening the door for him, I returned to the bunk. Romeo had left his key in a cupholder on the dash.

"You're going to have to stop locking me out," Romeo said.

"You're going to have to start using your key," I answered, sensing another vertebra begin to grow along my trucker's backbone.

Finally, we arrived back in Texas. Sometimes dispatch sent us to Dallas instead of our home terminal, Fort Worth. Today turned out to be one of those days. Though technically I could stay in the bunk and rest, like any team driver I helped Romeo build our new set of trailers for the short journey back to Fort Worth.

While we drove around the terminal and found our new trailers Romeo told me about his childhood, where he'd grown up, then more about his marriage and divorce. While he backed up the dolly near the trailer, Romeo went on about his struggles with his weight, his wife's infidelities, etc. Hearing this stream of personal information, I kept wondering, "Why is he telling me all this?" Then I speculated: Romeo must see driving with a woman as his opportunity to jam pack several date's worth of disclosure into a working week.

Romeo decided not to back the dolly right up to the back trailer with the truck. He wanted to "walk it back." We both climbed down from the truck cab and met behind it at the dolly. Romeo and I stood on opposite sides of the dolly rolling toward the back trailer. We gripped the sides while the unconnected brake lines and chain hooks rested in the metal basket at the nose of the dolly. Our back trailer awaited on a downhill slope. Working on an incline made the dolly harder to handle than usual. We struggled with the weight of not just a heavy object, but a heavy object on wheels going downhill.

"My wife was a slut, but she was my slut," Romeo confessed.

The dolly started to gain momentum while we walked along-side, keeping it under control.

"That must have really hurt your feelings," I said, searching for something supportive to say.

The dolly rolled faster and faster.

"I don't care because I'm a cocky bastard!" Romeo announced and with a flourish he quickly let go of the dolly and stepped back, jerking an arm stylishly in the air.

Romeo's actions took me by surprise. My hands still gripped the dolly, which then slammed against the back trailer and came to a crashing stop. The chains that bore the heavy hooks flew into the air then plunged downward. One of the hooks smashed against my left hand. Though I wore heavy gloves, they gave little protection to flesh and bone pinched between two heavy pieces of metal, that of the dolly and the chain hook. I tore off the glove and saw a purple bruise already forming across my left thumb.

"Shit! I hope it's not broken!" I exclaimed, tentatively moving the injured digit.

"Sorry," Romeo offered. "I don't want to bruise up the pretty ladies."

With our set built Romeo drove us to Fort Worth where we switched out trailers again, and I prepared to drive back to Tennessee. My thumb felt sore, but I could move it. Going by the old theory of: 'If you can move it, it's not broken,' I carried on.

I drove out of Fort Worth on our last run of the week. Soon Hilda would return. I had been hoping that somehow, magically, Hilda would find that home-time job she wanted or win the lottery. Sadly, no such luck.

Romeo and I talked on the way to lunch. "I don't know what to do about driving with Hilda," I volunteered. Over the week I had already described to Romeo conversations with Hilda and the driving habits I'd observed.

"Tell Wayne you need a new co-driver."

"I don't know if it's that simple."

Romeo laughed and looked at me out of the corner of his eye as if he shouldn't have to suggest such an obvious solution. "Just tell Wayne you need a new run," Romeo spoke like changing co-drivers was no big deal. Yet, I wondered how Wayne would take such a request. I'd finally gotten a permanent run that paid well, and after a couple of months I wanted to ask for a switch. Was it really easy, like Romeo made it sound? If Hilda returned to this run permanently, and in all likelihood she would, I just might ask Wayne what my options were.

Following lunch I drove on to Texarkana while Romeo rested. I stopped at the Covered Wagon then got back on the highway and crossed over into Arkansas. Rolling along, I thought about what a welcome break driving with someone different had been. I'd also enjoyed driving this run at a more typical pace without frequent or lengthy stops. Because of speedier driving I'd seen the forest in Kentucky and other parts of the route in daylight for the first time. If I'd been wary of any stretches of the road, seeing them clearly had helped demystify the surroundings and relieved that wariness.

In general, I'd begun to notice a dissipation of a lot of the wariness I'd felt starting out, simply by gaining confidence behind the wheel. The more miles I had covered the more relaxed I began to feel while steering down the highway, along local roads and through busy intersections, or on the terminal yard while breaking up or building sets of double trailers.

One evening I noticed it quite pointedly while driving from Texarkana and heading toward Little Rock. I steered the rig around sharp curves that set the highway's path toward a bridge over the Red River. I'd found these curves frightening to negotiate on early journeys, slowing down for each one while other trucks sped by. Then I realized with a sort of dawning awe how easily I guided the truck around the arcs of the roadway with accuracy and aplomb and at normal speeds.

In my earliest trips I had alternately marveled at the speed and deftness experienced drivers displayed while often inwardly chastising them for unnecessary risk-taking. Now I recognized what they had known all along: driving confidently is a matter of practice. They performed maneuvers quickly, but with skill. While I could still be described as only a junior driver, I felt like I'd turned a corner both symbolically and factually. I'd graduated from the status of frightened rookie to, well, junior driver and added another vertebra to my growing backbone along the way.

I'm a cocky bastard!

* * *

We drove up to the Cleveland hub, got our new trailers and headed back. Throughout our time together Romeo kept trying to be a Romeo. He continued sitting up front part of the time I drove. Sometimes we did natter on like an old married couple while driving around the yard building our set or negotiating our way through a bustling truck stop. On the other hand, Romeo kept making quips about how much he wanted to get me in the bunk or to see me without clothes on. It's not like females need males to make it that clear what their interests are. Just harping on about those interests isn't witty, but silly and occasionally annoying.

While I drove along one day, Romeo sat in the passenger seat and began to relate his woes with a dating service. He'd go out with a girl once then never hear from her afterward. Again he told me he must just be too much of a nice guy. I laughed.

"What?" he asked. "You don't think I'm a nice guy?"

"Mmm, you're not a *mean* guy."

"Then I'm a *nice* guy."

"Sort of."

"What do you mean?"

"Do you talk to your dates the way you talk to me?"

"Sure."

"You tell them you want to sleep with them and shower with them?"

Romeo responded with his heckling laugh, then replied. "I don't know."

"You know," I said.

"Sometimes. Sure. I expect a girl to have a sense of humor."

"So you mean it as a joke?"

"No. I mean I want to sleep with them, shower with them, dance naked in the rain with them," he said, waving his arms in the air.

"But women don't take it as a joke, and you don't mean it as a joke anyway."

"What's your point?"

"It's just that the way you talk sometimes . ."

"Yeah, what?"

"A lot of women would consider the things you say vulgar."

Again Romeo emitted his heckle of a laugh.

I continued, "Most women are romantics."

Romeo didn't heckle this time. Instead, he just sat and stared out the windshield.

Eventually, we ended our time together, dropping the trailers from our latest run. I drove up to the terminal's pumps near the guard shack to fuel the truck while Romeo headed home. That would give Hilda and me one less time-consuming task on the following Tuesday.

Romeo climbed out of the cab and walked around to the driver side while I set the parking brake. I turned to open the door and saw Romeo's round face next to mine through the open window. He stood on the steps of the truck holding on to the side mirror.

"You want to come over to my house?" Romeo asked. Up close I could see the dense stubble on his tired face and detect the waft of a driver who wouldn't shower on the road.

"No, thanks. I have to get home."

"I have a fireplace. We could make some ice cream. I have an electric ice cream maker I haven't opened yet."

An offer of fire and ice from Romeo was not on my wish list. I made more excuses and finally Romeo climbed down the side of the truck. While he walked toward the gate, I sat and updated my logbook. Once he'd passed the guard shack and walked toward his car, I climbed down to the pavement below and began to fuel the truck. Alas, poor Romeo couldn't accept one of the truisms of trucking: If a co-driver is not interested, be prepared to take 'No.' for an answer. Yet, at least Romeo had tried to be romantic. I just wished he would try with someone else. Meanwhile, I had something to remember Romeo by. Over the next several days my bruised thumb ranged in color from deep purple to blue then faint green and yellow before finally returning to normal.

Love hurts.

Chapter 10: "I've got an easy run for you."

The first week of December Hilda returned to work. We built our set, and I drove the many hours to our switch out in Tennessee. After a long day I bunked down expecting to at least get some rest. Though at times driving with Hilda made that difficult to achieve, other times I could get a decent amount of sleep. It depended on how carefully Hilda drove. But while I lay back and closed my eyes in the darkened sleeper compartment, Hilda swerved onto the rumble strip. Not just once or twice, but at least every half hour or so. Sometimes every quarter hour. Ear plugs made no difference. The sound echoed through the truck.

I stood up in the sleeper and peeped out the curtain to see if Hilda was texting. Instead she had a picture propped up on the instrument panel of the dashboard. While driving along, she gazed at the photo until the loud noise of rubber tires on the ridges of the asphalt rumble strip jolted her back to reality. Reluctant to confront her so soon after her return I lie back down in the bunk. Every time my mind surrendered to sleep for a few minutes, I also felt jolted back to reality when the rig swerved onto the strip again. My reality included wondering if Hilda would drive off the road or into another vehicle.

We arrived in Cleveland that morning and both sat in the driver compartment after building our set of trailers. Though I wondered how expressing concerns about Hilda's driving would cause her to react, I'd gathered a few vertebrae in my backbone

131

and felt I should ask. Maybe some words would persuade Hilda to be more careful, after all.

"I noticed we went onto the rumble strip quite a few times last night," I began, batting my eyes with sleepiness.

Hilda glanced in my direction quickly, looking surprised. "So?"

"Did you have trouble staying awake or was the wind gusty?"

"No. What about it?" Hilda asked, then added. "I'm not saying I did."

"Did what?"

"Drive on the strip."

"Are you kidding?"

"Why do you mention it?" Hilda asked.

"Because I now have to drive back with almost no sleep. Every time I dozed off, the truck went onto the strip."

"Me? I just sleep through that."

"I'm happy for you, but I don't make it a practice to drive on the strip when you're in the bunk," I countered truthfully.

Every few weeks I edged onto the strip. Each time I felt a bit foolish. But talking to Hilda about driving felt like talking to a brick wall. After we updated our logbooks, I drove to our usual truck stop to refuel and eat. With Hilda's nearly constant meanderings onto the rumble strip, overnight I'd gotten so little sleep I trembled with exhaustion. Knowing that I would have to drive about ten hours with almost no rest heightened the sense of fatigue. If I stayed on this run, quaking with exhaustion every trip might become the norm. The lack of sleep would compile throughout the week. If that wasn't enough fun and games, Hilda had already returned to her regular self even before I'd said a few words to encourage more carefulness. Surely this run wasn't worth dying for or being constantly miserable.

Before heading back out for that exhausted drive through Ohio, across Kentucky and back into Tennessee I stepped outside the truck stop into the cold December wind. Someone was ready to call Wayne and that someone wasn't Hilda. Amazingly, the phone didn't ring into voicemail. Wayne answered and I spoke to him about Hilda's driving and my resulting lack of sleep. He already knew other issues, though I highlighted a few.

"Can I drive on another run?" I finally asked, using Romeo's suggestion.

"I can't just put you on another run," Wayne said, without addressing any of my concerns.

Wayne had no fear of a driver swerving in the lane for hundreds of miles day after day. He wasn't trying to get to sleep behind that driver. Naturally, one driver complaining about another shouldn't endanger the other driver's job. Of course, this run rightfully belonged to Hilda. I didn't expect Wayne to replace her, though I wished he would try to help her become a safer driver. I just wanted to trade my place so someone who wanted this run could take it. Driving with Hilda might not be for me, but this run paid well. Different people have different comfort levels with risk and with other drivers. Another driver must be out there who would team with Hilda. Then I might work another run. I asked again.

"I don't have another run open," Wayne repeated.

"I can't switch places with someone on another run?" I asked, testing the idea that changing drivers' runs must be something he had to do from time to time.

Romeo had made it sound simple, almost automatic. Maybe he was right in a way. Maybe if a guy called and wanted to change runs, Wayne would call around to see if another driver wanted to switch. I could never really be sure because it can be difficult to tell when you're being treated differently for being female. You don't always know until after the fact when you've been able to discretely compare notes with guys and find out they were respectfully offered more options. Or you check with the girls and they say, "Oh, yeah, you were screwed."

"What if Hilda drives off the road?" I asked Wayne.

"Maybe you just need a break. I can find someone else to help cover the run for a couple of days," Wayne offered.

Our conversation ended with a reluctant agreement on my part to think about Wayne's offer. For the time being I kept driving the run, gritting my teeth in hopes that things went smoothly, through that week and into another. But finally, I'd had enough. After my last run with Hilda I met Wayne in the dispatch office. I had made a decision. I told Wayne I'd rather not drive this run anymore.

"If you want, you can go back to subbing," Wayne said good-naturedly. "I think we can keep you just about as busy as you'd like to be. We have a lot more trucks than Sam."

The upshot was I could agree to one or two days of work at a time up to a full week of work. The downside was I'd be part-time and ineligible for the health insurance I had yet to qualify for anyway. Of course, I'd probably make less money overall, but the tradeoff felt worth it right then.

No regular route or run was ever going to be easy, nor did I expect them to be. Following the Cleveland run, I drove many times for Wayne, including a memorable run some weeks later.

"I've got an easy run for you," Wayne began.

"Who with?"

"No one," Wayne said, meaning a solo drive. By that time I'd accumulated the 25,000 miles rookies must drive before the company would trust them to go it alone. This was considered six months experience, though by what standard I wasn't sure. After all, one only had to be on a full-time run, driving ten hours a day at about 2500 miles a week for ten weeks to have driven that far.

Wayne explained the run.

"One of our teams had to leave their truck at the dealer in Memphis last week for repairs to the turbo." I didn't know what the turbo did exactly, though I'd later learn in no uncertain terms what a broken turbo meant for the drivability of a truck. Wayne continued, "Right now they're using one of the spare trucks."

"One of? How many spares do you have?"

"Just a couple," Wayne laughed. "If you'll ride up in the passenger seat, they can pick up their truck. Then you can bobtail back while they finish their run. Pretty easy, hunh?"

This run *did* sound easy enough alright. Bobtailing meant driving without any trailers. I wouldn't have to build a set of doubles, just get in, turn the key, and hit the road. A day's ride up and then a relaxing drive back without trailers and, possibly, few cares in the world. I was in.

Per Wayne's instructions I met Jack and Chan at the Dallas terminal early Tuesday morning with my little green bookbag over my shoulder and my shower bag in hand. Over the months I had decided that bringing along just about everything could make a huge difference in comfort on any trip. If a driver didn't need something on the road, she just brought the item back home unused. But if a driver left something at home that she needed, that could be a real pain in the ass.

At the dispatch office Chan, a friendly middle-aged guy with a pleasant face that sported wire framed glasses beneath his short dark hair, greeted me when I climbed into their truck. Jack, a younger, handsome bearded fellow in a plain white tee-shirt, sat behind us on the bunk. It soon became apparent that Jack had the unfortunate tic of making a scoffing sound, something like 'Kish!' in my direction. We had just met so his openly derisive manner appeared to originate from having to work alongside a female driver. Apparently that put a second crease in his ass.

Once on board I soon discovered that neither Chan nor Jack had full command of the English language. They nattered to each other in a foreign tongue, Jack sitting on the bunk with the curtain open while Chan drove out of the yard and headed down the highway toward Memphis. I sat in the passenger seat and looked out the window. When someone else drove, I usually only got to watch the scenery in snatches and grabs before entering the sleeper to get some rest. On the first part of the run today while Chan drove I could pass the time by getting a better look at the towns and countryside that went by for the entire eight hour run up to Memphis. Then I looked forward to an easy drive back before going home to sleep restfully in my own bed that same night.

In the meantime, I sat in a puddle of isolation while incomprehensible words flew over my head. For the first hour or so I wondered how much or how little of Chan and Jack's conversation pertained to me. Maybe none of it did, but I couldn't avoid feeling the way many of us do when two or more people can say anything, knowing that someone nearby doesn't understand a word. I found myself in this situation in a small metal box with two men I didn't know. Oh, well, I thought. It's only for a few hours.

After a while Jack closed the curtain to get some sleep, and I sat up with Chan exchanging what small talk we could both understand while watching the sun rise over east Texas. A few hours later we passed through Texarkana, and Chan continued the drive across Arkansas. By early afternoon we had reached Memphis. While Chan drove to the mechanic's shop, I paid close attention to the route he took. Instead of taking the loop that circled north of the city, Chan drove to a shop located on the south side. I would have to drive the route he took in reverse to find my way back to the Interstate and homeward. I made a mental note of the exit and the street names while we rolled along.

We arrived at the shop where Chan signed the repair papers a clerk handed him. Then both Chan and Jack put their gear in their newly fixed vehicle and bid me adieu. Well, Chan did. Jack scoffed, "Kish!" Oh well, I'll never have to see Jack again, I thought. So "Kish!" to him, too.

With the two of them on their way I settled my little green bookbag in the overhead bin of the spare truck and set my cell-phone in an empty cupholder on the dash. I looked at the phone's luminescent screen and wondered whether to turn it off. Who would need to call now? But I left the phone with the screen still glowing within reach and drove the tractor, sans trailers, back toward the Interstate. I figured Chan and Jack would go to the Memphis terminal and get their new trailers while I started the return journey. I felt washed with a feeling of relief. For one thing I didn't have to drive with the presence of mind as if my being reached 73 feet in length. The mirrors had no trailers in their reflections, and the bunk held no co-driver. I was free.

I crossed the Mississippi River and headed westward into Arkansas with no sense of hurry. I could take my time. With my newfound freedom I could park and eat at an ordinary restaurant like an ordinary person. Without trailers the truck cab drove like a big, stupid car. I could park practically anywhere.

Skipping easily across Arkansas, the sun began to set. I didn't like driving during sunrise or sunset, especially when facing the sun. The light from our closest star could make me wince, even with the use of sunglasses and window shades. Thus, the time looked ripe to stop for something to eat. Let the sun set in its own time, I decided. It will anyway.

For the last several months traversing this Interstate I had seen a billboard for a country restaurant alongside the highway in a small town. Did I dare to drive into unknown territory to explore it? Yes, I dared. I took an unfamiliar exit and drove down a country road. I would never have driven down such a narrow path while pulling double trailers, not knowing if a place to turn around even existed. Making a u-turn in a cab only, however? That was a piece of cake. Or in this instance, maybe a slice of pecan pie.

I pulled into the gravel lot of the restaurant and parked while the sun continued its downward journey to the horizon. I would have an unrushed dinner then enjoy a leisurely drive back to Fort Worth. After enjoying barbecued brisket, baked beans and corn bread, I pushed back from the table happy and full. Stepping into the pleasantly dim parking lot I carried a Styrofoam container with a slice of pecan pie. Stars began to flicker overheard. I got in the truck and drove back to the Interstate and headed westward again. The dusky sunset had ushered in a sense of peacefulness. The dashboard lights glowed and I settled into the rhythm of the road.

The truck hadn't rolled much farther when the ring of the cell-phone interrupted the peacefulness. Wayne's name popped up on the screen. I briefly contemplated selecting ignore and letting his call go to voicemail. In retrospect that's the least of what I should have done. I probably should have thrown the damn phone out the window. But, no, I dutifully answered the call instead.

"Hello?"

"Hey, Karen. It's me, Wayne."

Did he not think I could read his name on the phone? I wondered, but just answered, "Hey, Wayne. What's up?"

"We've got a little problem."

"Oh?"

"Yeah, the guys' truck has broken down again," Wayne explained. "I need you to go get them and let them use the truck you're in now to finish their run. I'll have to have their truck towed back to a repair shop."

"Alright," I said, thinking I must be near Chan and Jack's location. They may have headed back toward Dallas a little later because they had to go to the Memphis yard for their trailers, I reasoned. Since I'd stopped to eat, their location must not be too far away. "Where are they?"

"They're at Holladay."

"Holladay?" I asked, surprised. "The only Holladay I know of is in Tennessee."

"Yeah, that's where they are."

"What are they doing there?"

"They were headed to their butthead in Virginia."

"Virginia?" I asked, beginning to realize I'd never really been told their destination when Wayne originally set up the run. I had just guessed they went to Memphis and right back.

"Yeah, that's their regular run," Wayne answered. "Listen, if you go get them, they can finish their run. Just ride in the passenger seat like you did up to Memphis, and we'll pay you for the full run, too."

"All the way up to Virginia?" I asked, still grasping the thought that my easy run up and back in the same day had suddenly morphed into a potential ordeal of riding shotgun for two days nonstop with Chan and Jack.

"Yeah, all the way to Virginia. Where are you now?" Wayne's question interrupted my thoughts.

"I'm near Little Rock," I answered. "It'll take a while to drive all the way back to Memphis then on to Holladay. Probably about four hours."

"I understand. That's okay," Wayne said, sounding chipper and encouraging.

I'll bet it's okay, I thought, but didn't say so. I knew that if I didn't turn the truck around Wil and Wayne would lose thousands of dollars on just that one run. In addition, the cost of repairs and towing for the bum truck and the cost of bobtailing the tractor I drove would also have to be absorbed into the bottom line, along with all our wages. But I couldn't feel too badly for Wil and Wayne. I'd also heard from other drivers that Wil pocketed the safety bonuses the company paid for his drivers' good work, bonuses other managers shared with their drivers.

I had mixed feelings about this run now. I almost wished the cellphone had been off or that I had waited an hour or two before calling back. Yet to some extent, I felt glad to be of help. There is something about dealing with the practicalities of trucking that is satisfying. Anyway, Wayne had just said I'd be compensated for my time and trouble. So I turned around and started back east towards Tennessee and another couple days of God only knows what. I would not even be one of the drivers, but an extra, a spare wheel. I wasn't a third wheel or a fifth wheel or even a nineteenth wheel. We pulled double trailers. That's another two axles for a total of twenty two wheels. That made me the twenty third wheel on Chan and Jack's rig!

Since I doubted Chan and Jack would pause at a truck stop so I could shower, I decided to take care of business first. A couple of hours later, after waving hello to the Mississippi River for the third time that day, I drove another hour before pulling off to a Tennessee truck stop called the Jolly Trucker. Without trailers I found a close parking spot and entered the building. Walking in for a shower and a change of clothes I thanked my lucky stars for the forethought to carry everything along, even on what was meant to be a one day run.

After a quick shower I drove on to Holladay, arriving at about ten o'clock that night and finding the parking lot filled to the brim with all variety of trucks. Wayne had said Jack had parked the broken truck next to the truck stop's scale. Scales usually have a tall sign next to them. I soon found the stranded team and prepared to switch out tractors. I climbed down from the spare truck and met Jack. The turbo in their truck had given out again, Jack managed to explain. They could reach a maximum speed of only about 40 miles an hour, less than the minimum of 45 mph required on the Interstate. Anyway, their truck had almost no power to go uphill pulling heavy trailers.

As he had been instructed, Jack called Wayne to tell him of my arrival. Within seconds Wayne called me. "Hey, how you doing?" Wayne asked, practically chirping in my ear.

"I'm okay," I answered, wondering why he asked.

"Hey, listen. I know you must be tired," Wayne's voice took on the tone of a used car salesman in mid spiel. "How would you like a hotel room for the night instead of riding in the truck?"

Alarm bells went off in my head. Most "hotels" next to truck stops are actually motels, with rooms that open up to the great outdoors. Any passerby can see a lone female enter a room. Plus, many places of lodging I'd seen near truck stops were cheesy to say the least, many of them next to bars or stores that advertised adult videos. Such motels appeared to have a bleed over from the truck stops of prostitution and drugs.

"I don't think there are any decent hotels near here, Wayne."

"There's gotta be something," Wayne said, sounding upbeat. "The guys can drive you over to a nearby place, and I'll call the desk clerk with one of our company credit card numbers. That way you can get a good night's sleep."

"The only places I know of around here look pretty crappy. I wouldn't be able to rest anyway."

Wayne persisted in trying to sound like he was doing me a favor. My bullshit detector not only beeped, its lights twirled. This wasn't about my convenience. I had already sensed that employers often don't care about the convenience, comfort or safety of drivers. I felt that Wayne simply wanted to get out of paying me a share of the run he had eagerly offered a few hours before when the truck he needed was still in another state.

If I wasn't in the truck, I could hardly expect to be paid for the run. Wayne would pay for the distance I'd driven so far, certainly. But when the truck they had needed to complete the run had been four hours away from the trailers that needed to be pulled another several hundred miles, I'd been in for a share of the full run. Both Chan and Jack would still get their full pay. But Wil and Wayne would have a little less profit on this run if they paid me, too. Of course, they wouldn't have made this run at all if I hadn't turned around.

"Wayne, I don't think I could even get any rest," I repeated, picturing myself in some skanky dive with ragged furniture and stained bedspreads. I could just imagine cockroaches keeping me company while I waited on pins and needles for Chan and Jack to return. Of course, for Wayne a few miserable dollars spent on a cheap motel would be a sweet deal. I explained to Wayne that the places looked sleazy. Prostitutes and pimps frequented these motels with doors anyone could knock on or, for that matter, kick in. I'd be safer in the truck, no matter how inconvenient it might be. Only then Wayne changed his story.

"I don't know if I can pay you all the way up to Virginia and back."

"You told me *before* that you could."

"I'd have to ask Wil."

"You told me you would pay me for the run," I repeated.

It wasn't like Wayne or Wil were suffering. They both did very well. Yet, any appreciation Wayne should have shown for saving this run appeared to have evaporated. To me it looked like Wayne had used a sneaky bait-and-switch method, such that I fervently wished I'd pressed the ignore button on my cellphone when his original call had lit up the screen.

Wayne insisted that the guys drive to a place nearby that Jack had told him about to see if I wanted to stay there. If not, another exit awaited about twenty miles farther. But with the good truck hitched up to the trailers and headed to the butthead in Virginia, Wayne kept saying he couldn't promise pay for anything more than what I'd driven that day, from Memphis to Little Rock and back to Holladay, six hours of solo driving for at least two days on the road and saving the run.

We ended our call without any satisfaction for either of us, or at least not for me. Wayne told me to call him the next day to find out if Wil would pay for my time and effort beyond the miles I'd driven. At least I had managed a bit of assertiveness on the phone, refusing the suggestion to stay God knows where and under what circumstances. Could I transfer that firmness into the cab of a truck with a naysayer or even a scoffer present? My gradually forming backbone was up for more testing that night.

Jack and I switched out tractors like we were butting heads. But I had no trailers to take back anywhere and Jack's broken truck would sit here at Holladay and wait for a tow truck driver to come and pick it up. Both guys moved their sleeping bags into the spare truck again while I sat in the passenger seat wondering what would happen next. With Chan sitting on the bunk looking

141

out through the open curtains Jack drove nearby and circled into the parking lot of a shady looking motel. When our truck pulled in, so did a small car with a radio booming loudly. The car was driven by a man. A woman got out of the car and walked up to the door of one of the motel rooms. Another man opened the door and the woman walked in. The man in the car, her pimp, waited outside.

"I'm not staying here," I said.

"Kish!" Jack scoffed.

Thirty minutes later Jack exited the highway again near a large truck stop. He drove into the parking lot of a nearby motel. The place looked so run down I could hardly tell whether they were still in business. Half of the rooms didn't have curtains. The headlights of the rig lit up the interior of rooms with torn curtains or pieces of brown wrapping paper partially covering the windows.

"I'm not getting out of the truck."

"Kish!" Jack scoffed again.

Fuck him, I thought.

Another hour later, near Nashville, Jack exited the highway yet again. I walked from a nearby parking lot to the lobby of a bright, clean, modern hotel. The hotel clerk checked and found they were booked solid for the night. I returned to the passenger seat and Jack drove back onto the highway. The reality that I would remain onboard for the duration finally seeped through Jack's thick skull. We headed eastward with Chan still in the sleeper resting up for his turn at the wheel while I wedged my little green bookbag between the cold window and the seat's back so I could lay my head on it. I leaned against the bookbag listening to the winds whirling by outside and tried to doze. After a while, I noticed that the truck moved more slowly than usual. I wondered if the speed just felt slower because my eyes were closed until I glanced out the windshield. Flurries of snow danced around the truck, escaping into the night on either side of the rig as it cut gradually into mountain country. I looked at the speedometer that shone up from the dashboard into Jack's bearded face, his brow furrowed with concentration. Fifty miles an hour. Turbo or no turbo, there would be slow going tonight.

* * *

Over the next several hours Jack drove through the night while I caught bits and pieces of sleep. While leaning against the window I pulled out the armrests on both sides of the passenger seat. I wrapped up in my coat and settled into the seat, trying to make myself comfortable, my little green bookbag cushioning my head against the bumps and jolts of the road. I closed my eyes and dozed. From time to time the truck's movements awakened me when we hit a patch of rough pavement. The bookbag kept my head from hitting the unforgiving window and its metal door frame while cold wind sped by on the other side of the thin pane. I slept fitfully, sometimes roused simply by the discomfort of my desperate sleeping posture. Then for a few minutes I would look out at forests that climbed into mountains interspersed with the sparkling lights of towns.

Eventually, we reached the butthead in Virginia. Early morning light shone over a parking lot heavily interrupted by orange barricades marking off areas of new concrete. Jack and Chan exchanged trailers with the team that had been waiting for them. After a brief stay Chan started the drive back to Holladay, all the way down I-81 in Virginia and most of the way across Tennessee. Jack went back to the sleeper while I continued to sit up front.

Though morning had dawned, I'd had a very sketchy night's sleep. I continued to lean against the window and get what rest would come. Yet, once morning wore on, even napping became impossible. Often on a truck, you might feel like selling your left arm for a solid stretch of sleep in the wee hours of the morning. But if you sat in the front of the cab with sunlight streaming in during the day, just as often you got your second or third or fourth wind. At some point my brain awakened and any chance of sleep evaporated for the rest of the day. So I watched the scenery go by.

Some hours later Chan stopped for lunch. He wanted to eat while driving so I came back to the truck with a burger and fries. "You want to sleep?" Chan asked. "I can see if Jack's awake," he said, turning his head toward the closed curtains of the sleeper.

"Nah. That's okay. I couldn't sleep now anyway. Besides, if he's driving, he needs to sleep."

"You sure?"

"Yeah, but thanks."

After eating I sat watching the trees and fields go by. My thoughts returned to the phone calls with Wayne the previous night. I wondered what insight Chan might give on the matter.

"Chan, what would you guys have done if I hadn't brought the truck back to you last night?"

Chan explained that the first time their truck had broken down on a weekend. Not only did they have to wait for the truck to be fixed, but most of Wil's other drivers were too far to bring them back to DFW in their cabs.

That's right! I thought, this has happened before.

"What about the butthead in Virginia?" I asked.

"They cancelled it. They had to," Chan said. "We lost most of our pay for that run, too."

"Did you stay at a motel like the ones we saw?"

"No, we stayed at an okay place. Not like those kinds of places," Chan answered, grimacing.

Wayne had told me to call him the next day. I could just imagine Wayne giving an "aw shucks" explanation that he'd spoken too soon on his first position when he had said they would pay me for the full run, too. I wondered if Wayne would claim Wil had backed up his second position, that they wouldn't pay for the miles to Virginia that Wayne had originally promised. Whatever Wayne might have said I decided instead to call the big cheese himself, Wil. On instinct I dug my cellphone out of the little green bookbag that had been my pillow the night before and dialed Wil's number. Wil answered in his nasal voice and we exchanged some pleasantries. Once Wil indicated he knew in a general sense what had happened with this run, I began.

"I need to talk to you about my conversations with Wayne last night."

"Okay."

"Wayne told me I'd be paid for this run all the way to Virginia and back. Then after I delivered the truck to where the guys were stranded Wayne said I wouldn't get paid for any more than I'd driven."

"I know you haven't been driving for very long," Wil answered, as if politely informing me of what I must not already know. "But it's customary to pay drivers for the miles they drive."

"I've been driving long enough to know it's also customary to pay team drivers for the miles co-drivers cover," I found myself countering with the help of another newly acquired vertebra.

"What team are you a member of?" Wil asked, as if to point out that I didn't have a regular co-driver just then. But any relief driver is paid for the miles his co-driver covered, regardless.

"I'm running with the team of Chan and Jack who wouldn't have made this run if I hadn't delivered this truck to them."

Wil paused, then said, "You know I really do appreciate you." A phrase other drivers would laughingly mock – they recognized the expression Wil used when he wanted something from them.

"Then you won't mind paying me for the run."

"Did Wayne tell you he'd pay you?" Wil asked, though I'd already said so.

"Wayne told me I'd be paid for the full run, all the way up to Virginia and back."

"Let me check with Wayne."

Of course, I agreed. Yet, I also wondered what Wil already knew. From what I observed over time I formed the opinion that Wil and Wayne often played off of each other, claiming ignorance of the other's actions or declaring the other to be the primary decision-maker. But maybe Wil really didn't know what Wayne had said or planned that night. Maybe a cheap motel had been Wayne's bright idea all on his lonesome. I'd have to wait to find out if my time and dedication had been utilized or merely used. Either way at least I'd made the effort to stand my ground. I'd jumped rank and called the boss' boss, too. My growing backbone really got some good exercise.

Our conversation ended. I said, 'good bye' and Wil said nothing, his typical behavior. My phone beeped in my ear, telling me the line had disconnected. I didn't expect Wil to be effusive, though by contrast, Wayne, often ended his calls with drivers like he was saying good bye to his best buddy. Then I spent the rest of the day and most of the next night sitting in the passenger seat, wondering what good my association with Wil and Wayne did, if they took advantage of my time and effort without providing compensation.

Jack drove us from Holladay to Dallas. I didn't get another chance at the sleeper until Prescott, Arkansas, about an hour east of Texarkana and four hours from Dallas. Since Chan and Jack had a break before their next run began, it didn't matter if I took a snooze then or not. After over thirty hours of discomfort, I retired to the sleeper and slept solidly while Jack drove and Chan sat up front talking with him.

In time Jack reached the Dallas terminal and drove the cab near the guard's building that led to the employees' parking lot so I could go home before he and Chan dropped their trailers. I gathered my things and climbed down from the truck.

"Thanks for bringing us the spare truck. You saved our run," Chan called out with a wave of his hand.

"Sure," I waved at the duo, then turned and headed toward the exit.

"Kish!" From the shadowed recesses of the cab I heard Jack scoff one last time.

The next day off, payday, I drove to the Fort Worth terminal, walked across the yard, and entered the dispatch office. Wil kept a folder there that drivers placed logs and fuel receipts in. Our paychecks were left therein, also. Wayne, unlike most driver-managers, often spent time in the office chatting with dispatchers. He stood up when I walked in.

"I know what you came here for," Wayne said in his usual jocular manner. He handed me an envelope. I put it in a jacket pocket while we chatted briefly about future runs then I walked back across the asphalt to the guard's gate. I put my hands in my jacket pockets. The envelope. I took it out and opened the seal. The numbers showed that Wil and Wayne had paid the full and originally stated amount. I had stood up for myself and won another small victory. I had also developed some more on-the-road backbone and none too soon. On an upcoming run I would need it like never before.

Chapter 11: "You're not gonna cost me $300!"

If Wayne harbored any hard feelings about having to keep his word on the "easy run," he kept them hidden. The first time afterwards when he had called I listened attentively to his tone, wondering if any resentment would seep through in his voice. Happily, Wayne had sounded like his jovial self. Over the next few months I drove many times. Then one day Wayne called and after exchanging our usual chitchat, he got down to business.

"I've got a team that runs a butthead up to the Jolly Trucker in Tennessee."

Though I kept mum, I recognized the Jolly Trucker, where I'd stopped to shower on my way to meet Chan and Jack when their truck had failed.

"Both team members are taking their vacations," Wayne explained. "The run goes out and back every day."

I would be driving with Romeo.

Romeo didn't seem too bad to drive with. So far he had been conscientious behind the wheel. He never once veered onto the rumble strip. And if he came on a bit strong, both aromatically and flirtatiously, he made up for it by being generally cheerful.

Romeo and I met again at the dispatch office. As we built the trailer set, I noticed he had cooled his jets considerably while remaining friendly. Though he acted a wee bit wounded that I had said some of his earlier comments might be considered vulgar, I could live with that. In fact, it made the job a little easier to

147

simply get on with our task without having to wonder what would come out of his mouth next.

Romeo would start us out first this week in order to run the butthead alone that weekend. He'd wind up with six days of work for the week. I was happy to take a slightly longer weekend by completing just four days of driving.

The particulars of another truck always took a little getting used to. For instance, the gear box shifted slightly differently, and the thin, flat mattress had been replaced by an air cushion. Because neither of us had ever driven this truck before we didn't have a spare key. We couldn't lock the doors without turning off the engine that stayed on all week, partly because we were always on the go and partly because the truck cab had to be cooled or heated year round. I wanted to stop and have spare keys cut, but we never did make our way to Wal-Mart. I didn't know it at the beginning of the week, but that turned out to be a saving grace.

On our first day Romeo headed out of Fort Worth and across Dallas to the eastern side of the I-635 loop that seemed to be perpetually under construction. To turn onto I-30 and head toward Arkansas a driver had to negotiate several lane changes. The last lane change occurred just at a juncture where motorists also entered the highway. If they weren't watching carefully, the motorists could get pinched between another vehicle on their left and a concrete wall on their right. When driving along here many truckers kept an eye on the side mirror just in case they could help a motorist merge by varying the truck's speed. I mentioned this.

"I have right of way," Romeo said flatly.

"True, technically," I answered. "But if you can stop them from hitting one of the trailers by slowing down . . ."

"It's their responsibility to merge," he asserted.

Strictly speaking, Romeo was right. However, many truck drivers often look out for the safety of auto drivers who sometimes act oblivious to danger. On most occasions when I'd driven this stretch of road I had adjusted my speed when necessary to give more space to entering motorists who didn't appear to understand the layout of the highway. Maybe some motorists understood, but many people today drive with a sense of trying to see what they can get away with. Or so it seems. Either way most drivers did their best to avoid hitting them.

About an hour later we stopped for lunch at the small truck stop next to the barbecue joint where Hilda had guided our overheating rig months before. I grabbed my little green bookbag and gripped the door handle to exit the truck.

"I think I'll have the brisket sandwich. What are you having?" I asked.

"Ah, I don't know if I want to eat there."

"Aren't you hungry?"

"I'll eat here," Romeo said, nodding toward the truck stop next door that had a sandwich counter.

I wished Romeo well and walked over to the barbecue place where they loaded a plate with meat, beans, bread and salad. Topping that off with a slice of sweet potato pie, I returned to the truck ready to get some rest in the middle of the day. Romeo sat in the driver seat listening to the radio. A large soda rested in one of the cupholders while he chomped down on an ice cream sandwich. Packages of snack cakes lay on the dashboard.

"That's some dessert," I said.

"Dessert?! This is lunch," Romeo answered with his heckle of a laugh.

"Didn't you have a sandwich at the truck stop?"

"This is a *sandwich*," Romeo answered archly, wadding up the wrapper of the ice cream sandwich and stuffing it into the trash bag before opening a package of snack cakes. Romeo often bought ice cream, sweet baked goods or candy. I had noticed when first driving with him that his snack food choices were nearly to the exclusion of anything else. The closest thing to a meal I'd ever seen him eat was a burger. Not surprisingly, he often complained that he didn't feel particularly well. He wasn't ill, he said. He just felt lousy.

Unlike Romeo during our first weeks together, I wasn't interested in sitting up and chatting. So I bunked down while Romeo continued through the rest of Texas, across Arkansas and into Tennessee to our switch out at the Jolly Trucker. Since it was the first day of the driving week, I felt well-rested. Yet I settled down for a brief nap in the cool sleeper compartment, darkened by closing the heavy curtains. Ironically, perhaps, knowing that a ten hour drive lie ahead that night could enable me to relax enough to fall asleep in the middle of the day.

Romeo and I proceeded through our week without fanfare. Each midday we built our set in Fort Worth. Then Romeo drove the ten hours up to the Jolly Trucker where we met another team in the same spot and exchanged trailers at about midnight. Then I drove back overnight and into the next day. Each of us drove our full shift, never driving on the other's logbook. That suited me fine. This run didn't feel so tiring, though we both naturally got more tired once the week wore on to Wednesday and then to Thursday.

Finally, Friday, the last day of our week together arrived. We would make one more run up to Tennessee, then I would head home and Romeo would drive back out on his solo weekend run. Since he would be alone on Saturday, he would stay at the truck stop overnight. On Sunday morning he would drive back.

Romeo drove the rig through the traffic of Fort Worth and Dallas again, and I sat up until we stopped for a meal. Romeo pulled the rig into the same truck stop I'd paused at when we had first driven together months before. We each got something to eat then Romeo got us back on the road. I lay down in the bunk for some rest. I had the accumulated fatigue of the week folded in to me, but couldn't fall asleep. I should have been able to get at least a nap, like on our first day, but couldn't quite settle down. Hours later Romeo stopped at the Covered Wagon near Texarkana. I availed myself of the opportunity for a restroom break then returned to the bunk.

Evening approached. Finally, I fell asleep. I had gotten about an hour's rest when our rig pulled off to a truck stop again and I awoke. I stayed in the bunk while Romeo, unaware of my struggle to sleep, climbed out of the truck, went inside and returned with another large soda. Then he drove back onto the highway. I continued to lay in the bunk, the spell of my slumber broken. I rested as much as possible, but didn't get back to sleep. Romeo stopped a couple more times. Then the last couple of hours he drove continually, but I still couldn't doze off. Something just didn't feel right. An uneasy energy lingered in the air, though I couldn't imagine what or why. About a half an hour before our arrival at the Jolly Trucker I gave up and sat down in the passenger seat to put on my shoes.

We reached our destination at eleven o'clock. We pulled into the customary spot where we had met the other team the previous three nights. We had made good time, but the other team hadn't arrived yet.

We each went into the truck stop. Lunch had come and gone eight hours prior so I entered the restaurant and ordered a meal of chicken strips, fries and Texas toast. Mostly carbs, but the salad bar here boasted stale vegetables and dressings, sour cream and cottage cheese of uncertain expiration date, even during their busiest hours. Also, I had a theory that fried foods may be fatty, but anything dunked in hot grease long enough is definitely cooked. I asked the waitress for half of the chow on the plate and half in a to-go container. I ate from the plate then returned to the truck carrying the Styrofoam container. I would put the rest of the meal in the tiny truck refrigerator for tomorrow morning's breakfast.

I walked back to the truck and saw Romeo sitting in the driver seat so I climbed into the passenger side. Romeo sipped bottled tea and ate from a packet of cookies on the dashboard. An idea flashed in my mind. Instead of storing the fresh food, I'd offer it to him. Maybe he'd feel better with some real food in his considerable, bulging tum.

"Would you like some of this food?" I asked him, briefly lifting the container to eye level.

"No."

"I haven't eaten from it," I explained, setting the container on the corner of the wraparound dashboard between us. "They put it in here straight from the cooker."

Romeo just sat slumped against the wheel, gazing lazily out the windshield.

"If you don't feel so good, a chunk of meat and some potatoes will probably make you feel better," I offered hopefully.

Again Romeo despondently declined.

I stepped back into the sleeper to put the food in the mini-fridge. "Let me know if you change your mind." I placed the container on the cool shelf, closing and securing the small door.

While I rolled up my sleeping bag a truck engine rumbled, pulling in next to us. The other team had arrived at midnight. I put on my jacket against the chill night and climbed out of the truck to help. I grabbed my gloves and spun the landing gear of our trailers down to the ground so Romeo could drive out from under them. Romeo released the brake lines and power cord. The other drivers disconnected their cab from the trailers they had brought, also. Next I climbed back into the cab before Romeo pulled forward. I'd decided weeks ago that riding inside the truck when semi cabs vied for position in a quasi-lighted parking lot was much wiser than standing near large, rolling tires.

The other team hitched up to their new trailers and pulled into a fuel lane to take a quick break. Not long thereafter they drove out of the truck stop and back on the highway heading east. While they took care of their business Romeo backed our cab up to the trailers we would be hauling homeward.

I climbed down and started winding up the landing gear while Romeo attended to the lifelines. The lifelines are the service brakes that brought the colossal rig of tens of thousands of pounds to a stop several times a day. They fed from a long, blue rubber tube. Also, the emergency brake system that served as a back up to the regular brakes fed from a similar tube of alarming red. Between them a thick black power cord fastened into a large plug that supplied electricity to the trailers' markers and brake lights.

Finished with the landing gear, I checked to see that the fifth wheel latch had well and truly secured the pin, before stepping to the front trailer where Romeo attached the lifelines with his usual heavy-handed flair. He reminded me of a school kid who constantly tries to show off. First, Romeo pushed in the large plug that attached the power cord. Then he grasped the emergency brake line and lifted it toward the glad-hand on the front of the trailer. Next, he turned his attention to the service brake line. With a swift, hard push and a twist he attached the line.

"Dammit!" Romeo exclaimed.

"What's the matter?"

Romeo undid the glad-hand to the service brakes. He leaned forward and lifted his glasses off of his nose, inspecting the bracket on the trailer. "It's broken."

"What's broken?" I asked.

"Hold on. Let me try something," Romeo said. Then he reconnected the glad-hands and climbed into the driver seat. With Romeo in the cab I stepped forward and looked. A thick crack ran along the grooved contours of the metal bracket that played a crucial role in connecting the truck's brakes to the trailers.

Romeo turned on the pressurized air brakes. Immediately, air hissed out from the crack in the bracket. I reached up and felt the unmistakable, steady stream of cool air striking my hand. The high pressure brake system forced the stream of air out of the breach in the metal. The system couldn't gather enough pressure for the brakes to work. We couldn't go. Or even if we could have rolled, we couldn't have stopped, at least not with the service brakes. If the service brakes won't function, the emergency brakes do. However, the emergency brake system isn't a back up operating system. Its sole function is to bring the truck to a complete stop and hold it there. From highway speed to zero, the emergency brakes engage, if the service brakes fail while driving.

Naturally, emergency brakes are a safety feature, but not without risks. Suddenly coming to a stop can be dangerous, for instance when driving on slick roads or around a curve or in heavy traffic. The emergency brakes engage without the judgment a driver uses to brake gradually or intermittently. The emergency brakes mindlessly exert steady pressure no matter what. If conditions aren't conducive to a safe, rapid stop, things can go wrong, even with a standard 53' trailer. With doubles the dangers are magnified by the risk that the back trailer can jerk around, get slung into adjacent lanes and jackknife, or tip over.

Romeo stepped down from the truck's cab and looked at the bracket and glad-hand again. His hands grasped the service brake line as if trying to thwart an artery from bleeding.

"I'm gonna go to the shop," Romeo announced. He shut off the brakes once more and trudged past the fuel lanes to the 24 hour mechanic's shop that occupied one side of the truck stop building. I climbed back aboard and did what little chores could be accomplished while waiting, throwing away the truck's trash bag and setting out a new one, updating my log.

I sat in the driver seat using the steering wheel like a desk when Romeo returned. He climbed into the passenger seat and flopped down crossing his right ankle over his left knee. Then he picked up a book he had brought from where it rested on the dashboard and flipped through the pages.

"He'll be here in a minute," Romeo said, referring to the mechanic. We made small talk while we sat and waited. Romeo said he thought replacing the bracket would take at least a half an hour, maybe longer.

When the mechanic walked over with tools and a flashlight Romeo leapt from the truck to meet him. They walked behind the cab to inspect the damage. I stepped back into the sleeper and unrolled my sleeping bag. I had decided to get whatever rest I could before driving back all night. I already felt tired from the week's work and from less rest than usual during the drive up. Getting a nap, if possible, made sense.

From inside the sleeper and with our engine running I could hear only the vague sounds of Romeo's voice and another man talking just outside the head of the bunk's bed. The bracket and glad-hand, though on the trailer, were just a few feet away from the metal wall that separated the bunk from the outside. I had just settled things down when Romeo climbed back in closing the passenger door heavily.

"He doesn't think they have the part," Romeo announced. "He's going to take another look."

"Oh?" I asked, stepping forward out of the sleeper. Leaning an arm on the back of the driver seat, I looked through the window at the mechanic's back receding toward the shop's door. I asked Romeo, "Do you think I might have time to take a nap?"

"Probably."

I lay down and tried to doze, leaving the curtains between the sleeper and the seats narrowly opened a gap. I wanted to know when we were ready to roll. The curtains didn't cut much noise anyway. The lights from the parking lot peered into the sleeper a bit, but wouldn't prevent getting some rest.

The mechanic returned and Romeo lumbered down the side of the truck and walked back to speak to him. Again I couldn't make out their words, though they spoke quite a while.

"It's gonna be longer than expected," Romeo said when he returned to the cab.

Several minutes later I could hear the whir of machinery outside the sleeper like the sound of a dentist's drill.

"He's got the part?" I asked.

"No, but I've got it under control," Romeo said, flopping down into the passenger seat. "He didn't want to, but I talked him into getting it fixed so we can get out of here."

Believing Romeo knew what he was doing, I lay back down in the bunk. However, between the sound of the tools outside and Romeo's frequent visits out of the cab to check on the mechanic's progress, I got only a few scraps of sleep. Mostly I just couldn't relax. I wondered if this was just the bad luck of a bout of insomnia. But I felt an inexplicable restlessness stirring in my system. Once more I sensed that something just didn't feel right, and I *still* couldn't imagine what.

By 2 a.m. the mechanic returned to the shop. Romeo clambered aboard, slammed the passenger door shut and proclaimed triumphantly that the mechanic had finished his work. Reluctantly, I crawled out of the bunk. In the past two hours, I had been lucky to catch fifteen minutes of sleep. Once more I rolled up my sleeping bag and, picking up my little green bookbag, headed into the truck stop for one last break before leaving.

A misty cloud of exhaled breath proceeded me into the truck stop and back. I secured the collar of my jacket a little more tightly upon returning to the truck. Before climbing behind the wheel I instinctively walked past the cab to the front trailer to look at the mechanic's handiwork. What I saw astonished me.

Sticking out of the front of the trailer where a bracket had once secured a glad-hand and the rubber hose that led to the trailer's brake system, the now naked rubber hose jutted out of the wall of the trailer, like a bone without any muscle surrounding it. With absolutely no protection, nothing held the hose in place. The bare hose of the brake line rested on the sharp metal edges of a hole cut in the trailer by the mechanic.

By contrast a few inches away the emergency brake's bracket sturdily supported the connections to the backup system, holding them in place so they could work and flex correctly. The difference between the two brake line connections looked like the difference between a slice of steak and a piece of shoe leather. A chef could place shoe leather on a fine china plate with colorful garnish, and it would still look like a piece of shoe leather served as steak! I couldn't imagine driving a truck with this "fix" could be safe! It just didn't look right.

I climbed back aboard and addressed Romeo who had pulled his malodorous bedding down from the top bunk to the lower one. Clearly, Romeo still liked to challenge his immune system by not showering.

"Have you seen this brake line out here?" I asked.

"Of course. I'm the one who told him to do it that way."

"It doesn't look good," I said, picking up the work order off of the truck's dash. The broken bracket also sat on the center of the dash stuffed into a plastic bag.

"It'll be fine. We need to go. I'm scheduled to do the butthead tomorrow. Remember?"

"I'm gonna ask the mechanic," I said, climbing down from the truck, the papers in my hand.

"You don't need to ask the mechanic," Romeo said, his voice trailing off into the night while I walked away from the truck. Then he sat down in the driver seat and yelled through the open window, his voice sounding out more loudly, "We need to go!"

I kept walking. I'm the driver, the captain of the ship, and I'd just discovered another truism of trucking. The captain of the ship is no good without a mind of her own or a backbone. I would utilize all the vertebrae in my trucker's backbone that night.

I made my way through the chill nighttime air to the truck stop's repair shop and opened the door. Entering, I walked past walls lined with windshield wiper blades, lights and reflectors, nuts, bolts, and other mechanical whatnots. A young woman with strawberry blonde hair, wearing a navy blue uniform shirt stood at the counter behind a cash register.

"Can I help you?"

"I wanted to talk to the mechanic who worked on our truck," I said, my words lilting upward like a question.

"Yeah, he's here," she answered, sweeping her arm toward a short, sturdy dark-haired man in a mechanic's uniform who stood a few feet behind her. The patch on his shoulder gave his name which I don't remember, but let's call him Ray. He nodded his head upward and walked to the counter.

"I'm the other driver," I said.

"Yeah?"

"Let me ask you a question," I continued, looking into Ray's eyes. "Does that brake line look safe to you?"

"No, ma'am. It does *not!*" Ray spoke evenly but loudly, looking so earnest that I thought his gaze might tip me over backward.

"What do we need to do to have the kind of connection we drove in here with?" I asked.

"We can get the part, but not until eight this morning," he answered, his hands and arms turned upward in an apologetic shrug, looking like he had explained this all before to no avail.

"Okay, well, then we'll wait until morning," I said, glancing down and fingering the paperwork I had set on the countertop.

"I'm *so* glad we're not doing this!" Ray exclaimed, his shoulders falling with relief.

I looked up quickly. "What do you mean?"

"The connection on there now would have lasted only about a hundred miles."

We were more than five times farther from our destination.

"Then what?" I asked.

"The hose would get a hole in it from all the bouncing around from the road vibration. When the hose split the brake system would lose pressure and fail."

"In other words there's a chance we'd have had a wreck?" I asked, picturing the big rig running into cars when the brakes failed completely or the rig spun out of control when the emergency brakes engaged unexpectedly while rounding a curve or if they caused the rig to skid on damp pavement.

"Pretty much," Ray said, his face softening once he saw he was being listened to, probably for the first time that night.

"Any chance we would have made it okay?"

"It would be a matter of time before you had big trouble."

"Did he know that?" I asked Ray, referring to Romeo.

"I tried to tell him." Ray waved his hand in the direction of our truck. "He wouldn't listen."

Standing at the counter I looked more closely at the work order: the date, our company name and truck number, type of repair, and so on. My eyes ran across the space for driver name. I saw my name listed under the title of driver on the work order. Romeo had been the only one to talk to the mechanic so far. I looked to see who had signed the order and saw my name again. There in Romeo's scrawl my signature had been forged.

As the driver who had broken the bracket in the first place, fittingly, Romeo dealt with the problem. But Romeo had browbeaten the mechanic into an ill-advised repair and then made it look like *I'd* authorized the work. When the brake line failed, and that would have been a certainty one way or another, it would have looked like I was the one to blame.

"We'll wait until morning," I repeated. "About what time do you think you can start?"

"As soon as the part gets here at eight. Just leave the broken bracket on the steps outside the truck so they can see the part they're replacing. Another mechanic will be on duty then."

"Okay, thanks."

"No problem. I'm glad you came in and asked," Ray smiled, his arms spread with his hands knuckle down on the counter. He'd transformed from a man who looked tense enough to enter a boxing ring to slug it out to a guy who could be your best friend. He had become my best friend the moment his candor had saved us from being stranded or having an accident. The entire situation suggested the second trucking truism discovered that same night: Listen to your spidey sense. If something doesn't seem safe, it probably isn't!

Turning around I walked back through the shop and across the parking lot to the truck. I felt pretty sure that Romeo's grandiose manner when connecting the lines had caused him to break the bracket in the first place. Now I felt disgusted that Romeo risked both our lives in his cavalier fashion and angry that he'd used my name to do so. Romeo had once told me he was a cocky bastard. I believed him.

I climbed into the truck and took the old bracket out of the plastic bag on the dash. After setting the bracket on the catwalk outside for the morning mechanic, I sat in the driver seat to update my log. I'd have to log myself back into the sleeper. I didn't relish the thought of sleeping in the same compartment with Romeo, but felt I had no choice. At least there were two separate bunks. I'd sleep in one, him in the other. I didn't fear Romeo, but felt more repulsion towards him than ever before.

"We need to get on the road," Romeo's voice filtered through the closed curtains to where I sat.

"We have to wait until morning for a part," I answered evenly over my shoulder.

"What?!" Romeo cried, pulling back the curtains rapidly. I repeated myself. Romeo's heckling laugh echoed through the cab. "No, we're not!"

"Yes, we are. That brake line's not safe."

"Sure it is."

"The mechanic just told me it's dangerous."

"Bullshit! This truck is going back to Fort Worth tonight!"

"No, it's not," I persisted, standing my ground.

"Dammit!" Romeo shouted.

He threw a shirt over his bulbous stomach and, grabbing the empty plastic bag off of the dashboard, he climbed down the passenger side of the truck. My eyes followed him while he walked around the front of the truck and then, walking past the driver door, he took the bracket off of the catwalk. I didn't know what he might do next so I climbed down, too.

"Leave that there," I said, pointing to the bracket, my words floating in the mists of the night air. "The morning mechanic needs to see it."

"We're leaving *now!*" Romeo said, stuffing the bracket into the plastic bag then looking up at me to check my response.

"I'm the driver now, and this truck's not moving from this spot until I move it!" I answered, pointing at the asphalt beneath our feet.

Then Romeo, who claimed he drove only for fun, screamed to me, the world and the cold, starry sky, his free hand reaching palm upward in a beseeching claw. "You're not gonna cost me three hundred dollars!"

Romeo's weekend run or not, I wouldn't drive a truck, any truck, with the sort of makeshift repair he had insisted the mechanic employ. Once more I stood my ground. "I'm not driving this truck with failing brakes for your three hundred dollars!"

"I'm calling Wayne," Romeo said. He didn't mean such a statement like Hilda had often intended. I felt no fear of either Romeo or Wayne, but something else came to mind. What line of garbage might he try to feed Wayne, I wondered. Out of a natural sense of self-preservation, I called Wayne, too. Standing out in the frosty air I dialed the number. Voicemail answered. After all, the clock had almost reached 3 a.m. I left a message.

Romeo had walked to the other side of the truck and along the trailers. I could hear the sound of his voice from where I stood next to the cab. Soon Romeo walked back up to the cab and opened the door to climb in.

"What did he say?" I asked, wondering what Romeo hoped to accomplish.

"I got voicemail," Romeo said, climbing back aboard the truck. "I left him a message."

I climbed back aboard, too. Romeo already lay in the bottom bunk while I sat in the driver seat. How I'd get any sleep I didn't know. Then another thought formed in my head. I didn't trust Romeo. If I stretched out on the top bunk, Romeo's behavior had become so erratic, his tone so desperate that I wouldn't put it past him to wait awhile, then slip up front, put the truck in gear and start back to Texas himself. Once he took off down the road I would be trapped in the cab with him while Romeo drove the dangerous rig to the point of failure. No night is a good night to risk a crash. Now I had an inkling of why I'd felt so ill at ease since the evening before. Somehow my instincts had sensed impending danger and the need to counteract it.

"You take the top bunk," I said, strategizing that Romeo couldn't climb down and get into the driver seat without waking me, in case I did doze off.

"You're driving back. I don't want to have to move my bed again when we leave," he pointed out reasonably. Still I just didn't trust him. So I grasped the ignition key in the steering column and shut the engine off. Then I put that solitary key in my pocket where no one else could get to it.

"What did you do that for?" Romeo asked.

"I'm turning the engine off until morning."

"We need the heater."

I ignored Romeo. Then like a reprieve my phone rang. Wayne's voice spoke, "I got a couple of voicemails. What's going on?"

I climbed out of the truck and told Wayne as best I could what had happened: the glad-hand bracket had broken, the shop didn't have the part, Romeo had insisted on an interim solution that the mechanic considered dangerous. I tried to explain to Wayne the gravity of the danger the mechanic had explained to me.

"The mechanic said the brake line, as it is now, would fail in about a hundred miles," I informed Wayne.

"You can wait for the part, if you want," Wayne said, laughing as if he thought my call sounded like a sort of lark.

Then I also explained Romeo's frantic reaction and my concern that he might try driving the truck himself in its current condition to get back in time for his weekend run.

"I'm wondering if he'll take off with me in the sleeper, though I'm supposed to drive back," I said.

"He can do the weekend run whenever you guys get back, if that's what's worrying him. I don't have anyone else to cover it on short notice anyway. Where's he now?" Wayne asked of Romeo's whereabouts. I told him. "I'll call him," Wayne said, the lilt of a laugh still in his voice.

I got back in the truck where Romeo asked what Wayne had said. I told Romeo that Wayne would call him presently. Almost immediately, Romeo's cellphone rang. Then luckily for me and unluckily for Romeo, he decided to take his call outside, too. That's when I took my chance and locked the doors. I just didn't want the jerk in the truck overnight!

While Romeo stood outside talking on his phone, I closed the curtains, threw his bedding on the top bunk, and spread out my own sleeping bag below. Romeo ended his call with Wayne and knocked on the driver window. At first, I didn't answer. I could hear Romeo's voice, but couldn't make out the words. Possibly a lucky thing. The knocking on the window continued. After several minutes, I sat in the driver seat with Romeo's moon face on the other side of the glass where he stood on the steps of the truck. I opened the window a crack.

"You're gonna have to sleep somewhere else," I said.

"I can do the weekend run late," Romeo replied, thinking I would infer that waiting for the repair in the morning was now okay by him.

While I felt glad to see Romeo had accepted Wayne's offer, I just couldn't imagine staying the night in the truck with him, especially after his behavior a few moments earlier. Right or wrong, I had determined that one of us was going to spend the night outside the truck and it wasn't going to be me.

"Call Wayne and get a credit card number from him if you want," I said. "He can put you up in the hotel across the road."

"I need my stuff," Romeo said, referring to his sleeping gear.

Figuring I wouldn't be able to get him out of the cab if he got back in, I shook my head, no. "Good night," I said and rolled the window back up. Walking back into the sleeper, I closed the curtains. If Romeo wanted back in the truck, he'd have to break a window. Even in his earlier state, he didn't seem likely to.

My nerves shot, I lay down in the bunk on my sleeping bag and tried to rest. I looked back on recent events. I didn't think the challenges of this night could have been sidestepped. First of all, the driver who arrives at a butthead typically takes responsibility for the trailer exchange, unhooking and resetting the brake lines and power cords. I had cranked the landing gear just to be helpful. Then since he was the one who broke the part and with plenty of time still available on his log, looking into a repair had been Romeo's duty. Even if he'd turned it over to me and retired to the bunk, when I reported back that the repair had to wait until morning Romeo still could have gone ballistic, overeager as he was to get back for his solo run. Result? The same. Moreover, Wayne had laughed as if he took the whole thing as a joke. I got the impression he took my concerns as being merely those of a persnickety female. From my point of view only the mechanic and I appeared to care.

Just a precious few hours of available sleep time remained so I settled down into the bunk. With the engine off only the sounds of the nearby highway traffic filtered through the walls and windows. The clock read 3:30 a.m. About an hour of dozing followed until I awoke from the cold air that enveloped the truck and had seeped in from outside. I tried to compensate with the warm sleeping bag, but couldn't doze off again. The chill sunk through to my bones. Gingerly, I opened the curtains. Romeo was nowhere to be seen in the truck stop's parking lot lights. Naturally, he had escaped inside to warmer climes. I started the engine and heated the interior of the truck. Then one last thing came to mind. Though I felt tired, nonetheless, I set my watch alarm for 7 a.m.

In the early morning after a few broken hours of sleep I put away my bedding and exited the truck. The morning mechanic hadn't shown up yet and before he did I wanted lasting proof of the condition of the brake line in order to justify my actions to Wil or Wayne, if necessary. Coach had reminded me many months before, 'A picture is worth a thousand words.' Walking behind the cab, I took several photos of the repair that Romeo had authorized under my name the night before. Then I walked into the truck stop to freshen up before the return journey.

When I came back Romeo stood outside the locked truck with sleepy eyes and a new coating of stubble on his cheeks and chin. I unlocked the truck, and Romeo climbed in and went into the sleeper. We exchanged a few functional words, but said nothing about the previous night's events. Several minutes before eight the morning mechanic arrived and set to work on the front trailer's glad-hand bracket. An hour later the mechanic finished, and I took a copy of the work order with my genuine signature and the correct time and tucked it in my bookbag. Then with a suitably repaired truck I drove all the way back to Fort Worth, making a couple of routine stops, but not seeing hide nor hair of Romeo on the ten hour run.

That evening I drove into the Fort Worth yard and woke Romeo, who apparently had slept like a bear in a cave after a night on what I supposed must have been a chair or bench in the truck stop's TV lounge. Then I headed home while Romeo started the solo run he had so desperately wanted.

That weekend I printed the pictures. While some of the photos looked fuzzy, others came out clearly. Surely, I thought, anyone could see the problem of the primitive "fix" and understand why the truck shouldn't have been driven until repaired correctly, as the mechanic so strongly recommended. The following Monday I brought the printed pictures into Wil's offices. Wil, a dark blond with glasses, wore jeans and a white tee-shirt. He led me from the lobby into an individual office where he sat behind a desk and politely thumbed through the pictures while I stood before him.

"Sit down," Wil said, waving a hand at the seat in front of the desk.

"I'm not trying to get anyone in trouble," I said, hoping for, if nothing else, some understanding. "I just wanted either you or Wayne to see what I was talking about this weekend."

Wil leafed through the pictures for a moment longer. Then setting them down on the desk blotter he spoke. "What we strive for is driver safety, both for our trucks and for the motoring public," Wil said, sounding like a public service announcement.

"I got the feeling Wayne thought I was making a big deal over nothing. I thought one of you ought to see what it was all about," I said, referring to the pictures.

Wil repeated himself almost word for word: "strive, driver safety, motoring public." The words spilled from his lips sounding like he read them from cue cards. The repetition, the oddly formal word choice: to me Wil's words sounded like a canned response. He didn't speak about my actions in regard to the repair, whether he thought I'd acted responsibly or not. Not a word.

I offered to let Wil keep one set of the double copied pictures, maybe show them to Wayne. Wil declined and handed them back. Neither Wil nor Wayne ever gave me any feedback about this incident. Wayne had guffawed through the phone into my ear like he thought the whole situation silly. Then Wil had responded with an unusual robotic-sounding stance. If Wil had lost Romeo's weekend run, I wondered if he would have sounded so cordial when we met.

Not gonna cost

Before college and truck driving I had worked for an airline and knew they had been genuinely obsessed with safety. For one thing if a plane crashes that always makes the news and costs an airline millions of dollars regardless of the cause, be it weather, mechanical failure or pilot error. On the other hand if a truck crashes, the results affect fewer people and news coverage may be nonexistent. Word on the street is that trucking companies often settle lawsuits to avoid court proceedings in the public view and to keep financial details hidden. The costs, while a concern, are much lower than in the airline industry. A truck crash is usually earthshaking news only to the people directly involved or to their loved ones.

I don't know if it ever truly occurred to either Wil or Wayne that trouble of one kind or another had been avoided that night. One might be forgiven for thinking that at a minimum they should have considered it appropriate for a driver to refuse to drive a vehicle with brakes that certainly would have failed. Meanwhile, the fact that one of their drivers had the courage to stand up to a co-driver when he had shown his true colors seemed to mean nothing to them from my point of view. Instead, I had been laughed at by Wayne and felt I'd been treated dismissively by Wil.

More true colors?

Chapter 12: "I knew a call from you would fix the truck."

Not long afterward and without missing a beat Wayne called. "I have another solo run," he began.

Between runs with other drivers I could supplement my hours and, therefore, my pay. I'd still have co-drivers, just not all the time. The "easy run" hadn't really shown me what driving solo might be like. Returning a cab without trailers wasn't like building a set, delivering or exchanging it, then returning with another set to drop upon arrival. I'd already driven a couple of overnight solo runs, but because they were tacked on to the end of a week with a co-driver, so far I'd never built a set of doubles completely alone. Finally, I had a chance to find out what driving entirely alone would be like. While every day on a truck has challenges, maybe a solo run might be easier in some ways.

"There's a solo butthead this weekend to Meridian that I need to cover," Wayne said.

I had already been to the Mississippi town near the Alabama border with another co-driver, but didn't remember exactly where the truck stop was.

"I'll give it a go. Do you know the exit number?" I asked, naively.

"When you get the dispatch slip, it'll have the exit number on it. This run is pretty much a straight shot. Just take I-20 all the way across Louisiana and most of the way across Mississippi. The truck stop is right along the Interstate. You meet a guy out of

Atlanta. Be at Fort Worth at four in the morning so you can build your set and be out the gate by about five," Wayne instructed.

Privately, I decided to get there earlier, since both new and experienced drivers had already told me a first solo build could easily take a couple hours. From these past conversations with other drivers I knew an hour would be miraculous for a first time solo set up. Thus, at 3 a.m. on a chilly Saturday in mid-December I went to the dispatch office and got the slip with the trailer numbers destined for Meridian. The slip listed the trailers in the order they were meant to be set up. The heaviest trailer belongs in front and the lighter one on the back. If their roles are reversed, a heavier trailer in the back can create a force strong enough to flip the back trailer onto its side or even to flip the entire rig. Sam had cautioned against this phenomenon when advising me not to let the tail wag the dog. A heavy back trailer could gain momentum swinging from side to side. Any driver who "lost" or flipped the back trailer received automatic termination for driving too fast for conditions, no matter what speed the truck moved at when the flip occurred. One driver explained, unless the truck was parked and tornado-like winds lifted and dropped the back trailer or the rig on its side, a driver had no chance of mercy.

Yet, I became aware, too, that the dispatch clerks' choice of which trailer went first could not always be relied upon. After a driver builds the set and turns in the dispatch slip with the trailers' seal numbers, the staff member hands the driver a more detailed page for each trailer that lists the actual weights. Sometimes the back trailer weighed more. If the difference was slight, we proceeded out the gates anyway. If the difference was great, some drivers rebuilt the set rather than risk an accident. Not all drivers would rebuild or even notice that they should. Ultimately, dispatch workers should have checked the weights before producing the slip or at least shared the true weights with the driver before the set was built.

Starting the solo run, I drove the cab over to the dolly yard where dollies of various ages sat in a jumble next to a row of parked truck cabs. Most of the cabs remained out on the road, which made getting a dolly a bit easier in the cramped quarters of the small yard. Drivers were meant to park the dollies in straight lines so other drivers could back in and attach the big metal loop of the dolly's point to the hitch on the back of their cabs. As the week wore on, more and more drivers haphazardly pulled in and dropped the dolly somewhere along the edge of the yard next to the row of parked cabs before hightailing it home for a few days rest after a long week's work. I empathized with their eagerness to get home, but the dollies parked askew and butted up against the row of cabs sometimes made steering through the yard without striking a dolly or another truck cab similar to maneuvering a boat through a cove of jutting rocks.

I needed to find the dolly that looked most like something I could handle alone. That metal loop in the front of the dolly is what I had to lift onto the cab's hitch and later onto the back of a trailer. Over the months when co-drivers and I had selected a dolly, each had imparted his or her bit of wisdom about what sort of dolly to get. I had been told that shorter dollies are heavier since there is less leverage between the dual wheels with the large fifth wheel hitch that sat atop the dolly's axle and the pointed loop near the front where the brake lines and chain hooks and sometimes a built in power cord were attached. Longer dollies can be a bit easier to lift while dollies with a small, hard rubber wheel under the pointed loop are heaviest of all. I didn't see any dollies with that small wheel today. Instead, I found a dolly that looked lighter than the others.

I made sure to tuck the brake lines inside the shallow basket between the loop and the axle so they wouldn't get driven over or scraped on the concrete while being towed. Then I undid the latch of the hitch on the back of the cab and walked up to the point of the dolly. Squatting down to use my legs I lifted that point and walked it up to the hitch. The weight and the rolling of the wheels made it feel like the dolly had a mind of its own. But this wasn't my first rodeo. I had helped other drivers with dollies. I had made sure to do so in order to be able to set up solo. Still I felt relieved to get this and every step out of the way. Each step felt like a minor victory in a small battle to leave the terminal.

I clicked the latch of the hitch closed over the dolly's tip and drove around the building, past the lot where drivers left loaded trailers for the yard dogs, the small vehicles designed strictly to move trailers between the loading docks and the drop lots. If no freight was ready, an empty trailer might be dropped in the outgoing lot where loaded trailers awaited transport to another terminal or a butthead.

Entering the lot, I looked for the back trailer. Some trailers stood parked in the lot's open area, their back doors closed and the door latch sealed against theft. Most seals, composed of either a weak aluminum strip or a plastic ribbon, could be broken almost effortlessly with a pocket knife. Other trailers had a more rugged metal bolt seal. The bolt could also be broken easily with a cutter, but they provided a modicum of greater security. Mostly a seal showed a trailer's contents hadn't been tampered with, rather than physically preventing theft. All seals have a number written on them that, along with each trailer number, helps assure the correct trailers get taken to their intended destinations.

Looking for a match with the dispatch slip, I drove along glancing at the large numbers painted on the sides of the trailers. Some trailers stood parked in the middle of the lot and others against the doors of the dock. I spotted the back trailer destined for Meridian against a dock door and prepared to back the dolly up to it.

The dolly needed to be set straight in front of the trailer in order to back up the dolly's fifth wheel into the trailer's latch pin, the thick metal pin that hangs down underneath the trailer and connects to the fifth wheel hitch. But backing a trailer is easier than backing a dolly. The longer the object the easier backing is. The trailers we pulled were 28 feet long while dollies reached only about 8 feet in length. Consequently, when a driver backed up, the dolly could veer to the side more quickly than a trailer until the dolly became pinched against the tires behind the cab. In a mini jackknife neither the cab nor the dolly could move further backward until the cab pulled forward again to straighten up their alignment. Of course, with proper steering the dolly never touches the cab's tires.

With the back trailer to my right I turned the wheel of the cab to the left and drove forward a few feet in front of the trailer, hoping to create a straightforward presentation, but with a short backing distance between the dolly and the trailer. Then I began

169

what could be a quick and easy back up or the see-saw motion of backing and straightening then backing again while working to align the dolly with the trailer. Though I didn't know it this chill morning, the quality of the dolly's tires could make the wheels behave erratically when backed. Also, the grade of the pavement on the yard made a tremendous difference. The concrete that made up each terminal yard had been designed to be flat. More or less. Each yard's surface had subtle contours, however. Alone or with a co-driver, I often struggled to push a dolly uphill or, equally difficult at times, to prevent a dolly from rolling downhill. Each dolly is supposed to have a hand operated button that turns on the dolly's brakes. Many of them didn't work.

After using the truck to get the dolly close and straight in front of the back trailer, I climbed out of the cab and, grabbing a pair of gloves, walked back to unlatch the dolly from the back of the cab's hitch and roll it right up against the trailer. Because the dolly's wheels are heavier, the pointed loop in front of the dolly often wanted to rise up in the air or plunge downward. Holding on to the dolly I fought to keep the weighty point from either falling to the ground or rising skyward. Standing at the head of the dolly and rolling it back or forth while trying to prevent the whole contraption from giving into gravity felt like a sort of slow motion underwater dance and a definite exercise in appreciating the three dimensionality of space. Pushing, pulling, and balancing I managed to center the dolly against the black vertical stripe painted on the front of the trailer that indicated where the heavy pin waited underneath to be snapped into the fifth wheel of the dolly.

The cool air felt good while I struggled to roll the dolly back the last couple of feet. In rain or shine, night or day, cold or hot, handling a dolly, especially on an uneven surface really took some doing. When I rolled a dolly, positioned it, or hitched it up to a cab or trailer, the effort could take every bit of strength my body possessed. Not every female could set up double trailers alone. The only females I knew of who regularly built their own sets of trailers were taller than average for women.

One male co-driver had described the plight of a petite female he'd driven with who toiled to build a set alone and suffered a severe muscle pull in her back. In great pain she, nonetheless, drove out to a butthead and, after exchanging trailers, knew she couldn't get any rest in the required ten hour break. Instead of bunking down for that break, she drove back to the terminal immediately. Naturally, she had gone well over the legal limit of eleven hours driving per day and was instantly fired, as a result. He didn't know if she got any worker's compensation for that injury.

Before driving away or connecting the dolly to the trailer, a driver has to make sure that the door of the trailer is shut and sealed. At this early morning hour the workers who loaded the boxes were not around. But you never knew if dispatch personnel might be. A driver had to be sure no one remained in a trailer before backing the dolly under it. One driver had told the tale of a loader who had been in a trailer one day when a driver backed up, lifting the trailer onto the dolly's fifth wheel and engaging the pin with a not uncommon jarring motion of the trailer. Inside, a loader lost his balance when the trailer shifted and fell several feet into the bottom, breaking his arm. Loader or no loader, if someone had committed the oversight of leaving the trailer door open, I'd have to call or drive around to dispatch to get someone in the office to pull the door closed, seal it, and record the seal number before driving away from the dock. Happily, I found this trailer closed and sealed.

Next, I had to find the front trailer. A nearby trailer matched the number on the dispatch slip. I backed up to the front trailer's hitch until the cab's fifth wheel pin closed with a loud clanging sound of metal on metal. I climbed out of the cab, stood next to the grid of the catwalk and attached the brake lines and power cord between the cab and the front trailer. Then I stepped over to the landing gear, the thick posts that hold up the front of a trailer when no truck supports it. I pulled out the handle that rests alongside the trailer when the rig moves down the road. Clicking the mechanism into place, I spun the handle in a circle about forty times until the posts and their square footrests gradually lifted from the ground far enough to drive without scraping them against the pavement.

Hitching up to the front trailer to bring it over to the dolly and back trailer was a piece of cake. Backing up to the dolly and aligning with the back trailer was more of a challenge. A driver needs open area in front of the dolly. Sometimes other trailers or the corner of a building, a light post or an ill-placed dolly abandoned on the yard by another driver could make backing more difficult. On this day a row of three or four trailers parked nearby presented the difficulty. The front trailer had to be in line with the back trailer, but because of the other nearby trailers, the cab would have to be at an odd angle. Even with a clear area to work in, my lack of experience would have caused me to shuffle back and forth before getting the rig in position.

I drove the front trailer up to the dolly in an approach such that the rig could be aligned. Then I backed up, keeping an eye on the trailers close by. I didn't want to smash a headlight, bend a mirror or scratch the paint on the cab or the parked trailers. Backing up, the front trailer came too far from the mark. So I pulled forward and began again. I jockeyed back and forth several times, not quite getting it right. I felt frustrated, but kept trying. Until persistence and the eye of a helper saved the day.

Another driver parked his cab nearby and set a dolly in front of a trailer four or five dock doors away. Seeing my predicament, he then walked over and stood where I could see him in the side mirror. Then he motioned which directions to turn the wheel, this way and that. At times, I couldn't quite believe how far he suggested turning the wheel in one direction or another. But keeping an eye on those parked trailers in front, I followed his suggestions, backing up the front trailer right where it needed to be. I waved a simple "thank you" out of my open window, and he nodded an acknowledgement before climbing into his cab and driving off to find his front trailer.

We never spoke, nor were introduced. In the dim light of predawn, he simply stepped in to help another driver. I'd seen this sort of ad hoc assistance on the yard before. Often drivers help each other with or without being asked. Occasionally, random drivers asked me to help position a particularly heavy dolly or to wave a trailer back, holding up a closed fist to signal a stop before a trailer bumped a dolly. I'd never refused to help anyone else, and on the couple of occasions when I asked for help to open a stubborn hitch, for instance no one ever refused to help me. A camaraderie of: "We're all in this together," has got to be one of the truisms among good-natured truck drivers.

Though I felt triumphant at this stage, the set up wasn't complete. I walked back to the dolly and lifted the heavy pointed loop onto the hitch at the rear of the front trailer then got back behind the wheel. Carefully, I backed the dolly's fifth wheel under the back trailer. The back trailer lifted slightly once the dolly's slanted fifth wheel platform eased its landing gear off the ground. Slowly continuing backward the pin clicked into the dolly's fifth wheel loudly enough to be heard up in the cab with the engine running and the ventilation fans blowing.

Again I climbed down and set to work connecting the brake lines and power cord on the dolly between the trailers, a sense of relief washing over me. Once the dolly connected the trailers, the worst was over. After checking the lights and bringing the dispatch slip into the office with the seal numbers written down, I'd be ready to roll out the gate on my first bona fide solo run.

Two hours after starting my first complete solo set I lay the dispatch slip on the counter in front of a gray-headed clerk named Shawn. For an experienced driver two hours would be an unusually long amount of time to build a set unless something had gone unexpectedly wrong. Most experienced drivers took between thirty to forty five minutes. Months later a co-driver, who had only ever driven 53 foot trailers prior to working at our company, exclaimed, "I'm used to a fifteen minute turnaround!" With no dolly to deal with dropping a 53 foot trailer and backing up to another one felt like a walk in the park on the rare occasions I pulled them, with or without a co-driver.

Shawn checked the trailers' numbers and their seal numbers with the computer system. His eyes shifted back and forth behind his half glasses from the screen to the slip of paper on the desk.

"Are you sure the front trailer is 33185?" he asked.

"I checked each number religiously. Did I get it wrong?" I asked, feeling a sense of dismay begin to filter through me.

"The seal numbers don't match what we have here," he said. "Where are you parked?"

"Under the roof by the shop."

"I'd like to double check, if you don't mind."

"Not at all. I don't want to take the wrong trailer."

We walked out to the golf cart the clerks and managers kept to travel around the many acres of pavement that surrounded the terminal. Shawn got behind the wheel and I sat on the back bench grasping one of the poles that supported the cart's small nylon roof. Droplets of rain dotted the pavement behind us while the cart tilted from side to side turning around the corners of the building. I looked down at the toes of my black shoes where spots of rain turned tiny circles even darker. If I'd picked the wrong trailer, I'd have to rebuild the set. I wondered how many more hours that would take. If I could leave immediately, I would be on time. If not, my first solo run would arrive at Meridian late. My thoughts were interrupted as we scooted up next to the rig.

"It's the right trailer number," Shawn declared.

Sure enough, the numbers stood out several inches tall.

"Good! So I can go?" I asked, feeling relieved again.

"Hang on," Shawn said, stepping between the parked trailers to jot down the seal number. With his head tilted to see through his half glasses he looked like a librarian inspecting the numbers on the spine of a shelved book. "Looks like you're good to go," he said, completing his notation.

Moments later I left the terminal on a true solo run. Moving the rig through the streets on the way to the highway felt different from leaving the shop in Memphis with only a cab and a whole day to ramble back to Fort Worth. Today I had two trailers to pull and eight hours of driving when I could rely on no one but myself. Like any driver, if anything went wrong mechanically, I could call Wayne or the fleet service that had towed the overheated truck that Hilda and I had driven months ago. But it could take hours for anyone to reach a truck out on the open road. The phrase, "Where the rubber meets the road," became a little more real.

Three hours later just over the border from Texas I exited the highway for a break at a truck stop near Shreveport, Louisiana. I came to a stop at a traffic light then turned down the service road accelerating toward the truck stop's main building when the truck lagged. The dashboard warning lights came on, and the wheels rolled ever so slowly. The engine had died. Going at slow speed on the service road the truck's momentum quickly played out. Luckily, there was time to ease over to the side of the road so other trucks could pass by. Rolling to a stop, I set the parking brakes and turned on the hazard lights.

What now? I wondered. At least, the truck had come to a standstill close to a truck stop, if something needed repair. Naturally, first I would try to restart the engine. I ran through the procedure and some of the lights on the dashboard flashed off and back on, but the engine remained silent. I tried again then waited a few minutes. Then yet again. Still nothing.

A trucker headed the other way on this two-way service road stopped opposite me. The driver inside made a cranking motion with his hand. I rolled down the window.

"What's up?" he asked.

"The engine just died," I answered.

"You need help?"

I didn't want to give up trying to restart the engine just yet. Anything else seemed premature. I lifted my cellphone to eye level and, tilting it back and forth, fibbed, "Help's on the way."

I thanked him for stopping. He waved and drove on. He was followed by a couple of others drivers who paused to offer help.

This must be one of those days, I decided, when a call to the boss will cure the truck. I reached Wayne's voicemail and left a message then sat and waited. Every so often I tried to start the truck, thinking maybe I just hadn't done something right. After a while, the cellphone rang from the dashboard's cupholder.

"Hey, Karen. You called?" Wayne asked. I explained that the truck had died on the service road and wouldn't restart.

"Let me try it again with you on the phone," I smiled to myself, wanting to see if my whimsy might prove correct. I went through the steps once more. The engine rumbled back to life. "I knew a call from you would fix the truck, Wayne."

"Yeah, okay. Glad to hear it."

We said our good-byes, and after taking a break at the truck stop, I got back on the road and finished the run to Meridian uneventfully. Why the engine had died, I'll never know. Why didn't the truck restart the first several tries? Later I would learn that the computer components that manage the ignition system could just be damn touchy. In any event, the truck purred unerringly for the rest of the run.

At half past one in the afternoon I exited to the Astro Plaza on the south side of the Interstate just west of Meridian. The Plaza took up dozens of acres with a building that housed a store and café next to fuel lanes in the corner closest to the highway exit. The building looked like the architect had been inspired, perhaps, by the Jetsons television show. Everything appeared to have dropped down from the sky in this little section of eastern Mississippi like a drifting leaf that had floated through the race-for-space decade of the 1960s before alighting here.

Driving past the building I spotted several trucks with our company logo lined up in painted off parking spots. The parking spots continued behind the building to the far corners of the property. I drove past the parked trucks then circled around to pull up straight in the painted lines within the pack of company trucks. Some drivers, having already exchanged trailers, walked inside to eat lunch at the café. Other drivers exchanged trailers while I set the parking brakes. Still others waited for the driver they met each day to arrive. Our company's trucks continually drove in and out of the virtually empty parking lot that would be full by nightfall.

As Coach had done in Virginia, I picked up my cellphone to call the automated computer system to see what trailer numbers my truck should return with, but my phone had no signal. If I knew the trailer numbers, I would know who to trade trailers with. A couple of spaces over a guy in wire frame glasses walked past his cab. I climbed down from my truck and approached.

"Excuse me, are you from Atlanta? I've got trailers from Fort Worth," I inquired, using the only information I knew.

"Nah, I'm from Charlotte. Anyway I meet a guy from Dallas."

"My phone doesn't work, and I've never been here before. I don't know who to trade with."

"Are you driving the truck that normally takes this run?"

"As far as I know."

"Whoever you meet with will know your truck number."

I thanked him and returning to my truck sat in the driver seat and waited, completing the logbook's page for the day. I also spread my sleeping gear out on the bunk. I'd seldom slept in a truck that didn't have a co-driver behind the wheel, taking us towards our destination or returning us to our home base. This time I could get some rest before driving back myself, I thought, looking forward to the possibility. Some rest in a truck with the engine running so I wouldn't freeze in the cold night at a truck stop, alone. The thought of being alone in an unfamiliar place chilled me more than the cold.

A short time later a truck pulled up beside mine and a young dark-haired guy climbed out and walked around to my window. I rolled down the glass.

"Hi, I'm Todd," he said.

"Hi, Todd. I can't reach the system to call in. Are you from Atlanta? "

"Yeah, this is my regular run. I always trade out with the guys in this truck," he said, handing his paperwork up to me. He added, "I'll call in. That way the system will dispatch both of us."

All we had to do was switch out our trailers. Unlike building a set or even breaking down a set, trading trailers is a breeze. We each drove out from under our front trailer after lowering the landing gear. Then we each backed under the front trailer of the other's set. Raising the landing gear was the last step.

Afterward I marched through the sunny, cool afternoon air and entered the café. Rows of tables extended across the open space of the building to the right. Shelves filled with food and toiletries, heavy-duty gloves and lights and other trucking paraphernalia stood to the left. I walked into the café past customers already seated. Families with kids, but mostly truckers, eyed me with my company shirt and little green bookbag when I went by. I settled down alone at one of the gold-flecked, white table tops. A waitress came by with a menu and then filled the order with the welcome and easy banter of old-fashioned southern hospitality. I ate a grilled chicken sandwich and fries with iced tea before returning to the truck for a night's sleep starting at about two in the afternoon.

Laws required a break of at least ten hours before heading back home. Thus, I couldn't leave until midnight. But I felt slightly, pleasantly tired and remained hopeful about getting at least a good, long nap, having woken at two that morning to get to the terminal at three.

Once inside the cab I pulled forward a couple of rows nearer to the building. To relieve myself late at night, I'd use a plastic pee bag. But if necessary, I wanted to keep the walk to the building through the dark to a minimum. Then locking the doors, I secured their handles with the seat belt straps to slow someone down, if they did get a door open. If so, the belt would create resistance. Next I pulled out a large pair of men's brown rubber boots, bought just for solo runs, and set them in the middle of the cab floor where anyone looking inside could see them. Then I stepped into the sleeper compartment, closed the curtains and lay down. In the bunk I closed my eyes and wished for sleep.

While I rested, my whole body jiggled. The truck didn't move down the road, of course, rather it moved like a bowlful of jelly, vibrating with the engine. In the middle of winter, if I turned off the engine, in a short time the entire cab would be filled with freezing air. If it had been summer, scorching air. Though the cab shook, the jiggle and hum was a vast improvement over the bumpiness and noise of going down the road while someone else drove.

I lay still on my back for a half an hour, turned over on my side and lay still for a half hour more. Then I sat up and clicked on the radio, cursing my choice of tea for the lunchtime beverage minutes before trying to sleep. I hadn't thought about the caffeine content. Maybe I just needed some more time awake, I decided.

Opening the curtain that shut out the bright afternoon light, I slipped a CD from my bag into the truck's player. Then I adjusted the side mirrors so the sides of the truck and trailers could be viewed while standing at the curtain and without leaving the sleeper. I put in another CD when the first one finished. Then another. While the music played I flipped through an appropriately boring magazine filled with little more than advertisements.

The afternoon marched on toward evening. I turned the music off, closed the curtains and lay down again. But every time I reclined my sinuses stuffed up. I coughed and cleared my throat, blew my nose, tried resting on one side, then the other. Nothing worked. Opening the bookbag I took out an over the counter decongestant, swallowed a tablet with a drink of bottled water and lay back down.

Outside the sun's setting lessened what few rays of light slipped through the cracks of the curtain while I came to a gradual realization. My brain not only refused to trundle gratefully toward sleep, instead the neurons flicked on while the sun went down. What was the reason? I wondered. Was I this nervous or scared to be alone in the truck? I didn't think so. I'd been alone overnight before. First the tea, then the decongestant. My brain just didn't want to enter sleep mode.

Over the past couple of hours the sounds of other truck engines had come and gone. Opening the curtains I saw on either side trucks that had parked next to mine. I closed the curtains so the steady trickle of drivers that walked to and from the building couldn't see into the sleeper. Then I switched the light on and read some more, adjusted the air vents, then lay still with my eyes closed for long stretches of time while the hours crept by.

Mid-evening came. People all over America watched television and ate dinner before they slept in their own beds.

Late evening inched by.

Then midnight arrived. I hadn't slept, but legally I could go. Once on the road, I figured, sleepiness would come. Just then there was no point in waiting at the truck stop any longer.

I climbed out and walked around the rig, making sure both fifth wheel pins remained secure and all the lights still worked. The long rig took up two spaces, the back trailer reaching into the second one. A truck cab bobtailing, with no trailers, had parked in the space behind. After I left, no doubt, a tired driver pulling off the Interstate would consider himself lucky to back his 53 foot trailer into the vacated spot.

But first I drove the long rig far ahead so the trailers could snake out from between the trucks parked next to them. Then I drove up to the fuel lanes. Along the way, I peered around the truck stop. Far as the eye could see, row upon row of trucks filled the lot. Some of these men and women would sleep well tonight while I started for home.

Almost every run Wil and Wayne managed headed eastward from DFW. I had come up with a rhyme for coping with the myriad pathways and many directional signs that dotted the highway interchanges: 'East is least. West is best.' When a driver is dispatched eastward and home lies to the west, that is.

Maybe which direction to take seems obvious, but Romeo himself had once confessed to entering the highway and driving back for a few hours in the direction his co-driver had come before he realized his error and resumed the intended direction.

I followed the signs and entered the highway, heading back across the state of Mississippi. Back over the river at Vicksburg I steered the truck into Louisiana. Then I felt the sleepiness that wouldn't come hours earlier descend on me like a wave.

The rows of rigs that lined the truck stop parking lots and rest stops along the highway reminded me of camels gathered around forbidden oases. No room remained for one more long truck that couldn't back out of a nose-in space. I continued down the highway looking at the service roads littered with trucks parked on the shoulders. Their improvised parking places formed a monument to the desperation a driver feels when he or she needs a place to stop and rest, even risking a ticket for illegal parking to bring a rig to a halt and pull closed the bunk curtains.

The clock on the dash read several minutes past 3 a.m. when I drove hopefully into a rest stop in northern Louisiana. Trucks packed the parking lot. Slowly, I steered past the parked vehicles, careful not to clip the edges of a trailer or a cab. More trucks spilled out onto the shoulders of the entrance ramp that led back onto the highway. Though parking on the ramps was often illegal, too, these spaces may provide the only places available to exhausted drivers.

I had just promised myself to keep an eye out for signs advertising upcoming truck stops when a space came into view, in the dirt between the entrance ramp and the highway. Between two trucks enough room to parallel park a set of double trailers awaited. I drove into the tire treads of the last truck that had parked there and climbed into the bunk. I closed my eyes, my conscious brain shutting out like a light.

Only a couple of hours later I awoke. Knowing I would have to drive into the Fort Worth terminal and break down the set on my own was another challenge that in my inexperience left me feeling tense. Yet, maybe by just having the nerve to do a completely solo run I'd earned another vertebra in my trucker's backbone. I climbed down to check the rig, then pulled out from the rest stop grateful to have at least taken the edge from my exhaustion.

After a short time back on the road, it became clear that two hours of sleep wasn't enough. But I didn't want to stop again. I wanted to get back and drop these trailers then go home to get some real rest. My eyelids weighed heavy as manhole covers, and once again I quaked with exhaustion. With no co-driver to disturb I popped a CD into the player, cranked up the volume to the max and did a scream-sing along to the music. I pounded the steering wheel to the rhythms, turned on the cruise control and pounded my feet on the floorboards, too.

To stay alert in any circumstances I most often played "Now What" by Lisa Marie Presley or "Can't Take Me Home" by P!nk. If one of those CDs wasn't at maximum audio, then Shania Twain sang some of the best crossover country hits, or Patsy Cline's classics filled the cab. These women and others kept me awake and on the pavement for countless miles over many moons. More than one day or night they may have saved my life. Trucking may be a mostly masculine endeavor, but the morning of that solo run, I drove down the road with music from kick-ass chix blaring out of the speakers, estrogen streaming from the windows like billowing smoke!

Chapter 13: "That's when we knew we were screwed."

On a team run a couple of months later I met a co-driver who reminded me a bit of *Popeye* the sailor man. His thin hair and plain looks were accented not with a pipe stem, however, but with the near constant presence of either a cigarette or a lollipop stem. If not one of those items, then he chewed gum or sucked on a peppermint or a cough drop. When he got tired of those, Sarge dipped snuff and spat out the results into an empty coffee cup he kept sitting in a dashboard cupholder. He emptied that cup by rolling down the window while he drove down the highway and slinging the contents against the side of the truck. By the end of the week long brown streaks of dried tobacco juice and saliva painted the driver side of the sleeper compartment. Thankfully, Sarge's modern art canvas had no fragrance detectable while in the bunk. It remained merely an eyesore on the outside. When Sarge had nothing else to gratify his restless mouth he simply licked his lips or smacked them together. He appeared to be oblivious to the constant motion of this nervous habit. By then I had come to know and enjoy running with many co-drivers, whatever qualities they possessed.

Wayne had set up my first drive with Sarge when he called and explained the run. "I have a team of older guys who run up to Toledo out of Dallas," Wayne began. "One of them is out for the next couple of days for a doctor's appointment." Wayne's comment reminded me that when a team driver, whose route normally took him out two days at a time, missed work for any reason, he usually lost two day's income instead of just one.

"Who would I be driving with?"

Wayne had given me the name of the guy I would come to call Sarge from his service in the Army. I met Sarge at the Dallas terminal to start his run to Toledo at about midnight. We would get to the Ohio terminal about twenty four hours later. At the cusp of his senior years, Sarge had been driving a truck for a long time, though most of that time with a different company. At the Dallas terminal he quite expertly backed up the trailers and the dolly. Like any helpful co-driver I climbed out of the cab to set up the trailers each time he stopped. Some drivers stayed in the cab while the "yardman," or woman, cranked up the landing gear, positioned the dolly or hooked up the brake and electrical lines. Sarge kept getting out of the cab and proceeding with the set up like he was on his own, even after I had begun to assist. At his age, naturally, Sarge could be called "old school." Maybe he didn't want help or didn't want a woman to help. Maybe he had convinced himself that I couldn't possibly know how to hook up the lifelines. With either a man or a woman co-driver, it might be a point of pride to set up alone. I would gladly adjust to whatever his wishes might be so I asked sincerely.

"Do you want me to help, or just stay out of the way?"

"I'd rather have help than not," Sarge replied in a gruff voice altered by decades of tobacco use. So I helped anyway possible, sometimes just cranking the landing gear, if nothing else.

With our set built we headed out the gate, and I retired to the sleeper bunk, though not for long. At one in the morning Sarge drove our trailers through the gates of a nearby suburban facility. We dropped those trailers and picked up a couple more bound for Ohio. Personally, I didn't like having to pick up and drop trailers at different local places. Juggling trailers could be a necessary part of the job, but over time added many extra hours of work with more opportunities to risk a serious muscle strain or to enjoy being out in all kinds of weather with little or no additional pay. All our pay was strictly mileage based. Mileage between local sites doesn't add up to much. Thus, for driving, breaking down and rebuilding sets over a couple of hours or more, a driver might only receive five to ten bucks.

Sarge started driving again just before 2 a.m. and I went to the sleeper to rest in earnest. Five hours later we pulled into a small gas station in southwest Arkansas that also had some diesel pumps and a parking lot big enough to accommodate a handful of trucks. I climbed down from our truck and entered the station. Returning with a sausage and egg biscuit, I sat down in the passenger seat. Since driving a truck and not always having a familiar food choice nearby, I'd braved the risks of indigestion to dip into such comestibles as truck stop corn dogs, chicken strips, burritos, pizzas, and more. Along the way, I'd had quite good gustatory luck.

Sarge returned to the truck and climbed into the driver seat. "You wanna drive?" Sarge asked in his friendly, twangy tone.

I had begun to feel leery again of driving off the book. If pulled over, we could be fired if our managers discovered that one of us received a ticket when the other driver was logged in. Also, a driver could be blamed for the other's speeding if caught by one of the company spy vans. Or worse. What if I was the driver of record, the one logged in driving, and my co-driver had an accident? Naturally, whoever had been driving would have to speak with police at the scene. Then it would be a matter of time before our employers would know who had been driving versus who *should have* been driving.

Most recently I'd driven with Romeo or Hilda, and they both drove by the book. Maybe that was why I felt a bit taken aback by Sarge's instant expectation that we would drive a five and five, where each driver is at the wheel for five hours then trades out. Legally, each driver should be at the wheel for his or her roughly ten hour shift. Often drivers changed out every two and three hours, whatever suited them. But I wondered, why did Sarge instantly trust me to drive on his book? We had just met, but the practice was so common that it was almost expected by some drivers.

If I drove for Sarge, he would eventually drive on my book, too. I didn't yet know how Sarge drove, experienced or not.

"You haven't finished your ten hours," I said.

"We always change out here," Sarge answered, referring to his regular routine with his co-driver.

"If I drive, it'll be for ten hours. Are you okay with that?"

Sarge agreed and retired to the bunk. I would drive across the rest of Arkansas then through Tennessee and into Kentucky before we switched out again. That day Sarge and I logged what we drove and drove what we logged. That just felt better, at least right then.

With Sarge in the bunk I drove through Little Rock and into eastern Arkansas. Throughout the morning we went in and out of rainstorms. The gray smudge of a storm would appear on the horizon, and I would drive into the rain, slowing down. Then that storm would blow across the roadway, or we would simply outpace it into sunshine again. Wet and dry, over and over again. Such weather is a prime time for collisions. Often motorists skidded on the slicker rain slicked highways, expecting a car to brake or maneuver the same on both wet or dry pavement.

By late morning I saw the telltale signs of a slowdown ahead. Brake lights on vehicles of every size and description clogged both lanes in front of the rig. I slowed the truck then gradually came to a stop near the scene of a collision. Police cars with flashing lights parked across the traffic lanes. The crew from fire and ambulance vehicles worked clearing up the wreckage caused by some momentary inattention or a need for speed or, perhaps even, a fit of pique.

When the Interstate must be closed for a lengthy time, officers sometimes direct traffic onto nearby roads. From time to time, along with all the other traffic, I had to drive off the highway and follow the route of a detour until authorities re-directed traffic back onto the highway. To do so normally vehicles leave the highway on an exit ramp. But if there is no exit ramp between the closure and the line of vehicles filing off the highway police may direct traffic to make a u-turn and drive the wrong way up an entrance ramp in order to get off the highway.

Waiting in this slow down I remembered such a time. I had been driving while my co-driver rested in the bunk when we approached such a closure. On that rainy day police directed traffic the wrong way up an entrance ramp. My eyes scanned the road ahead trying to measure the geometry of paved surface and what I'd come to understand to be the turning needs of a 73 foot long doubles rig. Remembering Dutch's encouragement to take up all the real estate God gave and the highway department paved, I tried to visually gauge whether the width of the pavement offered enough space for a long curving u-turn with two trailers. I certainly didn't want to sit and wait for what must be hours of delay while the road remained closed.

By then I had developed a sensibility I suspect all truck drivers possess sooner or later – the drive to drive – that is the wish to go and go and go. Once behind the wheel, I seldom wanted to slow down or stop. If any delay presented itself in front of my windshield, my mind instantly started to seek a possible remedy to keep going, to slow if necessary and, hopefully, not to stop. Whether a road gator blocked the lane ahead or a wreck blocked the entire road or the weather simply slowed traffic, I thought, how can I get around this? A driver always wants to keep moving forward.

On that occasion a policeman in a yellow raincoat waving an illuminated baton had stood in the left lane where I would have to drive to have any hope of making it up that entrance ramp. He walked over from his position motioning cars up the ramp and approached the truck. He came nearer the driver window, and I stopped in front of the traffic that crawled along behind. Then the policeman climbed the steps to the driver side and grabbed hold of the side mirror to balance himself while I opened the window.

"You're the first set of doubles to come along," he had said, leaning up to the window then looking ahead at the path of the detour. "I know you can't back this baby up. Do you think you can make a u-turn and drive forward up the entrance ramp?"

"I think so, but I'll need both lanes, even the shoulder."

"Alright, I'll call back and hold off traffic coming up from behind," he said, tapping the walkie-talkie on his shoulder.

I thanked him. Then he climbed down.

"Take your time," he said, waving me forward.

Just as when a co-driver stopped for a break, I often woke when the truck began to trickle through the ebb and flow of congestion or the aftermath of a collision. I had wondered what my co-driver might think of the slow down. If she had been awake or woken up, she might have even heard my conversation with the policeman. But I never heard any stirring in the sleeper while I eased the truck forward. Maybe she was getting some good rest. I sure hoped so. Plus, I hoped never to talk to a policeman while driving on anyone else's logbook. I happened to have been logged into the driver seat already.

Beginning the turn, I had steered the long rig into the left lane and partway onto the shoulder, eyeing the entrance ramp on my right, too. Drivers call guiding a truck through a parking lot or around obstacles "threading the needle." So I steered the world's largest thread in a big curving loop that amounted to an extremely sharp right turn. I looked in the side mirrors, careful not to get the left tires off the edge of the pavement where they could slide or get stuck in the soft rain soaked soil. In the meantime, I hoped the brake lines between the trailers had enough give to stretch and not to snap, engaging the emergency brake system and stopping the rig in its tracks until a repair truck could be summoned.

I had imagined the truck's trajectory on the concrete lanes and asphalt shoulders. The rig rolled around the curved path. Turning the wheel sharply to the right, bringing the front of the truck across the left shoulder and left lane then into the right lane, a panicked thought crossed my mind. What if I'd been wrong?! What if I couldn't make this turn? Maybe I should have awakened my co-driver and asked her for another opinion on whether the rig could make this u-turn. I had wondered, should I stop and ask right then to avoid getting stuck?

No. Go and go and go!

With all due respect for safety I had discovered a new trucking truism: If I'm going to fail, I'm going to fail trying! I knew enough about a double rig's talents and limitations by then. What's more I knew how to guide the rig up to the edge of those limits. I kept moving forward. The front tires crossed the right lane then edged onto the right shoulder. The rig blocked the entire width of the highway like a giant metal snake. If Sesame Street's Big Bird had flown overhead, the letter of the day would have been 'U.'

The front left tire edged up near the farthest extreme of the right shoulder. The make or break moment had arrived. Either all wheels stayed on the pavement or some dipped into the muddy soil right next to it. I didn't want to off-road even a single bit, since a deeply textured surface could provide enough momentum to flip the back trailer over, even at low speed.

One doubles driver with our firm who had found himself on a closed off highway had tried to make it across the shallow dip in the grassy ribbon between the highway and the service road. The driver who told me the story had advised him against it, but he decided he knew better. His tractor and first trailer made it okay. Then with just a bit too much of a dip and a rise the back trailer pan-caked onto its side. Instant termination. No excuses. Any driver who flipped a trailer at any speed was dismissed. I imagined getting another trucking job with that record wouldn't be easy.

But on that day in my truck, the entrance ramp had finally stretched before the windshield like a runway in front of a pilot. The rig just had to straighten out before takeoff. The wheels edged along, remaining on the pavement. I only had to complete the turn. I began to feel the warmth of joy and relief wash over me, but the feeling quickly drained to my shoes with the sound of a loud rush of air. What had happened? I wondered. My head snapped to the right looking at the arcing trailers on that side. The rig still curled along, but the sound got louder. For a moment, a feeling of alarm stealing over me, I nonetheless kept crawling forward, kept looking in front and glancing to the side. All the trailers remained upright. Then in the gray-blue sky above a movement had caught my eye. The rotors of a medical services chopper thrashed the air while the craft zoomed overhead and zeroed in on the site of the auto collision. The loud noise had come from the chopper. That u-turn had been at low speed and on solid ground, but I felt like I'd added another vertebra on my expanding trucker's backbone.

Driving up the ramp that day and onto local roads a line of cars and trucks had filed off the highway and along a narrow pathway shadowing the Interstate. On detours the alternate path might be no more than a country lane. Then the rig spanned its share of the road from the middle paint stripe to the grassy shoulder. Often the Interstate lie within sight of a detour, but an entrance ramp might be miles ahead. Like a bizarre mechanical conga-line traffic could drive on for miles past farmhouses both used and abandoned, past fields shorn to a stubble that lingered in the rains, past barns, derelict sheds and tiny stores with neon signs flashing 'Open.' The word reflected across the mud puddles in their gravel parking lots. Eventually, a police car with lights flashing shone ahead like a beacon. Traffic slowed again and gradually drove up another entrance ramp, this time in the right direction. We were back in business.

But with Sarge resting in the sleeper I simply waited with motorists and other truckers until police cleared the road. Then traffic slowly uncoiled back up to highway speeds. Soon thereafter I drove into Tennessee, heading north at Nashville on I-65. Once the truck crossed the first few miles into Kentucky, Sarge came out of the sleeper and sat in the passenger seat. He instantly cracked open the window and lit a cigarette.

"I've got a headache," Sarge protested.

"Maybe it's from nicotine withdrawal," I teased.

"It probably is," Sarge replied firmly, taking the joke, but meaning every word of his response.

I drove along a stretch of I-65 that after several months still had workers laboring to widen the highway. While we coasted along the narrow lanes, Sarge and I chewed the fat. Soon Sarge asked "the question."

"What made you decide to drive a truck?" he asked.

I explained that I wanted a job then asked Sarge why he drove. Sarge described how, when he was a young man and had left the Army, he had taken a job driving from Oklahoma to the gulf coast of Texas and back each day. After practicing a week with an experienced man and having driven tractors, pickups and jeeps, the company assigned Sarge a truck of his own.

"You didn't go to driving school?"

"Didn't have 'em back in those days that I know of."

Knowing that every new driver I had met felt anxious starting out, I couldn't imagine driving a truck with so little training.

Then I asked if he'd been aware of the slowdown that day.

"I slept pretty good," Sarge said, flicking a bit of ash out the window. "What happened?" he asked.

"They had the highway shut down to clean up a wreck. At least we didn't have to leave the highway and drive on lanes even more narrow than this one. You know, how some detours can go on for miles and miles," I said.

"Hmm. On them little roads?"

"Yep," I nodded.

"They don't always think of doubles on detours. They can plan one at the last minute for an accident, you know? Them little roads can be tricky!"

Then Sarge explained that the first few times his regular co-driver had stopped at the Arkansas exit where we'd switched out driving, they hadn't been entirely familiar with the lay of the land. The exit led to an intersection with many roads, one to a nearby motel, one to another truck stop. The place we'd stopped at had a little road that went up to the diesel pumps right next to the southbound entrance ramp.

"You drove out of there going north," Sarge explained. "When you drive back out going to Dallas, you'll see. That little road that leads to the pumps has a sign." He moved his left hand in the air, over an imaginary sign, his cupped fingers emphasizing each word: "No trucks beyond this point."

"I thought that was the service road."

"Looks like it, don't it? But the service road is one driveway over," Sarge continued. "One day me and Dale, the guy I drive with, we was leaving there. He drove out, turned onto that little road. I was sittin' up here," Sarge said, pointing down at the passenger seat. "He started to drive down that road and we seen the entrance ramp was one road over from the road we was on."

"What did y'all do?"

"You know some of those roads go along the highway for a while then they have an entrance ramp a few miles down."

"Yeah," I nodded, having taken detours along similar roads.

"Well, the road went on a ways. Then it curved off into the countryside. That's when we knew we were screwed."

I laughed.

"It wasn't funny," Sarge corrected, lighting a fresh cigarette with the remains of one that he then stubbed out in a plastic cup.

"What happened then?" I asked, still seeing the amusing side of Sarge's dilemma.

"We found us a wide spot in the road. Then we broke that sonuvabitch down and rebuilt the set so we could head back in the direction we'd come. Cost us time and was a real pain in the ass. But there wasn't nothing else we *could* do."

A bit later we switched out at a Kentucky truck stop, and Sarge drove the rest of the way to the Ohio terminal. We arrived and did our turnaround, dropping the trailers we'd brought and picking up a new set to take back. Sarge had driven five hours from Kentucky. He would drive us back across Ohio and into Kentucky again where I would take the wheel. Thus, we each drove ten hours. As Sarge started back across Ohio, he looked like he could have used some sleep already. Once I'd had enough rest to drive my upcoming shift I sat up front to see how Sarge was doing. From time to time Sarge's eyes did a long blink or closed for a split second. Maybe I should have done the five and five, I thought.

We were a couple of hours away from the Kentucky truck stop where Sarge and his co-driver normally switched out. They did so first in Arkansas, then Tennessee, then Kentucky, then reversed that order on the way home. Since I couldn't sleep anymore, I stayed in the passenger seat to talk and make sure Sarge remained wakeful.

Often in the wee hours of the night or when the early morning rolled around, drivers parked to sleep, not only in the truck stops and rest areas, but also along the side of the service road. Parking where other traffic passes by looks a bit risky and is prohibited in some places. Again I noticed that many drivers risked a ticket to stop and sleep rather than fall asleep at the wheel. Their rigs lined service roads near exit and entrance ramps. At times drivers have nowhere else to go.

I asked Sarge what he thought of the practice. Between dips of snuff he explained that years ago even fewer places existed for truckers to stop. The Interstate didn't yet cover as many miles so drivers often pulled over on the shoulders of the narrow state highways to rest. They frequently slept in the driver seat because not as many trucks had sleeper compartments. Sarge knew some drivers who had done this, and they told him a little story.

"One night one of them boys pulled over on a dirt patch right next to the state highway and fell asleep," Sarge said. "Then a couple of old boys from his company drove by and seen him. They decided they'd have a laugh. They crossed the highway and pulled their truck nose to nose up to his. When they was stopped right in front of his truck they turned their headlights on bright and set off the air horn. The fellow who'd been sleeping ran out of that truck so fast . . . " Sarge laughed heartily, imagining the man's terror when he woke up, saw the headlights glaring at him through the windshield, heard the horn blaring and thought he was about to be hit head on.

I thought Sarge's story was funny and unintentionally poignant. Sarge just thought it funny. It is hard to fall asleep while laughing.

We made it to the truck stop and Sarge went inside to get a burger so he could rest without being woken by hunger. I needed to eat and take a break, too. I slung my little green bookbag on my shoulders to go inside, but before climbing out of the truck curiosity got the better of me. I picked up one of Sarge's cans of tobacco off of the dashboard and opened the lid. Feeling a little like a naughty child dipping into a cache of hidden cigarettes, I lifted the can to my nose and took a whiff. Just one sniff woke me up. I thought the stuff smelled strong as gasoline.

About the time I pulled in to our Arkansas switch out Wayne called. Sarge's co-driver would be out for the whole week. Would I cover the next run, too? I agreed.

While Sarge started the last five hours of driving to our home terminal we talked about Wayne. The only thing Sarge enjoyed more than a good joke was a good argument. In all the weeks we ran together we never once went out that we didn't have a nice, pleasant verbal fight with each of us finishing the discussion secure in the knowledge that the other met the definition of a complete idiot. Generally, to "win" an argument Sarge made a statement and simply repeated that statement against all counterpoints presented. For instance, that day we discussed how much money Wayne might make. Sarge insisted that, since Wayne wasn't a driver, he must make less. I insisted that, since he was a manager, Wayne must make more.

We could argue about anything, large or small. One day weeks later we rolled through Kentucky along the hilly stretch of highway thick with trees that I had once called the scary forest. Sarge drove through the afternoon hours while we talked about what it might be like to live in the woods we were passing through.

"There wouldn't be a damned thing to eat," Sarge opined.

"You could gather berries and hunt before building a garden," I said, recalling books about pioneers who'd had to find things to eat. "You know, if it was like the year 1800 all of a sudden and you were in the middle of nowhere."

"Nah," Sarge persisted. "There's nothing to eat out here."

"People survived on the frontier," I said. "They hunted and fished and gathered whatever else they could while gardening and even raising livestock."

"There's not a damn thing to eat out here," Sarge repeated.

Right when he finished that sentence the truck rounded a curve, and the windshield faced onto a meadow between two clumps of trees. Directly in front of us a flock of wild turkeys grazed, their magnificent plumage shimmering in the sunlight.

"There!" I exclaimed, pointing at the great American game bird. "If you had a rifle, you'd have dinner."

Sarge said nothing. Perhaps he thought, 'Damn woman! If I had a rifle, you'd be dinner for the bears!'

But he said nothing. Bless his heart.

We returned to Dallas. A gap of a few hours before heading back out presented enough time to go home, shower and change clothes. Sarge lived several hours away so he stayed with the truck, though he could shower in the terminal if he wanted.

Sarge and his absent co-driver had worked out their schedule so that Sarge always drove out first. As a substitute driver, I tried to adapt to my co-driver's routines, when possible. When co-drivers acted as if I should function exactly like their regular workmates did, I could have said, "Your regular co-driver's not here right now." Once when a co-driver behaved in an obnoxious way, I did say words to that effect. But over the months I began to take pride in being adaptable no matter what the circumstances. Even a trucker's backbone needs some flexibility. Thus, for our second run I decided to go ahead and drive the five and five with Sarge. Part of the time he would be driving on my book and vice versa. Getting a nap of a few hours was the best rest most team drivers could get on the road anyway. I understood why Sarge preferred the method. Instead of driving when rested, many times over the months I had had to wait seemingly endlessly for my shift to start only to find sleepiness knocking at my eyelids when my turn to sit behind the wheel finally came.

Five hours from Dallas Sarge paused at the same small truck stop in Arkansas. Then I drove us into Tennessee to the Jolly Trucker for a late breakfast or an early lunch. I parked in the gravel lot across the road, nearly empty at that hour. Then we walked to the truck stop in bright sunshine. The truck stop never did look beautiful. But at least the gleaming building looked welcoming in the light of day.

Sarge and I sat in the café where he got his usual grilled ham and cheese sandwich then slathered it with hot sauce. I mused that after years of tobacco use, Sarge must have about twelve surviving taste buds. The hot sauce no doubt woke them. In the meantime I tried my luck or rather risked my stomach lining on the buffet while it transitioned from breakfast to lunch. Naturally, I went for the lunch items reasoning that they were fresher. That day's special featured fried catfish, coleslaw, and hushpuppies.

Our meal over, Sarge and I returned to our truck. Sarge climbed aboard and entering the sleeper, started rolling up his bedding. I stood on the top, outside step by the driver seat. Facing into the cab, I gathered the wrappers and bottles leftover from my shift. I stuffed the items into a plastic bag to throw them away in a nearby trash can when a voice from the parking lot almost made me jump out of my skin.

"'Scuse me," the raspy female voice inquired. "Can I use your CB for a minute?"

Turning around I spied a woman standing a few feet away on the dusty, pebbled parking lot looking up at where I stood on the truck's step. Despite her boldly blonde hair, a cleavage-revealing purple blouse and matching short shorts she looked like her 50th birthday had come and gone several years earlier. The large, round lenses of her sunglasses glinted in my direction while a ring of bright red lipstick encircled her crooked teeth. The cigarette that she held between two fingers of one hand resting on her hip had to be one of thousands that had turned her skin to a leathery texture. Her other hand rested on a bright purple purse with a gold chain arm strap. Hollywood itself couldn't have created a more stereotypical-looking: Truck. Stop. Whore.

A bit flummoxed I replied, "No," without explaining that we didn't *have* a CB radio in this particular truck. Drivers had to supply CBs themselves. Neither Sarge nor his co-driver had sprung for one.

The woman turned around wordlessly in her high heel pumps and began to walk down the lonely looking country road that led away from the truck stop and the Interstate. I surmised that her pimp lived down that road and owned a CB himself. Maybe, he would have picked her up from her latest tryst, if she had been able to let him know the deed was done.

Eyeing some business cards for a truck stop masseuse that lie in the sun on the dashboard, I asked Sarge, "Would you have let her use the CB, if you had one?"

"Yeah," Sarge nodded.

"Even though she's a lot lizard?" I asked, using the term truckers call the women they keep in business.

Again Sarge said he would.

At the same time I felt bad for women trapped in prostitution others seemed to have passed up alternatives and accepted the world's oldest profession as their own. Such women and the men who pay them can make a truck stop feel less safe for law abiding women whether they are truckers or not. Even though I wore my company's uniform shirt, occasionally when I walked from my truck into a store, even from the fuel lane next to the building, sometimes men accosted me with offers of money for sex. I never answered any of them, just shot them a look meant to discourage them or shook my head 'No,' and kept walking. The phenomenon in trucking and elsewhere is just one of the conundrums of life on planet earth.

We continued on our trip with Sarge taking the wheel on my behalf. He drove on my logbook through the rest of Tennessee and into Kentucky. I slept what I could then sat in the passenger seat for the last several minutes before we switched out. Once we traded places again I would be back on my own log until we arrived at the Ohio terminal. But right then on the way to the next switch out Sarge and I chatted. While we did, I looked around at the scenery. From time to time I glanced in the side mirrors and back along the truck. Careful not to block his view of the mirrors I nonetheless noticed Sarge changing lanes a couple of times without checking those mirrors.

Then Sarge changed lanes again, almost hitting a small blue car driven by a woman sporting a dark ponytail. On the truck's right the car nearly swerved onto the shoulder, but the motorist managed to slow down enough to get behind our rig. I cringed, not only for her safety, but knowing that if she complained, the record would show I was behind the wheel. Sarge did not appear to notice her, though I didn't ask. With many years of experience, he wouldn't change. On later trips I simply elected to drive what we called a ten and ten, though our legal limit of driving remained at eleven hours per day.

Over a period of months Sarge and I drove together several more times. Then one week I noticed Sarge kept getting shorter. Or at least, the driver seat did. The air bag that held the seat up had a slow leak. With remarkable regularity the seat sunk and sunk until it needed to be raised. That would be nuisance enough. Unfortunately, the button a driver pressed to raise the seat had broken off. Sarge took a spare key out of a cupholder on the dash, inserted it into the notch the button had fallen out of and manually raised the seat once its short stature threatened to prevent him from seeing down the road the way he wanted.

Both Sarge and I drove a whole week with that awful sinking feeling. We both found the seat annoying, but like everything else in trucking, when yet another problem comes along you just roll with it. As the week wore on, the leak got worse and the seat sunk more frequently. It became our topic of conversation.

Driving down the highway on the way back to Dallas, Sarge exclaimed jokingly, "This seat should be in the middle of Wayne's living room, and he should have to sit in it."

I laughed. "I'm going to tell him you said that," I teased.

After the week of the sinking seat, I climbed wearily into my car and switched on the radio. Steering out of the company parking lot, I turned on the wipers against big, lazy raindrops that struck the windshield. Though it was a rainy night, when I pulled onto the darkened highway, I couldn't help but marvel at how blessedly easy it is to pilot a car versus a tractor cab pulling two trailers in a driver seat that has a mind of its own.

Chapter 14: "Yep, I trenched their front yard."

At any rate it's comforting to know a co-driver at least *has* a mind, even if some might appear to be a few light bulbs short of a Christmas tree. So far most of the men and women I had driven with had appeared reasonably intelligent, some very intelligent indeed. Others seemed to be perfectly acceptable drivers who have occasional flashes of brilliance while somehow living up to the stereotype of a trucker whose skull seems thicker than the rubber on the tires of a semi-truck. Stereotypes that may bring to mind expressions like dull as a doorknob or dumb as a bag of hammers.

Wayne called a couple of days after the week had started. "Hey, I got a run you're going to like," he began. "I've got a guy out for a couple of days. I need someone to finish the week for him."

The run to the Astro Plaza truck stop in Meridian, Mississippi took about eight hours one way. Sometimes Wayne spoke with a bit too much optimism about how long a run would take. He might say a run would return in the morning when it rolled in well into afternoon, and that was when we'd made good time. I found it better to do my own math when possible, adding hours for waiting on the other team at a butthead run or driving around the yard dropping and building our set on a terminal run. Drivers also stopped for the occasional meal or restroom break. Not to mention weather, traffic or construction zones.

Figuring time for this and that, I guestimated those sixteen hours driving back and forth would stretch to at least eighteen total, or with bad weather or other problems maybe twenty. Even so, a run that might include the time to go home for a nightly shower and a nap without having to find the time during the work day sounded tempting.

"Who's the co-driver?" I asked.

"His name is Doug. He'll be parked outside the Fort Worth dispatch office."

Accordingly, I arrived at the Fort Worth terminal at 5 a.m. and walked to the office. In a quiet corner under the fluorescent lights the truck sat parked. Dew coated the windows on this cool, spring morning. The doors were locked so, according to custom, I knocked on the window. Understandably, Doug would be resting in the bunk. A shadowy figure emerged from behind the closed curtains and unlocked the door. I opened the driver door and climbed aboard. Once I entered the truck, I wasn't able to get a strong first impression of Doug, since he simply receded mutely back into the sleeper. Even in my limited experience of several months, I'd never seen a driver who didn't at least greet his co-driver.

"I'm going to go get our dispatch slip," I volunteered.

No answer emerged from the sleeper. I went in the dispatch office, got our paperwork, then came back out and climbed into the driver seat again.

"Doug?" I addressed the closed curtains.

"Yeah?" a muffled voice replied.

"Just wanted to make sure this is the right truck," I said, since we'd had no conversation.

I slung my little green bookbag into the cubbyhole above the driver seat. The engine had been running when I arrived. Putting the truck in gear, I started off for the trailer yard, a dolly already in tow behind the cab.

Good practice made it essential to know Doug really was in the truck. If he had gone to the restroom or shower in my absence, I might have left the yard without him. Leaving without a co-driver on a team run really throws a wrench in the works. If that happens, a driver has to turn around at whatever point he or she either realizes the mistake or gets a call from Wayne. Drivers don't always exchange cellphone numbers so Wayne occasionally fielded calls from drivers who had been left behind during a break at a truck stop or a rest area, one presumes mistakenly. Though one driver admitted, he left a co-driver he disliked just to peeve him. Of course, he still had to go back and get the guy. Such mistakes or pranks could make a team absurdly late. On this particular run, since the turnaround was less than 24 hours, that mistake should only last one day. On a run with no time to spare, one that turned around immediately, such a boneheaded move could create a domino effect for the rest of the week.

I drove to the other side of the building in search of our back trailer while the curtains to the sleeper never opened. I'd gained more experience building sets on my own a few times by then, but still could have used Doug's help on this, the toughest part of any doubles run. An experienced driver who preferred to set up without assistance would normally say, "I got it," if he didn't want help. Though, usually, any driver expected to help his or her co-driver because the set up didn't belong to one driver or the other. The team had to hit the road together, thus they built the set together. A willingness to help was a normal courtesy that I extended to all my co-drivers, and which they had all extended to me, until I met Doug.

Naturally, Doug must have felt tired from the first days' work with his regular co-driver. Such tiredness is a given, not to be confused with recklessly waking or inconveniencing your co-driver. I had already sensed that an unspoken rule exists in trucking: that you expect to be tired, you expect to be inconvenienced, sometimes by being woken at odd times, but you respond to whatever the circumstances at hand happen to be without complaint. We all had to do that. Experienced drivers expected that of me, too.

While I circled the terminal locating our trailers, I wondered how anyone could get any real rest in the bunk while someone else built the set. While I backed the dolly and trailers, the truck changed direction every few seconds. I had to pull forward a few feet, back up a few feet. After several tries, I got the dolly lined up in front of the back trailer. Then I found the front trailer. Clang! Metal on metal resounded when the fifth wheel behind the truck cab snapped into position on the first trailer. Then I managed to back the front trailer up to the dolly. Back and forth, back and forth to position it just right. Next, I lifted the heavy dolly onto the rear of the front trailer and drove it under the back trailer. Clang! The other pin on the back trailer and dolly connected.

In the meantime the driver door must be open and shut multiple times. I climbed down and back up the cab steps after setting the dolly in front of the back trailer, then when hitching up to the front trailer, when lifting the dolly onto the front trailer hitch, then connecting all the lines and hoses between the trailers. Opening and closing the door each time. Finally, the set stood fully built. By the time I pulled out of the terminal the clock radio on the dash read 6:30 a.m. Ninety minutes had gone by while I completed a task a more seasoned driver could accomplish in half the time under normal circumstances. My time, while not ideal, was not unusual for my level of experience. I knew this from commiserating with other drivers, both new and old, who understood all that the job entailed.

I drove out of Fort Worth and paused for a break about four hours later at a small truck stop in Louisiana called the Dandy Lion. Then I drove across the rest of that state and entered Mississippi. Sometime just after the noon hour, while I steered the truck along, Doug poked his head out from between the sleeper curtains. I supposed he had slept well, and I was glad if he had. We were both safer, if each of us was well-rested while driving. Then Doug stepped out of the sleeper and sat in the passenger seat. With little introduction, he soon steered the conversation around to dating. Right away I got the impression that Doug was looking for a date with me after having merely sat next to each other for a few minutes. Sometimes that's all it takes, but it felt like an odd approach after a morning of so little interaction.

"It sure is hard to meet anyone when you're driving a truck," Doug said. "Have you dated any of your co-drivers or do you not like truck drivers?"

"I *am* a truck driver."

"Hunh," Doug said.

'Hunh' was one of Doug's most common remarks. Sometimes 'hunh' took the form of a question, sometimes an observation. Sometimes it was an expression of joy or of confusion. Sometimes

201

'hunh' communicated a combination of different thoughts or feelings. Doug got a lot of mileage out of 'hunh.'

"You're not against dating a driver then?" Doug asked.

"Not because he's a driver," I said, glancing at him.

Doug sat looking out the windshield casually chewing on his mustached upper lip before he asked "the question."

"Why do you drive a truck?"

"It's my job," I answered. "Why do you drive?"

"Hunh," Doug thought. "I guess it's my job, too."

Woods and heavy foliage whipped by the windows on either side of us while we both contemplated this, the smartest answer any co-driver ever gave when *he* answered "the question." Then Doug said, "It sure took you a while to set up this morning."

"I've been driving less than a year," I explained. "I've only set up on my own a few times. It's been some weeks, too. I've driven mostly in teams."

"Hunh," Doug offered.

Since he had brought up the subject, I took the opportunity to clarify, just in case he didn't know the etiquette normally involved in team driving. After all, Doug had been driving less than a year, too, according to Wayne and almost exclusively with Alex, his regular co-driver. Maybe he just didn't know enough to help co-drivers or to ask whether they wanted help.

"All the other times I've driven, my co-drivers were willing to help build the set, if I was driving out," I said. "If they were driving out, I've always helped them, unless they didn't want me to. Most of the time they wanted help."

"Alex always sets up on his own," Doug said.

Some drivers preferred to work alone. A driver at any skill level can benefit from the help of a spotter when backing, if nothing else.

"How long has Alex been driving?" I asked.

"A truck? For a long time, maybe twenty years," Doug said.

"Then setting up must not be that big of a deal to him."

"Probably not."

"Setting up is still kind of new to me," I said. "I appreciate it when someone helps."

Doug just shrugged like the nice guy he was. He never acted rude about setting up as a team, just clueless.

Finally, we arrived at the truck stop where we would change out trailers with another driver. I steered around the truck stop's main building onto the sea of asphalt marked off by white parking stripes. Immediately after I set the truck's brakes, Doug hopped out and walked into the building while I made the trade. Exchanging paperwork with the guy who met Alex and Doug's truck here every day, I apologized. We were a little late.

"No problem," the other driver assured.

We switched out our trailers then I, too, headed into the truck stop. I found Doug at one of the tables in the restaurant and sat down across from him. Once I could see him I noted that Doug was a good looking, honey blond guy. A dark green tee-shirt covered muscular shoulders. When he handled his cutlery and reached for his drink, handsome biceps bulged out of his sleeves, intermittently revealing the tan line between his lower arms and the lighter skin above. While we lunched Doug informed me that he was in his forties and lived with his mom. That didn't sound good, but considering he was out of town most of the week, it sounded understandable. Doug stayed in the truck and slept the few hours between daily trips in the bunk. Why rent an apartment for two days of the week when you live in a truck?

After lunch I visited the ladies' room then walked back to our truck to get ready to sleep while Doug drove back. Climbing into the cab, I stepped over a large box on the floor between the seats. I wasn't sure what the box was for, but some drivers had a variety of things they used to keep themselves awake or entertained while they rolled down the road – CDs, books on tape, food. There was no telling what Doug kept in that box.

I entered the sleeper and found the bed lifted up against the back wall, the storage compartment underneath exposed. Pushing the sleeping surface down and locking it in place, I unrolled my sleeping bag onto the bunk. Then I settled down expecting Doug to climb into our truck and begin the drive back to Fort Worth. If the truck was moving steadily down the highway, I might have a chance of catching a couple of zees. Instead, I lay down with a sense of anticipation that the driver door would open and shut at any minute. Then the truck would move in stop-start motions while Doug shifted the gears up to the highway entrance ramp. But Doug did not appear.

I tried to doze despite Doug's absence, but I kept hearing an odd buzzing sound. Over and over the sound came closer then faded away. Nevertheless, I tried to relax and get myself in the frame of mind to fall asleep in the middle of a sunny afternoon. Thus, when Doug pulled into the Fort Worth terminal, I would be ready to dash home for a quick shower and a solid nap before coming back to the terminal to start the process all over again. In any week, getting all the sleep possible during my co-driver's shift made sense. With some luck that rest could be supplemented with a deeper sleep at home during this week.

Yet, each time my mind started to drift into a restful state, the buzzing sound returned more strongly. Then the sound thinned out again, but never quite disappeared. And where was Doug, I wondered. I waited. More time passed. I looked at my watch. We had finished lunch more than half an hour ago. Generally, once drivers exchanged trailers they headed back immediately. I couldn't imagine what would keep a driver from wanting to complete his run. Then the buzzing sound penetrated the cab for the umpteenth time.

I climbed out of the bunk and poked my head between the curtains, squinting in the abrupt change from the dimness of the sleeper bunk to the bright, sunny, spring afternoon. Once my eyes had adjusted, I saw him. Standing on a strip of grass at the edge of the parking lot stood Doug. He operated a toy helicopter. With a remote control he sent the mini-copter far into the nearly empty lot of the truck stop. Then he steered the copter toward our truck, buzzed past the windows of our cab and then guided it back over his head. Before returning to the bunk, I looked on in wonder at the man-child standing obliviously several feet away, playing with his toy. The copter, that is.

At last Doug got back in the truck and put his toy helicopter in the box between the seats. I had settled back into the bunk before he had halted his diversion. Doug addressed me through the Velcro-closed curtain. "I usually keep this box under the bunk. Did you close the lid?"

"Yes, I've made my bed."

"Are you trying to sleep then?"

Feeling incredulous, I answered evenly in the affirmative.

"Hunh," Doug intoned without impatience, but with a hint of wonder that I might not want to be disturbed.

At long last Doug readied himself to hit the road. Before he left the truck stop he asked a question I only heard once in trucking. "Do you want me to announce when I stop?" he asked.

"What?" I replied, wondering if I'd heard him correctly or if maybe he had been a train conductor in a previous life.

"When I started driving with Alex I called out whenever I pulled into a rest area or truck stop," Doug explained. "He didn't seem to like that."

"I'm not surprised. If it's all the same to you, if I'm still sleeping when you stop, I'd rather keep on sleeping."

Doug often made unusual stops. I would later learn from Alex that Doug sometimes stopped in the middle of his shift to fly his copter at rest areas. Or, Doug told me himself, if he saw debris along the road, like a rope or a piece of wood, he'd pull over and pick it up. He'd find a use for it eventually, he said. Funny as that may sound, it went hand in hand with the genuinely bright ideas Doug often produced in dealing with practical issues and the mechanical adeptness of building and flying model aircraft.

Halfway back to Fort Worth I felt the truck pull into the dirt and gravel driveway of the Dandy Lion again. True to his habit, Doug drove into the fuel lanes and made a u-turn so that he faced back out of one lane headed the wrong way. The truck stop's windows flashed with neon signs advertising beer and gambling machines. I went in while Doug stayed behind and cleaned the truck's windows before going in.

The décor in the Dandy Lion might have been described as Early Redneck. Deer horns and racks full of ball caps with witty messages silkscreened onto them littered the walls. Shelves stocked with high-priced comestibles stood next to more shelves with statues, plaques, and an almost endless variety of knick-knacks. One might like to imagine that the inside of this truck stop was a brilliant marketing concept. More likely this was true, grade 'A' kitsch in its native environment.

After the break, Doug steered the truck while it swayed and bounced downhill on its way back along the driveway. A few hours later Doug drove up to our home terminal where he stopped outside the gate so I could go home.

"Do you want me to help drop the trailers first?" I asked.

"Nah. I got it."

"You sure?" I asked, wondering if delaying my short break might encourage Doug by letting him see that a co-driver willingly helped another.

"That's okay. Dropping is pretty easy," Doug said. I knew he was right. Given a choice between building and dropping, I'd always gladly take the latter.

I ran home to shower and rest then returned to the truck by the office to set up our trailers for the new day's run.

Building each set of trailers always has unique properties. Each time, whether alone or with someone else, complications may arise, expected or not. Not all experiences are negative, of course. Sometimes building a set went better than expected. Sometimes everything functioned seamlessly. Both trailers were readily found and happened to be near each other. The back trailer, the critical one for positioning, waited in a fortuitously clear placement without inconveniences like other trailers, light posts or the corners of buildings blocking the way. Then the dolly rolled right back in a perfectly straight position to the front of the back trailer. The front trailer backed right straight toward the dolly. All the brake lines and light cords functioned and clicked easily into place. Sometimes setting up was a symphony.

Sometimes it was a raucous din.

This time proved to be no symphony. The back trailer stood buried amidst other trailers. The guys driving the yard dogs almost always, perhaps 9,999 times out of 10,000 dropped each trailer on the yard so that the front stuck outward and could be pulled out from an aisle of lined up trailers. Somehow this one had been parked with the business end in the middle of the rows of trailers. Then other trailers had been parked all around. I would have to hitch up to the trailer blocking the front of our trailer and relocate it.

I dropped the dolly, hitched up to the offending trailer, found a new place for it, dropped it and returned. Then I backed between two trailers to get our girl. With a row of trailers next to this row, also, I didn't like my chances of backing the front trailer or the dolly at an odd angle between the trailers on either side. So I pulled our back trailer all the way out and put it in a spot that would make setting up easier. This was the first and last time I experienced this difficult placement of a trailer and for that I was grateful. However, because of this, I drove and stopped the truck over and over again more than usual while building our set. My door opened and closed each time I climbed out to wind down landing gear, hitch and drop trailers, whatever it took to get the job done. Doug lay silently in the sleeper bunk the entire time.

Finally, I got the set built and headed toward the gate. But alas, one of the trailer's tail lights had given up the ghost. I drove to the shop and waited in line behind other trucks. In time one of the mechanics fixed the light. Once our rig was ship shape, I drove out the gate toward Meridian. The clock read about three quarters past 6 a.m. We would arrive at the truck stop close to 3 p.m. — about 60 to 90 minutes late.

Hours later, again Doug popped out of the sleeper bunk once we approached our destination. He plopped down into the passenger seat and looked at his watch.

"You got out kind of late again, didn't you?" Doug asked pointlessly.

Nonetheless, I acknowledged the time.

"Why did you move so many trailers this morning?"

I explained the presentation I had found.

Doug replied with his characteristic, "Hunh." Then he added, "Alex usually leaves the terminal before six."

"Alex probably takes less than an hour to set up."

"Well, yeah, he does," Doug said.

"I'm setting up fast as I can. If you want us to get out sooner, you can help me set up the trailers," I suggested.

"Alex always does that," Doug said, leaning back and to his right. Doug turned slightly toward me, sounding surprised at the idea of any aberration from the norm. Apparently, my comments the day before about drivers helping each other hadn't given Doug the notion that maybe he should help, us being about equal in experience and this being a team run.

"If you don't want to help, all I can tell you is I've got a job to do, and I'm doing it right. That takes the time it takes," I said, employing another truism.

Neither of us had anything more to say, not even a 'Hunh.' Doug knew I would appreciate his help and that setting up on my own made us later than usual. His main concern was having time to play with his toy helicopter, but he wasn't willing to lend a helping hand in order to carve out that time in the day. What else was there to say?

Once again we arrived later than usual. My apologies to our colleague had already begun to feel like a bad habit. "I'm still kind of new," I explained. "My co-driver doesn't think it's part of his job to help set up."

"That's too bad," he said, shaking his head sympathetically.

Then he pointed out that one of the trailers he was giving us in exchange was "hot." He didn't have an odd attraction for trailers, nor was the trailer ablaze. He just referred to the paperwork which showed that one trailer was due in Dallas by midnight. We just had time to get it there, if we made a quick turnaround. After switching trailers, I tucked our paperwork into the small cubbyhole above the sunshade over the driver seat and let Doug know about the hot trailer. We would have to eat on the go so we could drop that trailer in Dallas on time.

"Hunh," Doug emoted when he realized he wouldn't have time to fly his copter in the truck stop parking lot that day. But something even more challenging troubled the valiant Doug. While I made my bed, he sat in the driver seat and thumbed through the paperwork from a couple of traffic tickets he had received a few weeks ago. Then he slapped the papers down on his right thigh.

"This ticket is due tomorrow," he declared.

After a call to Wayne, another co-driver was arranged to substitute for Doug the next day. Doug would take the day off to attend to business, but he still looked a bit down.

"At least you noticed in time," I said encouragingly.

"My next day off I was gonna rebuild my chopper's engine."

Instead of answering, "Hunh," I went inside to grab a turkey sandwich from the lunch counter then sat in the passenger seat to eat while Doug started the drive to Dallas. He decided to tell me about his tickets. Naturally, most commercial drivers feel strongly about tickets. They are a threat to their livelihoods, after all. Yes, I know: then don't violate the laws. But those of us who live in the real world know that stuff happens. Case in point: Doug's first ticket. A no brainer, he had been driving his own vehicle with an expired registration. Such a ticket may be foolish and costly, but at least it is not a moving violation. This type of ticket tells your current or prospective employer that you let some personal paperwork go unattended. Not a huge concern.

On the other hand some violations are considered reckless driving, like going 15 mph over the speed limit. But a variety of issues fall under the category of recklessness. Even if an employer wants to hire someone with a ticket, they may not be able to insure a driver with too many tickets or with tickets of the wrong kind. For instance, DUIs or DWIs can prove a real deal-breaker for anyone who wants to drive for a living.

Doug's second ticket, he said, was also in his own car. He had been waiting at a railroad crossing and before the flashing lights had turned off or the arms of the gates had gone up, he had driven around them.

"That doesn't sound good," I said, lifting a drink cup and taking a sip to wash down a bite of sandwich.

"The train had already passed," Doug said. "I didn't think it mattered."

Thankfully, I had no tickets on my record, but I knew that almost every CDL holder fights any ticket. Fighting tickets is just good business when you drive for a living. One ticket might not be such a big deal, depending on the nature of the violation. However, even an accumulation of otherwise innocuous tickets might spell bad news to some employers.

"So," I asked. "Are you going to hire a lawyer to fight your tickets?"

"Nah, I'll just pay them."

"Are you sure? Maybe a speeding ticket a bit over the limit would be okay, but I don't know how our company would look at that railroad crossing ticket. They might think that's more serious."

"It doesn't matter," Doug opined. "I'll just pay them."

After a few more minutes to let my lunch settle, I retired to the sleeper bunk to get some rest. I dozed, stretched out in the bunk with one arm over my eyes to block the strains of sunlight that always managed to leak in somehow. Despite ear plugs, I heard the usual road noise. Then a couple of hours into Doug's drive he sounded the air horn. Like a fog horn, though not as loud, not many drivers can remain asleep in the bunk when the air horn goes off. I lifted my arm from my eyes and raised my head, wondering what had happened. Had a motorist nearly careened into the truck? Were we about to have a collision? But our truck simply kept going.

An hour later Doug stopped for his break at the Dandy Lion. I got out, too. Afterwards while Doug drove back to the highway I sat in the passenger seat a few minutes for a change of scene.

"Did you have a problem earlier?" I asked.

"Hunh? No. Why?" Doug replied.

"I heard the air horn go off," I said. "I wondered if we almost had a wreck or something."

"No, I drove by a car with some kids pumping their arms," Doug answered, demonstrating the universal up and down motion that kids of all ages use to ask a trucker to blow the loudest horn on the road. I didn't bother to explain to Doug why blowing that horn needlessly could be an imposition to someone trying to sleep five feet behind him. But the thought reminded me of a time when I was a schoolchild in a bus full of kids, and many of us had made that same motion. That trucker had smiled at us and gently shook his head, 'No.' He pointed a thumb to the closed curtains of his truck's sleeper bunk. He had then set one hand on his cheek and tilted his head in a gesture of sleeping.

That week ended, and for a while I drove with other co-drivers, wherever Wayne needed someone to fill in. Then Doug and I were scheduled to work an entire week together again. The first day of the new week we happened to meet in the parking lot in the predawn hours and pass through the guard shack together. Next we walked to where the trucks stood parked.

"Who drove first last week?" I asked Doug while we walked across the asphalt in the coolness of the morning.

"Alex did," he replied.

I felt a bit relieved. Normally, that meant Doug would drive out this week, since teams usually switch out who drives first. Teams generally alternate their shifts so that both drivers become equally familiar with the route. Plus, if one shift or another has extra challenges, the team shares any burden. I'd happily help Doug set up the trailers every morning. Perhaps, such assistance would pave the way for the next relief driver who worked with Doug to have life a little easier, especially if that driver hadn't set up alone very often. I didn't care whether Doug helped me drop upon returning or not. Like he had said, dropping is pretty easy.

We climbed aboard our charge. Instead of starting the engine and driving to the dispatch office for our slip, however, Doug promptly entered the sleeper bunk. He took his sleeping bag from the top bunk and began to unroll it on the lower bunk. If he drove out, I'd be in the sleeper shortly so I called his name.

"Doug?"

"Hunh?"

"Don't you drive out this week?"

Doug sat on the bunk. "Alex always drives out," he informed me, pulling off his shoes in preparation to lie down.

"Don't you switch out? You know, take turns? I'll be glad to help you build the set," I offered.

"Alex always drives out," Doug repeated and slid the curtains closed.

Once more, Doug stayed in the bunk while I began to build our set. At one point I simply couldn't get the dolly onto the hitch behind the front trailer. I returned to the cab, climbed up the driver side and stood on the top step.

"Doug?" I called into the open door.

"Hunh?"

"I can't get the dolly positioned. Will you see if you can lift it onto the hitch? I've been trying for a while and can't budge it."

"Hunh," Doug answered, his characteristic monosyllable, sounding surprised by the request. Nonetheless, he climbed out of the cab and walked along the front trailer then stepped between the two trailers. With one muscular arm, Doug lifted the dolly into position then he strode back to the cab. I finished connecting the set and then sat down in the driver seat to update my log. I thanked Doug for his help, however brief, though I didn't point out the brevity. Doug appeared to take my thanks as if it were heavily owed to him, though this was his only help the entire time we ran his team's route.

Our week continued like the first one had. I set up every day alone while Doug waited in the bunk. Doing the best I could in the cool mornings, even on a day when rain had made it difficult to see on the yard, Doug never offered to so much as spot a back up. Rather again he expressed bewilderment that a driver with less than one year's experience worked more slowly than his regular co-driver who had decades of experience. But I kept my shoulder to the wheel, growing a new vertebra of determination in my trucker's backbone. I'd finish this week with Doug, and that would be that.

Meanwhile, one day before heading back Doug and I ate lunch at the café. During a pause I asked how things had gone with his tickets.

"Oh, I paid 'em," he said.

"Really? Both of them?"

"Yep."

Eventually, this week, too, drew to a close. We arrived at the truck stop, and I exchanged trailers for the last time with the driver Alex and Doug met each day.

"Good news," I smiled, handing over the paperwork for the trailers. "Alex will be back next week. No more waiting."

"That's okay," he answered with the kindness and patience I'd come to see in so many drivers. "You did alright."

The most peculiar run Doug took me on happened months later in the autumn on another route entirely. Again we worked together for a solid week.

As a driver goes out and back each run and gets used to the particulars of a highway, gradually more of the scenery and sights jump out at her. One day I had noticed a building next to the Interstate with old military equipment in front. That afternoon while we ate lunch Doug happened to mention it.

"Alex said it's a military surplus store," Doug explained. "I've been wanting to stop there for several months."

"Yeah? There are lots of places I'd like to stop," I agreed, thinking of all the sights I wanted to visit when unencumbered by a lengthy truck and an expected delivery time. Along the highways businesses and billboards advertised places seeming all the more attractive because we couldn't stop at any of them.

On our last day of this week Doug drove us homeward. After lunch I bunked down, dozing and sleeping a bit from the accumulated exhaustion of another week's doings. Then after some hours I awakened to the sound of our truck slowing. We eventually came to a stop. Doug must have pulled off at a truck stop or rest area to stretch his legs, I thought. I didn't feel hungry or thirsty and didn't need a break, so I just stayed in the bunk.

But the door never opened for Doug to walk into a truck stop. Instead, the truck moved forward again. Then it stopped for a minute or two, then moved again. A collision or road construction impeding the way would be a logical explanation for the pace of our progress. We'd had mostly good weather and traffic the previous several days. We must be due for a delay, I thought.

Lying on the bunk in the muted light with sunshine filtering through the cracks into the sleeper, I became increasingly puzzled at the pace and movements of the rig. Doug drove for a while, but not very fast or far. I could feel the truck go around a curve to our right. Then he drove a while longer and stopped again, this time for quite a while. Again I chalked it up to a delay, but I could faintly hear speaking. The radio played music, and the voice definitely sounded like Doug's. However, his tone lacked a conversational air, like it would if he spoke on his cellphone. Without being able to make out the words, I detected an urgency to his speech. But what driver doesn't curse traffic every now and then?

Then I heard the sound of the hazard lights blinking for several minutes. Finally, the truck moved forward again. This time for quite a while, though still not very quickly. We stopped and started yet again. Next I felt the truck taking a sharp left. Then the truck turned and turned and turned. It felt like Doug drove in a circle. Then the cab straightened out before turning back to the right again. When it did I could feel the trailers swaying in the back. Each one weighing many thousands of pounds, the loaded trailers rocked the whole rig while they moved side to side.

I could only imagine what Doug must be encountering. Perhaps, the police had detoured traffic off the highway in the manner Sarge and I had talked about. Like Sarge had said, not all detours took into consideration the requirements of doubles. Maybe this detour traversed small roads with deep potholes, really deep. Or maybe the way crossed over an old country lane where the road surface had been built bowed to shed water. Whatever the case, Doug drove at an extremely slow speed, though a back trailer can flip over at any speed if pushed enough in the right, or rather wrong, direction.

We seemed to have regained a straight presentation, and Doug drove on for a bit. Then he took another curve, this time to the left. He drove a bit more, stopped, then restarted and made a right turn. Finally, he shifted all the way up to top gear. Whatever had transpired, we had returned to highway speeds. All must be well. I rolled over on to my right side and gazed at the back wall of the cab, waiting to doze off again.

Once we approached Dallas, I stepped out of the sleeper and sat down in the passenger seat next to Doug to put on my shoes. I couldn't resist asking about our mysterious slowdown earlier.

"You know that military surplus store we talked about earlier?"Doug began.

"Yeah," I acknowledged, thinking maybe a detour had occurred near there.

"I decided to stop there."

"You did?" I asked incredulously. "Today?"

"Un-hunh," Doug answered in the affirmative.

"What happened?"

"I pulled over on the service road next to the store and saw their chain link fence was padlocked. They were closed."

"Yeah?"

"I went down the service road to get back on the highway, but it curved off onto a narrow country road. So I kept going along trying to find a place to turn around. I noticed a car behind me. I stopped so they could go around, but they wouldn't."

"Once you stopped for a long time."

"Yeah, they almost passed then, too, but another car showed up about a mile ahead. The car behind us had an old guy driving. I guess he was afraid to go. Well, after that car passed, I turned on the all-way blinkers and waited," Doug said, describing the hazard lights.

"The oncoming car had passed?"

"Yeah."

"The other car was still behind you?"

"Yeah, but I stayed put until he went around that time."

"You had found somewhere to turn around?" I asked, imagining a parking lot Doug could drive into.

"Not yet. I drove for a while longer. The road was getting smaller ahead, and I could see where it curved off again to who-knows-where. I knew if I headed down there . . . "

"You'd be screwed," I couldn't help but chime in, remembering Sarge's fateful words.

"Yeah, but I saw a house up ahead on the left. I drove into their driveway and turned around in their yard."

"Of a house?"

"Yep, I trenched their front yard," Doug said.

"What do you mean?"

"The tires left some pretty deep trenches in their lawn."

"Did anyone see you?" I asked.

"No. No one was home."

"What about on the road?"

"No."

"Except for the car that had been stuck behind you."

"Oh, yeah. Except for him, but he'd already passed by then."

I wondered what the people must have thought when they came home and found the tracks the truck had made, deep grooves circling around their lawn. Would they think this was a random act of vandalism? Would they realize the grooves had

215

been created by a semi, in this case a semi pulling doubles? They might not guess about the doubles. Maybe the curving arc of a rig pulling doubles, different from a long straight trailer, would even rule out a semi in their minds. Whatever they speculated, to say they couldn't have been happy has got to be an understatement.

If anyone, including the "old guy" behind our rig, had simply written down the cab's number or a trailer number and noted the date, time and location, they could have called our carrier and reported Doug's actions. If anyone ever asked me, I could truthfully say I'd been in the sleeper the entire time. The only information I had to go on was Doug's description.

Doug had been lucky on another count, too. He'd made his extremely tight turn to the left, therefore turning so that the brake lines connecting the two trailers moved toward each other. If he had made such a turn to the right with a brake line just a tad too short, they might have stretched to the breaking point, the way they would months later when I made a sharp turn in a truck stop parking lot. Then the rig would remain immobile until the brake lines were mended.

How hilarious it might have been, I wondered, if Doug had broken his brake lines and become stuck that day. I would have loved to have listened in on that call to Wayne. Perhaps, the conversation would have gone thusly:

"Uh, Wayne?"

"Hey, Doug, how's it going?"

"Wayne, I need a mechanic."

"What's up?"

"The brake lines between the trailers broke."

"Where are you now?"

"In a farmer's front yard."

"What the hell?"

As a bag of hammers.

Chapter 15: "See that man right there? I work for him."

A bias against truckers does appear to exist, that we are so stupid the only work we can do is steering a truck. What I found out was some co-drivers were sharp as a tack while others, not so much. Every level of intelligence can be found behind the steering wheel of a semi. I had driven with college educated co-drivers and had a degree myself. I'd held jobs crunching numbers at a computer where analytical skills were paramount. Some of my co-drivers had also worked intellectually challenging jobs before taking up trucking for their second or even third career.

Every job requires a certain amount of expertise. Since driving a truck is such a real-world, concrete job, drivers often have to be very clever about the details of their work, maneuvering in tight spots, dealing with technical problems, and figuring out logistical solutions on the spur of the moment. On many occasions I found myself impressed with the quick thinking, ingenuity and down to earth know-how of truck drivers.

Some members of the public will think drivers are thick regardless, but one group of people who should harbor some respect for drivers are the ones who hand them their paperwork. Yet, a bias about drivers' supposed level of intelligence may be a reason lurking behind the attitudes of some dispatch clerks, too. While most clerks are at least even tempered and some are also friendly or helpful, too often this turns out not to be the case. In fact, from time to time a driver has to deal with a dispatch clerk who behaves like he has a grass burr stuck up his ass.

* * *

One afternoon Wayne called with another run.

"I have a driver who's going to be out four days. He drives to Memphis one day then back to Fort Worth the next," Wayne explained. "Then do it again, out one day and back the next."

"It's solo then?"

"Yeah, it's a solo run. You want to take it?"

I agreed, though I had a question. My other solo runs had been buttheads at truck stops. A driver steered off the highway at the designated exit and was pretty much there. The so-called "easy run" to Memphis had been to a repair shop, not the terminal yard.

"I've never been to the Memphis yard," I said. "How will I know how to get there without a co-driver to show me?"

"When you go to dispatch ask for a routing. That's a sheet of paper with a map and the address, phone number and directions to whatever terminal you need."

"Oh, yeah, I've heard of those."

Wayne continued. "If anything seems unclear, call the Memphis terminal at the phone number on the sheet. They can give you any specifics."

Wayne gave me the truck number and told me the time to be at the Fort Worth terminal. Thus, I walked into the dispatch office at 8 a.m. the next morning to get the dispatch papers and a routing sheet. No other drivers were around. On the other side of the counter a clerk stood at the window. A tall, good looking man with red hair, he sorted through paperwork on the counter in front of him. I'll call him Van. In the way I'd seen other drivers do when they needed help from a clerk, I stepped up to the counter and spoke.

"Hi. I need a routing to the Memphis terminal."

Van looked up slowly, his head stopping as though it clicked into place like a robot's cranium.

"Let me set aside this work and do what *you* want," he said hotly and in an oddly loud voice.

"What?" I asked, his response so out of place I almost looked over my shoulder to see if he was talking to someone behind me.

"That's all I've got to do is hand out routings," he still spoke more loudly than normal, his eyes staring hatefully into mine.

See that man?

"You don't hand out route sheets?" I asked evenly, knowing his job included this simple task.

"No, I don't!"

"I've seen Carol and Jane give out routings," I answered.

"Then you can just wait for them to get here in a couple of hours."

I didn't know quite what to do. My feet shuffled, and I felt my face redden with humiliation. I had no idea if the routings were kept in a file, or I'd simply get one myself. If they were only in the computer, I had no access. Only Van appeared to be working in the dispatch office at this early hour.

"I need a routing to find a terminal I haven't been to before," I persisted, gripping the edge of the counter in front of me. "I don't have a co-driver to show me the way."

"See that man right there?" Van lifted his arm pointing toward the door of an office that was blocked from my line of vision by a wall. "I work for him," Van continued. "If you want a routing, you come around here and ask *him.*" Van swept his hand toward another door, the one between the small lobby that drivers stand in while getting their paperwork and the area where Van stood.

I felt very tempted to walk out of the dispatch office entirely, get back in my car and go home. To hell with this jerk, I thought. Angered by the clerk's pompous and irrational response, but determined not to let him stop me from completing my day's run, I walked through the door next to the counter and up to the dis-patch manager's office where a balding middle-aged man in a golf shirt sat at a desk in front of a computer.

"Does this company want any trailers moved today?" I asked plainly, cutting to the chase.

The dispatch manager, who had sat well within earshot of my conversation with his clerk, looked up at me, his face pinched with a look of discomfort. "What is it you need?" he asked, sounding apologetic perhaps, but offering no explanation or reassurance.

I asked for the routing again. While the printer whirred the manager made mindless chit-chat, which I supposed was meant to make up for the verbal reaming I'd just received for having the nerve to ask for the necessary information to perform the run. Van's hostility was all the more irrational, since he stood where

219

dispatch clerks normally stand when supplying drivers with any needed paperwork. The manager handed me the dispatch slip and routing, and I stepped out to the truck to begin setting up.

Meanwhile, I doubted the dispatch manager would have the courage or personal values to admonish Van for his unprovoked hostility and lack of professionalism. In fact, perhaps some error on the manager's part had caused his clerk extra work. Whatever the case, Van obviously felt comfortable throwing his weight around because his work was needed right then and, I suspected, because he was a male antagonizing a female. Which led to my second doubt, that Van would have spoken to a male driver with the venom he had directed toward me. If clerks or some members of the public considered truck drivers to be the low men on the totem pole, female drivers could be looked on as dirt under their fingernails. Negative attitudes are not the sole province of male clerks, of course. Some female clerks could win an Olympic medal in contrariness and inconsideration, too. I had already suspected this and would later learn for certain.

When I recounted this conversation with Van word for word to other drivers, more than one said, "I would have gone home right then." That wasn't just big talk. I'd been around drivers long enough to know that some would have made good on that statement. Yet, I also knew that if I had left such actions would have reflected poorly on me and left Wayne without a driver for the run. Luckily, I had enough vertebrae in my strengthening backbone to stay the course.

While I drove around the yard setting up the trailers I remembered stories drivers had told me about their experiences with dispatch clerks. The clerks' jobs, no doubt, have their own set of requirements and inconveniences. However, driving a truck can be inconvenience taken to the level of an art form. Because clerks can make a driver's work even harder, that prevents some from speaking out. Whether intentionally or by mistake, a clerk can cost a driver time and comfort.

For instance, one older gentleman I drove with described a day in which he and his co-driver had been told to back up to a trailer at the dock to wait for the rest of the freight to be loaded. They waited and waited. Four hours later they learned that they had been directed to wait at the wrong trailer. While in that case the clerk's error had been unintentional, the fact that two strong, smart, grown men thought they had to wait silently for that length of time speaks volumes about the reluctance drivers can feel about standing up to office personnel. Some of whom need to be stood up to.

I drove around to the front of the terminal, parked and went in to report the trailers' seal numbers to Van. Happily, this time he created no drama. Then I got back in my truck and rolled to the gate while recalling what another co-driver had once told me. While working for a different trucking company he had delivered a load to a manufacturer on a Saturday evening as he had been instructed. However, no one there could take delivery until Monday morning. The driver then had to insist that he be allowed back through the gate to drive his rig away from the factory to wait at a truck stop until Monday. As if he had no rights or needs, the gate personnel expected him to stay locked in the factory's grounds in his truck for thirty six hours with no restroom and no food, like a caged animal at their disposal. Such callous attitudes toward drivers can happen with frightening regularity.

I headed down the highway following the route that had become so familiar, out of the Fort Worth yard and across Dallas, taking I-30 east toward Arkansas. The sun shone on a beautifully clear, cool day. The truck rolled along in the right lane going the maximum speed the engine's governor allowed. The volume of traffic was regular, not heavy or light. Motorists passed by. Trucks with higher governors or none at all passed by, too. My comfort with driving had improved such that I listened to music, opened a water bottle, or ate from a small bag of chips propped up on the dashboard. I had come a long way in the months I'd been driving. Not just adding thousands of miles to my logs, but leaps and bounds to my confidence and skills.

While driving along truckers often greet each other. Not with the loud air horn, that some people request by moving their arms up and down. Not even with the quieter city horn in the middle of the steering wheel. Glancing out of the side window when their trucks pass, drivers often give each other a brief three digit wave with the thumb, index finger and middle finger, splayed stylishly like a friendly T-Rex. Many drivers don't even look at each other. Pass another truck and out comes the wave, an automatic token of camaraderie among truckers. Months had gone by before I'd even been able to see, never mind respond, to the trucker wave while I sat at the wheel. But in time I'd grown accustomed to giving and receiving the wave also.

A bright blue rig pulled up in the passing lane. The driver glanced over with a friendly wave which I happily returned just as I heard my truck's city horn honk. And honk. And honk. My left hand in mid trucker wave, my right hand on the edge of the steering wheel, I couldn't quite wrap my head around what I was hearing. I glanced again at my wave-partner, his forehead furrowed into a question while his rig passed mine. Puzzled myself, I returned both hands to the steering wheel. The much louder air horn could only sound with the pull of a thin silver wire that hung down near the edge of the windshield while the city horn looked and functioned more like a car's horn. Though the city horn sounded more quietly, it still made an irritating raspberry noise that continued to blare while the truck rolled along.

I stupidly looked down at the steering wheel and back up at the road while pressing the center button in a vain attempt to stop the buzzing sound. A passenger in a pickup in front of the rig turned and looked through her vehicle's back window with a question creasing her face as much or more than the trucker who'd just passed. I couldn't imagine driving another several hours with this constant loud buzzing and so began to push and pull the steering wheel experimentally in different directions to see if somehow the horn could be made to stop.

I wondered if a policeman could pull the rig over for causing a traffic disturbance. Surely some law must exist saying you can't go down the road honking the horn non-stop. Or I wondered if I would have to pull myself over and call Wayne for a time consuming repair. Maybe I could figure out which fuse to pull to disable the horn, though that would mean the truck wasn't safety compliant with two functioning horns. But then I discovered the trick. Pushing the wheel forward, the horn stopped as abruptly as it had begun. A wiring connection in the steering column must have become awfully close. Pushing the wheel forward provided enough of a gap in that wiring to stop the horn's incessant noise.

I drove on for a few hours before deciding to take a break.

One of the truisms of trucking has got to be that you constantly learn something new about yourself. Sometimes these lessons contain profundities about your character or will. Other times you learn a fairly meaningless detail. That day I discovered a previously unexplored tendency to pull back on the steering wheel upon exiting the truck.

Parked at a truck stop next to other rigs I stepped out onto the metal grid below the door obliviously grabbing the steering wheel only to hear the horn go off again. I quickly scrambled back into the seat and pressed forward on the wheel until the sound abated. Climbing back out, the driver at the truck next to mine lowered the squeegee he was cleaning his headlights with and looked at me quizzically. I hoped he didn't think my actions constituted horniness of another variety as in, "Honk, honk. Wink, wink. Hello there, big boy." Avoiding his stare, I looped my little green bookbag over my shoulders and headed inside for a break.

Once back on the road the truck glided up and down the hills of western Arkansas through Little Rock then across the rice flats heading east towards the Mississippi River. Every so often the horn would blare. Each time I pushed the wheel forward until it stopped. The truck crossed over the Mississippi River and into Memphis. I followed the directions to the terminal on the routing the manager had printed. Dropping the trailers, I then steered around the large building to the dispatch office where the rays of the setting sun had begun to glow. My not-so-favorite activity of building a set on my own loomed ahead. I hoped the dispatch office would provide the slip with the returning trailer numbers, if they were already known. That way I could build the set and rest, secure in the knowledge that my next step simply entailed steering out the gate after the required ten hour break.

A lady dispatcher I grew to think of as "NASA Control," or just plain "NASA," had other ideas, however. She gave the impression of organizing the receipt and dispatch of space shuttles, not mere trailers. With her hair in a pert ponytail and a radio walkie-talkie clipped to her shoulder like an actress in a police drama, Ms. NASA Control appeared just a tad too tightly wound. While she worked, she often leaned her head to one side in a quirky way when speaking.

"Hi, I'm covering this route for Reggie," I explained, knowing that dispatchers often learn a bit about the drivers they encounter on a daily basis. "Can I have the return slip?" I asked, handing Ms. NASA Control the paperwork I'd brought.

"Is Reggie here?" she asked.

"No. He's taking some days off."

"Do you have a co-driver?"

"I'm alone."

"You have to take a ten hour break before you can leave," Ms. NASA advised unnecessarily, tilting her head like she were speaking to a naughty child.

"Right. I'd just like to get the set built now before I rest."

"Not if you're solo."

"Pardon."

"If you're solo, come back in the morning for your slip."

"Are the trailers not loaded yet? Do you know which ones I'll be taking back?"

"It's not that. It's that you're solo," Ms. NASA repeated, moving her head straight up and then to one side in perky fashion.

"I'd just like to get the set built now, if you already have the numbers," I explained.

"You can't leave until your ten hour break is up."

"My break hasn't started yet."

"Come back in the morning."

"You mean you don't trust me to follow the rules, though we both know my time in and out of the yard is recorded by the guards at the gate and the logs I turn in *and* in the computer system?" I asked, referring to an electronic box on each trailer that clocks them entering or exiting each company facility.

Just then Ms. NASA heard a chirp on her walkie-talkie. Bending her neck, she pressed a button to answer a disembodied voice that asked which dock number to take a trailer to. Then Ms. NASA continued taking dispatch slips from other incoming drivers. She referred one driver to a large magnetic clip that held dozens of dispatch slips for teams and nighttime solo drivers arriving to start their shifts. I looked through the sheaf of papers for the number of the truck I'd just driven in. No dice.

"It's not there," Ms. NASA said.

Obviously, I was not cleared for takeoff.

I had arrived at six in the evening. Taking into account a brief trailer drop, I could leave shortly after four in the morning without inciting suspicion from anyone, even Ms. NASA Control. Meanwhile, I had eaten a sandwich at a truck stop before arriving, since the food available at any terminal is limited to whatever the vending machines supply. Nonetheless, I checked out the selection and put a $5 bill into a change machine. Ten hours is a long time. I had learned that the gnawing of a hungry stomach can prevent sleep. I bought a pack of crackers and a pastry just in case. After stopping by the ladies' room, I headed back to the sleeper cab that waited sans trailers beneath a fluorescent light.

I climbed aboard and settled in, spreading the sleeping bag on the bunk, setting out some CDs to play to unwind and hoping to get a long, restful sleep. I felt a bit better about bunking down at a terminal versus a truck stop. Truckers and travelers of all descriptions wouldn't be coming and going throughout the night hours. Pimps and prostitutes were nowhere to be found. I locked the doors, but didn't worry about a determined lot lizard knocking or a potential thief trying the door handle.

The most frightened I would ever feel staying solo overnight at a truck stop would be a night months later at the Jolly Trucker in Tennessee. The truck stop that could look so bright and cheerful by day, like many such places, could take on an edge of darkness after sunset that had nothing to do with nighttime. On that occasion I had to exchange trailers with a driver who had parked in the then crowded gravel lot across the street from the truck stop building. The depth of the lot extended dozens of yards from the road. That night the rig sat back a couple of rows in the poorly lighted lot. The entire truck stop teemed with drivers and trucks parked in every available space. Most of the lot near the building had parking spaces that a doubles rig couldn't be backed into or driven through. The few doubles slots right next to the building under the glowing lights had been taken hours earlier. In this manner I found myself at the end of a long week and in need of a shower. So I lugged my travel bag across the street, showered and bought a meal.

Close to midnight I browsed the overpriced groceries and supplies to see what might seem essential before dawn arrived. On impulse I purchased a tire knocker, a firm wooden tool about eighteen inches long and two inches in diameter with a metal tip at one end and a leather wrist strap at the other. In other words a big, glorified stick. Some truckers swear by the use of a tire knocker, claiming they can tell a flat or partially deflated tire from a good one by the sound made upon striking the tire with the knocker. The principle being the same as thumping a watermelon to check for ripeness.

With a manly uniform shirt on my back and a dark ball cap resting on my female head, my hair tucked in underneath it, I grasped my recent purchase in one hand. The strap wound through a drilled hole in the handle to prevent a user from dropping the instrument. I slid my wrist through the strap. Next I slung the shower bag over one shoulder and walked quickly toward my truck, trying to be inconspicuous as possible. First I crossed the truck stop's fuel lanes. After waiting for traffic, I crossed the busy street into the muted light of the gravel parking lot. Passing between two parked cabs, I looked under their long trailers to check that no one lurked underneath. I was making my way quickly between the two trailers when a bare-chested man jumped out of one of the cabs I had just walked past and started rapidly towards me.

"Hey!" he shouted over and over, each exclamation the one staccato word, "Hey! Hey! Hey!"

I looked back and saw him fast approaching. I didn't know what on earth he thought he might accomplish by shouting at me. Did he think I was a prostitute? Was he trying to buy or sell drugs? Did I remind him of his ex-wife? I didn't want to find out.

I also didn't want him or anyone else to notice which truck I climbed into. Nearing the end of the trailers, I could set out toward my rig. I stopped and turned in the dim light, lifting the tire knocker up with my free arm just to be sure he saw it. A beam of moonlight shone on the hard Tennessee hickory. Suddenly, the man had a complete change of heart and wordlessly, but rapidly, reversed his course back to his cab. Whether to stay there or to retrieve a device of his own, I had no way of knowing. I took a sharp right at the end of the trailers and broke into a run across the darkest part of the parking lot toward my truck with the heavy shower bag bumping against my leg and gravel crunching loudly underfoot. I glanced over my shoulder while I ran. Luckily, no one followed.

Returning to the truck, I kept the inside lights off, triple checked the door locks, and tucked the seat belts hard into the door handles to prevent them from opening easily. It was late on a Saturday night when many rigs had stopped for the weekend. If I had left that parking lot, the likelihood of finding another spot in the jam-packed truck stops or rest areas at that hour was slim, especially with the limited maneuverability of a set of doubles. Anyway, I'd driven the maximum number of allowable hours for that day. If a policeman checked my logs, getting a ticket would cost my job. Driving over an hour away to the nearest terminal the computer tracking would clock me going over the time limit, too. So I fell in to that rut we often reach where our options are limited bureaucratically. Thus, we dutifully follow the rules.

Because of that encounter I had a tough time getting any rest in the sleeper that night. Though I had secured the truck doors, the realization that it would have been relatively easy for someone to smash a window, get inside to commit mayhem then make an escape before I or anyone else could do anything to stop him made my blood run cold. Thanks to that jerk's inexplicable behavior all I could do was hunker down fearfully and wait for dawn.

I felt a bit wary anytime I bedded down on a solo run, whether at a truck stop or at a terminal. Yet, I didn't always feel at ease alone at any terminal, even in sunny daylight. Many times I drove unaccompanied onto the grounds of the Dallas or Fort Worth terminal yards to start a solo run or when returning from one. The terminals are huge facilities covering many acres. A large central building dominates each yard with smaller maintenance or mechanical buildings scattered here and there.

On weekends each terminal's yard fill with randomly dropped trailers. Drivers pull into the terminal, and in their eagerness to quit work and head home, they leave trailers everywhere, some-times nearly blocking the pathways. The scattered trailers form a sort of metallic Stonehenge. Any newly arrived driver has to search to find space to drop two more trailers. On any lot this sometimes meant dropping trailers without another human being in sight. With only a thin, chain link fence with barbed wire across the top and sometimes only one security guard on the other side of the building hundreds of yards away, I sometimes felt on edge. What if some whacko had climbed the fence? What if a driver or a clerk had skirted a background check – not that that was any guarantee – and decided to do something to the lone female? If I was attacked and called out, would anyone hear? If they heard, would they help? Maybe. Maybe not.

I often felt distressed by the bleak utilitarian nature of the trucking world. I understood the very real meaning of stickers on the backs of trucks with mottos like, "Trucks Bring Good Things." Many truckers wore tee-shirts that sported statements, true for many, such as, "Everything you wear, eat, or use came to you in a truck." Yet, at times the notion hung in the air like diesel exhaust that trucks, these behemoths of glass, metal and rubber, course through the veins of our country spewing pollution and sometimes killing or injuring people in collisions. In addition, up and down the highways and byways the paved shoulders are often strewn with animals killed by the tremendous weight of tires that roared across the pavement and then rolled over their hapless bodies. Thankfully, I'd never seen humans injured or killed in accidents, whether with trucks or cars. Animals were another story.

On occasion I'd climbed out of the cab after driving and seen big, three inch long moths embedded in the grill of the truck. They'd flown along and gotten trapped, roasting to death against the engine's heat. At different times I'd had to run over a rabbit or a possum. One night an orange and white cat had run out like a flash from the underbrush only to be crushed under the wheels before I could even think of avoiding it. I especially hated that. Cats being some of my favorite people.

My first co-driver, Dutch, in reminding me not to swerve to avoid animals had told me while shaking his head in sorrow, about a beautiful Collie dog he'd had no choice but to run down on

228

See that man?

a sunny afternoon one day in Arkansas. He couldn't slow down in time and a car drove next to him in the other lane, blocking a possible escape from disaster. He couldn't stop, nor could he collide with the car next to him. To his lasting regret the dog's owners and their child stood nearby calling for the dog to try to stop its progress onto the roadway, but to no avail.

Along stretches of the highways, I'd seen deer carcasses with hellacious injuries, like a quarter of a torso removed from the force of trauma, and wondered what sort of horror and pain that creature had had to suffer. A trucker didn't even have to drive over an animal to cause its destruction. Much later, when returning from a solo run to Tennessee I'd been driving along in eastern Arkansas and heard the thump of something running into the truck. I looked back in the driver side mirror hoping no motorist had bumped a trailer, a potential fatality for them. Instead, in the side mirror's reflection I saw the disintegrated remains of a red-tailed hawk ricocheting onto the grass median. About thirteen feet from the ground the bird had flown too low and struck the small window at the top of the sleeper compartment. Hitting the edge of glass and metal that moved at over 70 mph had torn the living creature asunder, breaking the window and leaving a broad streak of dark red blood along the side of the truck's cab.

Added to these incidents of destruction, I'd seen the grimness of truck stops with their ongoing and unstoppable drama of drugs and prostitution. Human misery could seem to hang in the atmosphere like unseen smoke. Being alone while delivering trailers to the terminals could highlight feelings of sadness or even revulsion. Everything at a terminal, every trailer, building and light post could look so soulless and lonely. Every imperfection stood out: the rusty panels on an empty, old trailer; the carcass of a dead bird on the pavement with its joyously bright plumage still blowing in the breeze over its rotting flesh; in unswept asphalt corners of buildings, the debris of metal bits, paper scraps and nameless grit swirling in the wind. At such times every random, dirty, neglected object loomed like a bad omen. Then I felt truly and profoundly alone.

* * *

229

Trucks and drivers would still come and go that evening at the Memphis terminal, but all would be from our company. None would be there without passing by a guard first. Anyway, I'd be in a locked truck right under a bright light. With that hopeful thought I stretched out on the nylon fabric of the sleeping bag, flipping through a magazine, listening to the music from a CD floating out of the speakers overhead and trying to make the best of it. The engine would hum along keeping the heater going during the chilly night. But just then the day was still young. The usual difficulties of taking breaks on a time frame came into play. No brain can automatically feel sleepy just because its owner must rigidly adhere to a schedule. I couldn't help but imagine how I would be reading or watching TV if at home. Then a few hours later after a leisurely bedtime shower I could slip between two crisp, clean sheets on my own comfortable bed. Instead, like a penned dog, I waited in my confined space hoping for sleep to descend.

A couple of hours later I dimmed the lights and turned the CD player off. Eventually, I dozed. When my thoughts started reaching bizarre proportions I knew my brain had entered dreamland. My subconscious mind wandered randomly over the mental static of the previous days and my anticipations for tomorrow, trying to make sense of what had been and what would be. But then a peaceful dream. I envisioned a field with a stream running among dark red and orange stones. I waded in the water, feeling pebbles under my toes and listening to the gentle waters run their course. Only this brook didn't babble. It blared! I sat upright in the darkened bunk, the sleeping bag falling away from my shoulders.

"What the hell?" I sat blinking to myself, halfway between sleep and wakefulness. Whatever light bled into the sleeper from outside provided the only illumination. My drowsy mind tried to make sense of my surroundings. For all I knew I could have been at home or in a truck or on the dark side of the moon. Then sense came back to me. Fort Worth. Solo run. Memphis overnight. Horn that won't stop honking. Dammit!

I whipped the rest of the sleeping bag off my feet and opened the Velcro strip of the sleeper curtain. The horn continued to blare, echoing off the metal sides of the building. I pushed the steering wheel forward until the horn shut off then contemplated my next move. If I turned off the engine, the truck would become unbearably cold. If I left it on, the horn might go off again. That thought alone would make dozing off more difficult.

I looked out the windows. Night had fallen. No other drivers were to be seen on this side of the building. The clock read half past midnight. Most dispatch staff go home for the night before that. I decided to go inside to check the mighty magnetic clip that had held a sheaf of dispatch papers earlier in the evening.

Pulling on a jacket, I got out of the truck and walked across the pavement. I entered the building filled with machines and conveyor belts with packages on them and not another human in sight. To my satisfaction, hours before official departure time the desired paper with my truck number on it waited between numerous others in the dispatch office. I unclipped the sheet and walked back through the deserted building and out to the truck. I might as well set up, I thought. I felt pretty sure more sleep was out of the question right then.

Putting the truck in gear, I drove around the building to the yard of loaded trailers. A few drivers here and there already worked on building their sets. I joined in, dropping the dolly in front of the back trailer listed on my dispatch slip, then bringing the front trailer over to line them up. After connecting the brakes and power cords, I drove the rig back under the fluorescent light outside the dispatch office and dozed while waiting for the magic hour of departure to present itself.

Later that day I returned to Fort Worth then went home for a shower and a night of rest in my own bed. The next work day I started out again to repeat the procedure. Set up in Fort Worth. Drive, horn blaring intermittently, to Memphis. This time I didn't ask Ms. NASA Control for the paperwork. I merely waited until the office closed. Once rested, I set to work again. Ms. NASA Control was a trip. But compared to another female clerk I would later encounter, she was a cupcake.

At the end of the work week I entered the Fort Worth office alone late in the evening to turn in the dispatch slip and put my log sheets in Wil's file. Several reports from the so-called spy van inspections waited in the file among drivers' logs and fuel receipts. The spy vans followed our company trucks in cities and recorded their speed. Good or bad, that speed was reported to the company and all relevant managers. I looked around to double check that no one waited in the break room or near the dispatch office counter then I thumbed through the reports.

One of the reports included Hilda's truck number during a month I'd driven with her. The report didn't list the driver's name. That's something Wil or his staff would look up. The truck had been driving up I-65 toward Louisville at night. The speed: excessive – going 71 in a 65 mph zone. The penalty: a loss of safety bonuses, the same bonuses co-drivers said some managers shared with their drivers. I'd heard on the grapevine that in total each payment could add up to thousands.

Hoping I hadn't been the driver caught speeding, I wrote down the date and time then put the reports back in the file. Hilda and I never drove on each other's logbook. Looking at the logs from the month in question would reveal for certain which of us had been at the wheel. I drove home wondering what I would find in the carbon copy pages of my old logbook from that month.

Once home I flipped through the pages of logs until I found the date. Uh oh! I'd driven with Hilda that week. I looked at the time. When the van had recorded an excessive speed I had been in the sleeper bunk! Someone had just cost Wil thousands of dollars, and it hadn't been the rookie.

Chapter 16: "Misery loves company."

Simon, the driver who had taken my spot on Hilda's route, appeared to be a jolly fellow, and he had a fat figure that would fit a Santa suit. Over the months we had run into each other several times on the yard. Happily, neither of us had been in a truck at the time. Each time we met, Simon had a funny comment to make about something, anything. He came across as a really nice guy.

My birthday fell on an upcoming Saturday in early spring when Wayne called. "Hey, I need someone to cover on Hilda's run."

"Not with Hilda, I hope."

"Nah," Wayne laughed. "She's taking some time off. You'd be driving with Simon. You know him."

"Sure," I replied.

Simon and I met at the dispatch office and were ready to head out in record time.

"I hope you don't mind eating on the run," Simon commented. "This express don't stop like Hilda's does."

While Simon drove us out the gate and toward east Texas, we discussed a couple of Hilda's traits. Simon reported that Hilda still swerved onto the rumble strip texting or when she propped a photo up on the dashboard to look at while driving. She had a high rate of absenteeism, as well.

Simon laughed. "She misses work – a lot."

"She did when we drove together, too," I remembered.

"Wayne told me she's always been like that," Simon asserted. "At least one week a month I don't know who I'll be driving with."

I had to admit to driving with different relief drivers on the route during the months Hilda and I had run together. Romeo was just the most noteworthy.

Simon shook his head back and forth while chuckling. "I'll tell you something," he said, one hand releasing and gripping the top of the steering wheel more tightly. "Hilda says, 'I can't get no rest with you.'"

"Oh?" I asked.

"Um-hmm," Simon continued. "I drive as fast as I can. I don't get there at one or two in the morning. She can't stand it."

He laughed.

"She still gets ten hours in the bunk. I know her. She likes to run a ten and ten," I said.

"Yeah, but I make sure she doesn't get ten hours *rest*."

"What do you mean?"

"I have my ways," Simon replied with a smirk.

"Hilda can really be something," I agreed. "But it's not like you *try* to keep her awake, is it?"

Simon just laughed again with what sounded to me like a hint of devious glee.

"Don't you know you're safer if your co-driver is rested?" I asked, with a feeling of foreboding edging into my mind. Simon just shook his head to himself and continued to gaze out the windshield with a private grin on his face.

After our chitchat ended on that disturbing note, I lie down in the bunk on my sleeping bag and tried to relax. Simon had driven out that day because this weekend he would drive a butthead on his own that Hilda and I had driven together a couple of times before I had accrued enough miles to go solo. The day was Tuesday, the first day of our work week so I felt fairly well rested. So far we'd only reached mid afternoon. Left to my own devices at home I wouldn't have gone to sleep until several hours later. Sleeping or getting any meaningful rest the first day out can often be difficult, but not impossible.

Different intrusions can make getting sleep difficult for the driver in the bunk. For one thing, the truck jostles and jumps while the tires roll down the road. Also, even at night when the sun has faded, streetlights and headlights from oncoming traffic leak into the sleeper compartment. Some drivers are awakened by the cigarette smoke produced by their co-driver, if it makes them cough. Or if the ventilation is on the blink, the compartment may feel too warm or too cold, depending on the time of year. Co-drivers stopping frequently can be a nuisance, too. But the grand-daddy of all sleep-depriving phenomena on a truck must be NOISE!

Ironically, some drivers listen to CDs or an iPod while sleeping in order to create their own background noise. Not everyone sleeps well with sounds directly pumped into their head, however. Many drivers use earplugs, but of all the noises in a moving truck, not many can be fully shut out that way. Ear plugs only reduce the level of noise from within and without. A driver doesn't have control over most sounds that find their way into a sleeper. Anyone can close the vinyl curtains, of course. But sleeper cur-tains are merely meant to block light and provide privacy. The thin partition doesn't restrain much noise of any kind. Besides, the curtains have gaps where they meet the floor, walls, and ceiling.

Random noises like the occasional siren or car horn bleed in from the outside. Neither driver can help that. Nor can either driver control the weather. At times rain taps loudly on the roof, or gusts of wind make their presence known with an insistent bluster that rushes against the cab while tugging it from side to side. The roaring sound of the tires on the pavement below creates the greatest noise overall. At least that's a constant or so-called white noise, unless the pavement is uneven with bumps, grooves, or gaps between the sections of concrete. Then rubber tires carry-ing tens of thousands of pounds strike repeatedly against the pavement making their own racket.

What drivers can control is the sounds originating from inside the truck, which likewise can be many.

Simon turned on the radio while he drove through east Texas toward Arkansas. Yes, radio sounds can be soothing. Music often provides a continuity and rhythm that can lull a listener to sleep, whether the selection is pop or country, rock or classical. Even the

sounds of voices reading news or calling a sports game, the into-
nations of on-air interviews or the dispensing of advice have a
cadence and welcome familiarity that can soothe. Naturally, all
sounds can become noise at high volume. Out of consideration
most team truckers keep the radio volume fairly low. With Simon
at the controls the volume sounded a bit high. But lying in the
bunk I noticed the sound didn't just come from the front of the
truck through the vinyl curtains. I could also hear sound drifting
down from overhead. Like other sleepers this one had stereo
speakers near the roof of the compartment. The speakers broad-
cast the same sounds of the dashboard radio or its CD player.

When resting on a solo run I often relaxed in the bunk while
listening to the radio or CDs with those speakers on. When I
drove alone and felt exhausted I turned on all the speakers full
blast to stay awake. But no matter what fade setting the person in
the driver seat used, all sleeper bunk speakers had their own
volume control. Anyone in the back could adjust the levels with
the bunk's control panel, at least ordinarily.

During the months I'd driven with Hilda, Romeo and other co-
drivers in this very truck, I'd become closely familiar with all the
controls, the way you do with any piece of well used equipment.
Resting on my back looking at the bottom of the top bunk in the
dim light I turned my head up and to the right looking at the
control panel. I reached over and turned the volume control knob
left, to the off position. But at the off position no final click indicated that the speakers had been turned off. The knob kept
turning. The whole feel of the volume control felt different, kind of
spongy. Plus, a circle had been worn around the circumference of
the knob where the plastic control panel cover had been scratched
through the brown, simulated wood grain until a ring of white
showed through. Someone had turned the knob all the way to the
right, to the highest volume, and then forced it further and
further many times until the knob could no longer turn the
volume up or down. Instead, the bunk's speakers remained stuck
on high volume.

That wasn't all. While he drove along through the piney woods
of east Texas, across the hills of Arkansas and onward into Tennessee, Simon also kept the CB or squawk box on. Many truckers

use the CB for alerts from other truckers about what might lay ahead: bad weather, lane closures, weigh stations that are opened or closed, among other things. Drivers often communicate to help each other change lanes and to avoid striking cars and pickup trucks. That's all very good and wonderful. In fact, it's fantastic when CB use makes everyone a little safer. But CBs are also used to tell jokes, flirt, and spout obscenities. Frequently, if a female spoke on the box, as one driver put it, "You would think that none of these guys had ever talked to a woman," such were the catcalls, raunchy invitations, and innuendo.

The trouble with a CB for the poor sap or sappette trying to slumber behind the thin vinyl curtain with an inconsiderate co-driver at the wheel is that the sounds are sporadic. The CB sits mostly silent in a plastic cubbyhole above the windshield to the right of the driver. A gentle glow of electrification makes the CB look downright homey, like an oddly technological form of a soft fireplace light. Then suddenly, SQUAWK! The CB earns its nickname when loud crackling sounds and voices burst out randomly, bouncing off the inside of the cab. I'd wager no one twisted a CB knob until it broke, not only because a driver had to buy a CB himself, but also because whoever sat up front retained sole control of the sounds that emanated from that contraption.

I unfastened the safety netting that I'd extricated from the top bunk before lying down and stood up. Next I felt like stepping out of the sleeper and whacking Simon on the head with a large, wooden mallet, but I had no such object. Anyway, he was driving. Instead, I rifled through my travel bag that sat on the top bunk until I found my supply of squishy, orange, foam ear plugs. Then I settled back in to the bunk and tried to get to sleep. With enough light blocked, the temperature at a comfortable setting and the sounds of road noise interrupted only slightly by a few swells of music, a driver could at least get a good nap that first driving day, if his or her co-driver kept interior noises down to a dull roar. So much the better to stay up all night and drive.

I put in the ear plugs. I had managed to doze off on similar days in like circumstances. But today the noises continued unabated. In fact, they worsened. I put a pillow on one ear and lay on my side, my other ear against the bunk's thin mattress. I tried

237

mentally shutting out the noises. My eyes closed in the cool, dark sleeper with music or news playing loudly overhead and the CB spouting out static or voices at unpredictable intervals. Nothing worked. I couldn't sleep a wink.

Eventually, Simon completed his shift and pulled into the same truck stop in Holladay, Tennessee where Hilda and I had always switched out. The road noise diminished once the truck came to a stop. Then the sounds from the radio filtered back unobstructed into the sleeper. With dismay I realized that Simon had tuned the satellite radio to an X-rated channel. I could hear a radio host taking calls from males who, no doubt, wanted to get letters published in Penthouse. What Simon listened to while he drove didn't matter to me, since I didn't hear it in detail anyway. Leaving such audio blaring once his shift was over and while driving with a female he barely knew seemed thoughtless at best.

Simon went into the truck stop to take a break, and I turned the radio off. After a break of my own, I returned to sit in the driver seat and start my logbook page for the day. Simon sat in the passenger seat. The radio blared again on the same channel, only louder. The driver controls the radio. I was the driver now. Using my trucker's backbone, I switched the radio to a music channel and lessened the volume.

"Let me know if I play music too loud," I said to Simon, hoping he might take a hint.

As he finished his log update and stepped into the sleeper, he answered, "You won't bother me." Then he closed the curtains while emitting a soft, sneering laugh.

Oh, well, I thought. At least tonight was the first night of the week. I had to drive overnight, having been awake for only four-teen hours or so. That's not a huge deal for a trucker.

So I began to revisit the traces of the run I'd driven with Hilda months before. I drove through the rest of Tennessee, turning north at Nashville and heading into Kentucky. I liked the high-ways there. The interstates in Kentucky had better pavement and lighting than most. The rest stops were the best I'd seen. Huge parking lots had room for scores of trucks. Plus, the large facilities looked well cared for, and often had an attendant present during the day. Hours into the shift I drove the distance between Louisville and Cincinnati with considerable ease compared to my earliest days. In time we crossed the Ohio River and then skimmed northward across the flat farmlands. Finally, I guided the rig through the gates of the Cleveland terminal yard.

Simon arose, and we dropped the trailers we'd brought. Then I turned the wheel over to him. Before getting the return trailers, Simon steered the truck over to the yard's fuel pumps. While waiting for both hundred and fifty gallon tanks to fill, I decided to use the time to clean the truck's side windows. The windshield required a long squeegee that the company terminal yards never provided, but truck stops do. Because of this drivers cleaned the windshield at truck stops, often at the end of their shift as a courtesy to their co-driver or sooner if an accumulation of bugs or grit became too much for good vision.

I dug out a roll of paper towels and a spray bottle of cleaner from a cubbyhole above the passenger seat and spritzed fluid on the passenger side window. Simon looked over at me then took paper towels and a spray bottle from above the driver seat and began cleaning the driver side window in similar fashion. Next I cleaned the passenger side mirrors. Again Simon looked at what I did and started cleaning the driver side mirrors. I got the odd feeling Simon thought this was some sort of competition. If I did anything on the passenger side – cleaning the inside window, the inside of the door, the messy step into the cab – I noticed Simon watching me. Then with what I sensed as defiance in his actions he did likewise on the driver side.

We finished fueling the truck, got our return trailers and drove to the truck stop that Hilda normally frequented. After enjoying a pizza in a different part of the truck stop while Simon had steak in the restaurant, we each returned to the truck. Then Simon drove us back through Ohio and Kentucky with the radio and the CB blaring. I had kept the radio on low and the CB off. Before stepping into the sleeper compartment, I asked Simon to please lower the volumes, just about the only time I would ever feel the need to ask another driver to do so.

"Humph," Simon answered noncommittally, his hand not reaching for either control.

239

Once I lie back on the bunk where the volumes should be a bit lower, the sound levels reached the heights that had kept me awake the day before. But I hoped that the tiredness of driving all night would cause sleep to follow. Much of Ohio is relatively flat with smooth roads. I had a full stomach, had taken a shower and changed into fresh clothes at the truck stop. I just needed to relax, use a pair of ear plugs and let sleep overtake my weary brain. Heading back across Ohio, I snatched light naps between squawks on the CB and the sound of the radio.

A few hours later Simon drove back into Kentucky and headed up the hill from the Ohio River when our truck's loud air horn sounded. Maybe Simon had to let a motorist know in no uncertain terms of the truck's presence before they ran into our side. Maybe. In the noisy truck I tossed and turned for a few hours more. Then approaching Nashville, Simon sounded the air horn again. Every 100,000 miles of driving I had to sound the air horn, truly needed to sound that horn maybe once. Maybe. How extraordinary that Simon should have cause to do so twice within just 500 miles. Either he was having astonishingly bad luck or something else was afoot.

About midnight we reached our switch out spot in Tennessee again. Between the honking air horn and all the blaring speakers I'd gotten two hours of sleep at the most in the past thirty six hours. I settled in behind the wheel and began the long journey back to Fort Worth. Whatever tiredness had soaked through me was held temporarily at bay for a few hours by the adrenalin of driving a big truck, my thoughts about Simon and his peculiar behavior, and the desire not to run off the road. Yet after several hours, sleepiness began to creep up on me.

Most drivers will tell you the worst hours for fatigue are from about 4:00 a.m. to sunrise. I turned up the air conditioning on this chilly night and directed the vents on myself. I listened to the radio, quietly. I moved my eyes from side to side and lifted and lowered my head alternately. When the sun rose behind the westward-heading truck the rays of light helped to reawaken my brain. Nearing Dallas, I pulled over for a break, driving into a fuel lane to squeegee the windshield to wake up a bit more for the drive in to Fort Worth. Then I grabbed a quick bite to eat. When

Simon took over driving later that day I didn't want to have to wake up to eat.

We arrived at Fort Worth, dropped and built a new set of trailers then headed back out for the last two day run. Simon assumed his position behind the wheel while I lie down to get what I hoped would be the sleep of the nearly dead. I felt so tired, I thought surely no level of noise likely to be produced on a semi could prevent getting some real rest. Then before we left the terminal Simon informed me that he, who wouldn't stop to eat like Hilda did, would drive out about two hours and park for lunch at a buffet. Whoever drives makes the call on when or where to stop. I told Simon I'd eaten and would stay in the sleeper to rest. I just asked that he lock the truck's doors. Then I dozed while Simon made his way out of DFW with the same volume of noise he'd maintained so far.

Two hours later Simon pulled up into a parking lot decorated with signs that read: No Truck Parking, followed by warnings about towing at the vehicle owner's expense. The truck swayed slightly when Simon's stout figure climbed down the steps on the side. I rose long enough to check the door locks. The clock glowed 2:00 p.m. Unusually, Simon had shut off the engine. I re-closed the curtains and lie still in blessèd near silence with only the hum of nearby highway traffic, an easy background noise to sleep through. If Simon ate like most drivers, he would be gone at least thirty minutes. At a buffet, with the caloric intake Simon needed to maintain the girth of his waistline, maybe longer.

I nodded off.

Exactly twenty minutes later a loud, baffling sound crashed down around my tired brain. Ga-Wump! My brief sleep amidst such exhaustion caused me to awaken in a mist of confusion. What the hell was that? I wondered. Had a car bumped into us? Was a tow truck driver hitching the rig up to his wrecker?

Opening the curtains, I peered out and saw the hood of our truck standing open.

"What the fuck is he up to now?" I muttered to myself.

Simon opened the driver door and pulled out a wad of paper towels from behind the seat.

"What's going on?" I asked quietly.

"Whadaya mean what's going on?" he replied, sounding like he found the question somehow offensive. "I'm cleaning the windshield."

"Why did you open the hood?"

"I can't stand on the hood, but I can stand on the engine braces." Simon answered, referring to metal bars in the engine compartment.

Standing between the seats I looked at the nearly pristine glass before me – glass that I'd cleaned a few hours before at a truck stop. Every co-driver I would ever meet cleaned the windshield at truck stops, the way I had first done on an early run with Buster and on many runs since then. Whether fueling or not, we cleaned windshields in a fuel lane. Quietly. Never, ever had I heard such bullshit.

I lie back down with a sigh.

A few minutes later: SLAM! The hood shut again, and Simon climbed back aboard to continue our odyssey. And what a bizarre one it became because just two hours later Simon had to blow the air horn again. Then again a few hours after that. Funny that he hadn't had to use the air horn all the way up to Tennessee at the beginning of the week. But apparently hellions suddenly came out of the woodwork and nearly careened into the truck while he sat at the wheel. The quieter city horn wouldn't do. The only way he could avert disaster was by using the horn guaranteed to interrupt his co-driver's rest.

By the time our rig rolled into one of the fuel lanes at the switch out truck stop in Tennessee, I'd enjoyed maybe four hours of sleep in the previous sixty hours. Drooping with exhaustion, I started filling out my logbook and readying to drive a 60,000 pound rig for ten hours with an outrageously slight amount of rest. But first, I felt curious to hear what Simon had to say about his frequent use of the air horn.

"You sure are having problems, hunh?" I began, once Simon sat down in the passenger seat to eat a sandwich he had bought in the truck stop.

"Problems?" Simon replied.

"Why do you keep blasting the big horn?" I asked, wondering if Simon detected the skepticism behind the question.

"Someone almost ran into us."

"Four times in the past day and a half?"

Simon made a snorting sound in his nose, a sort of a cross between a laugh and an indication of haughtiness.

"Let me ask you something," I said. "Do you get some good rest when I drive with the radio and CB turned down and the air horn doesn't go off every few hours?"

"I don't sleep well, ever, especially on a truck," Simon answered.

"Why not?"

"I've got a bad back."

"You can't sleep well so no one else will? Misery loves company. Is that it?"

"That's the job," Simon replied cryptically.

"I've had the job long enough to know it's not supposed to include *trying* to keep co-drivers awake."

Simon made no defense or protest. He just uttered another derisive noise, a sort of snuffling sound. Then he leisurely wadded up his empty sandwich wrapper, placed it in the bag it came in and went into the sleeper without saying more. He didn't need to.

Silence can be eloquent.

Of course, I wasn't the first driver to deal with fatigue, not by a long shot. Even when not dealing with a noisy co-driver, there are many ways of coping with the soft tiredness that congeals into hard exhaustion as the week progresses. One way was to stop and take a break. Normally, most drivers stopped twice in a shift that lasted between nine and ten hours. The change of scene could help a driver feel less tired. Often I would use the ladies' room, maybe get a candy bar or a bag of chips, and stretch my legs. Once behind the wheel again, the hassle of fighting fatigue returned when the monotony of road noise and the same old visuals of driving returned also.

On these occasions drivers might try a variety of ways to stay awake. Months before I had tried one of the vitamin potions next to the cash register at a truck stop. The lettering on the brightly colored bottles had boasted how the contents increased the user's energy for several hours. I bought one and swigged it down before heading out to the truck one night. Nothing. I noticed no feeling of extra energy. Same old tiredness.

Or I might sip a caffeinated drink, but the more a driver drinks the more she has to stop so that has limited appeal. Besides, I found that a caffeine or sugar alert wore off quickly and left me feeling more tired than I had been to begin with. Next to the cash registers truck stops sell tablets of mysterious looking, but perfectly legal substances in little, clear, plastic envelopes or in brightly colored boxes decorated with exaggerated graphics of things like fierce-looking predators. The wording on the packages also bragged of great amounts of energy for many hours. After the first purchase hadn't worked, I never tried any more of them. I also never tried anything illegal, though occasionally men loitering at truck stops clearly appeared to be offering drugs to passing drivers. Some of whom bought whatever was being sold. I supposed the legal stuff might have a real effect or at least act as a placebo. The illegal stuff must have unintended consequences, or it wouldn't be illegal.

Many drivers found something to occupy themselves through long hours alone at the wheel. Dutch listened to his case of CDs. Buster ate an array of snacks. Hilda made frequent stops. Like some drivers I used sunflower seeds. At first I shelled and ate them, but the salt content and natural oiliness proved too much over the long haul. What worked best for me was to tip a small quantity of sunflower seeds from the plastic bag into my mouth then swish some water around to rinse off most of the salt. Keeping the seeds in my mouth, I spit out the water into an empty drink bottle. Next I used my tongue and teeth to take each seed out of its shell, bite the seed in half, then spit seed and shell into the same empty bottle, one seed at a time. This way I didn't eat any. The practice wasted seeds perhaps, but the concentration required to perform this little act kept my brain alert when I wanted desperately to snooze.

Of course, what worked best of all was deep sleep. But sleep is at a premium when the choices are to bounce along in the bunk with easily interrupted, shallow sleep or to sit up and drive. To our company's credit they did have posters in the dispatch office saying things like: It's Your Call When to Drive. These notices suggested pulling over for a nap when needed. The company would rather delay delivery – and we usually had ample time – than risk an accident, the posters declared.

In addition, notices showing snow or icy roads encouraged drivers to wait if they felt weather conditions warranted a delay. In either case they only asked that the driver let dispatch know their status. Though I'd heard drivers complain that they got an argument if they called due to weather, I never felt the need to stop for that reason so I don't know personally. When it came to fatigue, I wasn't going to ask permission to take a nap. No one did. If any of the dispatch clerks I met had received such a call, I doubt they would have known how to handle it. If I stopped for a catnap, that was between me, my co-driver and the wind.

From time to time I napped in a parked truck, my co-driver silently tucked into the sleeper behind me while I remained in the driver seat. At such times I sought relief not from mere tiredness, but from flat out exhaustion. Exhaustion can take on a life force that every driver at some point fears could become a death force. A sort of gray, cloudy weight begins to build like a storm over the top of the head. Gradually, the weight presses down, seeping further into the brain, shutting down sections of synapses like the lights shutting off in a city blackout. If this condition goes unchecked, the eyelids start to weigh more and more until the head sags and then jerks upward when its owner remembers he is still piloting a vehicle weighing tens of thousands of pounds down a roadway at high speed in the vicinity of other trucks and automobiles, zooming past trees, bridge rails, and overpass supports.

That's why at truck plazas or rest stops drivers park and nap when they just can't keep their eyes open anymore and when they shouldn't try to either. When that happens different drivers nap in different ways. Most chose not to lie down in the upper bunk, if the truck has one, because they might sleep for too long. One fellow told of a co-driver who pulled over for a nap, climbed up on the spare, overhead bunk and didn't wake until shaken on the shoulder by him – five hours later. In the way I had leaned against the passenger window with my little green bookbag on the "easy run" with Chan and Jack, I had also done so in the driver seat of the parked rig when taking a catnap break on different runs. So, too, did drivers lean against the window in the driver seat with a balled up jacket, a roll of paper towels or whatever they found handy for a makeshift pillow. Other drivers keep a regular pillow in the overhead bin of the driving compartment for the specific purpose. While still other drivers just slump face forward over the steering wheel.

But while sitting in that driver seat and preparing to nap, the floor takes on a vision of loveliness. 'If only I could lie down,' the trucker thinks. And when the driver's vertical hold becomes harder to maintain, he thinks, 'Oh, what sweet joy it would be to place my body in a horizontal position!' Yet, like I did at first, he might think it impossible. The dashboard, seats and gear shifter don't leave a lot of floor space in a truck cab. Many times I gazed with fatigued desire at the floor, but ultimately settled for the seat. Until, that is, I discovered the trick is to lie on one side with both the waist and knees bent. With my feet in front of the passenger seat and my head next to the back of the driver seat I lie on my right side and rested my weary head on my little green bookbag for the half an hour to an hour of solid sleep I needed to carry on the journey to its next phase.

Almost unbelievably, one co-driver told me about a night when he was driving near New Orleans and made his way across Lake Pontchartrain Causeway, the longest continuous over-water bridge in the world. More than twenty miles span the waters of the large round lake and provide a link between I-10 and I-12. This driver was a dependable guy and told the tale in a matter of fact, not a grandiose, way, such that I didn't doubt him. Also knowing the difference between tired and trucker tired, this is what he said: the last thing he remembered that night was driving onto the bridge headed north. Almost half an hour later when his truck's cruise control blinked off for no known reason, and his truck slowed down, a motorist behind him honked a car horn, awakening him. He'd driven across the bridge and had no memory of doing so. He felt very lucky that the truck hadn't veered off to one side into another vehicle, or even worse for him, over the bridge rail into the waters of the lake below.

* * *

As it happened another form of water helped me stay awake that third night with Simon. A few hours into the drive north while steering the truck through Kentucky I sipped water from a bottle and unintentionally inhaled a drop of H_2O. Liquid dripping into my lungs caused me to cough loudly and for a long time, the sort of deep, bronchial clearing cough that makes one's eyes water. The sort of cough easily heard a couple of feet away in the sleeper bunk. Though I heard no noise emanating from the bunk, I wondered if Simon thought it a vengeful stroke of genius.

Hours later I had recovered from the coughing fit and drove down I-75 across the last few miles of Kentucky and the Ohio River bridge into Cincinnati. The typical morning commuters, cars and school busses, shared the lanes next to my truck while unrelenting sleepiness returned, knocking at the door of my brain, insisting to be let in. Though I moved my eyes around and tried every little trick I knew to stay awake, it finally happened.

One blink of the eyes lasted more than an instant.

Two seconds, perhaps.

Maybe three or four.

I jerked awake and looked around in terror.

I felt like a bucket of cold water had been poured over me. I had been asleep at the wheel of a very big truck in a major city during a morning commute while unsuspecting motorists and busses full of innocent children passed close by! Rejoicing that I hadn't struck anyone, raw fear kept sleepiness at bay while the city receded into suburbs and then countryside.

But partway through Ohio and still with only the four hours of fitful dozing accumulated throughout the week, I had been awake for most of seventy hours. Our destination awaited only a couple of hours away – a hop, skip and a jump to a rested trucker. Yet I felt so tired I could barely keep the truck in its lane. Now and again I had seen truckers dream weaving dangerously within a lane, barely in control. Once on a Kentucky Interstate I'd seen a trucker zigzagging so much I'd been afraid to pass him. Remarkably, each time he had passed a police cruiser with an officer watching traffic, he'd gathered enough self-control to make his way past them steering reasonably straight. Once out of their sight, he began to gradually lessen his control again. Eventually,

I'd gotten around him, shaking my head at the wonder of driving in that condition, never thinking I would become a dream weaver myself one day.

Another time while carefully passing a trucker in Arkansas I'd looked over and seen the man hunched forward, his hands gripping either side of his steering wheel like his life depended on it, because it did. Exhaustion etched into his features, his tired eyes stared straight ahead moving his rig down the road to meet his goal. When beginning my shift I'd often had to adjust the driver seat from the forward tilt that tired colleagues set it at in order to feel more wakeful while driving. But the man I'd passed that day in Arkansas didn't dare lean his back against anything. He sat on the edge of his seat, looking very like he was wondering how his trip would end.

Now I wondered how our trip would end. I steered the truck to the right, close to the shoulder stripe, only to find myself veering gradually toward the center stripe. Several times I had to jerk the wheel hard to keep from drifting into the left lane. Auto drivers nervously zipped around the swaying back trailer that threatened to jog in front of them at any moment.

A rest stop came up around the next bend. I pulled in and parked in one of the many vacant places. At 10 a.m. most drivers had begun their day's work while I could continue no longer. Desperate for an hour or so of uninterrupted rest I settled back in the driver seat and fell fast asleep. About fifteen minutes later I awoke to the sound of a loud and persistent beeping noise. I looked around, glanced at the dashboard, then realized the sound originated from the sleeper where Simon lay. After a long moment the sound stopped. I leaned my head back onto my bookbag and several minutes later dozed off again only to be awoken by the same beep another quarter of an hour later. This pattern repeated itself two more times. At which point, I furiously climbed out of the cab, cursing Simon aloud and walked around the rig to check that the fifth wheel pins remained secure. Then I climbed back aboard and drove on to Cleveland for the final time that week.

Once at the yard Simon rolled up his sleeping bag in the bunk while I steered the truck toward the office. I asked him about the beeping noise.

248

"I sometimes set my cellphone alarm, if I need to call some-one," he said.

"Who did you need to call this morning?" I tested.

"I don't remember," Simon answered.

Sure, I thought.

I parked the truck near the dispatch office and walked in with our paperwork. Two clerks worked behind the counter. One clerk, a middle-aged woman, glanced up with a friendly smile that instantly took on the look of a concerned mother.

"You look like death warmed over," she volunteered.

"Thanks," I answered, smiling wearily and handing her the paperwork.

Following our usual routine Simon drove south to the truck stop where we each normally showered and ate. One of my CDs lie on the dashboard. Before I could stow the disc in my little green bookbag, Simon picked it up and looked at the graphics on the cover of "Can't Take Me Home" by P!nk.

"Do you want to listen to that?" I asked.

"Yeah, I'll give it a listen," he said.

We completed our tasks at the truck stop. Then Simon headed back across Ohio with the CD music blaring. I reasoned that since it was my CD I wouldn't find the volume as intrusive. This was so, up to a point.

White noise might help smooth over disruptive noises, for in-stance wind from an open window. Our truck came equipped with small vent windows in the sides of the sleeper bunk. When the truck moved down the road at highway speeds with the vents open, the rapid movement of air produced a lot of sound. The springtime air in Ohio still felt quite chilly. Yet I found myself willing to take the chance of being cold to see if I could outwit Simon at his own game, by fighting random noise with the con-stancy of stronger white noise.

I opened the nearest vent. With a baseball cap that had our company logo and a light jacket around my head I adjusted the pillow in an effort to keep the wind from beating directly against me or into my ears where the results could be head-swimming dizziness. Ear plugs, too, would help prevent dizziness or an ear ache. Then I curled up and prayed for much wanted sleep.

My strategy met with mixed results. I grabbed a few zees, very few. Because it seemed Simon, unlike Santa, opened a bag of tricks, overcoming the white noise I had hoped would mask his antics. Simon returned to playing the radio loudly, letting the CB squawk, blaring the occasional air horn, only now he had another trick in his bag. For the first time all week Simon coughed. He coughed loud and long. And not just once, but every few hours. My incidental slip up with the water earlier appeared to have given Simon a new inspiration. Hilda, I imagined, would hear this new addition in the months to come. Meanwhile another truism of trucking formed in my mind: "A considerate co-driver is worth his or her weight in gold!"

Many hours later back in Tennessee I took the wheel for the last leg of our journey together. By this time I'd had at the most seven hours of sleep in ninety six hours or four days. Not for the first time I turned on the satellite radio and listened to a comedy channel to help stay awake. About halfway through my drive home with the scenery of Arkansas passing by the truck's windows, the station replayed a prank phone call. A man called a mechanic's shop and asked to speak to someone who he knew wasn't there. At first a mechanic in the shop answered the phone politely. The caller tried to sound like an older man who, perhaps, was a bit confused. Manic with tiredness I giggled a bit.

The prank caller phoned persistently over a period of days and each time remained in character, stupidly asking to speak to the non-existent person and arguing with his pitiable victim. I laughed softly. The mechanic who answered the phone calls over even more days became bolder until finally at his wit's end he shouted and cursed at the prankster. Then I laughed, not just any laugh, but orgasmic, soul-cleansing laughs until tears streamed from my eyes. I couldn't stop. I fought for breath, sweeping the tears from my eyes with the backs of my hands.

I remembered having done this once before with another co-driver, laughing at a comedy routine. When suddenly, the Velcro strips that sealed the vinyl curtains of the sleeper had ripped open

Misery loves company

loudly. I couldn't see my then co-driver, but had imagined him sitting on the edge of the bunk in the darkness. "Sorry," I had managed to sputter in the direction of the sleeper bunk before quieting down. A few seconds later the curtains had closed again. But this time with Simon was different. Giddy with exhaustion I laughed uncontrollably for miles and miles. Despite his scoffing sounds when he and I spoke earlier, Simon would not completely reveal his poker face. The sleeper compartment remained silent. But I knew, if Simon had heard when I'd choked on water, he heard the laughter, too.

A couple of hours passed. I drove the truck into Texas on that Saturday morning, my birthday. Simon came out of the sleeper and sat in the passenger seat until I could pull over at a truck stop at his request. Truckers commonly pull over at the next available stop when their co-driver asks for a break. I'd stopped for other drivers many times, and they for me. Male drivers usually do this when they need to use the toilet for a non-liquid restroom break. We chatted a bit while I steered the few miles until we reached an exit with an appropriate stop. Simon watched while I reached into the overhead cubbyhole for my little green bookbag. Then the whole bookbag plopped out onto my head and comically bounced to the floor. I glanced over at Simon who I'd expected to laugh, but his face remained a stone blank. Maybe a driver could add laughing to a repertoire of noise making, though first he would have to develop a sense of humor.

We paused at a truck plaza. Then I drove back onto the highway while Simon returned to the sleeper. A couple hours more and I pulled the truck up next to the parking lot at the company terminal in Fort Worth and set the brakes.

"Simon, we're here." I called back towards the sleeper and began to gather my things from the driving compartment to take them to my car. I moved to the passenger seat and waited. Trucking custom calls for the driver in the sleeper to open the curtains. I needed Simon to step out of the sleeper so I could get my travel carrier and sleeping bag, lest I open the vinyl partition and find him in a state of undress or filling a pee bottle or God knows what else. Simon shuffled up front and sunk down heavily into the

251

driver seat with the full force of all his extra weight, pounds that no doubt put undue strain on his sore back.

Simon turned to me, sleepiness creasing his face. "You want to come along with me for the last run?" he asked. "You get another day's pay. I'll even bake you a little birthday cake," Simon joked, his hands cupped around an imaginary treat that I pictured with pink frosting and a single bright yellow candle on top. One thing I would never again picture is Simon in a red suit with white trim. For all his apparent jollity, he was no Santa and no birthday prize. After four days of tortured wakefulness, I would have preferred to whack Simon over the head with that proverbial wooden mallet than go out with him again on any run. I went home to celebrate my birthday by taking a shower and crashing into bed for nine hours, then after waking briefly, sleeping for an additional seven hours more. The sleep deficit I had acquired while driving with Simon put me into deep sleep for sixteen total hours.

Chapter 17: "You need to hear this from someone."

Treating drivers like dirt is not the sole province of male clerks. I was about to meet a female clerk who reinforced that concept more than I ever would have liked to know.

The next Monday, fully rested, I stopped by Wil's Fort Worth office. Since I'd driven straight home after arriving in Fort Worth, I needed to turn in the logbook pages from the week Simon and I drove together. Wayne sat behind a desk smoking a cigarette while Wil stood nearby talking to him. Wayne greeted me in his typical overstated way, and I paused to speak to them both. As the conversation went along, I took the chance to bring up something that had worried me for several months.

"I'm not sure exactly what all should be looked at when inspecting a truck," I confessed.

"Next time you drive out one of us will show you," Wil said.

"That would be great," I answered, hoping for peace of mind that finally someone would make certain I hadn't been neglecting anything that needed checking.

"Hey, while you're here I have a solo run out of Dallas to Texarkana I need to fill three days this week," Wayne said. "The run is kinda short, but it gets you back home every night."

The run went up to Texarkana just past the Arkansas border and met a team out of Nashville.

"Sounds good. What time should I be at the Dallas yard?"

"Pick up the truck here at nine and be in Dallas at ten," Wayne instructed.

253

Driven Crazy ~ Karen Greenhill

* * *

Yet, the next morning when I arrived at the Fort Worth yard to pick up the truck cab neither Wayne nor Wil were there to show me how to conduct an inspection. Nor did either of them ever again offer to demonstrate this key element of trucking.

I found the truck by the number on its side and opened the door only to be practically knocked down by the stink of leftover food, B.O. and stale tobacco that the previous driver had left behind. Drivers on a regular route could keep their truck in almost whatever condition they chose. Many kept a clean truck. Not all. To start with every steering wheel in the business has at least a fine coating of grease. Many drivers bring along a package of baby wipes to clean the steering wheel and gear shifter, and so on, in the cab's interior. After tossing my little green bookbag in the overhead bin I cleaned the cab of this truck a bit while wondering who might drive it overnight. The trucks used for short runs were often shared by two solo drivers. One driver took the truck to Texarkana or Oklahoma City by day, the other to Austin or San Antonio by night, for instance. Most drivers made an effort to hand over the truck to their colleague in reasonable condition.

I bobtailed from Fort Worth to Dallas with the windows open and dutifully arrived at the Dallas terminal at the appointed hour. Sitting at the counter of the dispatch office was Julie, a short, brunette, heavyset woman. I looked through the window that separated the lobby from the office and asked for the paperwork for the run. She looked up at me accusingly and spoke.

"Where have you been?"

"I just got here. Why?"

"You were supposed to be here at eight," she continued with her mouth drawn into a scowl.

"My manager told me to be here at ten," I shrugged.

With no change in her expression Julie handed over the paperwork. I proceeded to build the set, not yet knowing that one of the truisms of trucking has got to be: delay, whether real or perceived, breeds delay.

As was often the case on the northbound end of this run, only one trailer had any freight. When that happened we still took two trailers for the sake of an even exchange of trailers between all

254

destinations. If trailer parity isn't practiced, eventually some places would have an excess of trailers and others, too few. When there wasn't enough freight for two trailers we drivers put the loaded trailer in front, since it was heaviest, and pulled an empty trailer in the back.

I placed the dolly in front of an empty trailer and rolled the loaded trailer in front accordingly. After latching the dolly under the back trailer, I started to connect the lifelines, cord to plug and brake glad-hand to glad-hand. I began to connect the glad-hand for the blue service brake line from the dolly to the front trailer when that trailer's glad-hand fell to the ground like it were made of clay. As a result, I couldn't attach that loaded front trailer to a back trailer. Worn from metal fatigue and corrosion, glad-hand attachments can easily snap off, a hidden point of weakness like the cracked bracket Romeo and I had experienced on our last run together. If the glad-hand had broken on the empty trailer, another empty could easily be substituted. But the loaded trailer had to go on this trip. That much was for sure.

I called the dispatch office on my cellphone to let one of the clerks know that the trailer needed a mechanic to fix the glad-hand. Naturally, Julie answered. I gave her the rig's location and explained the problem.

"What did you do to it?" she asked.

"What do you mean?"

"You must have done something to it."

"I tried to attach the brake lines, and the loaded trailer's glad-hand fell off," I explained, knowing that time ticked along while Julie gave me this unnecessary and naïve third degree, as if inconveniencing myself was somehow a goal of mine.

After Julie made a final harrumph, she called the shop's mechanic. Several minutes later a mechanic arrived in a pickup truck and looked at the broken parts. But he then had to go back to the shop and get a replacement glad-hand because Julie had only sent him out to see whether the brake coupling was really broken. Thus, Julie cost us more time. Meanwhile I sat in the cab and listened to the radio, waiting. After a long while, the mechanic returned and replaced the broken glad-hand.

By noon I drove out the gates. Arriving at the Texarkana truck stop three hours later than the regular driver on the route normally did, I apologized to the Nashville driver. He and his wife were most affected by the delay. Not the Dallas clerk whose schedule remained unaffected. Not much bother for me either, since I would go home that night. But the Nashville team drove back eight hours each way, no doubt resting in their truck at night. Typically for many a long-suffering, patient driver he good-naturedly waved away my apologies and explanation. That's trucking. He knew unavoidable things happened.

Plus, I knew to be at the terminal two hours earlier.

The next morning I arrived in Dallas bright and early at eight. Julie took a hasty look at her paperwork, glanced at the computer, and told me to set up two empty trailers for the run. In our company I'd never heard of deadheading, or taking empty trailers, for so many miles. Going only between Dallas and Fort Worth, drivers commonly took two empties. Yet, I was in awe of Julie's hasty instruction because Texarkana is almost two hundred miles from Dallas. The Nashville team would have to deadhead over five hundred miles farther with nothing in the trailers but some springtime air. I hadn't driven a completely empty rig for more than a few miles, since truck driving school.

"*Two* empties? Are you sure?" I asked in disbelief.

Julie insisted. Two empty trailers.

In amazement I exited the dispatch office and went to work. Alone again and with the usual struggle I built the empty set within easy sight of the dispatch office. The only dolly available that day was particularly heavy and awkward. Anyway dollies could be the bane of any set up. The point that forms the tip of the dolly can be quite heavy. Some drivers can back up dollies all day long and lift the tip without thinking about it. For me lifting the heavy tip and rolling it into position was often a challenge. I had to huff and puff and position myself like a weight lifter to pick up the tip of some dollies. If I had to push, pull, and maneuver a dolly it frequently required every ounce of strength I could muster. Of course, using the truck to roll the dolly around is best, but that doesn't work for every inch the dolly has to be moved or adjusted.

256

Finally, I accomplished the feat. Since empty trailers aren't pre-assigned, I returned to the office to report the trailer numbers I would be hauling to Texarkana. But of course, Julie had other ideas. She casually informed me that at least one trailer on the yard did have freight designated for Nashville, after all.

"Why didn't anyone let me know?" I asked, disappointed that the work of setting up was all for naught. Further, unjust as it was I privately speculated that telling me to set up two empties was Julie's way of punishing me for arriving the day before at the time I'd been instructed and for having the bad luck to have a glad-hand on the loaded trailer break off.

"We drove all around in the cart and couldn't find you," Julie said.

Luckily for Julie, lightning wouldn't strike her through the roof of the dispatch office. Some clerks have no reluctance leaving a driver to struggle a few feet away while sitting inside and clicking computer keys. I had been close to the office the entire time and had seen the golf cart the clerks drive around the yard sitting right outside their door. The cart hadn't moved in the time I'd been setting up. I said nothing about that. Instead, I asked an obvious question.

"Why didn't someone call my cellphone?"

"We don't have every driver's number," Julie answered indifferently.

"Do you have mine?"

With a sigh Julie flipped through a Rolodex finding no such record. But the fact that she had to check for the number meant she hadn't looked before then.

"Will you add my name and number to the file?" I asked.

Julie glared at me angrily and spit out questions like a hissing snake, "Which do you want first? The dispatch slip or your phone number in the file?"

Taken aback with her attitude I just looked at Julie unsure of how to respond. Throughout all of my dealings with Julie, I never responded in kind. Like most drivers in similar circumstances I simply kept trying to deal with the business at hand, despite the clerk's attitude, if it was hostile or otherwise lacking.

"Here," she tossed the dispatch slip on the counter in front of me.

There *are* dispatch clerks who just don't give a damn what they put drivers through. Like the slips of paper they shuffle through their hands, drivers are like nothings for too many of them. Clerks work in a heated or cooled building steps away from water fountains, restrooms, drink and snack machines. Clerks go home to their families at night. And if they don't sleep soundly in their beds, it isn't because they are in a truck bouncing along a highway at seventy miles an hour in all sorts of weather. Being a driver does have compensations such as, well, compensation. I doubted any ordinary clerk made the kind of money the drivers earn.

That thought was my only comfort while I walked out to break down my rig and rebuild it with a loaded trailer. I didn't want to have to move the troublesome dolly yet again so I disconnected the empty front trailer and retrieved the loaded trailer from a dock door. In order to connect the front trailer I then had to back the trailer hitch precisely up to the tip of the dolly. Since the dolly was still connected to the back trailer, the dolly couldn't be moved or adjusted, unless I could pick up the thousands of pounds of empty trailer manually. Therefore, if the tip of the dolly reached too high or too low to attach to the hitch of the front trailer, I would have to disconnect the dolly from the back trailer anyway, or essentially, start from scratch. Back and forth I worked the front trailer until everything lined up just so. Fortunately, the dolly's looped tip wound up at about the right height to the hitch, and after some struggle the components fit securely into place.

Thus, the set stood rebuilt with the front trailer carrying freight while the back trailer remained empty. I walked around the rig doing a final light check and climbed up the bumper of the empty back trailer. The back trailer's door was still up. Even an empty trailer may contain large pieces of plastic wrap, cardboard boxes, foam beads and other miscellaneous bits of packing material. We always closed the doors of empty trailers to prevent anything from falling onto the road or other vehicles.

The doors of the trailers raise up and down like window shades. To close them a driver had to grasp the door's inside handle, a black nylon strap made of the same material used for seatbelts, and pull the door downward with his or her body weight. I reached overhead and put my hand through the loop at the end of the strap. Then I wrapped the strap around my wrist, and grasping it firmly, stood near the edge of the door and stepped off into thin air, essentially rappelling down the back of the truck until my feet reached the ground below. Once on terra firma I grabbed a metal handle on the outside of the door and kept pulling down to keep the door from flying upward while I connected the latch.

Finally, I drove the completed rig up to the dispatch office and carried in the seal number of the loaded trailer. Julie checked the seal number with the number in the computer system. They matched. I took the dispatch papers out to the truck, climbed aboard, and headed out to Texarkana only slightly late this time.

At the tiny Arkansas truck stop where we butted heads the Nashville team hadn't yet arrived. By then I needed to use the restroom, but had driven straight to the switch out location. So I could either go or wait indefinitely if the team was delayed by weather or traffic. I slipped my little green bookbag over my shoulders and walked up to the small store inside the truck stop. But once inside I couldn't find a restroom door. The female clerk looked at me inquisitively.

"You looking for the john?"

I nodded.

"They're outside," she said.

Outside I approached the thin wooden door marked "Women." The door had no knob so I pushed it open and found myself standing in the worst truck stop restroom I ever encountered, and it had its competitors. The one-person restroom looked like it hadn't seen a brush, mop or broom for decades. Filth covered every surface. The tile floor looked like it had once been white. Now grime spread across the tiles, fading to black in the corners. Someone had stuffed a piece of paper where the doorknob should be, an attempt at blocking the view into the room. But flies had managed to navigate past gaps in the wadded paper. Insects buzzed freely in and out of the small room that lacked a stall or any attempt to provide privacy. Only a filthy sink and a filthier toilet occupied the floor space. A mirror with most of the reflective surface peeled away hung on the wall. Up above cobwebs quivered in the corners of the ceiling like forlorn ghosts. The very walls oozed yuck.

I stood in the room needing to pee and just couldn't bear to, even hovering was out of the question. Two words: splash up. If I had so much as washed my hands at the encrusted sink, they would have become dirtier than when I'd arrived. I exited the restroom and glanced at the men's room door. That one too had no doorknob, only bits of paper. Anyway both rooms must be hygienically challenged, to say the least. So I walked back to my truck and filled a large, empty Styrofoam cup with yellow fluid then went to "check the trailers." In other words, I dumped the contents in the dirt under the front trailer and climbed back up to the driver seat to wait.

The truck stop management had likely removed the doorknobs to avoid the restrooms being used not only by prostitutes, but for a place of rendezvous by male drivers. When I'd driven with Doug to Meridian we had sat one day at a table in the restaurant waiting for our lunch, making small talk.

"What's written on the restroom walls in the women's room?" Doug had asked.

I set down the drink I'd been sipping before answering him. "You might not believe it, but – political arguments."

"Hunh?"

"Yeah, like current events, what's in the news, who's running for president and why he or she is the one to vote for in one opinion or is a rotten stinker in another opinion. Why? What's on the men's room walls?"

"Cellphone numbers with notes to call if you want a woman. Some are driver to driver though, man to man. Like, 'Call me,' the number and the day's date so anyone will know if the guy who wrote the note is still at that truck stop."

Doug was a good-looking guy. Sometimes he got unwanted attention from other men.

"When I'm driving along," he explained. "Sometimes guys will come alongside and flash their lights at me."

"Not like a flash to change lanes?"

"No. These guys will pass and look over at me. They'll slow down in front of me so much I have to pass them. Then they come up behind the rig and flash their headlights three times in the side mirrors. After that they drive up beside me again, look over and smile."

"I guess they like the cut of your jib."

"They ain't getting anywhere near my jib."

We had both laughed at his good humored reply.

On a different run with a different driver, I had been steering down the road while my co-driver sat next to me. We passed two big rigs parked on a shoulder together, not in a spot where drivers normally might stop to sleep or use the restroom, just randomly. The driver of one truck signaled a return to traffic while the other driver walked back to his vehicle.

"Either drugs or sex," my male co-driver had commented, tilting his head toward the trucks to indicate the target of his remark. "And most of them dudes are married, ya know."

While I contemplated these facts the Nashville team pulled up alongside the rig at our platonic rendezvous in Texarkana. We switched out trailers, and I headed back to Dallas. Tomorrow was the last day I'd work this run for a while.

The next morning I arrived at the Dallas terminal at eight on the dot. I hoped the third time would be the charm. That day it would feel like a blessing if Julie simply performed her role and let me perform mine. But sadly, that was not to be the case. I received the dispatch slip from Julie and paused at a nearby tabletop where drivers can fill out paperwork. While I checked my logbook I happened to hear Julie in conversation with someone else. She turned to one of the typically, seldom-seen dispatch managers, who walked in and stood nearby in a white shirt and tie. She asked him a question. He answered. Julie said, "I concur." She turned to another dispatch clerk. "Do you concur?" After confirming I hadn't fallen into a time warp and stepped onto the set of a self-righteously scripted television drama, I marveled at the two-faced nature of clerks who abuse innocent drivers one minute then portray themselves in an exaggeratedly serious way to the managers the next.

Once again only one trailer contained freight headed eastward on this run, though each day I'd brought back two fully loaded trailers. After setting the dolly in front of an empty trailer I backed up to the front trailer at one of the dock doors, climbed out, and walked over to make sure the trailer was shut and sealed. I peered around the edge of the trailer at the dock door only to find a nearly full and open trailer with packages stacked inside. With dread welling up in my gut I called dispatch on my cellphone. When this happened the dispatch office normally sent someone into the loading area to shut and seal the trailer before the driver left the dock.

"Just drive the trailer around to the front," Julie instructed, referring to the dispatch office.

"You want me to drive an unsealed trailer to the office," I asked, knowing a staff member usually sealed the trailer first. My impression was that class "A" CDL drivers were normally not supposed to come into contact with the freight at our company. Doing so might bring us under suspicion. One driver had told me not even to pick up a fallen box off the pavement, but to call dispatch and let them know. Putting a package in the truck cab, even just to drive it up to dispatch, could be perceived as stealing.

"Drive it up front, and I'll seal it," Julie said

"Can you send someone to seal it here?"

Julie insisted I drive the unsealed trailer to the office.

Maybe I should have refused. But in that moment I didn't know what else to do. The trailer door needed to be closed so no packages would fall out while setting up or driving around the terminal yard. Trailers awaiting loading stood on either side and all along the dock doors around the building. The only way to close the door was to drive the trailer out a couple of feet from the dock. I did so then climbed up the back bumper and grasping the door's strap did another controlled fall to the pavement below to close the door. After completing the set I returned to the office with the dispatch slip.

"Did you close the trailer door?" Julie asked.

"Of course."

"Why?"

"So packages wouldn't fall out."

"Did you do anything in the trailer?"

"What do you mean?" I asked, befuddled by her questions.

"Did you do anything to the packages?"

"Of course, not," I answered, as I realized Julie meant to insinuate that I might have looked through the boxes and selected some promising looking ones that could contain valuables. All because Julie had refused to seal the trailer or have someone else do so.

"Humph," Julie looked at me. She turned to the other dispatch clerk, the only other worker remaining in the office, the manager from her earlier conversation nowhere in sight. "I'm gonna go seal this trailer." When she walked away from the counter toward the door to the lobby I heard her parting shot to the other clerk. "I have to make sure this bitch didn't steal nothing," she said, referring to me.

Perhaps, Julie thought I hadn't heard those words, or more likely, she had said them *so* I would hear them. Feelings of anger mixed with the sickening knowledge I was being done yet another injustice by Julie. One I felt powerless to stop.

Julie walked into the lobby where I stood and went outside to the truck. I followed along behind her, feeling I'd better keep an eye on anything she did. She walked up to the back of the front trailer and rolled the door open partway. With one hand holding the door open she bent forward and looked at some of the boxes nearest the door. She picked up one or two smaller ones and turned them in her hand. She pushed others back to see further into the trailer. Knowing full well what her actions implied, a couple of new vertebrae in my trucker's backbone made me respond anyway.

"What are you doing?" I asked.

Julie ignored me.

"What are you looking for?"

Julie finished her cursory examination of the boxes and closed and sealed the trailer door.

"Is everything okay?"

Julie huffed past me imperiously, avoiding eye contact.

"Well?" I said to Julie's retreating back while she strutted toward the office door. I followed after her while feeling the weight of the degradation she had heaped on me all week. I was reminded of how some people *look* to create conflict, either for their own entertainment or to establish themselves as top dog, at least in their own minds. Inside again Julie walked behind the counter and updated the computer.

"Is everything okay?" I asked, through the window that separated us once more.

Julie printed out dispatch papers with the new seal number and slapped them down on the counter before me. She turned to the other clerk again.

"I'm going to take a smoke break," Julie said.

Julie walked back out the door, never responding to or looking at me. Yet Julie's message came through loud and clear. She had taken it upon herself to treat a random driver like a piece of shit. And she wanted to be sure I knew she felt that way. Not all dispatch clerks are like Julie or Van and every trucking company is the better for it. While most clerks are fair and even-tempered, some have favorites among drivers. Even someone like Julie, it turned out, didn't treat all drivers miserably.

I picked up the new dispatch papers and returned to the cab of my truck. From my vantage point in the driver seat I could see Julie standing with her cigarette several feet away next to the steps that led up to the dispatch office. After days of unprovoked insolence and abuse from Julie, I'd had all I could or would take. Some drivers fear standing up to clerks because of whatever crap the clerks might fling their way in the form of delays, disrespect and more difficult tasks. I had passed the point of caring. I climbed out of my rig and marched over to where Julie stood. I walked up a few feet away and faced her.

"Let me tell you something," I began.

Just then another truck rolled up, driven by a woman with a mop of curly hair. That driver, Ms. Mop Hair, greeted Julie like they were good friends.

"I'm talking to my friend now," Julie said, stepping to one side in an effort to avoid me.

You need to hear this

"I know you won't learn anything from this, but I'm going to tell you anyway," I persisted, stepping back in front of her.

Julie turned away facing the truck that rolled to a stop, the driver, Ms. Mop Hair, looking at me with confusion on her face, her brow furrowed. I stood my ground, looking at Julie.

"Hello, how's it going?" Julie called upward to the curly haired driver with the exaggerated friendliness and upbeat voice of someone pointedly playing innocent.

I spoke to Julie, "You are by *far* the rudest person I've ever met in the *entire* company system!"

"What's going on?" Julie asked Ms. Mop Hair whose brow furrowed at me more than ever. "I'm on my break now," Julie said out of the side of her mouth to me, her friend still looking down at us from her driver seat.

"You need to hear this from someone," I continued speaking to Julie. With both arms straight down by my sides and my hands formed into fists, I shouted to Julie at the top of my lungs, "You are a complete and utter ASSHOLE!"

Turning on my heels, I strode back to my truck.

Of course, Julie wouldn't learn. Ms. Mop Hair would forever believe that I was the asshole, but somewhere, sometime a mere driver had been the one to tell Julie what she ought to hear.

I was that driver.

Chapter 18: "You can go to hell!"

My next co-driver was retiring, certainly not in the sense of reticent or demure, however. That Monday my cellphone rang. Wayne's name popped up on the screen. I pressed the answer key.

"Good news," Wayne enthused. "A place on a route is about to open up."

"Oh, yeah? Who with?" I asked, wanting to know the all important, potentially deal-breaking or deal-making information. I wondered, into whose hands does he want me to entrust my life, liberty and pursuit of happiness.

"Her name is Margie. You've probably seen her around the yard. She's tall and has long hair." He paused, his voice drifting upward to nudge my recollection.

"Yeah, I know who you mean."

There were not a lot of women on the yard. While many guys blended in, for better or worse, us girls stuck out like sore thumbs. Or make that: like gems in the sun.

"It's a real easy run from Fort Worth to Tennessee and back daily."

"That doesn't sound too bad," I admitted.

I might get the job permanently if, Margie, the senior driver on the run wanted to drive with me, too. But first while Margie visited with her grandkids for a week, I would run with her co-driver. Then in a few weeks, I might start the run permanently when her co-driver left the job.

You can go to hell!

The next afternoon I met Margie's co-driver, a woman I'll call Diva, at the dispatch office. Diva was a middle-aged woman with a mound of fanciful curls piled high atop her head. Her fingers sported a complicated manicure with arching claws decorated with swirls. From one nail dangled a charm with a gold metallic rim around a sparkling stone.

We greeted each other, and Diva seemed nice enough.

We got our dispatch slip and headed to the dolly yard to grab that lovely, heavy piece of equipment that all doubles drivers relish working with.

"We always get a dolly with a crank wheel," Diva informed me. "They are easier to move around and set up."

Previously, my co-drivers had avoided the dollies that have a support wheel under the tip or point in the dolly's front. Ideally, the hard rubber wheel held up the heavy dolly making it easier to place the large metal loop of the point over the hitch. The little wheel, about the diameter of a saucer, was then cranked up and out of the way once the trailers were connected so that it didn't drag on the pavement while driving.

"Really? I've heard they're too heavy," I answered, backing the cab up to a likely dolly with a crank wheel, as I had just been instructed. The parking brakes hissed their readiness to hold the cab where it stood. Sitting in the passenger seat, Diva paused, bending her head down, her eyes looked into mine over the top edge of her mirror lens sunglasses.

She asked, "Who told you that? Guys?"

"You're the second woman I've driven with, so, yeah."

"Mm-hmm. Let me tell you something. Those guys don't use the little wheel."

"What do you mean?"

"They think they're he-men. They don't crank the wheel down to the pavement. So of course, they think it's too heavy."

"Do you think they're trying to be tough?"

"No. I think they're fucking stupid."

With that forthright announcement we both climbed out of the cab and walked to the back of the truck. I put on a pair of work gloves while I walked back. Diva, with her nails glistening in the sun, had to forego such a precaution. Diva waited while I operated the hand crank, lowering the small wheel to the pavement. With the front of the dolly supported by the wheel we rolled the dolly onto the hitch of our truck. Then I turned the hand crank in the opposite direction to lift the small support wheel off the pavement. It was still an effort to move the heavy piece of equipment, but there was no heaving the point of the dolly from a position on the ground to waist level, nor a struggle to prevent the point from rising or falling. What a fine suggestion this is, I thought. No more of the other dollies for me. If a crank wheel dolly was available, I'd use it instead.

Without further ado we built our set and headed for the gate. I took the dispatch slip in to the office to report the seal numbers on each trailer. Then I drove out the gate toward Tennessee, to the Jolly Trucker, the same place Sarge and I had stopped to eat on many occasions. I had been to the Jolly Trucker with other drivers and had stayed there overnight on solo runs, including the time I'd been glad to have that hickory tire knocker at hand. There Diva and I would exchange trailers with a team from the New York City area. We would then head back to Texas to start all over again the next day at about the same time. We would be constantly on the go all week with little time to spare.

Diva set up camp in the sleeper bunk and then sat in the passenger seat while I steered through the heavy traffic on the way out of Dallas-Fort Worth.

"One thing Margie and I always do: we make sure to stop and eat somewhere before getting down the road."

I agreed to stop at a truck stop with a fast food place we could both dine at.

"We switch out at Little Rock," Diva continued, plainly.

"At Little Rock?"

"We drive a five and five," Diva reported authoritatively.

I had traded driving with others since starting out. I had driven on their logs, and they had driven on mine. Just as many times as the practice had helped my co-driver to rest when tired and to drive when rested, so it had helped me. In fact, this often unspoken agreement between drivers had first helped ease me into driving. But the subject had usually been broached with a hint or, at most, a request. Many drivers treated the illegal practice like it

You can go to hell!

was the norm with their regular co-driver with whom they were familiar. Almost every driver I subbed with except Buster and Diva had treated the question like a personal choice. If a driver didn't want to trade out, she was normally under no pressure to do so. Consequently, I found Diva's announcement that she *expected* us to drive off the book a bit of a surprise.

"I don't know if we should do that," I said.

"Why?"

"We could get caught and fired."

"We won't. If we didn't trade out, by the end of the week we'd both be too exhausted to think," Diva explained. "Margie and I do it all the time."

"I've heard that it's not a good thing to do," I said, deciding to go by some recent advice from other co-drivers. I insisted we drive our own hours.

A few hours later with the last rays of the day's sun projecting over the horizon I drove into the parking lot of the Covered Wagon truck stop outside of Texarkana where I'd first stopped with Coach many moons prior and several times since. I drove our rig around to the diesel lanes. Even with several months of experience I didn't like the tight fit of this truck stop's parking lot, but the store with snack bar and clean restrooms was at the perfect distance for a pit stop after driving out of DFW.

I steered the cab around in a leftward sweeping arc, keeping an eye on the trailers at the same time. The trailers looked straight enough to pull ahead without any problem when leaving. Sort of. I climbed out of the truck with my trusty little green bookbag over one shoulder and glanced back at the trailers. They're okay, I thought to myself. But while I entered the building and walked to the restroom a little cloud of worry began to form over my head.

Several minutes later I walked to the front of the store and bought a drink and some chips. While I paid for my purchases, the little storm cloud of worry floating over my head began to shoot out branches of lightning. My business completed I stepped back outside into the rapidly darkening parking lot. Fluorescent lights on tall poles buzzed overhead with electricity and freshly formed clouds of confused insects. I walked up to the truck and climbed

269

into the driver seat. The curtains to the sleeper bunk remained closed. Apparently, Diva still rested inside. If so, I was glad the stop hadn't awakened her, as they so often woke me.

I turned off the parking brakes while engaging the pedal brakes. I put the truck in gear and slowly pulled forward, my eyes checking the trailers' position by switching between both sets of side mirrors. Gradually, the problem reflected in the mirrors became obvious. I had to stop. My little worry cloud had burst. I sat drenched by my own personal storm of stupidity.

The back trailer was at too much of an angle to pull forward without colliding with the bollards. Made of concrete and metal, the large posts called bollards protect vulnerable fuel pumps from being struck by vehicles. The bollards at truck stops can stand about four foot high, tall enough to strike the side of an errant trailer. At the Covered Wagon rods of reinforcing metal escaped from the three foot round diameter tops while ancient yellow paint flaked from the bollards' sides. The driver side of the rig came too close to the bollard on that side. I had misjudged the angle of the trailers when driving into the fuel lane.

Okay, I thought. Don't panic. No truck had pulled up behind us so I put the gear in reverse and eased back. In almost no time the back trailer, already in an awkward state of geometry, went helplessly askew. I pulled forward as much as I could until the back trailer neared the concrete bollard on the driver side a second time. I put the truck back into reverse and tried again. Almost instantly the back trailer showed a mind of its own, going off at an awkward angle. If I persisted, I could find myself in a slow speed jackknife between the front and back trailers.

Forward once more. Only so far forward and yet again it became clear that the lower edge of the back trailer would bump against the closest bollard. I set the brakes and climbed out of the truck. When in doubt, Get Out And Look. It's one of the truisms of trucking. Some trucking companies even have stickers affixed to cab windows with the letters: G.O.A.L. But the more informal way drivers have of putting it is, "Don't hit shit!"

I walked back along the side of the trailers. The back trailer sat close to the massive bollard, but with more space than I dared to move toward the concrete structure without a spotter. Another

270

bollard, just like this one, stood on the other side of the truck. If I didn't strike this one, I might strike the other.

I went back to the driver seat and backed up the truck as far as I dared. I walked back to take another look. With no way to steer the back trailer that trailer had gone askew once more. I couldn't get any closer to the bollard without help.

'Shit!' I thought.

There was nothing else for it. I would have to wake Diva and confess my foolhardiness. She and Margie had been driving for a while. Maybe Diva would know what to do.

I climbed back into the driver seat, but this time I turned in the seat and addressed the closed curtain. "Are you awake?"

"What's wrong?" Diva answered immediately, apparently awakened by the truck rolling back and forth while I had tried to free it from between the pumps.

"I seem to have gotten into a pickle," I explained. "I can't pull away from the fuel pumps without scraping the back trailer against concrete. But I can't back up to straighten out either."

Diva didn't reply, but I heard the unmistakable sounds of a co-driver stirring. A few minutes later she emerged from the sleeper wearing an oversized nylon jacket over her uniform. She climbed outside into the cool late spring evening. Then I stayed in the cab while Diva directed. She stood outside the truck within sight of the mirrors and gave me hand signals. Not the middle finger salute that I might have deserved, but rather gestures of 'Keep backing,' or 'Stop.' In this way I pulled forward and back trying to make progress, trying to straighten the trailers so they could make their way through the fuel lanes.

Like driving in the crowded dolly yard, the procedure felt like steering a boat through a rocky cove. But Diva helped prevent backing into the bollard on the passenger side. Then she walked around and helped me not to strike the bollard on the driver side when pulling forward. With Diva's help I could drive further forward or back with less risk of hitting anything, much more so than on my own. We did make a bit of progress, but mostly just seesawed back and forth. Plus, after all that rocking motion the truck cab bent away from the front trailer at an odd angle to the right where I sat facing out the windshield while the back trailer still bent more to the left. From a bird's eye view we were gradually forming the letter "S." The only thing that sat straight was the front trailer couched between two expensive diesel pumps connected to a flow of flammable liquid.

We struggled amidst the hubbub of truck drivers coming and going, getting fuel or stopping to park their trucks for the night. Some paused and watched a second. Most just glanced at us from their cabs. Some grinned. Some pinched their lips together and squinted their eyes. I chuckled imagining their thoughts: 'Damn women drivers!' I tried not to look at them too much. Observing them wouldn't help straighten our truck. Anyway, I was living out the theory that truck driving affords numerous opportunities to look and feel foolish.

Following several attempts, I climbed down from the driver seat and walked back to the trailers. I tried to gage our progress while Diva and I discussed our options. Would we have to break down and rebuild the set? We agreed that was the last thing we'd do. While we talked, a heavy guy in a red and white jacket and a black cap climbed out of the driver seat of a truck parked perpendicular to us, but with a front row seat to our goings-on. He walked over.

"Hey, I'm Tracy," he grinned cheerfully. "Looks like you got yourself into a real jam."

"Yeah, I called it a pickle, but you're right," I said sheepishly.

"Whatever it is, it's a shit sandwich, am I right?" Tracy laughed.

We laughed, too.

"Is the pup lighter than the front?" he asked.

Neither Diva nor I knew what Tracy meant. He explained that the back trailer was the pup. We did know that the heaviest trailer was on the front.

"You might try getting the cab up under the trailer," he said.

This suggestion baffled me because the cab and trailer were hitched together by backing the fifth wheel under the front trailer. But putting a truck cab up under a trailer means to back it *straight* under. Maybe that would help, I thought. Anyway it wouldn't hurt to try. I walked over and lowered the landing gear on the front trailer while Diva showed Tracy how close the trailers

272

came to the bollards. I undid the fifth wheel pin and lifelines then pulled forward, disengaging the cab from the front trailer. Then I backed the cab straight under the front trailer, reconnected the lifelines and raised the landing gear again. At least then only one part of the rig was crooked. Instead of an "S" the rig formed more of an "L," since the back trailer remained out of kilter.

With Diva on the passenger side and Tracy on the driver side I began anew to gradually ease the trailers forward, inch by inch. Tracy also turned his hand to suggest steering directions. Each time the back trailer came a little bit further up into the fuel lane than before. After several tries Tracy walked up alongside the cab.

"You may want to get back up under the trailer again."

I re-straightened the cab's alignment to the front trailer. The sun had set, and the air cooled. I noticed the chill while lowering the landing gear, and disconnecting and reconnecting the truck and trailers. But the adrenalin going through me, hoping I wouldn't have to break down the set, that I didn't hit anything, that something wouldn't go so badly awry that I would have to call Wayne, kept my blood pumping too quickly to feel chilled.

After readjusting the cab and front trailer again I climbed back up to the steering wheel where Diva stood within sight of my right side mirror and Tracy in the left mirror. Bit by bit I eased the truck into reverse and drive, until a chorus of angels singing in celebration felt appropriate to the occasion. Finally, as if the truck had never been stuck at all or had just been playing a lively joke on us, both trailers rolled forward, clear of the pumps and the massive bollards that protected them.

"Alright!" Tracy raised a fist triumphantly in the air. "No incident report to fill out."

Both Diva and I thanked Tracy.

"Sure," Tracy said. "You'd do the same for me."

During this whole difficulty I had truly wished Diva would take the wheel, if she thought that could make a positive difference. Quite rightly she didn't offer, and I didn't ask. Yet secretly I had even wished Tracy would take the wheel. Of course, that would have been a big misstep to have a non-employee drive my truck, even though he might be a CDL holder, too. If he hit something, how would I explain to my boss that I had surrendered control of the vehicle to a stranger, however kind he might be? But though I might have wished someone else would take the wheel, it was important that I, the one who had caused the problem, was the one who also steered out of it. Not only based on principle, but for the practice. For one thing, after this I would never under-steer the trailers into a fuel lane. For another, I had a better idea of how to get out of such a situation from the best possible source: my own experience.

To her eternal credit Diva showed nothing but patience while we wrestled with the predicament I had steered the rig into. That she had bothered to help at all was entirely up to her good graces. Most co-drivers would have helped, too. I would have helped, if a co-driver had messed up thusly. However, Diva was not the driver right then, and I knew she could have told me: 'Tough luck. You got into it, you get out of it.' I felt I ought to show appreciation somehow.

"I'll drive to Little Rock where you and Margie switch out."

"Oh?"

"Yeah, it's the least I can do, since I woke you up with all this trouble," I said. "We'll drive the five and five this week, if you want to."

Diva nodded and climbed back into the truck's sleeper bunk.

My ten minute restroom break had eaten up just over an hour. Not only that I had eaten some humble pie along the way, and it had tasted a lot like a shit sandwich.

Even after my not-so-illustrious start to the week we arrived at the Jolly Trucker at an hour before midnight, plenty of time. Not least of all because the team we were meeting hadn't arrived. Diva had driven us in from Little Rock, and she parked alongside a wall at the Jolly Trucker where she and Margie usually met the New York team. The wall stood on the same side of the street next to the truck stop itself. Unlike my visits here with Sarge, we didn't have to cross the street. Lucky thing, too, because this run arrived long after sunset on a typical day, though the headlights of trucks and motorists coursed up and down the nearby road continually.

Before leaving the parked truck Diva handed me a spare key.

"We always lock it," Diva said. "Especially after hearing that trucks can be hijacked."

I remembered hearing a news story of a man who had forced a trucker at gun point to drive across three counties before police stopped them. Thankfully, no one was hurt, but the story had certainly gotten my attention, too. Hijacker or not, I was happy to lock the truck. Not only was it nice to know everything left in the truck would still be there when we got back. It was also a relief to know no one would be waiting in the sleeper for the woman or women he'd seen go into the truck stop.

We walked across the parking lot that glowed with a bluish tinge from the truck stop's large signs, one on the building and one high overhead on a pole, both designed to be read from the highway. From our seats in the restaurant next to the plate glass windows our truck was clearly visible. We could see when the other team arrived and be ready for them.

"Thanks for your help at the Covered Wagon," I said.

"You're welcome."

"I'm glad I had a more experienced driver with me."

"How long have you been driving?" Diva asked.

"Almost a year," I answered.

"Me too."

"Really? Oh, well, together that's almost two years."

"Mmm," Diva answered noncommittally.

Midnight arrived and passed while I learned that Diva had only ever driven the second of each five and five shift for the first few months she was on this run. By her own choice the first time she'd driven the weekend solo run had been the first time she'd driven the segment from Fort Worth to Little Rock driving out or from Tennessee back to Little Rock on the return. Driving a highway in the opposite direction isn't entirely the same thing, especially for a new driver. Each direction of a highway has its own nuances and challenges.

I felt less surprised by that revelation than by her admission that often when it rained she had pulled over to the nearest truck stop and let Margie drive. That had been their practice until only fairly recently. Only lately had Diva begun to get used to driving in wet weather, but she still hated the same curves I'd found challenging, especially on the part of the drive she was less familiar with.

"How long has Margie been driving?"

"About five years," Diva answered.

If Margie and I were going to be a team, having a more experienced co-driver offered a bit of a sense of security.

After eating I took advantage of the wait to take a shower. The gap between the other team's arrival and ours ate up two hours. At least that meant a chance to shower and change.

The New York team drove up next to our truck at one a.m. and we switched trailers. Then I drove us back to Little Rock. Next Diva drove us from Little Rock to either Dallas or Fort Worth, wherever the trailers were destined. Our trailers were usually destined for Dallas. That meant dropping the trailers we'd brought from Tennessee and building a new set of trailers each morning in Dallas before we could head back to our home terminal in Fort Worth. Then we had to drop those trailers in Fort Worth and build another set to take back up to Tennessee. Our stop in Dallas each morning cost us another two hours, partly for time on the yard setting up and for fueling. Plus, the two DFW terminals were almost an hour apart, if weather and traffic cooperated.

In the meantime I laid down on my sleeping bag in the bunk in Little Rock. While Diva took over the driving, I rested for the next few hours. Finally, I woke from a catnap and gazed at the slits of light that intruded into the sleeper. I sat up and opened one of the small metal side vents to find out where we were and could tell that Dallas was less than an hour away. I had no more sleep left in me so I stepped between the curtains of the bunk and sat in the passenger seat to put on my shoes, readying to exchange trailers in Dallas.

"When we get to Dallas Margie always helps me drop and get the next set ready, okay?" Diva said, sounding a bit like a schoolteacher telling a child how to complete a simple task.

"Sure," I answered. "I always help my co-driver, unless they don't want help."

"Margie always helps me drop and get the next set ready," Diva repeated, seemingly oblivious to my affirmative response. Diva continued, "We work as a team, and there is no 'I' in 'team,' as far as I'm concerned."

I just nodded, wondering why she thought I'd gotten up and readied myself. Officially, I would have been within my rights to stay in the bunk while Diva worked this midday drop every one of the days we drove together. But I had never shirked helping a co-driver set up. Only if a driver said he didn't want help, would I sit idly by. I'd also never had a co-driver refuse to help me or, except in the case of Doug, one who simply wouldn't. But since Diva had brought up the subject, I thought it bore mentioning that I'd like help on the Fort Worth yard at the end of the week before heading back out for the weekend solo drive.

"I don't mind helping every time we have to drop and set up," I said. "I know you're leaving for a long weekend Saturday, but if you wouldn't mind helping me before you go, I'd really appreciate it."

"Not a problem," Diva assured. "Margie and I always help each other set up before a solo weekend."

I felt glad to hear that and looked forward to helping and being helped. We entered the grounds of the Dallas terminal and went to work. While we rolled from the drop yard, where we left the trailers we had brought in, to the dispatch office then to the fuel pumps then on to the loaded trailers, I kept noticing that Diva expected me to do things a certain way.

After dropping the trailers and getting our next dispatch slip, we went to the fuel pumps to take advantage of the opportunity to fill up with diesel without waiting in line at a truck stop or navigating the passage of trailers through the fuel lanes, my recent predicament at the Covered Wagon notwithstanding. Diva pulled up to the pumps and set the parking brake. I sat in the passenger seat for a moment and thumbed through my logbook, entering our new trailer numbers on the log sheet for that day.

"Well?" Diva said.

I looked up. "What?"

"We're at the fuel pumps," Diva announced.

I opened the door and climbed down to set a pump handle into the passenger side tank. Fueling up the truck wasn't particularly difficult. Two pumps had to be operated simultaneously, but fueling is certainly not a strenuous activity. Often just one driver fueled. Like other drivers I'd fueled up trucks on my own many times. But if Diva wanted me to operate one of the pumps, that was no big deal. I'd often done so for other co-drivers.

I opened the cap to the tank on the passenger side, inserted the nozzle and checked to see if the pump was working yet. It wasn't. The driver side controls turned on both pumps. So I stood and waited for the pump on the driver side to click on. In a few seconds I checked my pump again. Nothing. I waited some more. I speculated maybe Diva was having trouble finding the fuel card or negotiating her fearsome claws around the pump handle on the driver side.

While waiting I gazed beyond the small square of roof that covered the fuel pumps. The sky shone a beautiful soft blue that day with wisps of clouds here and there. A couple of red-tailed hawks circled overhead. Lots of hawks flew along the highways, using the thermal heat rising off the pavement to lift themselves skyward. They often hunted small animals along the roadways. I'd seldom seen hawks eating road kill. More often turkey vultures hunched over the decaying remains of highway drivers' latest victims. But the Dallas terminal was surrounded by grassy fields lined with woods. A prime place for the hawks to swoop down and catch field mice and other small prey.

"Well?" Diva's voice interrupted my thoughts. I looked toward the front of the truck. Diva wasn't there. I looked toward the back. She was nowhere in sight.

"Up here."

Directly above my head Diva leaned out of the passenger window, the fuel card placed between two highly polished nails. "That other pump ain't gonna turn itself on, you know."

There are a lot of drivers who, right then, would have walked off the truck. But after that week I would never have to drive with Diva again. If I walked off right then, my sudden absence would put Wayne in a bind. Plus, Diva had been helpful and patient when I'd gotten stuck at the Covered Wagon. I sighed and, reaching up, took the card from Diva's predatory-looking claws in one mousy hand before walking around the front of the truck to start the driver side pump.

After fueling, we headed over to the loaded trailers. To my surprise Diva got out of the truck to help position the dolly. She also whirled the crank on the landing gear with gloveless hands, while my gloved mitts connected the brake lines and power cords. I guessed it was easier to palm the landing gear crank than to grasp and turn the connections to the trailers, which were frequently oily and grimy, therefore requiring gloves.

Once our new set had been built, I climbed back into the passenger seat. Next we needed to drive to the dispatch office so they could confirm the seal numbers on the trailers. Whoever was officially behind the wheel, in this case Diva, normally wrote the numbers on the paperwork and carried them inside.

"Did you get the numbers off of the seals?" Diva asked.

"Me? No."

"You're supposed to."

"Yeah, if I was driving."

"Margie always writes down the seal numbers and takes them in," Diva said, peering at me once again over the tops of her sunglasses, the dispatch slip extended in her hand. I whisked the slip of paper out of her hand and climbed back out of the truck. Shaking my head to myself, I retrieved the seal numbers from the trailers.

Evidently, Diva, who had only driven a brief time before beginning her current run, thought she and Margie had worked things out according to some universal template. I had never seen that non-existent template. I couldn't read Diva's mind either. Further, I had discovered in working a variety of runs with different drivers that each team had their own routine and customs. While I had come to pride myself on being adaptable to co-drivers' expectations, I had never before met a co-driver who expected me to automatically know her team's routine.

I finished writing down the numbers and carried them in. The phantom Julie still haunted the dispatch office. On a couple of days I lucked out, and a different clerk handled our paperwork. But sometimes it was Julie who accepted the incoming paperwork and dispatched the rig to Fort Worth. For whatever reason she didn't try to menace my efforts that week. Had my commentary, delivered with such high volume and energy that it felt like the soles of my shoes had levitated a few inches, made a positive difference?

Diva drove to Fort Worth while I tried to catch a quick nap in the sleeper. Back at our home terminal we went through the whole procedure again, minus the fueling. We wouldn't have to fuel again until the next morning. We dropped the trailers from Dallas and picked up two new ones headed to New York by way of the Jolly Trucker. I became the driver of record so I wrote down the seal numbers then parked next to the dispatch office. After reporting the numbers to a clerk, I returned and prepared to drive out the gate.

"Where are you going now?" Diva asked.

It sounded like an obvious question, but I played along, telling her I was about to start the run back up to Tennessee.

"What about the inspection lane?"

"What inspection lane?" I asked.

"This is the second day you've driven past it," Diva informed me. "Margie always stops there for a tire check. I'm not in enough of a hurry to go back out without a tire check."

Nor was I in such a hurry. One of my trucking truisms was: It takes the time it takes. What surprised me most was that no one had ever mentioned the existence of an inspection lane where drivers could at least get the tires checked. Not even Wayne or Wil when I had expressed my concerns about inspections that day in their office.

I circled around the terminal and pulled into the inspection lane next to the shop. A metal roof stood over a spot long enough for a cab pulling doubles to park out of the rain or in the shade, depending on the weather. A couple of uncovered spaces marked out with yellow paint stripes on the asphalt next to the roof also awaited outgoing rigs. I had seen drivers parked under the roof on many occasions. Some co-drivers had written down the seal numbers and carried them to the dispatch office while parked there. I had even parked there myself to get a light replaced when I'd driven with Doug. Yet I had never been aware that anyone checked any of the tires while we were there. Most of the time truck drivers were the only workers present. I'd had to go into the shop to ask someone to fix the light months before, even though rubber strips like the ones at old fashioned gas stations lie across the path the trucks drove over. The strips make a bell ding when a tire goes over them. I wondered if the ding sounded on those strips anymore or if they were simply ignored.

Diva and I drove back out three more times to finish the week's run. We stopped and switched out drivers at Little Rock each shift according to her team's custom. I waited almost an hour each time Diva's turn to exit the sleeper bunk arrived. We met a New York team each night and exchanged trailers. Sometimes at midnight, sometimes at 2 a.m. or later. Each team's arrival times varied when they met harsh weather or congested traffic. On each day's return Diva drove first to Dallas, then on to Fort Worth. The whole week we worked each drop and set up together, regardless of who was the driver of record.

Finally our last day of the week arrived. Saturday morning Diva drove to the Dallas terminal yet again. After we built the set I wrote each seal number on the back of the dispatch slip the same way I'd done all week. The front trailer's seal number topped the list then our dolly number followed by the back trailer's seal number on the bottom. Thus, we were ready to turn in our paperwork so Diva could drive back to Fort Worth. Once there I would head back out for a solo run with a week's worth of bone-weary tiredness weighing down on me. Then after resting overnight I would drive back alone on Sunday.

Diva drove our rig up to the dispatch office.

"I'm really tired. I'm gonna try to get a nap while you drive back," I said, turning in the passenger seat to stand up and walk into the sleeper.

"You mean you're not going to take these numbers in?" Diva asked, wagging the dispatch slip under my drowsy nose.

"The seal numbers are on the back of the slip."

"How am I supposed to know which is which?"

"They're in the same order. Front trailer on top, then the dolly number, then the back trailer," I said, pointing out the way every driver I knew wrote the numbers down.

"Margie always takes them in," Diva stated adamantly.

281

"Didn't you hear me?" I answered, finally deciding to use my hard earned backbone with Diva. "I'm going to try to get a little sleep before we get back to Fort Worth."

"Margie takes the slip into the office," Diva repeated.

"You're the driver of record. I'm supposed to be in the bunk," I said. "Can't you take it in just this once?"

"Margie does it."

"I'm not Margie."

Again Diva looked at me over the top of her sunglasses. Her eyes glared with anger like an actress out of a B movie, but she meant it. For real. Then Diva opened the door and climbed down the steps of the truck.

"You can go to hell!" Diva shouted at the top of her lungs and slammed the driver door – hard! So hard the 60,000 plus pound rig pitched a little to one side.

Whatever sleepiness might have settled into my brain whooshed right out into the stratosphere with the wind off of that slammed door. My mind churning out four letter words by the second, I stepped back into the sleeper and drew the curtains closed against the late morning sun. I didn't understand what the big deal was. Everyone I'd ever driven with just took in their own paperwork without complaint or even comment. Perhaps, I was lucky Diva hadn't scratched my eyes out with her talon-like nails.

I had to give Diva credit for her kindness at the Covered Wagon the first day we'd driven together. And for introducing me, however incidentally, to the use of crank wheel dollies and to the existence of the tire check lanes. But after Diva's last performance I definitely couldn't get that much-needed nap on the way back to Fort Worth. Instead, I'd have to settle for seeing the back of Diva disappearing over the horizon instead.

Diva drove to the Fort Worth terminal and pulled the rig into the long driveway next to the parking lot. Though she hadn't said anything, parking there right then pretty much served as an indication she was leaving without helping set up for the solo run as promised. Just a couple of hours after I had dragged my exhausted ass out of the sleeper bunk for the fourth time that week to help her drop and set up in Dallas, she abandoned me at the starting gate for asking her to do her job just one time like everyone else. With rapid motions Diva began to gather her goods together to take them to her car.

While she worked I sat down in the driver seat and readied myself to take the rig into the terminal after she finished. Standing on the passenger side steps Diva tossed her belongings to the grassy ground beside the driveway the way drivers sometimes did for easy retrieval. Then she prepared to descend the steps of the truck just as I glanced down at the dashboard and spotted an unfamiliar phone charger still hanging from an outlet. I unplugged it.

"Is this yours?" I asked, imagining the inconvenience of a cellphone dying from low battery power sometime that weekend. Looking up at the charger that dangled in my hand, Diva's face froze in an expression of surprise. "Thank you," she managed to answer. Then she grasped the charger from my hand with her clawed fingers, climbed down the truck steps and walked to her car.

I had a feeling there *was* an 'I' in 'team,' as far as Diva was concerned.

Chapter 19: "Do you believe in spidey sense?"

So far I'd driven with two ladies and felt lucky not to have been in a catfight. I had gotten along with neither of them while I'd gotten along well with almost every one of the guys, even if some more than others. I wondered if driving with another female again could work out. Sure, risking life and limb every week and almost every day not knowing who would sit behind the wheel while I bunked down had been loads of fun. But maybe taking a regular route again would be worth another try. Team drivers don't have to get along like a house on fire. They just ought to behave with reasonable respect and not walk all over each other.

A few weeks later, Diva had opted to leave her job. Following Wayne's instructions, I planned to meet Margie at the dispatch office at the same time of day Diva and I had met. I already knew the truck number and who to look for. I had seen Margie around the terminal several times during my first year. As Wayne had mentioned she was tall, thin and had long hair down to her waist. Both Diva and Margie were about twenty years older than me, technically old enough to be my parent. Maybe driving with Margie would be sort of like driving with a mom, I hoped.

We'd never been introduced, but Margie had been kind enough to warn me one day while I sat in a driver seat during a solo run, waiting to pull an entire rig up to the crowded pumps at the Fort Worth yard. The trailers wouldn't have fit in the small area that surrounded the pumps. At her suggestion I'd unhitched from the front trailer before fueling. Standing next to the pumps with the

284

scent of diesel in the air I had felt grateful when I looked around at the unique geometry of the pumps next to the shop and tire lanes beside the guard shack at the single entry gate to the entire facility. Margie had been right. I would have gotten stuck and would have had to break down the whole rig just to get on my way. The resulting mess would have grossly inconvenienced many other drivers who needed to get to the fuel pumps or get a tire change or just drive out the gate. Margie had saved me from spectacular embarrassment and a very real, technical challenge.

On our first day of driving together Margie and I met and began to build our set. By then summer had arrived, and the heat burned full force, radiating up from the concrete on the yard as we worked. Diva had been correct about this much: she and Margie had worked as a team. Every time the dolly needed repositioning Margie and I stood on opposite sides and worked together to place the heavy piece of equipment wherever it needed to be. At about half past noon I steered our completed rig into the tire inspection lane. After getting a green light from one of the men that the tires checked out okay, we drove around to the dispatch office to turn in the paperwork. Then I guided the truck out the gate. We would stop for lunch shortly. Then I would drive us all the way past Memphis to the Jolly Trucker.

Once again a team from the New York city area would either be waiting when we arrived or would eventually join us to exchange trailers. Then Margie would drive us back to Dallas where I would exit the bunk to help drop and build the way I had done so for Diva. Then we would return to Fort Worth and start the whole procedure all over again. Every week we alternated who drove out. The driver who drove out from Fort Worth for the first shift did the solo weekend run. Our run had originally been meant for two drivers five days a week, according to Margie. But the nearest thing Margie had to a permanent home was staying with family in Oklahoma. Such housing arrangements are not all that unusual in trucking, since being on the road often makes maintaining a home unnecessary if a trucker isn't married to a non-trucker or doesn't have young children.

Driven Crazy ~ Karen Greenhill

Right then I drove out of the gate and pulled over. I had to get a sleeping bag and travel case from my car into the cab of the truck. We also hadn't decided where to stop for lunch. Before climbing down from the truck I began the first of our daily discussions on which truck stop would get our lunch money.

"Where do you want to eat?" I asked.

"Wherever you want to stop is fine with me."

"Where do you normally stop?" I asked, falling back on the practice of adapting to my co-drivers. Margie mentioned a place Diva and I had stopped at when we had driven together. After loading sleeping gear on the top bunk, I piloted the truck to our lunch stop. Then I started the long drive northeast while Margie bunked down.

Ideally, we met a team at the Jolly Trucker between 11 p.m. and midnight. Each day the teams we met alternated. On any given week our truck met Team A on Tuesday, Thursday, and Saturday while Team B met us on Wednesday and Friday. The next week Team B met us Tuesday, Thursday and Saturday, and Team A on Wednesday and Friday. The run from Fort Worth to the Jolly Trucker was the flip side of runs from Texas to Virginia that I'd taken with Coach or later with Jack and Chan. The fly in the ointment on such a route was each time one of the other teams arrived late that could make us late the rest of the week. The team driving the shortest distance ran constantly to meet the other two teams. Running the shorter distance, we had no gap in time to catch up like the teams we met did. Our run back and forth could take an entire twenty four hours, including fueling, building our sets and coping with delays.

By contrast the teams we met had a forty hour run that left every forty eight hours. Therefore, they had an eight hour gap to rest or make up for delays. With no such gap in our time we busted our butts to drive back down to Dallas where we dropped and set up to go back to Fort Worth and drop and set up again before driving hard to meet the other team the next night, if a delay had occurred the night before. Besides, unlike a linear driving assignment, trucking on a regular route involves making daily rounds at hubs or buttheads. If we gained time or distance,

286

we only waited longer for trailers one way or another. We still had to be in Dallas, Fort Worth or at the Jolly Trucker at or near an appointed time each day.

Naturally, delays inevitably happened when routing trailers halfway across the continent. When drivers meet regularly they often exchange cellphone numbers to let the other team or driver know if they've been delayed. Margie had the phone number of a guy we traded trailers with. Like all the New York drivers we met on this run, Ivan originated from eastern Europe. Unlike many of his co-drivers he spoke enough English to have a phone conversation. The days we met Ivan's team we often received or made a call to him to check on each other's progress.

Margie turned out to be a good-natured lady who was careful in her driving. I couldn't recall even one time she had eased the rig over onto the rumble strip, though she must have done so once or twice. In the following weeks Margie and I got into a pattern of working together. At the start of the week I might call Margie while she completed her drive in from Oklahoma. I had a half hour drive compared to her hours long, weekly commute. I could bring in lunch so we didn't have to stop to eat once we hit the road that first day. Sometimes that could save us valuable time.

"Let's see, I'm near a taco place, a hamburger joint and a pizza parlor. Do any of those sound good?" I might ask.

"Bring me a beef burrito, and I'll pay you back."

Over time I got the impression I could depend on Margie when the chips were down.

She could depend on me, too.

Neither of us could depend on the tire inspection lane.

We started our week by leaving the Fort Worth yard at about noon. On such days workers manned the tire inspection station when one of us pulled the rig in for a tire check. Getting the tires checked, however, was not always an easy task. Many days a mechanic would appear from the shop when we drove over the rubber strips that should sound a bell in the shop. He would write the trailer numbers on a clipboard and check all the trailer tires. If any of the tires on either trailer needed changing or one of us brought to his attention a broken glad-hand connector or a damaged trailer light, he replaced or fixed the item. Driving an average of five days a week with a hodgepodge of random doubles trailers at least two or three tires needed replacing each week. Many more needed air added.

Some guys even checked the cab's tires that were the driver's responsibility to check. In fact, one day a mechanic refused to let us leave unless Wayne replaced a bad front tire on our cab, a so-called steering tire on the front axle. Wayne had arrived and driven the truck to a nearby shop and back. The whole transaction cost time and money. Money well spent, I thought, being one of the drivers who had to live or die by that tire. And kudos to the mechanic who required the replacement.

Anyone who has had a tire blow out in a car going at highway speed knows how hard maintaining control can be. A trailer tire failing likely wouldn't cause a trucker much trouble, likewise if one of the cab's drive tires failed. But each of those axles had dual tires that share the load. If such a tire fails, usually the other tire remains. But the front axle only had a single tire on each side. I didn't even want to imagine how hard it must be to control a big rig when a steering tire fails. Neither Margie nor I had noticed a problem with the tire. I wondered how long it had needed replacement and if I could have spotted the need myself, if I'd ever been shown how to do a thorough inspection.

If we addressed any problems, we drove out on our run with a little more security that all would go well, safety-wise. Of course, sometimes as our week progressed one or both of the teams we met arrived late. Or we experienced delays of our own. Then we might leave the Fort Worth yard after 2 p.m. the following day. On days like that all bets were off on whether anyone would remain in the mechanical shop to replace trailer tires, lights or anything else.

The mechanics arrived at 6 a.m. and left about eight hours later at 2 p.m. if possible, after finding half an hour to eat lunch sometime during their shift. The mechanics also had trailers and dollies sitting in the shop awaiting repairs. To be sure they had other things to do besides replacing tires, though the inspection lane with air inflation equipment and racks of tires nearby clearly indicated that part of their job, too.

288

Believe in spidey sense?

At some point in the early afternoon nobody could be found in the shop. The departing mechanics locked the doors and no trailer tires could be inspected or replaced by onsite personnel. If a driver detected a problem with a tire, he would have had to call his boss to authorize a repair truck from a fleet servicing company to come out and do any work. Most drivers wouldn't want such a delay. However, many simply didn't check their own tires. Yet, the company runs a 24 hour a day operation. Trucks and trailers with little or no in-depth inspection by drivers, including myself, left the grounds of every facility all through the night and day on a regular basis. With a lick and a promise hundreds of drivers head out each day, system wide, never quite sure if one of the trailer tires might unpeel a long strip of metal-reinforced rubber onto the roadway in front of motorists or other truckers while they zoom along.

Even before two in the afternoon, we often struggled to get the trailer tires inspected before heading out the gate. Since I had learned of the tire lane's existence and ran with a co-driver who always stopped there, I got the trailer tires looked at every time possible. Many days a mechanic walked out when our rig pulled up, but often no one did. If a mechanic did step out and start checking the tires, I looked in the side mirrors for several minutes while updating my logbook before climbing down from the truck to record the seal numbers on the back of each trailer. Writing down the seal numbers gave us a chance to check on the status of the tire inspection or to make sure a mechanic really did replace a light or give the dolly some needed minor repair.

If no one ventured out from the shop after ten minutes or so, then I ventured in. Often I found a mechanic in the shop or its office. Depending on the time of day, the mechanics may have left for a lunch break, or they might be sitting at a picnic table in the shop. Presumably even then someone should be on duty, taking lunch earlier or later. Sometimes one or two guys would be in the midst of repairing a trailer or dolly. Even then, *someone* should be assigned specifically to check tires. At any time if I asked one of the guys, he might say, "So-and-so is supposed to be doing that."

"Where is he?"

"I don't know."

Even during their regular hours I sometimes couldn't find any mechanic around at all. On several occasions the only person around had been a mechanic sitting behind the shop, his back leaning against the wall, sleeping. You can imagine his surprise and our team's popularity when I woke him and asked him to check our trailers' tires.

Whatever it took I ferreted out one of the mechanics. After a little small talk: "Hey, how are you? How's it going? The weather sure is cold/hot today. I'm glad we did/didn't get rain, too. They keep you guys awfully busy. Bet your kids are looking forward to the holidays/vacation. Guess, you're looking forward to clocking out while we head down the road, lucky guy."

Somewhere along the way I would say something like, "Can we get a tire check before we head out the gate?"

Many guys happily obliged. Many acted reluctant. Once a mechanic even claimed his job didn't include tire checks and replacements. Maybe he hoped the pesky gal drivers would stop asking. We never did. I had to grow another vertebra in my trucker's backbone just to regularly seek an inspection when mechanics so seldom offered to do their jobs. But Margie and I had determined to follow another of the truisms of trucking: take advantage of every safety check available. I still didn't feel sure what all an inspection should include, but I would get the tires checked, if possible. Every time we arrived at the shop when it was open either Margie or I worked diligently to make sure someone checked the trailer tires.

Just a couple of persnickety females.

Having a compatible co-driver felt like a blessing. Shortly after Margie and I began to drive together we had a conversation about co-drivers in general and Diva in particular. I described some experiences I'd had with various co-drivers.

"Lots of drivers would be really cool to hang out with, but being in a truck with them for days is another thing," I said.

"It *is* really hard to find someone compatible to run with," Margie said. "But even Diva had her strong points."

"Yeah. She helped me that time I nearly got the trailers stuck at the Covered Wagon."

"She didn't complain?" Margie laughed.

"No, but the rest of the time she pestered me about everything. Like in Dallas, she absolutely did not want to go into the dispatch office with her paperwork."

"You know why, don't you?"

"Because I almost got stuck at the Covered Wagon and didn't want to drive a five and five?"

"But you did drive a five and five after that."

"True. Why then?"

"Diva couldn't stand Julie," Margie volunteered. "They'd had words a few times."

"Really?" I laughed. "That's not too difficult to imagine."

Unlike the mostly even-tempered and helpful clerks at the Dallas terminal, I had found Julie to be quite an exception. Despite a few favorites, a clerk may treat some drivers like they are as welcome as a rash. On the other hand Margie encountered no problems with Julie. In fact, Julie favored Margie the same way she favored Ms. Mop Hair, the woman who had witnessed me telling Julie off. What's more Margie and Ms. Mop Hair were friends, too. Margie informed me of a name to go with the face and the hair, Shirley.

Meanwhile Diva was exceptional in other ways and appeared oblivious to how demanding she could be.

"Diva acted the same way with me that she did with you," Margie revealed.

"I just do my job," I said. "And if possible, make my co-driver's life a little easier."

"Me too," Margie agreed.

We had stumbled upon another vital trucking truism: When you can – make your co-driver's life a little easier. Such consideration eases a difficult job, especially when the philosophy applies in both directions. Margie made my life a little easier by respecting my wish to take some time to shower either at the truck stop in Tennessee or at the terminal in Texas. If the team we met showed up soon after our arrival in Tennessee or were already there, we usually turned around and came right back. Then I took a shower at the Fort Worth terminal after we had finished building our set. While I showered Margie waited patiently in the truck, updating her log or catching a nap. I really appreciated her cooperation and thanked her.

Because of her kindness, naturally, I didn't mind waiting for Margie when she had a doctor's appointment one afternoon. We built our set together. Then while I drove the truck to the inspection lane Margie left on her errand. After our tire check I pulled the rig around the building near the dispatch office, parked and went inside to shower. When I returned Margie was still gone. Then she called my cellphone.

"I'm near a pizza place," Margie said. "You want me to get a pizza to go?"

"Sure."

We agreed on the toppings, and I pulled our rig out of the gate to wait for her. Margie hadn't appeared unwell. Maybe she had just gone in for a checkup. I certainly didn't want to pry.

Several minutes later Margie returned, and we set off again.

The next week Margie drove out in order to do the solo run that weekend. She had driven five hours all the way from her home in Oklahoma just to start the week. Even making good time, the run to the Jolly Trucker took about nine hours in good weather and traffic. Often the drive up took ten hours or more with delays. That meant fifteen hours or so of non-stop fun for Margie on the first day of the week, not counting time to build our set. We had the art of building a set down to about thirty minutes, both of us working hard to position the dolly, crank the landing gear and so on.

For the first few weeks Margie and I had driven the shifts known as the ten and ten. She and Diva had driven a five and five, perhaps at Diva's request. Of course, Margie and I were just becoming familiar with each other. Maybe Margie preferred a ten and ten, I speculated. Or maybe she just didn't know if she could trust me to drive on her logbook yet. As usual, I found the ten and ten more tiring than a five and five. At the start of the week, having taken a nap on the drive up, ordinarily I felt okay driving from about midnight until our arrival back in Fort Worth. Even on the second or third day, adrenalin, nervous energy and the desire to avoid a collision often kept me alert. By the last day or two of the week, especially on a night shift, most drivers struggle to stay awake, particularly just before sunrise. This was my week to drive nights.

About five hours after leaving Fort Worth Margie drove the rig up to a truck stop on the outskirts of Little Rock. While in the sleeper I'd woken when the truck had slowed down and then shifted from side to side on the access roads and into the truck stop parking lot. After a few moments I felt the rig roll to a stop. Then I heard Margie's voice through the sleeper curtain.

"Karen?"

"Yeah?"

"I'm pretty beat. Do you want to drive?"

"Okay," I said, grabbing my little green bookbag. "Do you want me to drive back here so we stay on a ten and ten?"

"That wouldn't be fair to you if the other team is late."

"You want to drive a five and five?"

"At least for today."

"I don't mind if we drive a five and five all the time," I offered.

"You know if we get stopped, we could be fired."

"I know. Do you believe in spidey sense?"

"Yeah. I know what you mean."

"Maybe we could drive a five and five, and if either of us ever feels like we shouldn't, she can say so."

Margie agreed, perhaps because she wanted to or perhaps because she needed to. I thought she also found the ten and ten needlessly tiring. After all, I became thoroughly exhausted by the end of the week in the best of times. In addition Margie had a persistent cough. By the end of each week I began to take on a slight cough myself. Over each weekend with plenty of sleep I got over the cough. Maybe Margie didn't.

I climbed down from the truck and walked away from the diesel pumps and the small store. Across the parking lot red neon lights shone from the truck stop's restaurant. I went inside and used the cleaner, more spacious restroom in the restaurant before heading back to the truck to finish our drive.

A team doesn't have to get along like a house on fire, though one night heading back toward Memphis in the wee hours I'd seen that very sight. About half an hour into the drive an unusually bright and pulsating light became visible on the north side of the highway. When our rig neared the spot I slowed to take a look and for the first time fully understood the expression: "engulfed in flames." A modest wood frame house stood just off the highway completely swallowed up by a yellow, gold and orange blaze. For all I knew people might be trapped inside. I fished my cellphone out of the cupholder on the dashboard and dialed 911.

"Units are already on their way," the emergency dispatcher explained. "But thank you for calling."

The high pitched wail of approaching sirens came into hearing range before our call ended. While trucking I called 911 any number of times. I'd called when a car bumper lie crossways in a lane of traffic on the highway one night in Memphis or in rural Texas when cattle had broken through a fence and wandered onto the highway where a vehicle might have a potentially dangerous collision striking such heavy animals, or when woods burned alongside the highway. Though they could have been part of a controlled fire, I didn't know. So I had called.

One night in Arkansas an entire highway of truckers had chattered over the CB about a drunk driver who swerved repeatedly back and forth across both lanes. No trucker wanted to try to pass the drunken motorist and be the unlucky S.O.B. to catch the car under their trailer. I wondered if anyone had called the police so I dialed 911. The dispatcher who responded said she was unaware of the problem. I gave her the mile marker numbers while we passed them. Then, thankfully, the motorist pulled over into a rest area. I gave that final bit of information, wondering if the drunkard would stop and sleep it off or return to traffic before police could intervene. Maybe an officer could prevent the drunk killing an innocent person that night. Often once a trucker made such a call she might never know what ultimately happened.

What happened to the burning house would be impossible to see in the dark of subsequent nights. The structure stood in a sparsely populated area with no nearby streetlights. I had to wait for my turn to do the solo weekend run to see what remained.

* * *

Believe in spidey sense?

I never felt completely at ease over-nighting alone in a truck, and the environment at truck stops often had issues. One need only sit in the cab of a truck to observe evidence of prostitution. Pimps drove up in small cars and delivered prostitutes to trucks at all hours of the day or night. Not only that, but drug sellers often tried to start conversations with truckers while they walked through the parking lot to the building, or sometimes, to Margie or me while we traded trailers with the New York team.

"I just shake my head or say, 'Not interested.'" Margie explained.

Sellers promptly moved on to find someone who was.

From time to time drug addicts hit on drivers for cash. A clean driver had to take a similar tact then, too. Truck stops are not the place to make charitable contributions. The recipients of such funds not only may use them for bad ends, some would gladly cut a driver's throat as soon as look at him. Most drivers I met knew to avoid bad medicine, literally and figuratively.

One week when I'd driven with Doug we had both encountered a man on numerous days begging for money. Each day the same man would stop Doug while he walked inside or the man paused at the driver door when Doug sat behind the steering wheel. Instead of ignoring him the way most drivers would, Doug rolled down the window while I sat next to him in the passenger seat witnessing their conversation.

"Hey, buddy," the beggar who'd hit Doug up for cash on previous days began. "I've got a car loaded with the wife and kids on the other side of the building and not a dime for gas."

The day before he'd said he needed bus fare to get to a funeral. Each day his story changed, but his face remained the same.

"If you don't believe me, walk around here with me, and I'll introduce you to the family," the beggar had said, pointing to a deserted part of the parking lot hidden from easy view by corners of the building.

"Hunh," Doug had exclaimed pleasantly, then said to the beggar. "You know, I can't stop here without someone hitting me up for money."

Even Doug knew not to give him anything though. After Doug had closed the window I asked him a question.

"You know what he'd do if you followed him over into that corner, don't you?"

"What?" Doug asked.

"He'd pull a knife on you and take your wallet."

"Hunh."

Afterwards I'd glanced into that corner on my way into the building that day with Doug. Nothing was there. No car. No wife and kids waited, of course. The beggar had moved on to another truck, probably with yet another story.

Occasionally on the nights Margie and I drove to the Jolly Trucker we saw someone abandoned, waiting with luggage on the walkway just outside the main building of the truck stop. He or she would look hopefully at the cars exiting the highway and steering toward the parking lot. Anyone might guess at each person's story. Young or old, male or female, of any race or creed. Maybe their bus trip had reached completion, or they missed the call to re-board, since busses did pause at the truck stop. Or they'd gotten into an argument with their ride. Most seemed only temporarily inconvenienced. Some appeared to have chosen the life of a transient. Others' presence just didn't jibe with the usual goings-on at a truck stop.

One night after the heat of the day had dissipated, a young, blonde woman of about thirty stood outside wearing a light jacket, her luggage at her feet. I figured her boyfriend, maybe a trucker, had kicked her out of his rig and left her. She probably didn't have much, if any, resources. I wondered if she felt hungry.

After eating half of a meal and getting the rest to go from the restaurant, I returned to the truck. I pointed the woman out to Margie who had already noticed her.

"Do you think I should offer her this?" I asked Margie, indicating the Styrofoam container full of warm food.

"I don't know, but I don't think she would do anything bad if you tried," Margie said. "It's up to you."

I climbed down from the truck and walked over to the woman.

"Would you like something to eat?" I asked, opening the container lid to let her see the fried chicken strips, French fries and thickly sliced bread.

Believe in spidey sense?

The woman said nothing and avoided eye contact. Close up I couldn't help but notice a large bandage wrapped around her face, almost comically, like Bugs Bunny would wear for a toothache.

"The food is fresh. No one's eaten from it," I assured her.

The woman turned a little to one side, facing away. Still silent, having never looked right at me.

I walked back to the truck with mixed emotions. I felt a bit foolish, but also glad I had tried. If I had been in her shoes, the world would have felt a little less cold if someone at least offered help. Maybe the offer lifted her spirits, even if she couldn't accept that help right then.

"She wouldn't take it," I reported back to Margie

"I'm not surprised," Margie said.

"I don't think she could have eaten anyway."

"Why not?"

"I think her jaw is broken."

On the first available morning after seeing the house ablaze next to the highway, I headed back in the bright daytime of a Sunday morning. Passing the house's location, I looked over. To my surprise the inner walls remained. The outer walls had been peeled away, even part of the roof had withstood the blaze.

I wondered whether over a period of weeks I would see the damaged house rebuilt or torn down. I hoped the small dwelling, perhaps uninsured or unused, wouldn't remain in ruins. Seeing an abandoned house, I couldn't help but think of all the living that must have occurred there. All the drama and comedy of life that takes place in a house. The struggles and sorrows, the joys and the laughter. Carpenters build an ordinary house. Then a family moves in and, by their living, transforms a house into a home.

I might witness the gradual metamorphosis of rebuilding or see the remaining structure reduced to its foundation. Because of the house's position in an unlit area and our late hours of arrival and departure from the truck stop I could only ever see the house once every two weeks when returning on those Sunday morning solo trips. That was, if I stayed on this run.

More drifted on the wind than the smoke from a fire.

Chapter 20: "I'm not a racist. I'm a supremacist."

While Hilda had often taken a week off at a time, more and more Margie began to trim weeks by starting a day or two late or ending her week early. On her days off I drove with a substitute co-driver. At first I didn't notice Margie's time off all that much. If anything, I might have wondered how she could afford it. None of the drivers had vacation days. If you don't work, you don't get paid. That went for holidays, too. I didn't know why Margie missed work and hadn't questioned her absences. She was an independent, grown woman, and driving seemed to be what she wanted to do.

At the beginning of each week Margie and I met on the yard to build our set. Quite often the dispatch slip listed the heaviest trailer last, instead of first. In order to avoid cracking the whip or having the back trailer swing around the truck if the driver had to stop suddenly, we reversed the order, putting the heaviest trailer in front where it belonged. Since the original listing of which trailer went first came from an estimate of expected freight, we got into the habit of asking Carol or Jane what the actual weights amounted to when we received the final dispatch slip. Maybe a third of the time we had to reverse the order of the trailers before building our set.

Typically, we drove around the yard, both of us up front in the seats trying to spot our trailer numbers and ready to get out to move the dolly or connect a trailer. Off in the distance on hot summer afternoons, heat rose in wavy lines above the asphalt and

298

concrete. While we sat and one of us steered around the yard, we talked.

"You know," I began. "I think you're the only person I've ever driven with who hasn't asked me why I drive."

"I just figured you needed the job."

"Exactly!"

"I started because of my ex, Rex."

"Rex the ex?"

"Yeah, he had been driving for a long time. He wanted to be an owner-operator, but didn't have the credit."

Then Margie explained how Rex had used her good credit rating to get a truck, among other things.

"You must have been making good money then."

"But as soon as we made any money, he spent it."

Margie went on to describe how a relative of Rex's had even expressed concerns about him leaving her "holding the bag" when the time came to pay the bills. After a while their outlay exceeded their income. Eventually, they couldn't meet the truck payments. But Margie had in her possession a card that could help her make a good living on her own – a commercial driver license or CDL. She had come to work for Wil and Wayne while Rex took a driver job at a company hub in another state.

After building our set I drove out the gate and parked so each of us could get anything we needed from our cars. Typically, I got a six pack of water bottles and my luggage. As a practice left over from my days subbing, I still took almost everything home at the end of the week. The way I saw it, you never knew what truck you would drive in, regular co-driver or not.

We settled in, then began our discussion of where to eat.

"Wherever you want," Margie typically said.

"I dunno. Are you hungry for any particular type of food?"

"Wherever you want to stop is fine with me."

Sometimes I had a preference. Other days I felt open to suggestions. And when Margie wanted to stop somewhere specific I wanted her to have her say.

"How about Arby's?" I asked. "You see the little cowboy hat floating over my head?"

"Yeah, if it's a sombrero does that mean you want tacos?"

"Yep, and if it's a tall chef's hat that means pizza," I answered. "You'll have to let me know what hat you feel like wearing next time."

At times while the other remained in the sleeper either Margie or I might get something to eat. We frequented a gas station near Dallas which sold good mini-pizzas. Some days whoever drove into Dallas pulled over and got a couple of pizzas and ate one while driving in. Then when the other exited the sleeper at the Dallas terminal to help out she had her own pizza or maybe a pastry from Arby's waiting for her.

Margie drove out to the truck stop near Little Rock where we switched out. Then I sat behind the steering wheel and drove back out onto the nighttime highway. Touching the back of my hand to the glass side window I estimated the outside temperature. Over time driving on many different routes I'd honed this skill by checking my guess against the illuminated signs advertising car dealers, churches and so on that often included the current temp. I'd become adept at saying to myself something like, "It's in the low 40s." Then while the truck rolled along, the signs by the highway shone 43, 41, 42.

I had become more adept at driving, too. I still felt a bit of wonder that the activity of driving a big rig, which felt so energizing by its nerve-wracking nature early on had become so trite that I sometimes struggled to stay wakeful while driving. Steering tens of thousands of miles along curves and up and down mountains hundreds of times and in all types of weather and at all hours on the clock had finally made driving a semi sleeper cab with double trailers routine. I also gained confidence guiding the trailers through tight spots both on the terminal yard and at truck stops. Such minor triumphs felt satisfying, but I hadn't planned on driving a truck indefinitely. I had considered trucking a stop-gap measure and an opportunity to experience life beyond the suburbs, driving the trucks I'd looked at in wonder since childhood. Yet, I had a reliable co-driver and had settled into driving more than ever before.

Then Wayne called one Monday morning. "Hey, Karen," he said. "You're gonna start out the week with a guy named Keith."

"Oh? Is Margie okay?"

"Yeah, she'll be back in a couple of days."

Our week started on Tuesdays. Accordingly, I met Keith, a cheerful guy from Jamaica. We drove that first day without incident. On the second day Keith and I had built our set on the Fort Worth yard when Ivan called my cellphone. The transmission had gone out on Team B's truck. He estimated they would arrive at the Jolly Trucker at about 4 a.m. I rejoiced. A gap of a few hours meant I could go home and take a proper shower in a clean environment. Keith and I agreed to park the truck for a few hours and meet back at the yard later. But what, I wondered, would Wayne think if he found the rig seemingly abandoned for hours on the Fort Worth yard. I had better give him a call just in case.

"Hi, Wayne."

"What's up?"

"We got a call from the other team. They've had a breakdown so they're delayed about four hours or so."

"Oh, really?"

"Yeah, I'm gonna run home and leave the rig here next to the fence by the tractor yard. I just wanted to let you know in case you saw the truck parked here with no one around and wondered what was going on."

"Okay, thanks for letting me know," Wayne answered.

With that I happily ran home.

The next day Margie came back to work. She had visited the doctor's office again. We built our set then waited for a minor repair to be completed. Meanwhile we had nothing to do but sit in the cab and talk.

"Are you okay?" I asked, hoping all was well.

"Yeah, I'll be okay." But the doctor had said she was ill.

"Did he say anything about smoking?"

"I don't smoke in his office."

True, Margie could smoke if she chose, but on this occasion I persisted. "I wish you'd stop."

"Yeah, I know you do," Margie replied, likely reflecting on a couple of previous conversations. Margie was a truly considerate smoker. I felt concern for her well being, not annoyed by smoke.

We worked hard that week to make up for the delay caused by the New York team's transmission failure. But as a result, the day of Margie's return we didn't get back out of Fort Worth until after 3 p.m. nor to the Jolly Trucker until 2:30 a.m. when we met Team A. For the first time ever they acted miffed at our late arrival. Since we had different native languages, I tried to explain across our communication gap that the other team had been much later the night before. Oddly, they didn't take the delay in stride like almost all drivers do, and the way they had done so before that night.

If we'd been lazy or inconsiderate, the other teams would have had a valid point. Usually, however, truckers don't dawdle when on the road. They go. I'd waited for other drivers many times on different runs to different places and never questioned a late driver. Other drivers had waited for me without complaint, too. Every time I'd waited for another driver I had returned the favor. We simply exchanged paperwork and trailers then went our separate ways. These incidents brought to light another of the truisms of trucking: never hassle another hardworking, well meaning driver.

Nonetheless, we kept working hard to meet Ivan and his co-driver on the alternating night. We arrived a bit earlier, at 2 a.m. Though neither Margie nor I blamed him, Ivan apologized for their earlier delay. But we both knew these things happened. We drove back to DFW and managed to get Margie out for her solo run at a respectable 1 p.m. so she would arrive at about 10 that night, if traffic and weather permitted.

Soon after, Margie took a couple of weeks off. Wayne assigned in her stead a dude I'll call Eddie, a short, skinny guy with more tattoos than you could shake a stick at. Whenever Margie took days off odd things seemed to happen. The first day out things went normally. The second day I got a call from Wayne while we headed eastward.

"The New York team is running pretty late. They had some sort of an engine problem," Wayne began. "You'll meet them a couple of hours further east at the Nashville terminal instead of the truck stop."

"Okay, I'll call Nashville for directions," I answered, knowing each truck has a small, laminated card tucked into the cubbyhole above the driver seat with each terminal's phone number.

"They're really making a habit of being late," Wayne continued. "I called in on their last delay."

"What do you mean?" I asked.

"I called the head office when they were late with transmission problems. The same manager has both teams driving old trucks with too many miles on them."

"Oh! I had no idea. I just called you as an FYI. I didn't mean for anyone to get in trouble."

"Don't worry. I took care of them," Wayne said.

Or he had taken care of *us*, only not the way he thought.

Another oddity occurred during that time. I unintentionally stumbled upon a way to have a mechanic actually wait for a truck's tire inspection. I had driven into the tire inspection lane and had to do the usual song and dance to get anything done. One of the brake lines on the dolly needed replacing, too. The lines connected the power of the brakes between the trailers sending pressurized air all the way to the back trailer from the front of the rig. As with tire checks, I kept an eye out to make sure the repair got done and done correctly.

Standing on the opposite side of the dolly, I stopped to chat with Antonio, the mechanic doing the repair. Antonio stood a bit shorter than me and had dark hair and a goatee. We discussed the usual things like weather. I also mentioned how tiring driving can be because of the difficulty of getting good rest in a moving truck. Antonio looked surprised by that comment. I figured he'd never driven and just didn't know. Over the years I'd decided a safe area of discussion with an unknown man was his children. So while we chatted I asked Antonio about what presents his kids looked forward to getting for their birthdays. Antonio and I spoke a while longer. Then with Antonio's work done Eddie and I left for Tennessee.

The next day in Fort Worth Eddie went to the restroom while I pulled the rig into the tire inspection lane. This time Antonio had waited for my arrival. He quickly inspected the tires. All the lights and the dolly worked fine. Like any other day I had climbed down from the truck to retrieve the seal numbers from each trailer. I wrote down the seal number from the back trailer then walked forward and stepped between the two trailers to get the seal number off the front trailer when Antonio approached. With a sly grin on his face he stepped between the trailers, too, and immediately looked me in the eye when I glanced up. The dolly stood to my left, a trailer in front of me and another in back and Antonio to my right. In the relative privacy of this boxed-in location Antonio let me know what was on his mind.

"If you ever need any *help*, I can do that for you?" Antonio volunteered.

"What?" My mind reflected over whether Antonio meant the trailers or tires needing mechanical attention. Then I realized he wasn't talking shop.

"You know, like if you need some *rest* in the sleeper," he explained, tilting his head toward the front of the truck.

Slightly stunned I just looked at Antonio and said nothing.

"If you ever need any *help*, I'm available," Antonio repeated, lifting his eyebrows with a knowing look. "Just let me know." Then Antonio stepped away, letting me pass, never turning his eyes from mine nor washing the grin off his face.

Still a bit astonished I returned to the cab. Alone. I hadn't recovered quickly enough to ask Antonio what his wife might think of him *helping* another woman. Apparently, Antonio misinterpreted my remarks about the lack of restfulness in a truck. Maybe he had also taken my small talk about his kids as an attempt to learn whether he was attached. When Margie returned to the run I told her about Antonio's proposition and laughed at my own surprise. Funny, too, what it finally took to find dedication to the tire inspection lane in a mechanic!

But right then Eddie and I had to travel all the way to Nashville to meet the New York team. At our pace Nashville was too far for one driver to travel from Fort Worth in one shift. We had arranged our time so Eddie could run solo that weekend. He drove out for his entire shift then turned the driving over to me for the last couple of hours to the Tennessee capital.

304

One of the good things about our run up to the Jolly Trucker was we switched drivers at the same time we switched trailers, whether running a five and five with Margie or a ten and ten with Eddie or anyone else. Margie tended to stay up front regardless of how long the other team took to show up, though many nights estimating the length of our wait proved impossible. We had contact with Ivan only some of the time. At other times he drove another run or took days off, too.

If a delay stretched out on the nights I drove in, I leaned against the window with my little green bookbag for a pillow or laid on the floor between the seats or occasionally climbed on the top bunk to get better rest. One way or another whoever drove up to the Jolly Trucker waited to trade trailers while the driver who drove back overnight got all the rest time available.

That night I drove two hours to Nashville and went inside the dispatch office shortly after midnight. According to a clerk, the computer showed an ETA for the other team of 4 a.m. I went back out to the truck and spoke through the curtain.

"Eddie?"

"Yeah?"

"Dispatch says they're not gonna be here for about another four hours. If you don't mind, I'd like to try to get some sleep on the top bunk."

"Won't bother me," Eddie declared.

I stepped into the darkened sleeper to climb onto the top bunk about five feet above the floor of the sleeper. Setting my right foot on the edge of the desk that had a slip resistant edge for this very purpose, I reached up to the grab bar on the high shelf behind the driver seat and hoisted myself up and over into the bunk. I settled in and tried to get a nap.

Whatever time the New York team arrived I'd have to get up and drive back until my shift ended. I really wanted some sleep. But the anticipation of waiting and the uncertainty of not knowing how the rest of that week would go with this delay, not to mention sharing the sleeper compartment with a relatively unknown guy, made dozing off difficult.

Now and then I pressed the light button on my watch. Soon one a.m. came and went. On the bunk below Eddie rested quiet as a mouse or a sleeping man. I closed my eyes. Every so often the sound of trucks driving to the trailer yard interrupted the constant hum of our engine working the air conditioning. I still tried to get a bit of sleep. 1:30 a.m. 2 a.m. 2:15 a.m. Finally, I dozed off.

Knock. Knock. Knock.

Yuri, a member of the New York team, knocked on the glass of the driver side window. I looked at my watch. Just after 2:30.

I climbed down from the bunk and stepped out of the sleeper to trade trailers. Yuri and I exchanged paperwork wordlessly. That night I drove back across Tennessee and partway into Arkansas. My eyelids pulled heavily downward by the time I drove up to a truck stop. I'd done my ten hours. Eddie's turn to drive had arrived.

This small truck stop had no room anywhere for doubles in their tight parking lot. In many truck stops a painted stripe runs crossways several yards in front of the pumps. Generally, the paint stripe gives drivers a visual aid to pull forward so at least someone behind can fuel while they pay for their fuel, or often in our case, if we couldn't find better parking. Such paint stripes are placed with standard 53 foot trailers in mind. In a longer doubles rig a driver really needs to pull up a few feet beyond the paint stripe to get the caboose clear of the pumps, not only for the driver who might fuel up behind, but also for the drivers walking back and forth in front of the pumps on the way from their parked trucks.

Yet some doubles drivers drove up only to the stripe, leaving the back trailer too close to the pumps. Evidently, those drivers never looked back in the mirror and saw drivers squeezing by next to the pumps to get around the back of our rig. Even with many years of experience more than one driver parked as if he didn't know his rig reached back farther than a standard one. Unfortunately, this truck stop barely had room in front of the pumps to steer back up a driveway and onto the highway service road. Pulling a few feet beyond the stripe would block the driveway. Pulling up to the stripe would still block the pumps.

So when I saw the pump closest to the building unoccupied, I pulled the rig up next to it and went inside. When I came back Eddie stood leaning against the building, smoking a cigar. While I set my sleeping bag and pillow in the bottom bunk Eddie remained outside, chomping the end of his cigar. A hundred years prior he may have made a believable cowboy. The grimace on his features while he faced into the morning sun made the image nearly complete. If he'd stood six foot tall, he might have conjured up images of a gunslinger at the O.K. Corral. At five feet five, Eddie looked more like Yosemite Sam. Yet, someone was about to challenge him, though happily not to a shoot 'em up.

Eventually, Eddie put out his cigar against the concrete wall of the building and climbed up in the driver seat. I stayed in the sleeper getting ready to rest, knowing there was no point in dozing off until we got back on the highway. Then Eddie decided to update his logbook. Sitting on the edge of the bunk with the curtain slightly open I told him the name of the town so he could write it down. Next Eddie took the paperwork out of the cubbyhole above his head to record the trailer and seal numbers on his logbook page when a different knock resounded through the entire cab. Not the sound of knuckles on the glass this time, but the sound of a fist on the side of the sleeper.

Bam! Bam! Bam!

I stood up and stepped between the seats. Eddie and I both looked down at another modern day cowboy outside the driver window. A tall man with a brown handlebar moustache, white button down shirt, blue jeans, boots and western hat yelled unintelligible words, no doubt choice in their selection. The gist of his commentary? He wanted our rig the fuck out of his way. We had parked at a pump long enough to fuel. The angry driver had waited behind us and seen Eddie with his cigar standing leisurely nearby. He had seen me go in the building and out several minutes later. Then we had stayed a few minutes longer. Now he wanted us out of there.

"If someone wants the numbers on my log, that's their tough shit," Eddie said, throwing his logbook on the dash and hastily snapping on his seat belt. Eddie put the truck into gear, headed down the driveway to the highway and onward. I covered my amusement by making sympathetic remarks. Once the rig rolled onto the highway I lay back in the bunk with the trace of a laugh on my face. For both regular trailer or doubles drivers it's a good policy never to block a fuel lane longer than necessary. Funny, too, how tough-guy Eddie folded like a house of cards the second someone stood up to him.

The days progressed and, conversationally, I asked Eddie about the many and elaborate tattoos covering his arms. At first he called them symbolic, but didn't say much else. Then as we continued to drive together he became more open and made bolder statements. Eventually, he volunteered that his tattoos signified his beliefs about race. Messages and symbols reflecting his thoughts on race, he said, were hidden in the ink.

Despite the diversion to Nashville that required hours of additional driving, we made good time. According to custom, I helped drop and build in Dallas and Fort Worth. Since the diversion had altered our schedule, Eddie and I didn't switch out again until getting back into Arkansas. Then I drove up to the Jolly Trucker at half past nine in the evening. Not only were we not late, we had reached our destination early. I took advantage of the time to grab a shower in the truck stop and get a bite to eat. Then while Eddie remained in the bunk I waited. And waited. Half past midnight the other team made it. Without any comment from me about their tardiness we traded trailers, and I headed back to Texas.

But now I understood what Margie meant when she had said a driver having to wait for the other team to arrive *and* drive partway back from the trade wouldn't be fair. Waiting time is down time, not part of the ten hour driving time. This way whoever waited for the trade *and* drove back had to be up for an unusually long amount of time. While Eddie snoozed in the bunk I had dozed in the driver seat. Eddie had grown even more comfortable making remarks about the extent of his philosophical stance on race. Since it seems people with Eddie's opinions on race often have limiting opinions about women's roles, I wondered what Eddie might think of a woman working a so-called man's job without a husband or boyfriend. Some people misinterpreted a woman in such a job or simply resented her, whether they made ignorant assumptions about her sexuality or not. Would my being a tall woman, taller than Eddie, whose job required her to wear a man's uniform shirt affect his behavior? Would Eddie think he had the right to do something to me, or had he thought so all along? I decided bunking up top was no longer an option in case Eddie's notions about race accompanied ideas about women truckers.

The next night we met the team who had cut their run short by meeting us in Nashville. This time a traffic snarl had slowed *our* progress. I drove into the truck stop parking lot at about one in the morning, but at the right place and only a couple of hours off of the ideal arrival time. Just two days before this very team had caused us the extended drive to Nashville. We had never caused them more work.

But with his face tilted up in a look of defiance, Yuri asked. "Where have you been?"

Though the question reeked of gall and stupidity, perhaps the time had come to get it back into his head that delays happen. Yuri had met us in Nashville a couple of nights before due to his own delay. He had been late on numerous other occasions, too, therefore he should understand what happens in trucking. Just deal with it, without comment or complaint.

"Making up for your delay," I responded not quite accurately, but thinking he might get the point.

"Our delay was two days ago."

"The team we met yesterday got here late, too. Then we met some traffic today," I explained, hoping reason might soak into this driver's head.

"We leave early to get here on time," Yuri said, rapidly pointing his finger down at the asphalt.

"I'm happy for you, but we don't have a gap of several hours to catch up," I said.

"You should be here at eleven, midnight tops," he insisted, sounding a little proud he knew a slang expression like 'tops.'

"Listen, you've got no room to complain," I answered evenly, but employing a little discretionary use of my trucker's backbone to make the point. "When we drove all the way up to Nashville to meet you, I said nothing."

"Humph," Yuri grabbed the paperwork from my hand and stomped away without further ado for that night.

But this new attitude of confrontation and argument didn't just come from Yuri. Once Margie and I drove together again, whomever we met with rare exception tried to argue if our team arrived later than theirs. Of course, our NYC colleagues acted like *our* tardiness was a serious fault. If they fell behind, they thought that was okay. Naturally, *they* always had good reasons. Not that we ever asked or pressured them in any way. Nonetheless, occasionally they gave reasons for their delays, mentioning a mechanical breakdown, slowed traffic due to an accident, or a particularly heavy rain that had slowed their drive. These same incidents could delay us, as well. If they turned up late, neither Margie nor I ever mentioned it. But the next time we showed up late, one of them would.

Either the NYC team drivers couldn't understand the realities of trucking anymore or their obstinacy became a game they played. At least a couple of them did exude genuine surliness, hostility lurking under their gruff faces when they handed over their paperwork and in broken English tried to place blame on us, if we had arrived later than them. But then the next night Ivan would sweetly try to explain: "See, we leave the first day early," he began, "So if there is delay, we can get here on time."

I attempted to explain just as sweetly. "We are one team meeting two teams. If one of your two teams is late, that can put us behind the next day."

All to no avail.

Ultimately, Wayne calling the company's head offices about the New York teams' lateness appeared to have served as a catalyst. Perhaps, their manager had told his men to give us hell for whatever Wayne may have said or done. Because it sure looked like Wayne had stirred shit into the broth, and there was no way to get it out. After trying to explain a few more times to the other teams' drivers when they complained, I simply handed over our paperwork, took theirs and walked away ignoring any complaints about our arrival time. Since explanations went unheard anyway, the only thing to do was simply to ignore attempts to create pointless conflict.

* * *

Eddie and I pulled into the Dallas terminal on our last day and dropped the trailers we'd brought in. While we worked, once again Eddie spoke openly of his attitudes about race, how he didn't want to have any interaction with non-whites. He called himself a separatist, saying he thought only whites should live in the US.

So I asked him. "Would you drive with someone who's not white?"

"Sure."

"You would?"

"Yeah."

"It wouldn't bother you, if you hate them?"

"I don't hate them."

"You don't?"

"I'm not a racist. I'm a supremacist," Eddie answered. "I could work with a black, a Mexican, whatever. They'd never know how I really feel."

"They wouldn't?"

"I'd never show them."

Again I wondered what Eddie might have felt but not shown the weeks he and I worked together.

The following Tuesday Margie and I met as usual and built our first set of the week. With Margie back at work I hoped her time off had provided the rest she needed. Driving is tough enough when a trucker feels well. We had completed the first run up to Tennessee and returned to the Dallas yard to drop and build when Margie's phone rang. After her conversation, Margie clicked off the phone and returned it to the clip on her belt.

"That was Carol," Margie said, referring to a dispatch clerk in Fort Worth.

"Oh? What's up?"

"My ex is over at Fort Worth."

"Is he?"

"When we get over there will you do the driving around the yard?"

"Sure."

"I don't want him to see me."

We arrived at the Fort Worth yard and dropped our trailers. I went in for the dispatch slip and, as promised, steered the cab around the yard to find our next trailers while Margie sat on the bunk with the curtain open so she could see out. No one could see her in the unlit sleeper from the brightly lit outdoors. She hopped outside into the day's heat to help move the dolly, but climbed right back in again. We had our set built, and I steered around a corner on the way to the tire check lane when, from her position seated in the sleeper, Margie saw Rex drive by.

"That's him," Margie said.

Like a typical trucker, both on the highway and on the yard, Rex waved the three finger T-Rex trucker's wave when he drove by. I waved back while noticing a flash of gold on Rex's hand. I mentioned it to Margie.

"I'm not surprised he still has his rings. That's one of the things he spent our money on," Margie explained. "In fact, one time he lost a ring in the sleeper of our truck while I drove."

"You found it later?"

"We looked for the thing. It was on a night I drove and nearly froze my butt off. Rex had left the A.C. on max on a cold night. The switch on the dashboard broke, and I couldn't turn the air conditioner off. The next day all he had to say was, 'Well, I guess you didn't have trouble staying awake.'"

"I know what you mean," I said, recalling how difficult sleeping can be when you're cold while warmth can encourage sleepiness. On more than one occasion I'd advised new drivers only to switch the heat onto their feet if they must. Then I asked, "What about the ring?"

"We turned that cab upside down looking for it."

"How did he lose it?"

"It just slipped off his finger while he slept. We never did find that damn ring."

We started the week with Margie driving out because she wanted to drive the solo that weekend. Thus, she jumped right back in with a tiring six day work week. She'd had a bit of rest, but still didn't feel up to 100%. Nonetheless, we ran the week together, working like a team. After a day or two I couldn't help but share with Margie some of the things Eddie had said.

"I think Eddie just tried to fill your head with talk," Margie said.

"What do you mean?"

"He's new on the job, and he wanted you to think he's tough."

"Why?"

"Maybe he thinks he'll get treated better by his co-drivers."

"The things he said, that's no way to win friends."

"Just to sound big if nothing else."

"I hope you're right."

"Yeah, I think so."

A few weeks later we would learn that Eddie had been put on a regular route with a black guy as his co-driver. Eddie's co-driver might never know the attitudes encoded within his tattoos.

Chapter 21: "My spidey sense is tingling!"

I felt happy to be a gal driving with another gal. Margie had returned to the run, and we were back in business. I enjoyed driving with most guys. The pragmatism and easygoing nature of men can make them a pleasure to drive with. Growing up surrounded by brothers and male friends made me feel more at home with guys anyway. Though at times I felt like the world's tallest woman. I often felt like a giant when standing and talking to a group of women. I might suddenly notice that the second tallest woman stood a petite 5'5" or so while I stood 5'10" and sturdy. As a child I'd gone through school with other kids calling me all sorts of names because of my height: Too-Tall or Alice the Goon, after the giant *Popeye* comics character. I'd long outgrown any hurt or annoyance at schoolyard terms. And anyway, I'd been wearing schoolgirl clothes at the time classmates made such comments.

Then in a men's uniform in the trucking profession at my height and build I discovered I could appear to cut the figure of a man to some onlookers. For instance, on a random day I had walked into a truck stop and steered my work shoes through the aisles of the store, my head down looking at the tiles on the floor when I entered the women's restroom. A woman gasped. Not at my presence, at least. But then I looked up and followed her eyes to the man who had innocently followed me into the restroom. With an embarrassed laugh he promptly exited. Like so many truckers he stood shorter than me. With my head tucked down he

314

hadn't seen my longer hair. Most significantly he left me with the knowledge that he had thought he was walking behind a guy.

If from the back and in the men's uniforms we wore someone might mistake me for a guy then even from the front my appearance might ping someone's gaydar, leaving them *wondering*. So long as they didn't try to use that as an excuse to limit or to mistreat me in some way, their assumptions didn't really much matter. But if they did try to harm me, it mattered both for my right of self-preservation and because of the principle involved: that a person is a person, and no one has a right to treat anyone badly based on assumptions about their appearance. If we're honest, we all know in our society that questions about sexuality are still used by some to discredit and harm others socially if not physically.

On the first day of a new week Margie and I built our set and headed out to Tennessee. Summer temps in the 90s or 100 plus can feel like a hot frying pan has been turned upside down over the land while it bakes in the sun. Little wind stirs, and the heat feels like a weight pressing down. But summer had begun to fade into autumn, and cooler temps on the yard didn't press down quite so hard. The nights at the Jolly Trucker became cooler, too.

Like always we drove back to Dallas the next morning with our trailers, dropped them, took on fuel and headed over to Fort Worth. If we needed to move freight between the two hubs, we might back up to a loaded trailer and carry an empty trailer behind it so we brought two and took two. Unless Julie, who liked Margie and considered her a friend, decided to send us over with a 53 foot trailer instead. After checking to make sure the door was closed, we simply backed up to the 53 footer until the fifth wheel pin snapped into place, connected the brakes and lights, wound up the landing gear and took off. This procedure felt like a holiday after struggling with a dolly and lining up the rig just so in order to build a set of doubles. Pulling a long trailer cut our turnaround time from about an hour if we also fueled in Dallas to well under a half hour, if we fueled elsewhere.

Sometimes Fort Worth needed a long standard trailer. Sometimes I suspected Julie just cut Margie some slack. Julie certainly wasn't doing anything to help me. Unlike Diva, I frequently interacted with dispatch staff. Julie never resorted to the kind of abuse she had directed at me before. But she reserved special privileges for her favorites. I just happened to be working with one of her favorites. That favoritism might show itself in the form of permission to take one short trailer instead of two. In that event we still kept our dolly, if we found it easy enough to work with. Though we had to trade trailers every day at the Jolly Trucker, we usually got back the dolly we had started out with later that week. We generally used the dolly the first New York team had chosen at their terminal, unless something broke on it or we deemed the dolly especially difficult to handle. Then we might trade that dolly for an easier one at the Dallas hub, if any were available. Once the week had begun in earnest every team or solo driver had a dolly on the back of her truck. So we might find ourselves stuck with what we got, if we couldn't make life a little easier by finding a lighter dolly.

On days Julie sent us back with one short trailer Margie and I often put the dolly on the back of the one trailer. Though the dolly wasn't supporting a back trailer right then, we still needed it in Fort Worth to build our next set. We connected the dolly to the trailer's lights. No motorist should rear end a lighted dolly or bump into its side when visibility slackened at night or during bad weather. If Julie felt really generous and freight requirements remained light enough, she might send Margie and me back with no trailer at all, especially if we had been delayed for hours by the other team's late arrival at the Jolly Trucker or because of road conditions along the way. On those occasions, since we couldn't connect the lights from the dolly to the cab, technically we weren't supposed to pull the dolly off the terminal grounds. No dolly lights meant theoretically a motorist might not see the heavy piece of equipment behind the cab. But since we drove between the two terminals during the day, only a rainy, gray day could cause a potential problem. Margie preferred to drop the dolly in Dallas. Often I took the risk of driving back with an unlighted dolly, if we considered it easier to use. Otherwise we dropped the dolly and sped back on our own, picking up a different dolly in Fort Worth.

Spidey sense tingling!

Each morning in Dallas we took a quick break before finding out what excesses of effort we might have to deal with before driving to Fort Worth. Building sets of doubles takes effort when a driver is well, let alone tired or ill. Margie seemed well enough sometimes. Other times she tired out quickly.

On a typical day we walked inside the Dallas terminal and through the office toward the restrooms. Along the way, we met none other than Ms. Mop Hair or Shirley. Shirley was the driver who had pulled up seconds before I told Julie exactly what I thought of her. Weeks before Margie and I began driving together Shirley had seen me say my piece to Julie then march back to my truck and drive away. Shirley had no clue about the days of abuse I had endured before that moment. I could only imagine what Shirley might think of me.

While all three of us walked to the restrooms Shirley kept up a loud, mostly one-sided conversation with Margie who smiled with amusement at her friend's exuberance. Shirley exclaimed with childlike energy and enthusiasm at just about everything. Driving. The weather. An uncomfortable shoe. The sandwich she planned to have for lunch.

Then Shirley went on to work her solo run. After we parted from Shirley and returned to our truck I couldn't help myself. With the lilt of humor in my voice I said, "I'll bet she got in trouble at school for speaking out."

"I'll bet she did," Margie agreed with a light laugh.

We built our set and carried on driving that day. We usually arrived in Dallas in the late morning or close to noon. Shirley's run sometimes placed her at the terminal at the same time of day. Occasionally, we met Shirley on the way to or from the dispatch office, or we saw her in her truck driving around to find her trailers. She and Margie chatted when they met or talked on their phones while we each built our sets.

After driving together a while a couple of Margie's comments and questions sometimes left me wondering if she was *wondering* about the tall, sturdy woman she drove with. Margie didn't seem to make any assumptions about me early on so I started to think, why now? Was it just by appearance? Not everyone misread me. Men still flirted with me when they didn't outright offer to *help*. Male co-drivers asked me out or otherwise expressed interest. One married co-driver told me he'd like to replace his wife with me, but I don't poach husbands. However, I did date single guys. So I couldn't be sure appearance was totally at issue, though some people jump to conclusions.

Had Shirley jumped to a conclusion and shared her thoughts with Margie, perhaps fueled in some way by our one previous encounter when I had told her friend Julie off? For that fact, did Julie make something up, as a form of revenge for my telling her what she needed to hear? Or could Diva have gossiped to Margie in order to bestow a special parting gift before she left trucking for good? Diva had emphasized more than once how she and Margie had taken *separate* bunks when they had been snowed in at the Jolly Trucker months earlier. The emphasis had struck me as odd and unnecessary.

Margie appeared to harbor no ill will towards me despite whatever bug someone might or might not have put in her ear. She may have wondered on her own, or I may have misinterpreted what Margie thought about me altogether. But I speculated what such suspicions might mean to my fate on this run. The senior driver rightfully had control over who she drove with.

But some things remain beyond anyone's control.

On a sunny, but cool day Margie and I built our set in Fort Worth. That week I drove out as if to do the solo, but Margie wanted to run five days instead of four to make up for her recent lost time. After leaving the tire inspection lane, Margie drove the rig through the bright afternoon light up to the dispatch office to turn in our paperwork.

"Now we don't have any tail lights on the back trailer," Margie announced, setting the brakes on the truck.

We sat in our truck next to the office, facing the gate. The power cord between the trailers had worked loose on the short trip of a few dozen yards from the tire check. We had two power cords, one of which was nearly useless. Margie only kept the bad cord on the truck to have something to turn in to Wayne or Wil if someone stole the good cord. If someone, even at a company facility, stole a cord and the driver had nothing to turn in for a replacement, the manager might charge the driver $50 for the cost of a lost cord. I didn't think Wayne or Wil would do that, but Margie may have thought differently. Our only problem being that from time to time we mixed up the two nearly identical cords when taking one from the storage hatch behind the driver seat.

"I'll check it," I said.

"That's okay. I will," Margie answered.

"I'm driving to Little Rock," I said, referring to the nearest city on our five and five switch out.

"It doesn't matter."

Indeed, it didn't matter if you had a co-driver you trusted. I imagined a lot of women felt the way I did – that having a man on the truck gave at least a psychological boost of confidence, as if when something did go wrong having a man around somehow provided an extra layer of protection. But if you have a co-driver you can depend on and at least one working cellphone, either of you can call for any extra help needed, which in most circumstances was all a guy could do anyway.

"We just checked our lights, and now they don't work," I said.

"It happens."

"I once told both Wil and Wayne I wasn't sure what all to do for an inspection."

"I think it's just what Rex showed me: check the lights and tires."

"In some ways driving with Rex must have been reassuring."

"Yeah, in some ways," Margie said. Then with her head bent over her logbook and with an air of studied indifference Margie asked a question that seemed to have hung in her mind of late. "Have you ever driven with a boyfriend?"

"I didn't get into trucking with a boyfriend. I thought I might meet a guy once I started. After all, there are lots of guys in trucking. But most are married or not right for me."

"Not right in what way?" Margie asked.

"You know, like Romeo."

Margie knew Romeo. I had described my experiences with him.

319

"Then there are guys like Doug," I continued. "Really good-looking and a nice guy, but maybe not the most dependable," I laughed. "It's like the saying goes: the odds may be good, but the goods may be odd. Not that the odds are all that good, it turns out."

Margie laughed politely. "But you can go out on weekends with a guy, whether he's a driver or not."

"True. But most weeks by the time I catch up on sleep, do laundry and run errands, the new week is here," I said, remembering the struggle of the first year or so just to become comfortable driving a truck and getting established in a run. "Working this kind of job just takes up so much more time than a regular job."

"I know what you mean. I'm so busy driving, too," Margie said.

"Once you're in a truck, and the guy is married, otherwise off limits, or not someone you would consider dating, you don't have the chance to meet anyone else."

"Maybe during one of your longer weekends . . ."

"Yeah, you're right. If we want steady boyfriends, we each have to go out there and find them." I tugged on the ill-fitting uniform shirt that hid whatever curves I possessed. Our shirts were tailored for men, meaning my top half was covered by a piece of fabric that wore like an old potato sack. "It might help if I wasn't wearing something like this," I added.

Margie smiled. After our talk, Margie climbed down to check on the loose power cord while I waited up front, filling out my logbook. A few moments later Margie climbed back in the truck, picked up her cellphone and started dialing.

"I'm gonna have to call Wayne," Margie said, shaking her head.

"What's going on?" I asked.

"There's some sort of leak from one of the packages in the front trailer. It's right above the lifelines," Margie said, referring to both the power cord plug and the glad-hands for the brakes.

"Okay, but why call Wayne?" I asked naively.

"I don't know what's leaking."

"What can Wayne do? Have the trailer re-opened?"

"If it's hazmat, it might corrode the lifelines," Margie explained, having undergone special training. Our carrier only shipped hazardous materials in small enough quantities the laws did not require such training for all drivers. I did not yet have the hazmat endorsement on my CDL.

"Someone will have to identify it," Margie continued. "If it's dangerous, they'll have to clean the trailer before we can go."

I imagined a delay of hours and remembered a story another driver had told me about a trucker who spent an entire weekend waiting at a remote truck stop in the Rockies because of a package leaking in his trailer. On Monday a hazmat team had arrived, dealt with the package and discovered its contents: shampoo.

"What did it look like? I mean, any color?"

"It's just brown. Sort of thick, but a liquid," Margie said.

I puzzled for a moment then climbed down from the truck to take a look at the rear of the front trailer. There I saw a thick, brown gunk oozing out from under the trailer's back door and dripping on the lifelines. Instinctively, I leaned forward and took a sniff. Syrup. Maple syrup. Feeling a bit relieved, even triumphant, I walked back to the cab and climbed back into the passenger seat.

"It's syrup," I announced.

"What?" Margie turned her head from her phone conversation with Wayne.

"I smelled it. It's syrup."

"You're not supposed to smell a leaking package in case it's dangerous, like a chemical."

"Oh," I responded, thinking how harsh or deadly chemicals can be. Just a whiff of ammonia in high school chemistry class came to mind. A leaking package could contain just about any substance known to man, possibly far more dangerous than dilute ammonia.

"Never mind," Margie said, speaking into her phone. "Karen says she thinks it's syrup."

I could hear Wayne's swaggering manner of speech coming over the phone even from across the truck's cab. "I wouldn't worry about a little spilled syrup," Wayne said, no doubt relieved he didn't have to send someone out due to my ignorance of hazmat procedures.

While we settled in and started our run I remembered another story about a driver with a package that did leak a hazardous material along a highway for hundreds of miles before he knew about it. The trucking line and its insurance company had to spend millions to clean up the pollution caused to the environment.

Many times the teams we met arrived on time. But inevitably, one night the other team didn't arrive at the usual time. The delay came at the end of a week when Margie had driven out from Fort Worth. I rested in the still and quiet bunk of the parked truck conked out from several days of driving. To my surprise I awoke from a deep sleep at the sound of Margie's voice at three in the morning.

"They're here," Margie said from the driver seat, and she climbed down from the truck to exchange paperwork and perform the other tasks of trading trailers. Her words gave me time to awaken. Luckily, neither of us considered trading trailers to be all that challenging. Whoever drove in could easily accomplish the trade on her own. But something else weighed on my mind. With the switch completed we sat up front updating our logbooks. Margie sat in the passenger seat while I sat down at the steering wheel. I couldn't help but ask.

"What time did you get here?"

"About eleven."

"You sat up here for four hours?" I asked incredulously.

"Well, yeah. They weren't here yet."

"Did you get any sleep?"

"Some."

"You could have gotten on the top bunk."

"I could have," Margie answered. "But you need your sleep. You're driving back."

Even so, I still felt a bit amazed so I tried again.

"It won't bother me if you climb upstairs when the wait looks like it'll take a while."

"Today's the last day of the week. I'll be okay."

Yes, luckily the last day of the week meant more real rest soon. After getting what rest she could in the bunk while I drove back, we each had an entire weekend to recuperate.

Even so.

Spidey sense tingling!

From time to time I had gotten on the top bunk when I'd had to wait for one reason or another, even if my co-driver happened to be male. Sometimes I had let a male co-driver know I didn't mind if he hit the top bunk, if he needed to sleep. Some guys hesitated to do so before that reassurance, lest they freak out a female co-driver. Sharing a sleeper compartment had nothing to do with sex in these instances. True, I would not share a sleeper with any guy, like Romeo for example. But if a guy seemed okay, I didn't hesitate to let him know, he was welcome to take the top bunk. One tired guy plus one tired gal equals separate bunks. It seemed unspoken and obvious that separate bunks would be used guy or gal. Thus, with two gals I had even less hesitation about sharing a sleeper compartment. I hoped Margie saw it the same way.

By late autumn Margie tired out more and more quickly. Like a watch with a broken spring she became less resilient than in the first months we had driven together. Halfway through the week we agreed to take our lunch break at a barbecue place just east of Dallas. I pulled off the highway and into the parking lot. Entering the lot, I steered toward the usual place where trucks parked, guiding the cab and trailers to the right in a tight arc to fit in the space between two other trucks. Just when the rig straightened out I heard an odd sound. Then the brakes acted funny when I brought the rig to a halt.

"That's weird," I said. I put the truck back in gear, and it wouldn't budge. "The brakes are locked up."

"You may have snapped a brake line," Margie explained.

"A brake line? Where?"

"On the dolly, between the trailers."

I climbed down from the truck and walked back to the dolly. Sure enough the brake lines hadn't reached quite far enough to stretch fully into a tight right turn. The dolly's brake lines had snapped off. Then those same lines had gotten run over by the dolly's tires. I stood looking at the brake lines pulled taut between the glad-hands on the front of the back trailer and the wheels of the dolly almost directly underneath. When the brake lines broke the emergency brakes had engaged. Now the rig couldn't move until the brake lines were fixed. The brake lines had been endangered alright, but not by any corrosive liquid. Rather the last

323

mechanic to install brake lines on the dolly had measured them too short.

I walked back to the cab and climbed behind the wheel.

"You're right," I told Margie. While I dug through my little green bookbag for my cellphone Margie retired to the sleeper with the curtains slightly open. I dialed Wayne's number.

"Hello?"

"Hi, Wayne? We've got a little problem," I said.

"What's that?"

"I made a sharp curve in the parking lot," I explained, giving him our location. "The brake lines on the dolly snapped."

Wayne gave me permission to call the fleet service. I phoned and told them our location east of Dallas. Inexplicably, they decided to send someone from Fort Worth. I called Wayne and explained our even greater delay waiting for the mechanic. Then I turned toward the sleeper compartment and spoke.

"It's gonna be more than an hour, if you want to get something to eat."

"Nah, I'm too tired. You go ahead," Margie said, lying on her side in the bunk.

"You want me to get you something for later? It'll keep in the fridge."

"That's okay," Margie answered. "I just don't feel like eating."

I knew that feeling. There comes a time when the brain just wants to sleep and hunger subsides for a while. Yet, food also builds strength. Each driver has to strike her own balance.

"I'm gonna lie down while you eat," Margie said. "It'll get my feet up."

"Why do you need your feet up?"

"My ankles are swelling."

"Have they ever done that before?"

"Yeah. The doctor gave me something for it, but it gets worse when I sit up."

I climbed down from the truck, closing the door quietly. In addition to her ankles swelling Margie just looked exceptionally tired. Much like the blazing summer heat from previous months her weariness seemed like a weight pressing down. Maybe the brake lines snapping had been a blessing. Without the truck moving perhaps Margie could get a bit of solid rest. I hoped so for both our sakes.

After sitting down to a meal at the barbecue place I returned to the truck. Still no mechanic. But soon I wished I hadn't tried to build strength with food. My stomach felt awash with nausea. Something I'd eaten hadn't gone down well. It wanted to find its way back up. I sat in the driver seat. The engine rumbled while I grimaced out over the bright parking lot, glancing in the side mirrors to check for the service truck rolling up. I felt hot and prickly behind the windshield in the afternoon sun. Conscious of Margie in the sleeper and not wanting to disturb her, I determined not to lose my lunch in the cab. I didn't want to imagine what misery filling the cab with the stench of vomit would cause us both. I grasped the door handle, ready to bolt outside if the seemingly inevitable took over my body.

Waiting in misery, I began to *wish* I would vomit. After almost an hour of feeling hot and queasy I climbed out of the truck and walked along the trailers. I stopped and leaned over with my hands on my knees, willing my stomach to deposit its contents on the surface of the dusty gravel parking lot. Before anything could happen a service truck pulled up. A man behind the wheel spoke.

"You ___?" he asked, referring to the company name.

The name was stitched on my uniform shirt and cap. The cab and trailers had the name plastered all over them. The letters on the trailers alone stood out about four feet high. I straightened up from my leaning position.

"Yes," I answered flatly.

Though my stomach churned, lunch stayed out of sight. The mechanic set to work while I returned to the cab, the grip of nausea gradually receding. I kept an eye on the left side mirror to see when the mechanic finished. No doubt he had a work order he needed me to sign. Eventually, he walked up below the window and waved. I opened the door and climbed down.

"All done?" I asked.

"Almost," he answered. Then walking back toward the dolly with a metal part in each hand, he said over his shoulder. "I gotta show you something."

I followed him back to the dolly. He stopped and turned, in each of his hands his fingers covered a metal tube that connects a brake line to a glad-hand. "I got some bad news," the mechanic began. "I don't have the right part. I'll have to go back to the shop. May be a couple more hours." He looked at me, his face straight, but his eyes sought out mine with a slight intensity.

"Oh, that's not good," I responded blandly. "I'll have to call my boss and let him know."

"Just kidding!" the mechanic announced and spread his fingers to reveal identical brake couplings in each hand. "I just need you to sign a form."

After looking at the brake lines between the dolly and trailers to make sure our would-be comedian really had completed the job, I signed the paper and walked back to the cab to continue the rest of the drive up to the Jolly Trucker.

The next day Margie decided she wanted to run a ten and ten again so we began working regular shifts. Margie hoped ten hours in the bunk would make her feel more fully rested once her time at the wheel arrived. Also, a longer rest period gave her more time to put her feet up. But sitting at the wheel for longer stretches of time, built up more swelling with each shift, also.

On the next to last day of the week I drove the full shift up to Tennessee while Margie rested in the bunk. After I had traded out trailers Margie began driving back to Texas while I bunked down. Once we returned to Fort Worth we only had one more run for the week. But about four hours into our return from Tennessee Margie eased the truck off of the highway. I opened the sleeper curtains and looked out. Margie had stopped at a Wal-Mart near Little Rock that had truck parking. Our rig rested in a spot between other rigs.

"I don't think the back trailer has lights again," Margie said.

"I'll bet it's that bad cord."

"You want to check it?" Margie asked, standing and stepping over to the passenger seat. I noticed her face appeared pale and she looked bowed by weariness. "Do you mind driving for a while?" she asked.

"I don't mind," I said and rolled up my sleeping gear before climbing down to check the back trailer lights. The old cord had worked loose again. I replaced it with the good cord. I returned to the cab, saying we needed a piece of brightly colored tape to mark one of the cords so we could tell them apart. Margie had already rolled out her bedding.

"Are you sure you're okay?" I asked.

"I don't know. I have more fluid build up."

"In your ankles?"

"Yeah, them too, but fluid is also building up in my chest and stomach. The doctor gave me some medicine, but it's not doing much good." Margie stroked her hand across the midsection of her company shirt where her normally flat stomach bulged. With the congestion she felt in her chest, too, she could only take shallow breaths.

"That sounds serious," I said, remembering a schoolmate's mother who had died unexpectedly when her lungs had filled up with fluid while she slept. She, too, had been a long-time smoker with a cough. I told Margie the story.

"Well, thanks," Margie said.

"Sorry. I'm just really worried about you." It was true. I wasn't sure what was wrong, but I really didn't think Margie could go on much longer.

"I know, but I'll be alright," Margie asserted.

"Are you gonna try to finish the week?"

"Yeah. I guess we can just do the five and five, after all," Margie said.

"My spidey sense is tingling!"

"You're worried we'll get pulled over?"

"No. I'm worried once we get back to the Jolly Trucker to switch out you won't be able to make it back. I don't want to have to call an ambulance for you."

"I'll get what rest I can," Margie said. "I can't afford to take too much time off anymore."

"If you're worried about the money, I'll split the solo with you this weekend, even if you go home," I said in an effort to encourage Margie to feel better about taking the rest of the week off. In my naiveté I hoped a slightly longer weekend was all Margie needed. But Margie remained determined to stay on the truck.

I got the truck rolling and placed a call to Wayne, telling him what I knew of Margie's condition. Then I drove the remaining five hours through Arkansas and east Texas. When we got to the Dallas yard Wayne had called dispatch. While Margie remained in the bunk I only had to drop our trailers then bobtail back to Fort Worth. At our home terminal Wayne would have our set built and waiting. He was a lifesaver that day, maybe literally.

I drove to the Fort Worth yard and backed up to the new set of trailers that Wayne had already built. Sadly, I was about to use my trucker's backbone, not for the safety of the vehicle, nor to stand up to anyone's carelessness or behavior. Indirectly, I felt I had to stand up to the best co-driver I'd ever had – for her own sake. While Margie remained in the bunk, weak and exhausted, I walked into the dispatch office and met Wayne. He stood leaning against the counter. Carol sat behind the open dispatch window, listening.

"Wayne, I don't think Margie can finish the week. She's really sick."

"Yeah?" Wayne answered, the word sounding more like an acknowledgement than a question.

I told him my concerns that Margie might need urgent medical care once we arrived at the Jolly Trucker. Then I explained what Margie had told me about fluid building up in her chest.

"If you want to do today's run solo and drive back the next day alone, I'll get someone else to cover tomorrow's run," Wayne offered.

"I don't know if she'll agree. I already tried to get her to take a day off," I said.

"I'll talk to her," Wayne said, walking toward the door.

"Tell her again I'll split this run with her," I added, hoping that would help Margie to get the rest she needed.

I stood next to the counter with Carol on the other side and waited. Carol knew Margie and thought highly of her. We chatted for a few minutes until Wayne returned. Thankfully, Margie had agreed. She couldn't make the arduous drive all the way up to Oklahoma, though. She would check in at a local hotel for the

Spidey sense tingling!

weekend and call the doctor she had visited recently to see if she needed different medication.

Meanwhile I had to drive the nine to ten hours back up to the Jolly Trucker after finishing the last half of Margie's shift. Of course, I couldn't share my concerns about that with Wayne without telling him I'd driven on Margie's logbook and that in the last twenty hours or so, I had sat at the wheel for about fifteen of them. Instead, I simply drove out and back across east Texas, the shining sun and adrenaline keeping me going as on many other trips. Then the sun went down and hours of fatigue caught up with me.

The day before I had driven the entire shift up to Tennessee. Then after a break of about four hours I'd driven five more hours returning to Texas. I had just finished another five hours back to Arkansas. Too many hours with only a brief break had passed when I pulled the rig off the road just a few exits from the Wal-Mart we'd visited that morning. At the truck stop that Margie and I usually switched out driving, I no longer cared how late a sleep break would make my arrival at the Jolly Trucker. I just needed to rest. Luckily, the huge truck stop had space to park a set of doubles. Pulling the rig into a spot I made sure the doors were locked, pulled the curtains closed and crashed. No alarm clock. I would wake up when I woke up. Simple as that.

Hours later I woke and began the last four hours of the drive. Ignoring comments about lateness at the Jolly Trucker, I switched trailers with Yuri's co-driver in the chilly night air. Then I secured the rig again. After an overnight stay I would drive back alone, drop the trailers and go home a day earlier than expected. Next Tuesday the new week of driving began. At the Fort Worth office Carol or Jane would hand over a dispatch slip at the counter with our truck number on it. I hoped to see Margie there.

Chapter 22: "I want this driver off the truck."

If your regular co-driver is meeting you at the dispatch office, Wayne doesn't have to let you know. That's a given. On Monday my cellphone rang. Wayne's number appeared on the screen. Reluctantly, I answered the call, imagining what it must mean.

"Hey, Karen," Wayne's voice came through the phone and told me to meet a driver the next day who I'll call Dopey, for reasons that will become evident. Then Wayne added, "Margie is in the hospital."

"What's the matter?" I asked.

"The doctor gave her some medicine over the weekend, but she didn't get much better."

After talking to Wayne, I called Margie's cellphone. From her hospital bed she told me what had happened. On Friday of the week before while I'd headed out for the unexpected solo run, Margie had phoned her doctor. The doctor called in some prescriptions for her. Margie filled them then drove to a nearby hotel, too tired to drive home to Oklahoma. On Saturday Margie's condition hadn't changed much.

"Sunday morning I felt just as bad," Margie explained.

"As you did on Friday?" I asked.

"Pretty much."

"What did you do?"

"I called the doctor again."

"Did you need different medicine?"

"The doctor said, 'If what I prescribed hasn't made much difference, you need to get to a hospital.' So here I am."

We talked for a while before I had to ask. "Do you know when you'll be driving again?"

"I don't know.

"Do you know *if* you'll be driving again?"

"I hope so. But it's gonna be a few weeks. Maybe even months."

For the time being, it was back to the rodeo clowns.

God help me.

During one of Margie's weeks off Dopey and I had already driven together. Dopey, a 40-something guy of average looks with rounded features, built the set quickly and ably. He didn't want help, but disconcertingly drove the truck with heavy feet, jerking the rig forward and back when he repositioned to set up the trailers. Sitting in the passenger seat felt like riding a bucking bronco. I heard myself resort to the typically female question, "Are you mad about something?"

No. Dopey was just dopey.

We made the first of our trips together, and Dopey appeared alright that first week, even cheerful and fun. For instance, one evening when Dopey drove us through Arkansas he stopped for a break at a small truck stop. We both went inside then happened to walk back to the truck at the same time. Partway there Dopey walked up to the cab of a semi that resembled ours. He opened the door revealing another driver innocently filling out his logbook in a different company's truck.

"Get out of my truck!" Dopey shouted jokingly.

Everyone laughed: Dopey, me, the other driver, another driver walking past, even a cashier who'd stepped outside for a smoke. Both trucks were parked close to each other. Dopey had really mistaken another truck for ours. Dopey's response was amusing, and his reaction made him more agreeably human.

Then with Margie in the hospital Dopey and I drove together again. However, this time Dopey acted oddly "out of it." He became totally confused by ordinary experiences, like reading our paperwork or building the set. One memorable day on the Fort

Worth yard Dopey's moves looked particularly unnatural. He displayed an exaggerated cautiousness in his actions. Resembling a man whose next step might cause him to fall from the ledge of a high building, Dopey walked in a decidedly wooden manner. On the terminal yard that day Dopey forgot to set the parking brake upon exiting the truck cab, causing the rig to roll unattended with other trucks, trailers and worse, other drivers, nearby. As we both stood outside the truck, tons of weight rolled across the pavement, unchecked. Fortunately, Dopey climbed back up into the truck, jerking on the parking brake and jolting the rig to a stop before it hit anything or anyone.

Moments earlier while we built the run-away set Dopey had methodically backed a trailer up to a dolly trapped between two other trailers. It turned out to be the wrong dolly, one abandoned by another driver. I had gotten out of the truck to help and noticed the dolly's number wasn't the same as the dolly we had started out with.

"Are you sure?" Dopey asked.

I retrieved the dispatch slip from the cab. The slip had our dolly number written on it. Then I spotted our dolly a few trailers away. While we stood there, the incorrect dolly between us, Dopey had stared deeply into my eyes. I innocently returned his glassy-eyed stare while Dopey looked searchingly at my face like a man trying to see through a dense fog. Later with 20/20 hindsight I believe Dopey had been trying to detect whether I recognized his condition. Not familiar with it, I had not. Then he had driven a full shift up to Tennessee while I naively remained in the sleeper.

The next day while driving around the Dallas terminal in the places we'd driven before, Dopey became lost. Not surprisingly, most truckers have an excellent sense of direction, especially in places they have already driven. I kept my concerns to myself while quietly directing Dopey around the Dallas and Fort Worth terminals along the paths Dopey couldn't remember, the same ones he and I had traced previously. In addition, Dopey began having trouble reading the large and readily visible numbers displayed on all sides of each trailer, which led me to wonder what else he could no longer see while driving.

Later during a break at a truck stop I sat at the steering wheel preparing to drive back out while Dopey sat on the edge of the bunk. We had been talking about this and that. The topic of solo driving came up. Dopey claimed our company didn't allow women to drive their trucks without a male present.

"It's against company policy," Dopey declared absurdly.

Not even beginning to discuss how that idea didn't match reality either morally or legally, I quietly explained I had driven alone for the weekend solo run just days before and had done so on numerous occasions. Dopey wordlessly closed the curtain to the sleeper, but did so with such vigor he appeared ridiculously angered by hearing facts that didn't mesh with his assertion.

At the Jolly Trucker that night Dopey made a further attitudinal revelation. From time to time Margie or I had what we called a "pee bomb," a plastic bottle or bag that needed to be disposed of for obvious reasons. Normally, we each took care of our own "bombs." But because Margie's departure happened unexpectedly she let me know over the phone that she had left a "pee bomb" under the bunk so I could throw it away. To avoid trouble at work we threw them away at the Jolly Trucker rather than at a company hub. Dopey had been so quick more than once to get in the sleeper at the Jolly Trucker I finally had to explain to him I needed to get the bottle from under the bunk.

Moments later Dopey snarled, "I bet that was *your* piss bottle. This is why I hate driving with females. Women are *disgusting*."

This from a guy who regularly left a full pee bottle of his own out in the open on the sleeper floor. If all that wasn't enough, Dopey began expressing opinions not too far from Eddie's. For instance, Dopey stupidly claimed black people were a mix of human and gorilla. By his own words, evidently, I had a co-driver who spoke with open hatred toward me, as a woman, and who expressed ignorant beliefs about others, while unable to function normally himself. Dopey reminded me of Robert Louis Stevenson's characters Dr. Jekyll and Mr. Hyde because Dopey often struck me as a character hiding behind a mask, leering out occasionally to show his true nature.

In general, maybe safety can be put on a back burner in a workshop in the boondocks or some other isolated place. But when a profit is turned by sharing the public roadways with millions of innocent motorists and their passengers, safety really should come first. Thus, trucking includes a responsibility to care about more than just moving the truck down the road. With poor vision, poor motor control, a bad memory and a strikingly bad attitude I wondered what Dopey might do next. Could he black out while driving? Would glimmers of an angry side explode in some unforeseen way? To say he gave me the creeps was an understatement. I had become the senior driver on this run and had developed a fairly decent backbone. The time to call Wayne was fast approaching.

That evening at the Jolly Trucker I walked into the women's restroom and dialed the familiar number.

"What's up, Karen?" Wayne asked.

"It's Dopey."

"What about him?"

"Wayne, something is wrong. I think he's either drunk or on drugs. I don't know which, but something is awfully wrong," I said, giving my point of view.

Regardless Wayne wanted me to drive with Dopey from then on. "It's not easy to find good drivers," Wayne said.

I repeated my concerns.

Wayne asked why I thought what I did.

I explained in more detail what I'd seen Dopey do or not do. His mood swings and mysterious confusion at the familiar, his posture and movements that, in my opinion, resembled a man clinging to sobriety by the skin of his teeth. Wayne remained unmoved. He simply kept repeating that hiring drivers wasn't easy, though many trucking companies hire drivers on an ongoing basis as they change jobs, retire or leave trucking for various reasons. Nevertheless, Wayne still expected me to put my life in Dopey's hands every workday without complaint.

With no foreseeable solution we ended our call, and Dopey and I returned to Fort Worth. I had already arranged to take the next day off for a dental appointment. That gave me time to think before the last two days of the week. From my perspective Wayne appeared to brush off rather serious concerns and remain determined to keep Dopey on the run. Maybe just because Dopey was a guy? The good ol' boy system? After all, my spidey sense told me driver-managers might not like a gal with a trucker's backbone.

A couple of days later the morning air had cooled from recent rains when I walked onto the terminal yard at Fort Worth to build our set. But first, where *was* Dopey? I called Wayne again.

"Hey, Karen."

"Hi, Wayne. I'm here at Fort Worth, and Dopey isn't around."

"He hurt his back. He'll skip today," Wayne informed me. "If you want to run solo today, I'll have him cover tomorrow's run."

"Maybe he hurt his back lifting a case of vodka," I joked.

"He'll be back on the truck Tuesday," Wayne responded, ignoring the humor.

"You still want me to drive with him," I asked, repeating my concerns.

Wayne then indicated the obvious, that Dopey had passed a drug test before hiring. His pre-hire test had been weeks ago.

I had to nip this situation in the bud. "Wayne, I can't drive with this guy," I insisted, employing my fully grown trucker's backbone.

"What do you want me to do?" Wayne said, sounding irritated.

"I want this driver off the truck."

Wayne sighed impatiently. "I'll see what I can do."

With that noncommittal remark we ended our call.

Drug tests are common practice in trucking because the government requires them. When a driver takes a job or changes jobs, he or she must take a drug test. Any driver Wayne and Wil or other driver-managers hired was tested, as I had been before working for Sam. Plus, a company can call in any driver they employ at any time to take a random drug test. Even on days off an employer could call in a trucker for a random drug test. It would seem lawmakers meant such tests to be unexpected, and therefore, unplanned for by the driver.

On the few occasions the dispatch office sent me in for a random test, normally, Wayne called me earlier that day or a day or two before. I speculated I couldn't be the only driver who he gave prior notice. But also, I wondered how Wayne knew. He spent a lot of time hanging around the dispatch office on buddy-buddy terms with dispatchers and their managers. I didn't know if the company normally let driver-managers see the list of drivers selected for testing each week or not. Common sense suggests the list *should* be kept confidential for the company's dispatch managers' eyes only. But somehow Wayne always knew when my name appeared on the list for random drug testing.

Since Wayne had called me when I had to take drug tests, it seemed plausible he could inform Dopey beforehand, too. Previously, I had regarded Wayne's warnings as needless, but with Dopey's performance in mind, I found such warnings more disturbing. This brought to light a previously unexplored trucking truism: random drug testing means less if drivers are forewarned, or the public deserves safe and sober truckers.

Yet, moments beforehand a clerk might tell a driver when a co-driver had been selected so he or she could come into the office. Then a driver only had time to drive to the nearby clinic that conducted testing. The clerk wrote down the time he or she handed the driver the drug testing paperwork at the company terminal. Then a clinic worker wrote down the time of the driver's arrival at the clinic a few minutes away.

Ending the call with Wayne, I walked into the dispatch office where Jane sat at the desk behind the window. "Where's your new co-driver?" she asked.

"He's not here."

"They want him for a drug test when he gets in," Jane said.

"Wayne said he's taking the day off," I explained.

To me Jane looked concerned. After handing me the dispatch slip, Jane got up from her chair and walked into a dispatch manager's office. Maybe one of the office staff, like Jane or Carol, had observed something odd about Dopey's behavior. Of course, possibly, Dopey's name just happened to come up for testing.

Regardless, as Jane said, Dopey had been chosen for a drug test and would take it. Later Wayne would tell me Dopey passed. But based on Wayne's previous warnings to me before my drug testing, I wondered what had happened and in what order. Did Dopey have time to dry out or otherwise prepare for testing? I had missed a day myself and didn't know how many days Dopey missed. Dopey had at least one day off in the middle of the week, maybe two. Would home-time and 24-48 hours notice give a driver a chance to do something to clear out his system? Or maybe that explained why Dopey had become so ornery. Maybe he already knew a test awaited him and his moods and mentality disintegrated as he prepared for it. Or one could claim Dopey simply had a hot-and-cold personality coupled with extreme prejudices. But that wouldn't explain his physical symptoms like poor vision and motor control.

Whatever the case, I had refused to drive with Dopey. Thus, Wayne arranged for a different co-driver. He called to let me know I would be driving with Doug for the next week. I liked Doug. Though I felt more like a den mother with her overgrown boy scout than a driver with a colleague, at least Doug behaved like a genuinely good guy. He was also always clean and sober. Compared to Dopey, Doug was a genius.

For the next week Doug and I worked like a team. He helped build the set each day. He also became courteous and attentive. To what did I owe this gentlemanliness? After hinting about dating in the times we had driven together, Doug became more direct. He was temptingly good looking, too.

God help me, indeed.

Doug and I had a good week together and enjoyed each other's company. Plus, he wanted a new run. Could this be the run I'd hoped for with a compatible guy as co-driver? After all, word had come back that Margie was gone, from trucking anyway. In an era of speedy hospital stays, Margie remained in care for a couple of weeks before the doctors released her. A short while after she had checked out of the hospital we spoke on the phone.

"Wayne said I could come back to the run whenever I want," Margie explained.

"That's good."

"I just don't know if I ever can."

Margie never would return to trucking. Not long after Margie had left the run, Carol, the Fort Worth dispatcher who had been on duty during Margie's final run, cornered me outside the dispatch office to ask about her. "My dad and uncle both had those symptoms," Carol said. Carol sounded almost angry, but she spoke with passion because she cared. "They both died in their 50s. If she doesn't stop smoking, she could die too soon!"

"Maybe," I nodded. "Maybe she *could* drive for a while longer, but we might never know."

"Tell her to stop smoking," Carol said, her brow furrowed.

Right then Margie still needed time to rest. But the next time Margie drove, the trip would not be to Tennessee to meet a team at the Jolly Trucker. When she became well enough, Margie traveled to stay with friends. At least she could rest while deciding what to do next. And to Margie's enduring credit, whether she had suspicions about her co-driver or not, she never threatened my job nor showed me any unkindness.

As it should be.

Nevertheless, my partnership with one of the best co-drivers I'd ever shared a semi with had rolled to a stop. Driving a truck is an ongoing challenge. A team that works together well makes a huge difference in quality of life for both drivers. Because for all its apparent freedom, driving could feel like being trapped or "stuck in a truck." The stresses of being on the road working a risky job exacts a toll from every driver. Even with a compatible co-driver like Margie, I had written myself a note on the cover of a logbook weeks prior, underlining a couple of words. The message read: "I must quit. This job is too dangerous and is prohibiting other possibilities."

Chapter 23: "I'm gonna stop right here!"

Meanwhile Doug was still needed right then on his original run. So Wayne arranged for me to drive with Nick. A fifty-something who looked more mature than his years, Nick's features reminded me of a puppet. Like many older drivers Nick had begun a second career in trucking. He was almost completely unfamiliar with driving doubles or any commercial truck at all. He had never built a set. Knowledge that had seemed mysterious to me at the start had become ordinary. When a new driver came on board I would train them while my regular co-driver was out or if we were both subbing and I happened to be the senior driver. Once again I would show a rookie driver the ropes.

The next week on a cool but sunny Tuesday in December I walked through the guard shack, entered the Fort Worth terminal yard and met Wayne where he introduced the new driver. Nick looked like an okay guy, pleasant and smiling, chatty. Very chatty. Wayne left on an errand. Nick and I walked over to the tractor yard to get our truck then drove to the dispatch office to get the first slip of the week.

Nick was mostly a clean slate. Driving with a rookie I had to keep in mind all he might know or didn't yet know: how to back a dolly up to a trailer, that the full rig once built can only back up a few feet at most, that the trailers should be arranged with the heaviest in front, how to attach the lifelines. Don't forget the tire inspection lane. I hadn't known about that safety check for many

339

months, the better part of a year. Nick would know about it his first week.

We finished the set then I drove out of the gate at half past noon. Nick sat up front in the passenger seat. We would run the legally required ten and ten so shortly Nick should bunk down. But Nick acted so excited about his new job. If a new driver feels enthusiastic, that's a good thing. Right?

We stopped for lunch, ate and climbed back aboard the truck. Usually the nighttime driver retires to the bunk after lunch to get what rest he can, even on the first day of the week. I expected Nick to do so. He had driven a couple of runs already. He must have developed at least an inkling of how tiring driving can be, especially at night. But Nick remained in the passenger seat.

Sitting up for a while isn't completely unusual. Sometimes a driver sat up before resting, if driving with a friend. They might catch up and exchange gossip. Other drivers like to have a smoke or two before sleeping, or they want to check out the scenery on a route they've never taken or seldom seen. Sometimes a stomach demands its owner maintain it in an upright position for a while after eating. Maybe Nick had to do so, or maybe he had other things to think about or talk about. So Nick stayed in his seat talking while I steered the truck along the east Texas Interstate. And Nick stayed. And Nick talked. Before we knew it an hour had passed. Maybe Nick just didn't know he should bunk down soon. I had better mention it, I thought.

"You might want to see if you can get some rest," I suggested. "It's gonna be a long night ahead for you."

"Oh, I can't sleep," Nick declared. "I'm too excited."

So Nick continued to sit up. And he continued to talk. A rested co-driver is better than an exhausted one. And to drivers, sleep can be the most valuable commodity of all. After another hour I decided to try again.

"We'll be up there before you know it. Then you'll have to drive back all the way overnight. Why don't you see if you can get some rest?"

"Oh, no. I can't sleep now," Nick said with hyper energy.

"You may be surprised. If you make the sleeper dark and close your eyes, you can doze off, even when you don't expect to."

"I can't sleep right now," Nick repeated. Then he slipped right into another monologue about his ex-wife and stepchildren, the weather, his ex-wife, news and current events, his ex-wife and so on.

Driving at least an hour longer, I pulled over at the Covered Wagon truck stop for a break and welcomed the relief from Nick's never ending verbiage. Nick likewise got out and went into the store. About a quarter of an hour later we each returned to the truck and carried on our way.

I steered back onto the highway toward the Arkansas border. Crossing that state from Texarkana to Memphis took about four and a half hours. Then we had more than another hour's drive into Tennessee before reaching our destination. With a lunch and other breaks the total drive up took between nine and ten hours, if weather and traffic remained agreeable. Nick would have to drive all that time while reversing our path overnight, including the predawn hours when sleep knocks hardest at the door of a driver's brain.

Surely, I thought, Nick would go back and lie on the bunk. But no. He still sat up, and he still talked nonstop. With a tendency to tune into whatever spoken words float around, I found mentally disengaging from the stream of language difficult. Not only that but my driving time had become my time to listen to the satellite radio or play CDs. Driving was the only part of the day I didn't have to deal with a co-driver, build a set, or try to get to sleep myself. Maybe the difference in the words "sleep" and "rest" would strike a chord. I jumped into a rare gap in Nick's discourse.

"Just Arkansas now and only about an hour into Tennessee," I began. "You should get some rest, even if you can't sleep."

"Oh, I feel too up," Nick countered again.

"Even if you can't get a nap, just resting your eyes is better than nothing," I said, knowing such rest often leads to sleep.

Naturally, Nick declined and stayed up front talking while we continued eastward until the sun began setting behind us. Just beyond Little Rock traffic slowed to a crawl and then stopped. The Arkansas highway patrol worked to clear an accident blocking both eastbound lanes. The CB buzzed with news from other drivers saying the highway wouldn't reopen for over an hour.

Many truckers had pulled over to get a sleep break of their own. For miles up and down the highway trucks had pulled onto the service road or even the shoulders with their hazard lights blinking and bunked down. No one sat in either the passenger or driver seat in those trucks. But both seats in our truck remained occupied.

"This is just about the perfect time for you to get some rest," I said to encourage Nick. "The sun is setting, and the truck won't bounce while we're sitting here."

"I'm still not sleepy," Nick insisted.

I increased the volume on the radio that I had been trying to listen to in vain all afternoon, hoping Nick might take a hint. I would gladly have listened on low volume, if Nick went into the sleeper. Reminiscent of Romeo before him, who had wanted to stay up and flirt, Nick wanted to stay up and hear himself talk. Though Nick's excitement was somewhat understandable, even Romeo had been pragmatic enough to call it a day eventually.

I turned up the volume on the radio a bit more. No problem. Nick just increased his own volume. So we sat and Nick talked and talked. Then he talked some more. I looked out the windows at all the hapless motorists and truckers trapped in this traffic jam and wondered what needled them. Maybe the local auto drivers worried about family members waiting for them at home. How many motorists felt thirsty or hungry without the water bottles and food most truckers store on their vehicles? How many bulging bladders caused their owners to feel a growing or desperate need for a porcelain fixture? How many motorists had a passenger who wouldn't shut the fuck up?

I wondered how Nick's vocal cords worked with almost no break for what had already stretched to six hours then went to seven. Then eight. Finally, traffic began to inch forward. Gradually our speed built up. Yet ironically, we had also closed in on another truck stop. I pulled off the highway to visit a porcelain fixture myself before completing the drive. At last, thankfully, when I steered back onto the road Nick had given up. He retired to the bunk while I finished the last few hours in glorious peace.

I switched out our trailers with the other team at the Jolly Trucker. Then Nick's turn to drive us back had arrived. I gave him some of the words of guidance and encouragement other drivers had shared during my rookie days:

"Take your time. Go only as fast as you feel safe. Take a break whenever you need it. Oh, and do you know that at a truck stop doubles usually park in the fuel lane? Even though you won't fuel up, don't worry about finding a parking spot. Many truck stops don't have good doubles parking even during the day. At night on your shift most truck stops are full to bursting. You don't want to wind up heading into a place in a parking lot where you can't turn around, especially since you're not familiar with the truck stops yet. So parking in the fuel lanes at any truck stop will be just fine, preferable actually for this type of rig. And last but not least, don't hesitate to wake me, if you have a problem or a question."

My words to Nick before his night shift had been about the most he'd heard in a single stretch. I retired to the bunk immediately to get whatever rest possible. Not for the first time I empathized with experienced drivers who had trusted their fate to the gods and to my inexperienced hands early on. Now came my turn to bunk down, click the safety netting closed and hope Nick could handle whatever came his way.

The next morning I woke and sat in the passenger seat as we approached Dallas, the same way my co-drivers had sat up to guide me in along then unfamiliar highways. Nick needed to know which exits to take and what lanes to be in. A tad subdued by tiredness Nick talked less than the day before. This afforded a chance to familiarize him with a few points about the run.

"These trailers are due in Dallas," I began.

"I thought this run went from Tennessee to Fort Worth."

"It does, but we almost always drop trailers in Dallas on the way back. Then we build a new set there to take to Fort Worth." I double-checked our paperwork. "Yeah, Dallas is the destination for these trailers."

Then, speak of the devil, my cellphone rang. With the Christmas season nearing and package sorting at both terminals at a high volume Wayne had received a call from the dispatch office instructing us to take the trailers to Fort Worth.

"Okay," I corrected my earlier statement. "They *do* want us to take these trailers to Fort Worth."

343

"So this run is to Fort Worth," Nick countered.

"Today, yeah. With the holidays they want trailers wherever they can sort them fastest."

Going straight to our home terminal of Fort Worth always felt like a bit of a break. Skipping the Dallas terminal meant not dropping and building a new set before returning to Fort Worth, saving us the better part of an hour. Such dispatches rarely happened. Occasionally, we had a "hot" trailer due directly in Fort Worth. Usually, we had to drop in Dallas, even if a clerk permitted us to bobtail back to Fort Worth. But when we drove straight to Fort Worth we saved additional time with a more direct route, too. I explained this to Nick. He would get to see the route to the Dallas terminal another day.

As we progressed through the week, sometimes Nick needed explanations or instructions. Like any new driver Nick had a lot to learn, especially since he was pretty much brand new. Like many rookies I had felt afraid to make a mistake by *not* listening to experienced co-drivers. I'd driven with newbies before Nick, and they, too, had been ready to learn, even a bit afraid of goofing up. Drivers at any level of experience have many opportunities to look or feel foolish. Those chances are simply multiplied starting out. Yet increasingly, when I shared information with Nick or had to direct him in some way, he took on an air of resentment. Nick was the first rookie driver I'd met who acted annoyed by the need to listen to another driver. A reaction made even more ironic, considering how much Nick talked, and presumably, expected others to listen to him while he yapped almost non-stop about everything *except* trucking.

We did our turnaround in Fort Worth, dropping our set and building a new set before heading back out again. Nick sat in the passenger seat talking while I drove to our chosen lunch site. I had driven halfway toward the Dallas terminal, which we usually passed on the way out, if not on the way in, when I glanced at the paperwork and noticed the trailer weights.

"Oh, no!" I exclaimed. "The back trailer is sixteen thousand pounds."

"So?"

"The front is only nine. I forgot to check the final weights."

I called the Fort Worth dispatch office to check for sure, hoping the clerks had listed the trailers in the right order, after all. But, no, one of the dispatchers confirmed the weights. From here we could continue, or we could stop at the Dallas terminal and switch them. I weighed the probabilities. The risks of having a heavier pup, or back trailer, became worse on wet pavement. The weather forecast predicted rain later that day and evening. Stopping would cost us time, but I'd feel better if we switched them, the difference in weights being greater than usual.

The New York team often gave us sets of trailers built with the back heavier than the front, according to the paperwork. Margie and I had surmised they never checked or inquired about their trailer weights when starting out. Most drivers don't. Often most dispatchers didn't either, though it should be a part of their job. Rather than breaking down in the parking lot of the Jolly Trucker, we had always driven trailers back in the order the other team had delivered them. But heading out at least we could decide the trailer order. That made our run safer, and the New York team's return run, too. Stopping right then would also teach me to be on top of my game without having Margie along to remind me. I slowed for the exit to the Dallas terminal.

I drove the truck onto the Dallas yard and steered to a quiet area where we could switch trailers without getting in anyone's way. While we worked Nick kept glancing over at the terminal building. The main building has numerous dock doors. In warm states especially, the company often kept many doors open. Without a trailer backed against a dock door anyone could climb onto the dock and enter the building where packages awaited sorting. Workers were not always around when drivers walked through sorting areas on their way to the restrooms or to the dispatch office. Terminals also had stairs with ordinary doors spaced intermittently, mostly at the building's corners. Such doors were seldom locked in my experience.

"They sure do keep a lot of doors open," Nick observed.

"Yeah, they do and pretty much year round," I answered.

"I wonder if stuff ever gets stolen."

"From what I understand they watch the package handlers at these terminals pretty carefully."

"So things do go missing then? And they don't know why?"

"They may. I'd bet they catch and fire some people for taking things."

"Have you seen any security cameras inside?" Nick asked.

"In the sorting area? I don't know. I hadn't thought about it."

"At my last job, whenever I could take something, I would," Nick volunteered, referring to his former work as a repairman who went to people's homes.

I paused with a dolly brake line in my hand and looked at Nick while he stood, gazing at the terminal. Only in his fifties, but with thick white hair, Nick seemed grandfatherly. He could be anyone's next door neighbor, colleague or friend. He *looked* trustworthy.

"People must ship things like computers," Nick continued.

"If a driver like us has freight in his truck's cab, that's bad news," I offered. "It could mean getting fired or even prosecuted."

Nick ignored my comment, adding one of his own instead. "At my last job I stole a laptop computer, but I couldn't get a power cord for the damn thing anywhere."

I shook my head and noted for the umpteenth time how looks can be so very deceiving. For the next couple of days Nick continued to make comments about security, revealing more than a passing interest on his part. But on this, his second day, and with our trailers in the right order I climbed back up to the driver seat and drove our rig back out so we could stop for lunch.

After lunch, Nick could get in the bunk. Of course, he could get in the bunk nearly anytime. If he wanted to stop and eat on the way in, he could have done so then retired to the sleeper when his shift ended. From driving in last night I figured Nick must feel tired enough to try to rest earlier than the day before. But following lunch, Nick settled back in the passenger seat and began to gab again. First, I simply tried to tune Nick out. Then after a couple of hours I turned up the radio volume. But Nick kept on and kept on. He may have felt more tired, but like the Energizer bunny he kept going and going.

More than three hours had passed again when I pulled in to the Covered Wagon truck stop for a regular daily break. When we returned to the highway Nick continued to sit up front and talk. I didn't want to appear rude, but knew he needed to give up his constant chattering for his own sake. Once more I encouraged him to get some rest.

"Aren't you tired after driving in last night?" I asked.

Nick admitted to a bit of tiredness, but showed no signs of hitting the sack any time soon. You never know what's going to happen in trucking. Things might work out such that we became a regular team. If Nick learned the routines of team driving, that would benefit us both. So I tried to get Nick to see my side.

"Once you get used to driving, you'll start to look forward to your drive time as a chance to talk on the phone or listen to music or a comedy show on the radio," I explained.

But again Nick wouldn't take the hint. While I steered the truck into the winter evening the Arkansas pine trees lined the highway ahead in the glow of the headlamps. Nick stayed up at least an hour more before bunking down. He had only stayed up half of the previous day's eight hours of relentless talking. At least that was progress. Sort of.

The following morning when we reached the outskirts of Dallas once more I sat up front to show Nick the way to the Dallas terminal from an eastern approach. But Wayne called. Dispatch diverted our trailers to Fort Worth from Dallas again. Another break for us and a smug sense of satisfaction for Nick.

"Aha! We do go straight to Fort Worth then," Nick said with a hint of triumph, failing to note we only did so after a call from Wayne.

"Twice so far this week," I acknowledged.

"Wayne said this run is between Tennessee and Fort Worth," Nick repeated.

"Ultimately, yes. Usually with a stop in Dallas on the way."

Nick looked unconvinced. Did he think I was kidding, I wondered. Who knows what lurks in the minds of others? I wouldn't have guessed he had such sticky fingers, but Nick had freely admitted to being a thief. I wondered if his philosophy of taking what he could had contributed to an earlier job loss. Since he was already contemplating theft with his new employer, he might take advantage of the isolated and largely unwatched facilities when he gained enough experience to drive solo. Maybe he would try to filch packages or open them to see the goods inside. Further, if he put stolen goods in our cab and they were found, it began to occur to me he might deny knowledge and claim I had acquired them.

On our return Nick got to see a typical day. We drove to Dallas, dropped, fueled up and built a new set then headed over to Fort Worth. Another more typical occurrence, Nick, tired from a few days of relentless driving, went to the sleeper sooner. Every driver needs to rest, even if he doesn't want to.

Once we neared the end of the week when every line-haul driver feels most tired, Nick talked less and less. He went into the sleeper compartment after only a couple of hours each day while I drove all the way to Tennessee then switched trailers with the New York team. Then Nick took the wheel for another drive back to DFW.

Several hours after our last trailer switch of the week in Tennessee Nick steered out of the forests of east Texas on the way to Dallas when I stepped out of the sleeper and sat down in the passenger seat. The sun had been up for a couple of hours.

"Would you stop at the next restroom, please?" I asked.

"Okay, but I don't know where one is."

"There's a rest area about twenty minutes ahead," I said, giving him the exit number.

Several minutes later Nick slowed down and wound into the curving driveway of the rest area. Trucks lined the driveway on that Sunday morning. This particular rest area only had a small parking lot, filled with trucks whose drivers typically had no freight to pick up or deliver until Monday. Nick came to a stop and set the parking brakes where the narrowed driveway passed through the full parking area. Truckers don't normally park in driveways or exits unless other trucks and cars can get around their rig. I didn't want to insult the guy, but Nick would need to learn to give other drivers an out, if common sense hadn't provided him the instinct not to block in others.

"This isn't a parking spot," I explained quietly.

348

"It'll just be a few minutes," Nick answered curtly, once again showing the air of resentfulness he had built up all week whenever he needed new information or direction. He didn't want to be wrong, but he couldn't park blocking a driveway so I calmly persisted.

"A lot can happen in a few minutes."

Right then as if on cue a trucker rolled up behind us and honked. That trucker no doubt wondered why our truck had blocked the driveway. So Nick put our truck back in gear and moved forward. Fortunately, the driveway from the parking lot back to the highway had been built wide enough for trucks to park there, too. We saw another driver exit the facilities and walk back to his truck.

"There," I pointed, keeping in mind our long rig. "That guy's leaving, and there's room enough to park."

The other driver pulled out and Nick approached the spot. He steered the truck along the curb where the other truck had been. His approach wasn't perfect, but would certainly do. I put my hand on the door latch to exit, but before I could do so Nick began to pull away from the curb.

"What are you doing?" I asked.

"There's not enough room here," Nick insisted.

"You had it. It was fine."

Nick had already begun rolling farther down the driveway. He approached another spot with less space than the one he'd just left. I glanced in the side mirror to see how much farther the walk to the restroom buildings was becoming. Nick made a half-hearted attempt to steer into the second spot then steered back out of that place, too.

"What's the matter?" I asked.

"There's not enough room there," Nick insisted again with a quarrelsome tinge in his voice.

I said nothing.

Both spaces had enough room. But Nick moved onward having merely driven through the rest area without stopping except to block the driveway for a second and then swerve into a couple of spots for a split second each. Short of leaping from the truck I had no choice but to hold on until Nick stopped at an exit with enough room for a doubles rig. Behind us the trucker who had honked parked handily in the first spot Nick had refused while Nick steered back onto the highway.

"I really need to go," I reminded Nick, reasoning that even if he had decided to behave like an ass he wouldn't want to trap himself in a truck with a co-driver who had to relieve herself regardless of whether he stopped or not. Luckily, a truck stop awaited a few more miles ahead. I mentioned the exit number to Nick so he could be ready and sat waiting for the minutes to tick by.

Finally, we approached the exit and Nick slowed down and got off the highway. He steered the rig up to a stop sign and then down a lane on the way to the truck stop. We bumped along a gravel road then made another turn. The fuel lanes stood right in front of us, several yards ahead. Nick rolled towards them, but then turned a sharp right and took off into a section of the parking lot.

"You're not going to the fuel lanes?" I asked.

"No!" Nick announced huffily. Nick had used the fuel lanes all week because of what I had taught him, the way others had taught me. Driving a doubles rig into a dead end in a truck stop could cause us to break down and rebuild the set. But like Custer, Nick had decided to make his last stand. We passed several rows of parked trucks. Then Nick pulled into an area of the parking lot where other trucks blocked the way.

"Wait!" I said. "If you go up in here, we'll be boxed in and won't be able to pull through or turn around."

Solid lines of trucks had taken all the parking spots in front of us and on both sides. We couldn't nose-in then back out of spots that edged up to a curb. Nor could we back into those spots like most trucks. The few pull-through spots were taken. We couldn't wait for one without blocking the path for other trucks coming and going. But waiting was pointless if a driver had stopped for the day. Solo drivers might drive at night because of less traffic and sleep during the day when they found parking more easily. Anyway, pulling up behind another driver put us at his mercy. He may have parked for a few minutes or for his ten hour break. Blocking ourselves in meant either waiting for him or asking him to move. Asking another driver to move simply because you'd been too inobservant or careless to park wisely was no better than pulling into a campsite and asking someone to move his tent. He didn't have to move. Whether he chose to or not, you might get the broadside of his tongue complete with a trucker's vocabulary. Parking sensibly in the first place just worked better for everyone.

With hasty, indignant motions and a scowl on his face Nick steered in an arcing circle to prevent getting blocked in. At least he had listened before getting us trapped. He drove back down the lane towards another area of the parking lot where he could have driven near the building.

"Let's go up to the fuel lanes," I suggested.

But Nick had other ideas. Instead, he spoke the most prophetic words of his brief trucking career. "I'm gonna stop right *here!*" Nick nearly shouted as he turned the corner around a row of trucks, intending to park next to the nearest rig when an explosive sound burst in our ears. I leaned forward to look in the side mirror. Nick had driven the right side of the back trailer against the left rear corner of the truck next to us. With our rig brought to a crashing halt partway into a parking space our back trailer now sported a sizeable gash that had torn through the trailer's wall. The impact had peeled back the trailer's side like an old sardine can. Brown and white boxes showed through the gash and bits of metal and insulation lay on the asphalt parking lot.

"What was that?" Nick asked.

"You hit another truck," I answered plainly. Grasping the little green bookbag sitting on my lap, I opened the door. "I'll give Wayne a call, but first I have to go to the restroom." I climbed down and started walking toward the building while my cellphone dialed.

"Hey, Karen, what's up?"

"Hi, Wayne. Your new guy ran into some trouble."

"What happened?"

"We stopped at a truck stop for a break, and he ran the back trailer into another trailer in the parking lot."

"Ran into a trailer?"

"Yep, there's a hole in the side of our trailer."

"There is?" Wayne asked, sounding completely unperturbed and disbelieving, not an unusual stance for him. Sometimes I had a feeling if I called Wayne and had to explain that the sun rises in the east and sets in the west, he might respond doubtfully.

"Yeah. I'm going to the restroom then I'll take a closer look."

"What exit are you at?"

I gave him the number. Like other drivers Wayne knew the truck stop from the exit number.

"I'll call a repair truck to come out," Wayne explained. "They'll patch it, and you'll be on your way."

"Okay," I said, picturing the mechanic fastening plywood or sheet metal over the opening so no packages could fall out. In the interim hopefully Nick would not attempt to explore what packages his defiant actions had caused him to reveal.

A few minutes later I walked back out to the parking lot. Nick had faded into the background shortly after accomplishing his feat. In fact, for the first time all week the Motor Mouth Express had finally come to a standstill. Out of necessity I stepped up and handled the rest of the proceedings.

Luckily, Nick had been driving at a slow speed, maybe ten miles an hour. The driver in the other truck acted nice enough about Nick careening into his trailer. We exchanged information. I dug out the insurance card from the cubbyhole above the seats so the other driver could write the information down for his boss. Except for a knocked out light his trailer appeared none the worse for wear, but fluid dripped from the corner nearest the collision. I asked him about it.

"I'm hauling sides of beef," he smiled.

Nick had smacked right into a butcher's wagon.

While the other trailer appeared relatively undamaged our back trailer looked like it had been in a different collision. Unlike trailers used in some operations, such as thick-walled, stackable intermodal trailers or heavily insulated, refrigerated trailers, our trailers were thin and light. They mostly just needed to keep the rain off. Grit and bits of the trailer's siding crunched under my shoes when I called Wayne to explain the extent of the damage, estimating that the hole reached about five feet tall and two feet wide.

"Five feet tall?" Wayne asked, again sounding doubtful or apathetic. I wasn't sure which. God knows Wayne didn't want to spend any extra money, which was understandable. Yet, he may have failed to consider I didn't want to endure any inconveniences either. If I had to call, I simply related the facts.

Wayne repeated what he'd said about the repair truck patching up the gash. Before the mechanic got to us I went inside and had a sub sandwich while Nick waited in the truck.

About half an hour later the mechanic surveyed the damage and made his pronouncement. First he would have to cut away the sections of metal that had curled back from the impact site.

"You'll have to empty this trailer before I can cut the siding off," the mechanic said.

"Can't you just cover it?" I asked.

"It's sticking out too far."

"You can't cut it as it is?"

"No, it takes a welding torch" he explained. "There's a risk of catching these boxes on fire."

I called Wayne to let him know we needed another trailer. If the mechanic's tools set just one box on fire, the whole rig might go up. I could have driven the front trailer and cab away from any flames, but taking such a risk would be ridiculous. Quite rightly, the mechanic wasn't taking any chances.

"Let me talk to him," Wayne said.

I handed my cellphone to the mechanic. He described the trailer to Wayne estimating the gash at eight feet tall by three feet wide. Then he walked away. I couldn't hear the rest of what he said to Wayne. Some minutes later the mechanic walked over and handed the cellphone back. I put the phone to my ear.

"I'm gonna bring out another trailer," Wayne began. "See if you can park somewhere we can set the trailers back to back. That way it'll be easier to unload and reload."

So Wayne believed the mechanic or at least had to accept his decision.

Since we had switched drivers ten hours before, I logged myself out of the bunk and steered the truck to a nearby curb to wait.

From Wayne's location he would need a couple of hours to reach us. While waiting Nick got into the sleeper compartment and remained silent. By late afternoon Wayne arrived. He backed up the single trailer he had brought as close to the back of our rig as possible. Then the three of us began the grueling task of unloading a trailer, package by package into another one on top of the exhaustion of a full week of continual driving.

Due to the holiday season most trailers were packed full to the gills. This back trailer was no exception. We climbed up the bumpers and into the trailers. At first both Nick and I stood in the empty trailer while Wayne threw packages at each of us, always making sure we knew when he had another one coming our way. While we threw and caught boxes from truck to truck I thought about how people say, pack boxes like someone will throw them across a room or into a truck.

Stepping carefully in the trailers was essential, since much of the surface consists of elevated strips of metal rollers along the interior sides of the trailer and down the middle with narrow pathways in between. We walked or stood on the unsteady rollers or below them on the more surefooted floor, littered with bits of cardboard and wrapping. The challenge of fitting the boxes together had an element of puzzle solving to it, like 3D Tetris. We placed bigger boxes below and stacked lighter ones on top. We also took advantage of the space below the rollers. The rollers themselves helped move boxes of all sizes farther into the trailer.

About ninety minutes later, we had moved half of the packages to the new trailer. Naturally, Wayne felt more refreshed, having slept every night of the week in his own bed. The sun had set on a cold December evening, but our work kept us warm. We all took a break then reconvened to finish the job. This time at Wayne's direction I stood in the damaged trailer and carried or rolled packages of all sizes to Wayne and Nick where they stood in the single trailer. Many large and heavy packages had been loaded at the front of the damaged trailer. I managed to push or pull all but a few onto the rollers. Some I simply couldn't budge. Wayne stepped over the gap between the trailers and moved the heaviest packages onto the rollers. After another ninety minutes the three of us had moved all the packages. Wayne pulled the cargo netting down from the top of the completely full single trailer to prevent the boxes dropping out when a worker opened the door at the terminal.

"That's about as close as it could get," Wayne commented. He closed and latched the door then turned to Nick. "You can wake him now."

Sitting in his repair truck, the mechanic had long ago dozed off. He awoke, and by the glow of the truck stop's fluorescent lights he trimmed off the jagged edges of metal. I would drive the rig back. Wayne would drive the single trailer behind the rig to check that the damaged trailer performed satisfactorily. Before heading back to Dallas, we emptied the random bits of packaging that littered the floor of the damaged trailer so they wouldn't fly out onto the highway. The back door stayed rolled up so the hole in the side wouldn't create a pocket of air and make the back trailer swerve to one side or tip over. As Dorothy and Toto might attest, the rapid movement of air remains a force to be reckoned with.

Wayne and I each steered our respective trucks out of the parking lot at half past nine in the evening, over seven hours after Nick had decided not to heed his co-driver's advice. Too late for his own good Nick had run into an essential truism of trucking for any driver at any level of experience from rookie to seasoned pro: Don't be too proud to listen to another driver's advice, especially a driver with more experience or knowledge. And double that if the other driver is training you or you're new to trucking.

Chapter 24: "I can sleep behind you. You're a good driver."

What makes or breaks any team is character, consideration, and the drive to drive. Like anyone Doug wasn't perfect, but he had always been a good guy. We'd worked well together when he had helped cover the run. A driver could do a lot worse than Doug. Before I could fully ponder the matter, Wayne called that Monday and told me to meet another driver named Ned at the dispatch office the next day.

"What about Doug?" I asked.

"You didn't hear yet?" Wayne asked. "Doug got a notice from the state that his license is revoked."

"Revoked? What happened?"

"He had some tickets."

"Yeah," I remembered. "He had a court date for some tickets when we drove together."

"One of them was for a pretty serious violation."

"Driving around the arms at a railroad crossing?"

"He told you then" Wayne said. "That's considered reckless driving. For a CDL driver that means an automatic revocation. Once a license is revoked a driver can't work for the company for a year. After that he'll have to apply as if he's brand new."

"He can't drive for us then?"

"If he wants a class C license to drive his own car, legally someone would have to give him a ride up to the motor vehicle office so he could test for it."

* * *

On Tuesday at noon Ned and I met, built our first set and
drove out. Ned looked like a short version of Fred Flintstone with
lighter hair, only less of it. An older man, he had recently blacked
out when he suffered a serious heart attack. Yet, he seemed okay
by then. On first impressions his attitude appeared reasonably
positive, and he was careful in his work.

I drove the ten hours up to Tennessee where we switched out
trailers. With every new co-driver there comes a period of adjustment. Each driver gets used to the other. Any driver new to a run
gets used to the details of the run itself and with the habits and
routines in place before his arrival, at least in theory. As I had
done with other co-drivers and they with me, I sought to familiarize Ned with the run. When we got back to Fort Worth lucky Ned
ran home just a few minutes away to take a shower and change
while I dealt with the tire inspection lane and our paperwork. We
left soon after he came back. As a result, I didn't get my normal
shower at the terminal. So I mentioned to Ned that I would need
to shower at the Jolly Trucker before we headed back. But after
switching out trailers with one of the New York guys up at the
Tennessee truck stop, I had just gotten my shower bag from
among the luggage on the top bunk when Ned sat down in the
driver seat and put the truck in gear to start his drive back.

I could have said something. But I just felt too tired. Not only
physically tired, though that was true. I also felt tired of long
hours, unpredictable weather and nearly constant discomfort or
stress. Like I had told Wayne weeks before, I wanted a driver off
the truck. Only now the driver I wanted off the truck was me. It
wasn't because of Ned, who seemed okay in most ways. But he
wouldn't last forever either. On the contrary, it felt somehow
fitting that the new co-driver seemed like a potential colleague, if
I'd had the will at that point to get it through his head that he
wasn't the only one who needed to shower. No. That was just the
straw that I decided broke the camel's back. The real reasons had
accumulated over time.

Driving in all sorts of conditions with all sorts of co-drivers I
had gradually become burnt out like one of those crispy bits of
bread found in the crumble pan of a heavily used toaster. More
importantly, I felt a sadness gathering over a long period of time

with the realization that I belonged somewhere else in life. I didn't want to leave the run *because* of anything or anyone, but rather *for* those other possibilities I'd wondered about. If I chose to drive, I could work part-time again. Right then I wanted a break and an indefinite amount of time to rest and think. The week before Christmas I decided to give myself the gift of finding out what those possibilities might be. When Ned rolled into the Fort Worth yard the next morning, I called Wayne.

"Can you get someone else on the truck?" I asked.

"Yeah."

"I'd like to go home."

"Sure."

No argument. Wayne didn't sound like he was jumping for joy, but maybe he felt relieved that the persnickety female had gone, at least for a while.

After a couple of weeks off for Christmas and New Year's, Wayne called and asked me to do a solo run to Meridian, Mississippi, out a single day and back the next. Then he called back the same day. Dispatch advised one of the trailers had to arrive at Dallas that night so we needed a team. Wayne would be my co-driver. Wayne had built the set when I got to the Fort Worth terminal on the appointed morning. He drove out while I settled down in the bunk almost immediately. I didn't expect to get much rest, but didn't really have anything to talk with Wayne about. Anyway, as usual, Wayne's phone rang almost constantly while he juggled a never ending stream of issues with drivers and trucks. From the bunk I could hear the faint rumble of his voice on the phone while waiting for the hours to roll by. Just over the Louisiana border Wayne pulled into a truck stop parking lot. He steered into a fuel lane, and I went inside. When I came back outside Wayne had unexpected news.

"One of the dolly's brake lines is broken," Wayne said. "Will you walk over and see if there's a pull-through spot over there?"

Wayne pointed at the center of the lot where regular rigs filled most potential doubles parking. I walked over and found a spot Wayne could park in without blocking a fuel lane or getting stuck in a head-in parking spot. I turned and waved toward Wayne from the clear spot. Wayne put the truck in gear and dragged the back trailer with its emergency brakes locked up for several yards. Streaks of rubber for each side of the truck's tires left marks on the asphalt that looked like two pair of long black snakes had crawled over from the fuel pumps to the parking space.

Wayne called for a repairman while I returned to the bunk. We'd left Fort Worth at five in the morning. Later I would drive until close to midnight. This delay might afford a chance to grab a nap, after all. Wayne sat up in the driver seat fielding calls again while I settled back down. I had started to doze when Wayne got out of the truck. The opening and closing of the door woke me. Oh good, I thought, I can sleep better with him outside anyway. Then a few minutes later Wayne climbed back aboard. Wayne's phone rang again and he repeated the procedure: open door, step down, shut door heavily, stand outside talking with the driver side window down so voice is still audible in the cab anyway, reopen door, climb in, sit down, receive next call, repeat every ten minutes or so.

Maybe Wayne imagined his calls were of such a confidential nature he couldn't risk an ordinary driver hearing his side of a conversation once road noise couldn't drown out his voice. Maybe he just didn't realize I could not have cared less about his calls and wouldn't have tried to listen in regardless. At least we would only drive a day so getting good rest didn't much matter. More than an hour later, the repairman came and fixed the brake line. Once more Wayne assumed his position behind the wheel where he could no longer scramble outside for calls while steering down the highway.

Several hours later at Meridian we sat down across from each other at a booth in the café of the Astro Plaza. If I'd wanted to ask for another route, that would have been the time. But I didn't want another route. Instead between phone calls Wayne and I chatted about the weather, trucks and driving. Ned had a new co-driver, Wayne volunteered. Dopey. Well, drivers *were* in short supply and Wayne had never seen Dopey behaving erratically, as far as I knew. If he had witnessed Dopey at his worst, I could only wonder how Wayne might have responded.

Wayne and I passed a pleasant enough lunch time. Then Wayne retired to the bunk while I steered us westward, back to Texas. Wayne had told me I'd need to stop for fuel. About halfway through and running low on diesel I pulled off into a truck stop's fuel lane in Louisiana. When I returned from the fuel desk a bleary-eyed Wayne had stepped out of the truck.

"Where are we?" Wayne asked.

"Minden," I answered. "Did you get some sleep?"

"Yeah, I can sleep behind you. You're a good driver," Wayne answered. Laughing he added, "I can't say that about everyone."

I fueled up the truck, went inside and grabbed a bottle of Cherry Coke from the cooler and picked up a snack bag of nacho-flavored Doritos from a rack before pausing at the fuel desk. The clerk made small talk while I signed the fuel slip and took the receipt. Back on the truck I made sure Wayne was on board then pulled out the driveway to the Interstate. I'd driven almost an hour more before it struck me: I hadn't paid for the chips and drink! If we had been on a regular run, I could have paid next time and was dork enough that I would have. But I kept steering down the road, hoping the profit on the fuel they'd sold would help offset the loss from an unintentional shoplifting. Not that that was an excuse. Without further incident we returned to Dallas and dropped trailers before returning to Fort Worth.

For a while I drove as a substitute driver again. In addition to team runs Wayne also sent me out solo. Maybe up to the Jolly Trucker overnight or to Texarkana and back the same day. On one such occasion I'd readied a rig in Dallas for the three hour trip to Texarkana then discovered a broken trailer light. The mid-morning weekday hour meant someone would be at the mechanic's shop to replace the brake light. I pulled the rig into a repair lane and let the mechanic on duty know which light had stopped working. Then I climbed back into the cab and filled out my logbook, checking the side mirrors every so often to see when the mechanic finished.

Then another truck pulled up facing me. Two men inside recognized me and I them: Ned and Dopey. Both looked right at me. I couldn't hear them, but clearly one of them said something they both found hilarious. They laughed heartily with the sort of gleeful grin people wear when feeling cruelly superior. What a couple of jerks, I thought, and looked back down at my logbook, ignoring them. A few minutes later the mechanic came to my window with the repair slip to sign. I signed, got a copy, and then cranked up the window. While doing so I got another view of Ned and Dopey. They sat looking at me with somber expressions, like two suitably chastened schoolboys. But why?

When you work for a driver-manager long enough you not only get to know other drivers, you also get to know the trucks and their routes by the truck numbers. They may have noted the truck number and realized my run headed to Texarkana and back home that same day. A run with daily home-time is a rare treat in trucking. Meanwhile, Ned and Dopey had to drive almost non-stop between Fort Worth and the Jolly Trucker over 500 miles one way, relentlessly all week. How quickly they changed their tune when they feared I, a woman driver, might have a better slice of the pie. I clocked their response then put the truck in gear for Texarkana with the pair still looking remarkably somber. Somber and sober. In fact, that was the most sober I ever saw Dopey.

Meanwhile, I hadn't decided what to do next. Try a different driver-manager or maybe another company hub? Maybe another trucking company altogether? Go back to school for another degree? I had good grades and test scores. Or get an office job? If so, I could definitely go home every night. My reluctance to continue driving didn't mean I wouldn't cover a run when needed. Every so often I checked in with Wayne just to keep the door open.

Ironically, or appropriately, Wayne called me on a weekend to cover Sarge's solo butthead run for him. Romeo often drove that run, but was on a longer team run that week. I arrived at Fort Worth at seven on a Saturday morning to pick up Sarge's truck. At eight I steered up to the Dallas terminal where Julie and another woman worked that day. Julie handled the dispatch slip.

"The first trailer is on the yard," Julie explained, meaning the front trailer had already arrived at the Dallas terminal. She continued. "The back trailer is coming from the west coast. It's still on its way,"

"Do you know when it'll be here?"

"In a couple of hours."

A couple meant two to me. I located the front trailer for future reference and parked nearby. Setting the dolly was no use. The dolly needed to be set in front of the back trailer. I sat waiting until nine then ten. A few minutes before eleven I called Julie on my cellphone. The dispatch office closed at noon. I'd better check to see if a change of plans had occurred or further information had come to light. Past experience had taught me I couldn't count on Julie to volunteer such information.

"I wanted to check on the trailer that's coming in."

"What about it?" Julie asked.

"It's been almost three hours. Maybe the driver came in and dropped it. Can you check in the computer?" I asked, since the terminal yard covered many acres with large buildings surrounded by paved lots.

"It's not here yet," Julie said.

"Do you have an ETA?"

"Hmm. One o'clock."

The new ETA was another two hours away and conveniently after the dispatch staff had left for the day. Hmm, indeed. Julie sounded like she had pulled the time out of the air anyway. I called Wayne to let him know in case anyone ever asked why the run started so late. He would know why.

"Hey, Karen, what's up?"

"Hi Wayne. I just called because dispatch said the back trailer won't be here until one. I wanted you to know in case that affects your pay for this run."

"I sure do appreciate you waiting," Wayne said. Then because if I had flown the coop and left Wayne without a driver, it would have cost him the income from the run, Wayne added, "Go on over to that burger place that's across the highway. Turn in the receipt with your log, and we'll reimburse you for lunch."

"I'm in the truck I picked up at Fort Worth. I don't know if their parking lot can handle this cab," I said, imagining driving around auto drivers who zip around trucks unpredictably and might not expect a big truck, even just a truck cab to drive near them in a confined area.

"They have truck parking," Wayne said and repeated his offer. "Go straight at the light and turn right, down what looks like a sort of alley."

I waited a while longer then drove the truck cab out the gate and over to the hamburger place. They did have truck parking, but I decided to get the food and go. I didn't want to miss the incoming trailer. Missing this trailer might mean sitting and waiting even though someone had dropped the trailer and left on their way back home or parked for the night. Often drivers who ran wild, going wherever the company randomly needed them, parked near dispatch and slept in their trucks until the office reopened. I would have no way of knowing which truck had pulled in the trailer I was waiting for, even if the driver parked there.

I walked in, got food and drove back to the terminal where I sat point directly across from the only entry gate open that day. Like a birddog waiting for the ducks to land, I waited. Soon enough noon had rolled by and gone. Then one p.m. After yet another hour I called the Dallas office at two o'clock. Naturally, no one answered. Julie and the other dispatcher had left two hours prior. I wondered if the trailer had come in while I had gone to the hamburger place. I called the company's central office. Not every driver had their number, but Margie did and had shared it with me. The office could check whether the trailer had arrived due to electronic sensors that logged each one in and out of any company facility then sent the signal via satellite to the company's computer database. A man at the central office answered, and I explained the situation.

"They should arrive about five this evening," he said.

"Five? Are you sure? The Dallas office said they would be here at eleven this morning. Then they changed that to one in the afternoon."

"The manager of the truck called in himself earlier today. He said the driver hit heavy thunderstorms then had to wait several hours in a traffic jam."

I verified that we were talking about the same trailer then thanked the man for the update and hung up. If I had known the true ETA, I could have gone home at eight, rested and returned in the evening to start the run refreshed. Instead, the day was completely shot. If I went home now, I'd have to come right back almost immediately. The trailer's late arrival also meant having to drive up to Tennessee into the wee hours of the morning after a long day of waiting.

Tired of sitting I stood up and lay back at an angle on the sleeper bunk with my feet on the desk just behind the driver seat. With the curtain open I waited and watched each truck arriving. Every so often the sounds of a truck lumbering up to the gate filtered into the cab. I sat up just in case and read the trailer numbers while the drivers paused so the guard could make a record of each trailer's seal numbers.

It started to rain, a bit at first then harder. Evidently, the west coast driver brought the storms with him. I leaned back with my little green bookbag behind my head like a pillow and thought about what I wanted to do. Not about that day's run, but about life. About trucking.

If I wanted, I could call Wayne every Monday and be Miss Janie-on-the-spot, ready to go out and drive more runs. Or, since plenty of other fish swam in the sea, I could work for another manager, even move to another hub anywhere in the company system. With a clean record and demand for drivers I could work for another company entirely. The main issue? Right then I just didn't want to drive for anyone. If I'd needed to prove anything to myself I had done so long ago. I no longer felt afraid of driving a truck, of being a woman alone on the road, or of standing up for safety or fair play to any manager, clerk, co-driver or to any random nut job who happened to cross my path.

Trusting co-drivers with life or peace of mind was probably less predictable than the weather. Rain or sun, hot or cold; we all drove in winds that could knock a trailer over or storms that obliterated a driver's view of the highway in an instant. Out on the terminal yard moving the dolly or hooking up the lifelines in rain or sleet, in bone-chilling cold or flesh-melting heat. More than once moving a heavy dolly on a warm day I'd surprised a dispatcher with a face reddened by exertion in temps that had reached into the 90s Fahrenheit or hotter.

Even having a moment's peace or the opportunity to really think was a continuous struggle. Reading a book or writing with pencil on paper proved difficult in a truck. I'd learned that early on when I'd tried to jot down a paragraph or a verse or two. Not only was reading or writing on a truck difficult because of the inevitable jostling, but before long the fatigue of the job placed the necessary mental concentration beyond reach. The constancy of driving a regular route takes so much out of a driver that weekends feel more like a recovery than a break. Then once on the road again, trucking takes over with an enveloping thoroughness that prevents practically any other activities beyond the business at hand. Trucking is not just a job, but a way of life.

I'd never intended to take on that way of life permanently. I wanted to live a more typical life again. Many times I had driven along seeing people going about their ordinary lives and *craved* what they took for granted. While the rig zoomed down the road each evening I saw motorists heading toward their homes. I imagined them sitting down to a meal of almost any food they wanted instead of grabbing whatever the next truck stop happened to have in store.

After sunset, glimpses of light peered out from the windows of homes near the highway. The glowing lights held the promise of comfort. In those houses people began their day with a full night's sleep on a bed that, if it bounced in the night it was not due to the unevenness of pavement. Then they went to work or school wearing, if not precisely the clothes they wished for, at least something clean. They themselves were clean, luxuriating as they should in a warm shower or bath in the privacy and convenience of home whenever they liked. I longed to live like a person should – clean, fed, clothed, and housed.

Sitting back on the bunk, waiting, I heard the rain stiffen from a shower to a downpour. Lightning boomed in the distance, as I decided. Some people love the job. I enjoyed many aspects of it, but I had done all I wanted to with trucking right then. No way could a driver find out what possibilities lie ahead without a lasting break.

Reading trailer numbers on trucks entering the gate became harder and harder with gray sheets of water cascading downward. Yet from time to time in the crazy fashion of a southern thunderstorm the rain would abate for a few minutes before priming up for another deluge. The hours ticked by. Three in the afternoon then four. Five o'clock arrived and the minutes still passed without the trailer destined for Tennessee. Finally, at half past five a driver pulled in with the long awaited trailer. I practically leapt out of the truck cab and trotted up to the guard shack through a chilly drizzle. Standing beside his truck, I looked up at a handsome, brown haired, bearded man who sat in the driver seat.

"Hi, I've been waiting for your front trailer since eight this morning. It goes on the back of my set."

"Where ya parked?"

"Right there," I pointed. "Would you mind letting me show you where the front one is so we can switch 'em out?"

"Sure. Lead the way."

I couldn't resist jogging back to my truck through the strengthening rain. Luckily, the heavy company coat did a great job keeping out water and chill. By the time we got to the front trailer the rain had resumed flood-like proportions. In the spirit of the trucking truism "we're all in this together," a random, anonymous driver cheerfully helped build the set and send me on my way. I thanked him and headed out the gate over nine hours after arriving at the Dallas terminal that morning. The soonest I could get to the Jolly Trucker would be the next morning. Another driver had driven down from Ohio earlier in the day expecting to switch trailers that evening. He had a wait ahead of him, too.

Up through east Texas I steered past grassy fields as the sun set. Pine trees became numerous in the fading light. The Arkansas border loomed ahead. By the time the headlights skimmed along the forested highways approaching Little Rock my eyelids blinked more and more heavily. I popped a CD in the player and tried to stay awake, but the damage was done. Close to midnight I entered the parking lot of a truck stop and drove the rig to an empty pull-through spot. I couldn't help but make whoever waited up ahead hang around a while longer. I retired to the bunk and nodded off for a little sound sleep.

In the wee hours I finished the remaining drive. At last when the clock read half past six in the morning I steered the rig into the parking lot of the Jolly Trucker. I pulled alongside the truck whose driver had waited all night. He emerged from the cab refreshed and unperturbed. His girlfriend climbed out the passenger side and walked into the truck stop. Evidently, their wait hadn't been dull.

We exchanged trailers. Then I logged myself into the bunk while the Ohio driver started for his home terminal. I couldn't legally leave until after four in the afternoon. Sleep wouldn't be a problem though. Having made a decision helped me rest easier. I would take a break from driving and look into other plans. I could still do the occasional run, but the arrangement had definitely become short term, as far as I was concerned.

I did team runs for Wayne. Then in May Wayne called close to Memorial Day weekend. "I've got a run up to Texarkana and back for a couple of days," Wayne began. "Joe wants a longer weekend," Wayne explained. I agreed to do the run on Friday and Saturday so Joe could enjoy a couple of days extra holiday.

The first run on Friday went without a hitch. Up to Texarkana and back home for the night. That Saturday the drive up to Texarkana also went according to plan. Holiday traffic made the going a bit slower up I-30, but happily, no fender benders meant no traffic jams to wait out. I traded trailers with the team Joe met each day and headed back to Dallas. Lots of motorists made their way to or from a day at the lake or visiting family and friends. Across east Texas a steady rush of cars, pickups, and other four wheelers shared the highway with big trucks.

Approaching Dallas on I-30, the truck suddenly seemed to die, but the engine kept running. I turned on the hazard lights while the rig rolled along nearly without power. The truck slowed to about 40 miles an hour, then 30, then 20. I couldn't tell what had happened and wondered if the transmission had gone out. Starting out, I had feared a collision by losing control if the truck moved faster than I could keep up with. This was the other side of that coin. The slow speed made the rig like a stone in a stream with the flow of traffic eager to rush around it. I steered haplessly along, hoping no impatient or inattentive motorist rear-ended the back trailer, as the rig oozed along well under the minimum speed limit.

Cars began to clog the lane behind the rig. I signaled to take an upcoming exit that had a small truck stop. If the truck held out, I could get safely off the highway. After what felt much longer than the elapsed time, I steered the weakened truck around the spaghetti pathway of circuitous access roads. I kept wondering if the truck would stop responding at all, perhaps clogging a narrow highway service road. But when a traffic light turned green the truck responded, albeit at a snail's pace.

Eventually, I steered the slow-going rig into the truck stop parking lot. On this holiday afternoon the lot didn't have many trucks. Gratefully, I steered into a parking space and phoned Wayne. He didn't answer so I left him a message then got out to get a bite to eat. Afterward I returned to the truck and continued waiting for Wayne's call. I lay down on my side in the bunk and looked out a narrow gap in the curtains. About an hour later Wayne's call came in.

"Hey, Karen, what's up?"

I explained how the truck had performed and suggested the transmission might have gone out.

"Check the turbo gauge," Wayne instructed.

The orange needle of the turbo gauge pointed all the way down and to the right. Dead.

"Do you want to send another cab to take the trailers to Dallas?" I asked, since the rig had reached the DFW area, rather than a far flung corner of Texas or another state.

"Nah. You can bring 'em back."

"The truck maxes out at 20 miles an hour on level ground."

"Yeah. That's okay."

"On the highway?"

"Sure."

"You don't think someone could hit the back trailer? Without trailers maybe I can get up to 45," I said, referring to the legal minimum speed on Interstates.

"Aw, don't worry about it. Just bring 'em in," Wayne directed.

For the umpteenth time I wondered what else I could do. With hazard lights blinking I steered the rig back onto the highway and began driving the rest of the way in at slow speed, a process that would take a few hours instead of one. Driving the path back to the terminal, I remembered my first professional drive with Dutch occurred near a Memorial Day weekend years earlier. Somehow that made completing this run on this weekend more meaningful.

I thought back on all the things I'd seen and done, the people I'd met along the way from the truly excellent to the unique or eccentric. I looked back fondly on guys like Dutch and Coach who with kindness and patience had helped me get started. Even when Buster had told me all that could go wrong, he'd given me something to fight for and rebel against. Next Hilda in her way had taught me some of the practicalities of driving. From the start I'd gradually learned the need to stand up for myself. That gave me strength to defy Romeo and the unsafe repair. I'd driven with oldsters like Sarge and younger guys like Doug, helpful co-drivers like Margie or Coach and taxing drivers like Simon, self-indulgent drivers like Diva and Nick. A driver like Dopey was something else all together. But each co-driver had become a part of a longer journey.

I realized that I had faced down my fears, as I steered the slow truck along pavement that rose and fell each time a highway overpass crossed a major road. The variations in pavement affected the speed of the rig. On the gradual declines the struggling rig got up to almost 40 mph from the momentum of a weight of about fifty thousand pounds that day. On inclines the engine struggled to reach 20 mph with power applied fully.

While steering at these varying speeds I remembered how I'd started out dependent on co-drivers to show me the way, but I had become a confident solo driver. I had developed the skill of driving not just any commercial rig, but a doubles rig. Years after my debut drive with Dutch I felt in complete control at any speed, having gained enough confidence to drive a rig like my own car. I'd learned you didn't have to be a man to drive a ten-speed stick or to have and use your very own trucker's backbone.

The hazard lights made a muted ticking noise while motorists zipped around the sluggish truck. In heavy traffic a backlog of cars seeking an adjacent lane waited for a break to join the stream of speedier traffic moving next to them. With the sun setting motorists snuck around the back trailer in the darkening light. Headlight beams reflected from the side mirrors as I thought how I had remained a CDL holder, earning a living trucking longer than the statistics predicted. I felt pleased, even if I had bent the rules when necessary. Not to ignore or disrespect safety, but rather to enhance it, like driving when a co-driver became ill or exhausted. Where the rubber meets the road, we drivers had made the final decisions. I wouldn't have had it any other way!

In the super slow truck I approached the first of two different points on the way to the terminal where the only route for traffic to get from one highway to another ran over elevated single lane bridges. Each time I felt apologetic towards the auto drivers who rolled slowly behind the rig, trapped between two concrete walls on each side and the truck in front of them. I could only press the pedal to the metal while the heavy rig moved like a derelict amusement park ride along the enclosed lane. Steering between those walls I thought, if someone had told me what was in store behind the wheel of a semi-tractor trailer, I wouldn't have known whether I could get through all the ups and downs. That must be why we don't always know what's ahead up the road. We might not know how we could bear the challenges and hardships and might give up without trying.

With my little green bookbag and trucker's backbone I had gathered a list of truisms, little life lessons to apply outside of trucking. I decided that must be the last truism of trucking, to apply those lessons elsewhere. Finally, I reached the Fort Worth terminal and guided the weakened rig, as it limped into the confines of the fenced yard. I dropped the trailers then parked the cab and walked through the guard gate to my car. Even if my journey up to then had to end with the whimper of a nearly conked out engine, I much preferred that to ending things with a bang. T. S. Eliot might have approved.

I tossed my little green bookbag onto the passenger seat of my car and, cranking up the engine, steered for home.

Epilogue

I drove out of Dallas/Fort Worth for the years covered by this book. Afterwards, I left the DFW area and relocated to Memphis, driving out of that city before leaving trucking permanently, eventually earning a master's degree in library science. The only trucking company I drove for was the one in this book. I drove the company's trucks proudly and felt a sense of duty in being a safe and considerate CDL driver.

On a recent auto trip I retraced the drive between the two population centers of Memphis and DFW. I remembered the exit numbers to a couple of favorite stops. Weigh stations and truck plazas stood out in my mind. In Texas the independent Covered Wagon truck stop had declined in business, since a national chain truck stop had moved in a few miles down the Interstate. At the truck stop in Arkansas where Margie and I had traded out driving so many times I noticed a new floor in the restaurant and the absence of a monitor that had shown a list of runs available to independent drivers. Replaced, most likely, by the increased Internet connectivity of so many modern truckers.

Then nearby, I drove up to the Wal-Mart that Margie and I had stopped at on her last run. The store had closed the parking area set aside for truckers. Several signs declared parking for cars only, and a tall arch of metal poles had been built over the driveway with a height lower than the typical 13 feet, 6 inches of semi rigs. Signs warning of the height limit and about towing made it crystal clear truckers were no longer welcome there. I wouldn't be surprised if part of the reason for the change at that store had been because trucking brought drugs and prostitution close by, something the retail managers would not want next to their store. Such issues follow the trucking industry, it seems.

One of my last co-drivers out of Memphis was a male who parked our rig next to a mall in Southaven, Mississippi, ostensibly so we could each pause for a meal at the restaurant of our choice. The instant he parked, a man in a motorcycle zoomed up beside us. My co-driver, who I'll call Earl, got out and stood beside him, looking back at me while I started to get out of the rig. Earl's behavior appeared unnatural to me so I sat down on the bunk with the curtain gapped slightly open and watched. After ex-

371

changing just a couple of words, both men stood silently looking at the truck while I waited inside. Neither made a move or spoke after their initial greeting. Clearly, they were waiting for me to leave the truck.

Finally, I gave up and turned my back on them to climb down the side of the rig. When I turned around the motorcyclist sped off and Earl came back to the truck. I asked him who the man was, and Earl said the man wanted to talk to him about what driving for the company is like, though they had both stood next to each other wordlessly while I had waited. Once back on the road, the fact that Earl wanted to do practically all of the driving supported my strong suspicion that he had bought speed from the cyclist.

What, I wondered, is safety like for trucking lines without many resources to draw on for drug testing, maintenance, and training? Will things change in trucking? Some may change incidentally, but most will never change. We cannot stop the world from being worldly, after all. Nonetheless here is a book that gives the public a glimpse into some of the many aspects of the world of trucking, from the wonderful to the weird. I thought you have a right to know.

Yours faithfully,
Karen Greenhill
September 2015

PS – The burned house was rebuilt.

Appendix: The Truisms of Trucking

1. The driver is the captain of the ship.
2. The captain doesn't sink the ship!
3. Only the captain operates the controls.
4. Expect the unexpected.
5. Courage is not a lack of fear, but enduring in the face of fear.
6. No one can get used to your challenges for you.
7. The best laid plans of trucks and drivers often go awry.
8. Good team drivers must show mutual respect for each other.
9. If a co-driver is not interested, be prepared to take 'No.' for an answer.
10. The captain of the ship is no good without a backbone.
11. Listen to your spidey sense. If something doesn't seem safe, it probably isn't.
12. We drivers are all in this together.
13. If I'm going to fail, I'm going to fail trying!
14. Doing the job right takes the time it takes.
15. In trucking you constantly learn something new about yourself, large or small.
16. A considerate co-driver is worth his or her weight in gold!
17. Delay breeds delay.
18. Get Out And Look! Or in other words, don't hit shit!
19. Take advantage of every safety check available.
20. When you can, make your co-driver's life a little easier.
21. Never hassle another hardworking, well-meaning driver.
22. The public deserves safe and sober drivers.
23. Never be too proud to listen to a more experienced or knowledgeable driver.
24. Apply trucking truisms elsewhere in life.

CPSIA information can be obtained
at www.ICGtesting.com
Printed in the USA
LVHW091136150420
653547LV00001B/57